To Live Peaceably Together

Historical Studies of Urban America

Edited by Lilia Fernández, Timothy J. Gilfoyle, and Amanda I. Seligman
James R. Grossman, Editor Emeritus

RECENT TITLES IN THE SERIES

Mike Amezcua, *Making Mexican Chicago: From Postwar Settlement to the Age of Gentrification*

William Sites, *Sun Ra's Chicago: Afrofuturism and the City*

David Schley, *Steam City: Railroads, Urban Space, and Corporate Capitalism in Nineteenth-Century Baltimore*

Rebecca K. Marchiel, *After Redlining: The Urban Reinvestment Movement in the Era of Financial Deregulation*

Steven T. Moga, *Urban Lowlands: A History of Neighborhoods, Poverty, and Planning*

Andrew S. Baer, *Beyond the Usual Beating: The Jon Burge Police Torture Scandal and Social Movements for Police Accountability in Chicago*

Matthew Vaz, *Running the Numbers: Race, Police, and the History of Urban Gambling*

Ann Durkin Keating, *The World of Juliette Kinzie: Chicago before the Fire*

Jeffrey S. Adler, *Murder in New Orleans: The Creation of Jim Crow Policing*

David A. Gamson, *The Importance of Being Urban: Designing the Progressive School District, 1890–1940*

Kara Murphy Schlichting, *New York Recentered: Building the Metropolis from the Shore*

Mark Wild, *Renewal: Liberal Protestants and the American City after World War II*

Meredith Oda, *The Gateway to the Pacific: Japanese Americans and the Remaking of San Francisco*

Sean Dinces, *Bulls Markets: Chicago's Basketball Business and the New Inequality*

Julia Guarneri, *Newsprint Metropolis: City Papers and the Making of Modern Americans*

Kyle B. Roberts, *Evangelical Gotham: Religion and the Making of New York City, 1783–1860*

Amanda I. Seligman, *Chicago's Block Clubs: How Neighbors Shape the City*

Timothy Neary, *Crossing Parish Boundaries: Race, Sports, and Catholic Youth in Chicago, 1914–1954*

Julia Rabig, *The Fixers: Devolution, Development, and Civil Society in Newark, 1960–1990*

Aaron Shkuda, *The Lofts of SoHo: Gentrification, Art, and Industry in New York, 1950–1980*

List of titles continues after the index.

To Live Peaceably Together

The American Friends Service Committee's Campaign for Open Housing

TRACY E. K'MEYER

THE UNIVERSITY OF CHICAGO PRESS

CHICAGO AND LONDON

The University of Chicago Press, Chicago 60637

The University of Chicago Press, Ltd., London

Published 2022

Printed in the United States of America

31 30 29 28 27 26 25 24 23 22   1 2 3 4 5

ISBN-13: 978-0-226-81781-1 (cloth)

ISBN-13: 978-0-226-81782-8 (e-book)

DOI: https://doi.org/10.7208/chicago/9780226817828.001.0001

Library of Congress Cataloging-in-Publication Data

Names: K'Meyer, Tracy Elaine, author.

Title: To live peaceably together : the American Friends Service Committee's
campaign for open housing / Tracy E. K'Meyer.

Other titles: Historical studies of urban America.

Description: Chicago : University of Chicago Press, 2022. | Series: Historical studies
of urban America | Includes index.

Identifiers: LCCN 2021029493 | ISBN 9780226817811 (cloth) | ISBN 9780226817828 (ebook)

Subjects: LCSH: American Friends Service Committee. | Discrimination in
housing—United States.

Classification: LCC HD7288.76.U5 K54 2022 | DDC 363.509173/2—dc23

LC record available at https://lccn.loc.gov/2021029493

♾ This paper meets the requirements of ANSI/NISO Z39.48-1992
(Permanence of Paper).

Contents

Introduction

Freedom to live where one chooses is a basic necessity for a free, democratic community.

BILL MOYER, Open Communities

In 1951, the American Friends Service Committee (AFSC) launched Housing Opportunities Programs (HOPs) to challenge residential segregation by race in Chicago, Philadelphia, and Richmond, California. Jane Reinheimer, a white Jewish woman born and raised in Philadelphia's Germantown neighborhood, became the main staff person for that city's program. Trained in sociology at Swarthmore College and the University of Chicago, Reinheimer had begun volunteering in 1947 for the AFSC's Race Relations Committee. Deciding that the organization had "an unusually large number of good people, doing an unusually effective work," she remained associated with it as a paid staff member or volunteer for over fifty years. As her first task for the Philadelphia HOP, Reinheimer tried to persuade real estate developer William Levitt to sell houses to Black families in his second Levittown development in nearby Bucks County. For two years, she met repeatedly with Levitt and other businessmen while lobbying federal officials to exert pressure on the housing industry—enjoying access in part because she "had the look of such a respectable person." She also collaborated with members of the National Association for the Advancement of Colored People (NAACP) and local unions and conducted research for an unsuccessful lawsuit. In 1954, Reinheimer concluded in her characteristic understated manner, "Our approach to those in the housing field has not been fruitful." The other HOPs proved equally unsuccessful, prompting her to note more caustically that the "general approach" of developers "seems to be that if you ignore the people [who need housing] they will somehow disappear in smoke."[1]

Reinheimer next turned her attention to a grassroots effort to persuade white suburban homeowners to sell to Black families. For the next several years, she spent nearly every day advertising houses for sale on the "open market," recruiting and advising Black buyers, negotiating with recalcitrant financial institutions, and assuaging the fears of neighbors. In the years that followed, the HOPs tried a variety of tactics, including sponsoring their own housing developments, cooperating with integrationist builders, lobbying white suburbanites to open their neighborhoods, and employing nonviolent direct action to change real estate practices. Many years later, Reinheimer drew from her "level-headed understanding of the dynamics of social change" when describing the AFSC's experimental approach to the fight for equal housing opportunity: "When you have struggled for many years with deep-rooted and wide-spread problems, without eradicating the problems, you cannot become attached to one set of methods or . . . solutions. You are forced to reexamine your operations, to abandon old approaches, to attempt new methods, [and] to reassess the premises upon which programs have been based."[2]

This book tells the story of the AFSC Housing Opportunities Programs and their contribution to the movement to create "free, democratic" communities. It explores how a relatively small group of citizens motivated by their spiritual and humanistic values understood the inequities caused by residential segregation, and it explains their vision for how people of different races might live together. Their experience reveals the on-the-ground, local, and daily ways that private and public actors created and defended segregation, minimizing the amount of integration the AFSC and others could achieve. But it also demonstrates how social activists drew from their core principles—in this case pacifism, reconciliation, and an optimistic view of the innate potential for good in every human being—as resources for coping with failures and persisting in working toward their goals. Finally, this study examines the strategies people in the AFSC used to challenge housing segregation and how their tactics changed over time. As Jane Reinheimer explained, the staffs of the AFSC housing programs experimented to see what worked, evaluated their efforts, and retooled as needed. In that process, they responded to changes in government policy, the ups and downs of the economy, and the rise of other contemporary social movements. In turn, the AFSC pioneered, modeled, and nurtured many of the strategies adopted by other groups. Thus, the story of the HOPs demonstrates how social movements act and interact, and how they develop a distinctive modus operandi for a given problem and context.

•

In April 1917, a small group of members of the Religious Society of Friends, or Quakers, gathered in Philadelphia and formed the American Friends Service Committee as a vehicle through which pacifists could serve people devastated by war. The new organization recruited young men, negotiated with the federal government to release them from military service, and sent them to France as part of the Haverford Emergency Unit (HEU) to undertake humanitarian relief work. This first program foreshadowed the extent to which the AFSC would work with government officials, cooperating to further the organization's goals without compromising its principles. The makeup of the HEU established another pattern that would hold throughout the AFSC's history: the volunteers did not have to be Friends but only were required to share key Quaker beliefs, most important pacifism. After the armistice, the HEU remained in Europe to contribute to the reconstruction effort, replanting fields and building houses for displaced families. Other AFSC volunteers joined the HEU recruits, and the organization began to feed European children on both sides of the conflict, including over one million young Germans, over the next several years.[3]

At the end of the war, AFSC leaders turned their attention to the home front, creating the Home Service Section to provide young people with opportunities to address social problems within the United States. Drawing from Quaker history, the Home Service Section initially placed volunteers in African American and Native American schools, reservations, and settlement houses. This domestic program expanded in 1922 when the AFSC fed the children of striking miners in West Virginia, mimicking its experience in Germany. The feeding programs, both foreign and domestic, taught the AFSC how to stretch a meager budget, a skill that would prove useful in the coming decades. They also reflected the organization's goals of reconciliation and serving the humanity in all people, regardless of their side in a conflict. The founders of the AFSC hoped that by focusing on good deeds rather than ideology, they could unite and appeal to Quakers holding different political and spiritual beliefs. The volunteers' encounter with endemic poverty and inequality would make that neutrality harder to maintain over time, however. In 1924, as the need for wartime relief and reconstruction faded, AFSC leaders rededicated the organization to "practical Christian service in times of peace" and established four sections to carry the work forward: Foreign Service, Home Service, a Peace Section to promote opposition to war, and an Interracial Section to address the "hostility between the races."[4]

In both the domestic and the foreign missions, AFSC founders sought to apply Quaker principles to social problems. Although those principles had evolved in a variety of directions since the seventeenth-century formation of the Religious Society of Friends, most leaders in the AFSC came from the progressive and liberal wings of Quakerdom and so adhered to a social justice–oriented interpretation of core Friends beliefs. At the center of the AFSC's mission lay the idea that all people had within them a part of "the Light of Christ," or an "Inner Light," also known as the Inward Light. Attending to the light led to the awareness of personal sin and opened a path to salvation. But recognizing the divinity within all people also prompted concerns about social problems and a desire to do something about them. Early Quakers' embrace of the spiritual equality of all people led them to reject ministers and priests. It also persuaded many Friends to challenge the gender and racial inequalities of the eighteenth and nineteenth centuries. Friends in the AFSC expanded on these notions of human equality, arguing that because every human had a spark of the divine, none could be "ignored, degraded, or exploited."[5] All people had equal value and thus, they contended, deserved equal respect, dignity, and opportunity to reach their full potential. The belief in the Inner Light also led Friends to reject the use of violence against any person. The Quakers' historic Peace Testimony denounced violence and participation in war; in the mid- and late twentieth century it also led AFSC members to adopt nonviolent strategies for addressing social conflict. Finally, Friends believed that to hold these principles or have a concern was not enough. Faith was not real unless it was expressed in action.[6] More conservative Friends often disagreed with how the AFSC interpreted and acted on Quaker beliefs, creating ongoing tension between that organization and some branches of the religious body, especially Midwest Evangelicals, who resented the AFSC's liberal dominance. But the organization's domestic program also attracted and welcomed individuals of other faiths or with no formal religious affiliation who shared its vision of equality and commitment to nonviolence.[7]

The inspiration for the AFSC's Housing Opportunities Programs was the postwar shortages of decent homes for African Americans and hardening patterns of residential segregation, which Quaker leaders viewed as the most significant threat to interracial peace. Between 1925 and 1933, the number of new housing starts in the United States had dropped from a high of 937,000 to less than one hundred thousand. Construction then bottomed out during World War II, because the federal government allocated building materials to the military effort. Meanwhile, housing demand rose, particularly in major urban areas experiencing the Great Migration, the movement of African Americans from the South to northern and western states that had begun in 1915. Old and decrepit housing stock already plagued many inner-city neighborhoods, and when approximately one million people moved to defense industry areas during the war, they found subdivided houses without basic conveniences. Newcomers squeezed into the homes of friends or family, lived in Quonset huts, trailers, or other temporary shelters, and waited for vacancies that never came. At war's end, returning servicemen and the rising numbers of marriages and births exacerbated the problem. There simply was no room.[8]

These conditions disproportionately affected African Americans. Consequently, though its programs often included Asian Americans and Latino Americans, the AFSC focused primarily on the housing needs of Black families. Between the start of the Great Migration and the early 1950s, for example, the Black population in Chicago grew by over two hundred thousand people, including approximately sixty thousand migrants from the South who arrived during the war. Newcomers found few residences available to them. In North Philadelphia, just blocks from the AFSC headquarters, the African American population grew from 97,155 in 1940 to 164,107 ten years later. Meanwhile, in the entire city only seventy-four houses available to African Americans went up for sale. In Richmond, California, the approximately fifty thousand war workers, most of them African Americans, who had moved there faced perhaps the worst housing situation in the country. They found themselves living in temporary housing squeezed into an area of about seven hundred acres.[9]

Beginning in the 1930s, the federal government adopted policies to invigorate private home construction and ameliorate deteriorating housing conditions. President Herbert Hoover's Home Owners' Loan Corporation paved the way, but the Federal Housing Administration (FHA), created by the National Housing Act of 1934, proved the most enduring and important agency over time. The FHA provided federal mortgage insurance and established minimum construction standards, thereby reassuring private lenders and encouraging them to invest in home loans. In 1944, the Servicemen's Readjustment Act, commonly known as the GI Bill and administered by the Veterans Administration (VA), which made low-interest, long-term loans with low down payments available to returning soldiers and sailors. The second prong of the federal government attack on the housing shortage was the building or subsidizing of low-cost rental housing, beginning with 1937 Housing Act loans to local housing authorities. Significantly, the law left decisions about whether and where to build in the hands of the local officials.

After the war, federal involvement in housing expanded to meet the ongoing shortages. In 1947, as part of an executive branch reorganization, Congress created the Housing and Home Finance Agency to oversee the work of the FHA, the Public Housing Administration, and the Home Loan Bank Board. Two years later, the 1949 Housing Act declared that the government would ensure a "decent, safe and sanitary home in a suitable living environment for every American family." To that end, Congress greatly expanded the FHA mortgage program, which fueled dramatic growth in new private housing. The act also allocated funds for eight hundred thousand units of public housing. As low-income housing advocates soon discovered, however, those units proved slow in coming. Finally, the Housing Act responded to local city planners' concerns about the deteriorating conditions of urban neighborhoods and resulting declines in property values by providing federal funds for redevelopment projects carried out by local authorities, spurring a national urban renewal movement.[10]

By 1950, the housing shortage had begun to lift thanks to a boom in the construction of single-family homes fueled by the demand of returning veterans and their families but underwritten and shaped by federal aid. FHA mortgage insurance enabled home seekers to obtain long-term financing to buy a house more easily. The agency's priority on new construction encouraged buyers to seek a home in the rapidly growing suburbs. Builders could secure in advance a guarantee of mortgage insurance for homes in their developments, providing them with a marketing tool to attract customers. Innovative construction techniques also speeded the home building, and local governments eagerly provided the necessary infrastructure for new subdivisions. As a result, in 1950 new housing starts had climbed to a new high exceeding 1.6 million units, and competition raged among rapidly expanding construction companies to build on available land outside the cities. Over the next few years, the pace showed no signs of slowing down. In 1954, *Fortune* magazine reported that nine million people had moved to the suburbs in the previous ten years. In the Philadelphia area, seven hundred thousand left the city between 1950 and 1960; during the same period, close to one million people relocated from Chicago to surrounding communities.[11]

But nearly all these new suburbanites were white. Beginning with Kenneth Jackson's groundbreaking *Crabgrass Frontier*, historians have amply documented the extent to which government policy, financial and real estate institutions, and white residents' actions combined to make and keep it that way. The FHA and the VA continued loan policies developed by the Home Owners Loan Corporation that favored homogeneous neighborhoods and restricted African Americans' ability to receive mortgages, particularly in all-white subdivisions, a practice soon known as redlining. Until 1948, courts enforced restrictive covenants on deeds that prevented the home buyer from reselling it to a minority and in some cases to a Jew. That same year, in *Shelley v. Kraemer*, the Supreme Court ruled such covenants unenforceable, but real estate agents venerated them, and they continued to shape selling practices. The developers of the new suburban tracts openly advertised policies against selling homes to African Americans and controlled resales to prevent minority infiltration. Mortgage institutions refused to grant loans both to individual Black families and to developers interested in building integrated communities. Real estate agents, meanwhile, abided by professional guidelines that prohibited "introducing to a neighborhood . . . members of any race or nationality, or any individual whose presence will be clearly detrimental to property values in the neighborhood." When a Black family managed to purchase a home in a white community despite these obstacles, residents used harassment and violence to drive them out. Such practices effectively barred African American families from the new suburban housing. In Philadelphia, for example, 120,000 new houses were built between 1956 and 1963, but African Americans had the option of buying only 347.[12]

Excluded from the new suburban housing, African Americans competed for homes in urban neighborhoods with working-class whites who had not joined the trek out of the cities. The Black population of major northern and western urban areas continued to grow as veterans and others sought better economic opportunities. Increasingly, Black families searched for housing on city blocks bordering African American areas, in so-called transitional neighborhoods. Once Black families moved into a transitional block, real estate agents encouraged whites to move out by fanning fears of plummeting property values. Some white residents decided to stay and fought what they viewed as an invasion. Chicago became particularly notorious in this regard, with one local civil rights organization documenting fifty-nine attacks on Black families between 1943 and 1946, including twenty-nine bombings. Incidents of violence in transitional neighborhoods continued well into the 1950s. More often, whites left for other neighborhoods or distant suburban havens, while African Americans remained concentrated in the city. At the same time, civic leaders took advantage of urban redevelopment programs to condemn and clear inner-city residential neighborhoods, usually home to low-income African Americans. Federal policies mandated that local governments relocate the displaced to better housing, and public housing absorbed much of the demand. But city officials resisted building additional public housing units, maintained segregation in those they opened, and located projects for African Americans in undesirable locations. Thus, while the new suburbs became places of racial exclusion to which whites felt entitled, city neighborhoods suffered turmoil and conflict, with African Americans restricted to marginal accommodations.[13]

Although scholars have documented this story well, they have devoted less attention to the activists who challenged housing discrimination, particularly in the era before the passage of federal fair housing legislation in 1968. The NAACP employed its legal strategy early, winning the overturning of city laws mandating segregation in 1917 with *Buchanan v. Warley* and then waging the long fight that culminated with *Shelley v. Kraemer*'s nullification of restrictive covenants. In 1950, the National Committee against Discrimination in Housing formed to conduct research, lobby for legislation, and pressure the housing industry to end discrimination. The next two decades would bring private efforts to build and sustain integrated subdivisions and stabilize a racial balance in neighborhoods. In some suburban neighborhoods, fair housing councils worked to attract and welcome Black residents. And in a few northern and western cities, most prominently Chicago, the direct-action campaigns of the civil rights movement focused at least in part on securing antidiscrimination policies for housing. Ultimately, open housing advocates turned their attention to securing and enforcing state and federal legislation.[14] This study explores the work of those advocates who tried to break down the "wall between" whites and Blacks—to use activist Anne Braden's metaphor—by examining why they chose a particular tactic and how it worked on the ground; why they moved from one approach to another and persisted despite repeated failures; and how they combined elements of different strategies in an evolving social movement.[15]

In his survey of the freedom struggle in the North, historian Thomas Sugrue called the AFSC the "most visible white-dominated group in the civil rights movement besides the communists."[16] While Sugrue spoke of the freedom struggle broadly, the statement accurately describes the campaign for open housing. In the 1950s, only the AFSC and the National Committee against Discrimination in Housing actively promoted housing integration, and only the AFSC had both a national program and paid local staff working full time on the issue in urban centers around the country. When other leading civil rights organizations and grassroots organizers turned their attention to residential segregation in the 1960s, they recognized the AFSC's leadership and looked to it for expertise. Most important, the organization pioneered many of the tactics used by "open housers" and directed the most sustained and focused effort on the issue. Thus, although it tended to work in the background, promoting local leadership and eschewing large publicity or fund-raising campaigns, the AFSC was a backbone of the early open housing movement, making its history a revealing window on the pre-1968 struggle against residential segregation.

The richness of the sources in the AFSC's national archives enables close attention to questions of how social activists faced failure and kept working, and how and why strategies for challenging residential segregation changed. People in the housing program understood they were working in a field with relatively little organized action. Because they wanted other groups to benefit from their experiences and continue the work, the staff regularly produced daily, weekly, and monthly reports that ran for several single-spaced pages, describing meetings attended, recounting whole conversations, and assessing progress. Barbara Moffett, a former journalist who directed the community relations work of the organization from 1956 until her death in 1994, including all housing programs, insisted that staff members "meticulously document what was happening at the local level."[17] The resulting notes contained detailed narratives of events such as a Black family's move into a white neighborhood, a demonstration, or an encounter with a real estate agent, government official, or banker. Some writers proved quite introspective in their evaluations of their own behavior and questioned whether their response reflected the organization's values. They offered heartfelt expressions of their belief in fundamental equality and the possibility of reconciliation, and sometimes they made sly and sardonic observations on the difficulty of achieving the latter. The level of detail and the reflective nature of these reports convey the personality of the longtime staff members, their motivations and changing views of suitable tactics and strategies, and what sustained them in the work.

The organizational structure of the AFSC along with Quaker traditions and practice contributed to the abundance of material. Most of the organization's programs were conducted through regional offices around the country, including in Chicago, Boston, San Francisco, Pasadena, and Greensboro, North Carolina. But local and national advisory committees and ultimately the national AFSC Board of Directors approved all initiatives of these offices. To facilitate this oversight, the local program staff produced quarterly reports that described housing problems, the reasons for their concern about the issue, justifications for the tactics employed, results seen thus far, and arguments for continuing the effort. Because Friends believed in consensus decision-making and considered everyone's perspective important, the discussions about a new program or direction could be lengthy, and the meeting minutes often contained nearly full transcripts of the debate. Out of concern for the spiritual well-being of the local activists, staff from around the country periodically gathered to share ideas and decide how to move forward, and national leaders regularly visited local offices to witness the program in action and offer advice and moral support. The practice of the organization was to record a full account of all such meetings. Such proclivity for documentation affords scholars access to the day-to-day work in the equal housing movement as well as the motivations and personal reflections of those who fought for the cause.

The AFSC identified housing segregation as one of the most significant threats to racial peace in the immediate postwar years, and it made challenging that injustice the centerpiece of its civil rights work in the North and the West. This study explores how the organization made that challenge. Chapter 1 introduces the Housing Opportunities Programs and examines their earliest efforts to overcome residential discrimination through lobbying public officials, pressuring builders, and developing integrated housing projects. Chapter 2 tells the story of the fair housing councils, which in the late 1950s and early 1960s absorbed the largest share of the HOPs resources. HOP staff developed the councils to help African American families move to the suburbs and to influence white public opinion, with the goal of creating democratic communities in which people could freely choose to live together. Growing frustration with the failure of the fair housing councils to change residential patterns and inspiration from the campaign to end Jim Crow segregation and disenfranchisement in the South in the early 1960s persuaded AFSC housing staff to adapt nonviolent protest techniques to push for equal housing laws. Chapter 3 examines the staff members' growing understanding of the systemic nature of housing segregation and their embrace of direct action, which culminated in their participation in the Chicago Freedom Summer demonstrations in 1966. Chapter 4 demonstrates how, throughout their existence, the HOPs spoke truth to power by using personal connections with powerful people and officials to influence state and federal housing policy, lobby for new legislation, and press for enforcement of existing laws. The final chapter details how regional office staff, motivated in part by the Black Power movement and the War on Poverty, organized inner-city African Americans to control and improve their own housing, seeking to forge democratic communities of a different kind, in which low-income minorities determined their own living conditions.

Together, the stories in the pages that follow demonstrate how and why the AFSC staff members' understanding of housing inequality and strategies for overcoming it evolved. During their long campaign, the housing staff confronted resistance and violence, ever-larger and more creative barriers to progress, mounting frustration and despair, and often minimal results. Their failures taught them more about the mechanisms sustaining segregation, and those lessons pushed them to adopt more systematic approaches to attack it. In the process, they developed new strategies, modeled them for others, and nurtured independent organizations to pursue them. Over time, the housing staff embraced the outlook and strategies of contemporary social movements—the urgency and moral power of the Black freedom struggle, the use of nonviolent direct action, the language of grassroots empowerment, and War on Poverty–inspired community organizing—and incorporated them into their Quaker-based values and practices. Thus, the story of the HOPs demonstrates how mutual influence, adaptation, and sheer persistence enabled the AFSC to forge a nonviolent, community-organizing, and empowerment-based approach to fighting housing inequality.

Equally important, this story reveals how and why, despite multiple frustrations and failures, the housing activists in the AFSC kept trying. They believed that people should live in communities that valued and respected them as equal human beings, communities where they could reach their full potential. Housing segregation prevented African Americans from doing so while generating polarization and tension that threatened peace. The solutions the staff pursued reflected a commitment to nonviolence and reconciliation that involved bringing people together and forging better understanding, and AFSC members judged any new strategy against these core principles. Faith in the light within others gave Quakers in the AFSC optimism about human nature and the ability to effect social change. Their belief that they had a responsibility to follow where their conscience led, even though working through a small organization with few resources, limited power, and modest success, gave them hope and the determination to keep trying, experimenting, and trying again. In the end, and most personally, I tell this story to convey their vision for how people might live together but also to understand and draw inspiration from their persistence in making that vision a reality.

1. Getting Started

Launching the Housing Opportunities Programs

In the spring and summer of 1952, James Cassels, working for the AFSC out of its Chicago office, repeatedly tried to persuade Philip Klutznick, president of American Community Builders, to sell a home in his new Park Forest subdivision to an African American family. Klutznick admitted he "had a guilty conscience about the fact that no Negroes lived in Park Forest," but he claimed he had too much invested in his development in that suburb and so could not risk integrating it.[1] In the summer of 1953, in the wake of violence against the first Black residents of the Trumbull Park public housing apartments in South Chicago, AFSC staff and volunteers attempted to bring about peace and reconciliation between them and their white neighbors, only to witness the number of Black families dwindle and the spirits of those who remained falter. Later in the decade, AFSC personnel offered help to private businessmen who wanted to build a subdivision open to African Americans in suburbs along Lake Michigan's North Shore, but they met unrelenting resistance and hostility from nearby residents, the real estate industry, and local officials, which derailed the plan.

These efforts were all part of the Chicago Regional Office's new Housing Opportunities Program (HOP), one of several such initiatives established around the country in the early 1950s. As their name suggests, the HOPs strove to secure equal access to housing for African Americans in either the burgeoning new suburbs or the older but previously all-white city neighborhoods and public housing projects. Staff in these programs were equally concerned, however, about "how peaceful and constructive their welcome will be."[2] That is, they were mindful that the process by which integration happened would determine whether the new neighborhood would become a true community. As the Chicago stories demonstrate, in the early years of the HOPs the program staff and volunteers tried a variety of approaches, responding to local conditions in different urban areas. Many of the staff doing this work for the AFSC were not Friends but had expertise in community relations, and they were driven by a belief in the inherent dignity and potential of all people. Nevertheless, while recognizing the "need for experimentation" in addressing the housing problems of African Americans, the HOPs always grounded the strategies they employed in Quaker values.[3] Thus, at every point in the evolution of the AFSC's housing integration work, persuasion, reconciliation, and nonviolence informed its approach to the problem. Reflecting this set of guiding principles, the first HOPs in Chicago, Philadelphia, and Richmond, California, set out to persuade those in power to do their part to change residential patterns and to foster mutual understanding between parties in conflicts over housing.

Yet the story of the HOPs' early years is a litany of failure, frustration, and disillusion—with a few silver linings—as their staffs tested different tactics and struggled to keep the new programs afloat. AFSC regional office leaders quickly realized that "the area of housing represents the worst area of American life as far as putting democratic belief into practice." Moreover, the problem worsened as discriminatory practices by developers in the suburbs and the displacement of Black families in the cities due to urban renewal programs intensified segregation. Finally, although each city had sympathetic people who might be counted on to support increased housing for African Americans, and from whom the HOPs drew to organize a welcome in the suburbs, the AFSC was the only national organization with paid staff working at the grassroots level on residential integration per se. Given this "uncharted territory" full of minefields and challenges, AFSC leaders explained, "much of our work is highly experimental, and subject to the discouragements of such pioneering activity."[4] In the early 1950s, that was putting it somewhat mildly. Nevertheless, the HOPs' early experiments and disappointments helped the AFSC understand housing segregation, demonstrated what strategies for overcoming it had limited impact and why, and, more positively, affirmed the organization's dedication to integration and revealed resources for accomplishing it.

The AFSC's Background in Antiracism and Housing

AFSC leaders viewed race relations as a foremost concern from the organization's early years. In 1924, when Friends debated the role of the now permanent AFSC, Rufus Jones, the chair and one of the group's founders, suggested two priorities: "Quaker peace work" and building "better interracial relationship[s]." Acting on the latter, the organization established an Interracial Section, with the charge to study "Negro, Japanese, Mexican, and Indian problems," "break down prejudice," "cultivate friendship and fellowship," and increase understanding and mutual respect. Members hosted educational programs and facilitated personal contacts through student exchanges and lecture tours. The AFSC's focus on intergroup communication and understanding resembled the priorities of the ecumenical Christian interracial movement that had responded to anti-Black violence during and after World War I. But by explicitly linking racial antagonism to conflict at home and abroad, the AFSC reflected its Quaker roots. Members worried that if the "growing feeling of hostility between the races" was not checked, "it [was] only a question of time until wars [would] be fought between the races." Moreover, a peaceful world could not exist as long as racial prejudice and nationalism kept "alive the war-spirit." Despite the ardor of a few key members, however, the Interracial Section never aroused widespread support from Friends and so was "laid down," or discontinued, in 1928.[5]

For the next decade, a small group of Friends struggled to create a new institutional forum through which to express their concern about race relations. In 1927, the AFSC's Peace Section collaborated with prominent African Americans to form the American Interracial Peace Committee to organize Black antiwar activity. However, the committee survived only until 1931 because of a lack of funds. In 1933, the AFSC launched the Institute of Race Relations, a yearly summer seminar with lectures by white and Black social scientists about the challenges facing African Americans in the areas of employment, housing, and health. The attendees then discussed how they could act on the lessons they had learned.[6] The looming threat of war abroad in the late 1930s increased the urgency with which some Friends agitated for the reestablishment of a race relations section. In the fall of 1937, thirty groups or individuals wrote to AFSC executive secretary Clarence Pickett in support of the move.[7] Though the national board deferred action, Rufus Jones asked a small committee to investigate what more the organization could do. The outbreak of World War II interrupted these conversations as the AFSC's attention moved to the work of its Peace Section.[8]

In Detroit in June 1943, racial tensions caused by an influx of white and Black war workers into the city and the resulting competition for jobs, housing, and social space erupted into three days of rioting that sparked nationwide fears of an imminent race war. The atmosphere of crisis convinced the AFSC's leaders that "race relations constitute the area of greatest friction in our social order at the present time and probably will continue to do so for years to come." Wartime dislocation, "social bitterness," the federal government's forced relocation of Japanese Americans to internment camps, discrimination in defense jobs, and concerns about postwar unemployment contributed to growing racial antagonism. Jones, in his introduction to the organization's 1943 annual report, noted that in response to suffering overseas and at home, "Americans are increasingly aware of the need to find fellowship across the barriers of race and color with their own countrymen." In December 1943, the AFSC formally established a Race Relations Committee.[9]

The AFSC was not the only faith-based organization focusing its attention on racial reconciliation at the time. Indeed, in the 1930s and accelerating during and after the war, many denominational and ecumenical agencies began addressing social issues in general and the problems of bigotry and intolerance in particular. Although some Protestant church bodies in the late thirties had decried the bad treatment of African Americans, the tensions of the war years, as exemplified most dramatically by the Detroit riot, led northern denominations and the national church press to support the end of discrimination in the military and in employment. They remained notably silent on housing, however. In 1946, the Federal Council of Churches affirmed this shift by condemning segregation in the church and in society and calling for its member denominations to work toward abolishing it. Meanwhile, concern about race relations started to manifest in the Young Women's Christian Association (YWCA), campus ministries, student organizations, and the work of ministers who, often lacking their own congregation, acted through groups like the Fellowship of Southern Churchmen or the pacifist Fellowship of Reconciliation. These groups and individuals forged a subculture that exposed young people, including many of the men and women who would eventually join the AFSC, to a religious perspective on racial equality.[10] They also spawned church-based and interdenominational committees around the country, which worked locally for better human relations and would partner with the AFSC throughout its Housing Opportunities Programs.

Some of the AFSC's most common and steadfast religious collaborators came from the Catholic Interracial Council (CIC) and Jewish organizations, which likewise became more outspoken about racial equality during the war and postwar years. Rev. John Lafarge, a white Jesuit, had formed the CIC in New York in 1934. Based on the principle that prejudice sprang from ignorance, the CIC published information about African Americans for white Catholic audiences. It soon became more assertive, however, supporting an antilynching law and the wartime Fair Employment Practices Committee. After the war, the organization spread to other cities, including Chicago and San Francisco, where it campaigned for equal housing for African Americans, often more assertively than local diocesan officials would have preferred.[11] In the same period, three national Jewish organizations—the American Jewish Committee, the American Jewish Congress, and the Anti-Defamation League of the B'nai B'rith—shifted from defending individuals against anti-Semitism to attacking prejudice more broadly. Sharing with the CIC the conviction that lack of understanding nurtured biases, these organizations invested in social science research to combat stereotypes and sponsored educational campaigns of films, lectures, and print material. Over time, they also used the courts and lobbied for legislation against discrimination, including in housing. They combated housing segregation, not only because restrictive covenants often targeted Jews alongside Blacks, but because, like the members of the AFSC, they understood it as underlying all other forms of separation.[12] The AFSC shared with the CIC and these Jewish groups the convictions that all prejudice was interconnected, education and personal contact could change minds, and in the wake of a devastating war, combating discrimination was even more urgent.

In addition to these shared beliefs, the new AFSC Race Relations Committee grounded its work in Quaker principles, promising "to continue in our times, the Friends' ministry to those who suffer from intolerance and strife between men—in the knowledge that intolerance and injustice brutalize both the perpetrators and those who are victims, and stunt the human personality." Drawing from the idea that faith must be expressed in deeds and that concern must lead to action, committee organizers declared they would move past the conference and dialogue approach that had characterized the AFSC's earlier interracial programs. Instead, the racial crisis of the 1940s demanded shared work on concrete problems, particularly in northern and western cities where tensions were escalating. Thus, the Race Relations Committee would collaborate with African Americans to secure housing and jobs while continuing to foreground the "spiritual aspect of this problem."[13] After the war as Cold War hostility escalated, committee members also connected their mission to the Quaker Peace Testimony, arguing that the "improvement of race relations at home is one of the most essential steps toward validating our work for world peace." Because "mutual respect among races" was becoming ever more central to the achievement of peace at home and abroad, the committee proposed that race relations be a "persistent and pervading aspect of the entire program of the American Friends Service Committee" and asked for additional staff and funding.[14]

In response, in 1952 the AFSC created the Community Relations Division (CRD) to address social tensions and sources of conflict within the United States. The division was headed by a national secretary—Richard Bennett, a Friend who had gotten his start with the AFSC in the post–World War I relief program—and overseen by a national Community Relations Committee. Regional offices then set up community relations programs and hired their own staff. Consequently, many of the regional office initiatives grew out of local conditions and the concerns of Friends nearby, producing a range of programs on a variety of issues. From the start, advisory board members stressed the need to include African Americans on staffs and in committees, a quest that housing program directors would pursue with mixed success. By the same token, AFSC leaders recognized that these programs would be difficult to support with local fund-raising and so sought grants from outside sources, starting with the Ford Foundation and Fund for the Republic. The fund-raising challenge stemmed in part from the fact that many of the division's projects would engage the AFSC in "tension areas." Though community relations leaders recognized the potential pitfalls of doing so, they looked forward to the opportunity to be a "reconciling witness" in such situations. Although the work of the CRD expanded over the years to include programs in Indian relations, the migrant labor system, prisoner rights, and economic justice, among others, the division always gave its highest priority to the conditions and treatment of Black people.[15] Simply put, AFSC personnel believed that the United States could not be considered a democracy as long as African Americans could not "eat a sandwich at a roadside stand," "find a job worthy of their talent and capabilities," or "choose a neighborhood in which to live."[16]

One of the AFSC's first race relations programs after the war focused on helping African Americans achieve the second item on that list. Equal employment opportunity was a hot topic in Philadelphia, and the AFSC had already weighed in on it by supporting the rights of African Americans to be hired and treated equally during a tense wartime hate strike by white transit workers. The first secretary of the Race Relations Committee, G. James Fleming—an African American who was regional head of the Fair Employment Practices Committee—signaled his own priorities when he announced at an early meeting that "the most important service of the AFSC race relations work is to increase job opportunities for minority groups." In this atmosphere, Frank Loescher, a white sociologist at Fisk University, suggested that the AFSC create a job placement service to help African Americans break into new areas of employment. The national board agreed and hired Loescher to come to Philadelphia to start the new Job Opportunities Program (JOP). He proposed a process of carefully screening and recruiting highly qualified African Americans and pursuing negotiations with employers to encourage them to hire. His approach reflected Quakerly ideals of reconciliation and mutual respect along with the conviction that working together would benefit both Blacks and whites. But the process also closely resembled the Urban League's Pilot Placement Project, as both emphasized "individual merit" rather than "group opportunity," according to historian Stacy Kinlock Sewell. Initially, Loescher worked with the Philadelphia NAACP to press local department stores to hire more African Americans. Over time, the

JOPs spread to regional offices around the country. While the employment service would be overshadowed as the Community Relations Division increasingly emphasized housing, the JOPs lent their name and their model of working one-on-one with Black job seekers to the early Housing Opportunities Programs.[17]

The AFSC's concern for housing stemmed from the organization's early years, when it provided homes for people displaced by war and economic disaster. As part of its reconstruction work in France, its Haverford Emergency Unit repaired damaged structures and set up a "house factory" to construct two-room homes for refugees. In that project, AFSC volunteers linked housing to their spiritual values. As one volunteer recalled, "The reason we wanted to mend houses was that it would give us a chance to try to mend hearts." When the Great Depression led to mass unemployment in the United States and the displacement of Appalachian coal miners from company housing, Clarence Pickett, the AFSC's executive secretary, argued that resettling mining families onto farmland where they could build their own homes would move them "from relief into self-support and the recovery of dignity." Beginning in 1934, the AFSC recruited volunteers for summer work camps—short-term projects involving young participants who lived together for the duration—to build houses in the New Deal homestead program. Then in 1937, the organization purchased two hundred acres of farmland in Fayette County, Pennsylvania, and created the Penn-Craft community. There it helped fifty mining families build their own houses and create a cooperative to own and manage the community. In a system the AFSC labeled self-help housing, the group of families took out a loan from the organization for land and supplies and used their labor—their "sweat equity"—as a down payment. AFSC leaders believed that self-help housing, with its shared labor and cooperative ownership and management, could provide homes for low-income or insecure families while fostering "spiritual and cultural values."[18]

In the 1940s and early 1950s, AFSC leaders regarded self-help housing as a promising method to meet the housing needs of African Americans and build integrated neighborhoods. During the war they partnered with Flanner House, an African American settlement house in Indianapolis, in a housing construction program for low-income Black families. The project combined the Penn-Craft model of cooperative construction with funding from the AFSC, foundations, and local donations. Delayed by wartime shortages of materials, fund-raising difficulties, and barriers thrown up by local government officials, Flanner House Homes began slowly. While waiting for funds and for the bureaucratic logjam to break, Fred Reeves, the Quaker hired by the AFSC to oversee the program, worked with a group of Black war veterans to organize a cooperative association that would oversee the planning and construction once building began. In a process that would be typical in self-help housing and throughout the CRD programs, by 1950 the AFSC devolved leadership of the project to Flanner House. Ultimately, the project built 175 houses and became a model for urban self-help.[19]

In the late 1940s, AFSC officials began to eye the dilapidated apartments just north of their headquarters in Philadelphia as a site for another cooperative self-help experiment. By this time, although they acknowledged that Flanner House had filled a need, they decided that creating a segregated all-Black neighborhood would be setting back the clock. Any new self-help project would have to be integrated. At the same time, federal slum clearance programs seemed to offer the opportunity to work with government officials as well as new sources of funding. AFSC officials thus proposed to use the Penn-Craft model to renovate existing structures, cooperating with the local redevelopment authority and securing private bank loans insured by the Federal Housing Administration. African Americans already living in the neighborhood participated in the planning and were among the first families to sign up to renovate and buy one of the new homes. Soon, however, the AFSC got a taste of how difficult it would be to build integrated housing. Because of constantly shifting local and federal policies, resistance from banks, and bureaucratic obstacles created by strict FHA construction policies, the Philadelphia Self-Help Cooperative took over ten years to complete (fig. 1.1). Still, by most measures, it proved to be a success. The residents paid off the loans and became financially self-sufficient as a cooperative by the early 1960s. But AFSC officials, disillusioned by the red tape encountered in the project, concluded that self-help housing would not work in urban areas, nor would it produce a significant degree of residential integration. Thereafter, leaders of the housing programs warned regional offices away from self-help—though other parts of the AFSC, primarily the migrant farmworker program in California, would later return to the approach to solve the housing problems of poor communities.[20]

Launching the Housing Opportunities Programs

In 1951, after conflicts over housing near the regional offices dramatically drew attention to the violence that residential discrimination could cause, the AFSC began to prioritize enabling African Americans to "choose a neighborhood in which to live." Attacks on Black families moving into formerly white neighborhoods first caused alarm among Chicago Friends. In 1947, riots erupted after a group of Black veterans moved

FIGURE 1.1: First families move into the Philadelphia Self-Help Cooperative on Christmas Day, 1952. Courtesy of the American Friends Service Committee Archives, Philadelphia.

into the previously all-white Fernwood Park public housing apartments. After cooperating with the Chicago Housing Authority, the Welfare Council, and the Commission on Human Relations to calm the situation, the leaders of the AFSC Chicago Regional Office began exploring ways to combat discrimination in the sale and rental of housing. Specifically, they would use a "quiet, consultative and educational approach" of "top level conversations" with people in the housing industry to encourage them "to develop a voluntary fair housing program." Borrowing language from the Job Opportunities Programs, they proposed creating a Housing Opportunities Program that would "gather evidence of the practicability of heterogeneous communities," circulate educational literature, and cooperate with other groups interested in open housing. While the Chicago Regional Office waited for approval for the proposed program from the national AFSC Board of Directors, violent attacks against a Black family who had moved into the white Chicago suburb of Cicero highlighted the urgency of the problem.[21]

On July 11, 1951, a mob of four thousand to five thousand whites surrounded a twenty-apartment building in Cicero's northwestern corner. Angered that the family of African American veteran Harvey E. Clark had moved into one of the apartments, the crowd threw stones and smashed windows, broke in and vandalized the interior, and set fires to furniture, debris, and the building itself. According to eyewitnesses, the police, who had previously threatened both the owner of the building and the Clarks, did little to stop the crowd. The next day, the county sheriff persuaded the governor to send National Guard troops, who along with county police encircled the building and kept the now ten thousand attackers at bay. By three o'clock in the morning of Friday the thirteenth, National Guardsmen had dispersed the crowd but stayed on patrol to make sure that no nonresidents came near. Although it was not the first time that white mobs had driven a Black family from its home in the Chicago area, the Cicero riot quickly made national and international news. With headlines such as "Terror in Cicero," "Ugly Nights in Cicero," and "Cicero Nightmare," popular weekly magazines made Chicago a poster child for racial violence. Meanwhile, journalists abroad circulated the news of the riot as an example of the hollowness of American democracy.[22]

A month after the first attack on the Clarks, Community Relations Division secretary Richard Bennett visited Chicago at the request of local civil rights groups to investigate what the AFSC could do to help. Back in Philadelphia, Bennett told a meeting of national AFSC leaders that "Cicero is not an isolated community or a very special case" and that what happened there could "happen almost any place in and around Chicago and at almost any time." Indeed, the "terrifying" thing was that the residents there were "little different than any other all-White group in America." He suggested that while the AFSC should cooperate with the immediate efforts by other groups to reduce tensions in this specific case, the CRD should also look for a longer-term solution to the problems the riot epitomized. To accomplish the first, the AFSC partnered with the Chicago branch of the Catholic Interracial Council to hire a community organizer to spend six months in Cicero facilitating a peaceful move-in of African Americans. For the longer-term project, the CRD approved the Chicago Regional Office's request for a Housing Opportunities Program. The new HOP's goal would be to accomplish integration "peacefully and with some degree of consent" from white neighbors. Specifically, the HOP would attempt to persuade real estate professionals not to discriminate, "create a responsive atmosphere" for integration in all-white suburbs, build housing for open occupancy, and reconcile tensions in urban neighborhoods undergoing transition. James Cassels, a former conscientious objector who had built a local cooperative housing project, became the first HOP director.[23]

The HOP idea quickly spread to other AFSC regions, beginning with Richmond, California, just north of San Francisco. Richmond had boomed during World War II when its shipyards attracted migrants from around the country, including approximately thirty thousand African Americans from the South and Midwest. The federal Lanham Public War Housing Act of 1940 funded the construction of public housing units for defense industry workers, but it came with the provision that after the war the buildings would be torn down and the property returned to private hands. The fate of these public housing units, and the question of where the new Black residents would reside after demolition, got caught up in debates about slum clearance and urban renewal. Businessmen who wanted land for commercial or industrial uses pushed aggressively to close the war worker housing. Meanwhile, migrants in the unincorporated areas north of the city known as North Richmond had built their own ramshackle houses out of whatever materials they could find. After the war, local officials and developers wanted to use new urban redevelopment programs to clear those structures and convert that space for industry. Under federal law, city officials had a responsibility to help displaced residents from both the shuttered wartime housing and the redevelopment areas find new homes. But new private housing available for sale or rent to Blacks was "non-existent" in the area, public housing was insufficient to accommodate the demand even for temporary shelter, and "influential groups" "bitterly opposed" any effort to build more of the latter. A housing crisis, especially for African Americans, was brewing.[24]

As in Chicago, a mob attack on a Black family's home triggered the formation of the Northern California Regional Office's HOP. In 1952, Navy veteran Wilbur Gary and his wife, Borece, who lived in the Harbor Gate Temporary War Housing Project, heard rumors that their community would soon be demolished and replaced with a supermarket. Gary started looking for a new home with the help of Neitha Williams, an African American real estate agent. She found the couple a place in Rollingwood, an all-white war worker subdivision. The Garys purchased the house on the first of March, and on March 3 a cross was burned on their lawn. On March 5, vandals also attacked Williams's home. A local white attorney offered to pay the Garys $1,000 over the purchase price for their home, but they refused. Then on March 6, the Garys' first night in the house, a mob of approximately two hundred people circled the property, throwing rocks and threatening to burn the place down. Unintimidated, Wilbur Gary marched out to the lawn and declared that they were not leaving, and if the mob torched the house the family would "come back and live on the empty lot." The local branch of the NAACP and the Civil Rights Congress contacted their members, who started arriving to the home to support the family around ten o'clock that night; the situation consequently calmed and the crowd dissipated. Although violent incidents continued against both the Garys and Williams, the family remained in their home and were befriended by some white neighbors and local union members.[25]

In the weeks after the attack on the Garys, some of the family's supporters asked the AFSC for help. The president of the Richmond Council on Intergroup Relations reached out to local Friends, including Josephine Duveneck, a white woman who during the war had been involved in aiding Japanese Americans in the internment camps and had worked on housing conditions for African Americans. These Quakers agreed to ask the AFSC to employ an organizer to help Black families displaced from war housing move peacefully into previously all-white subdivisions. Not long after, a group of businessmen and attorneys who worried that repeated conflicts over housing would increase racial turmoil in the community formed the Richmond Committee for Better Housing in the Bay Area and seconded the request for AFSC intervention. The Friends in the regional office eagerly agreed that this was a worthy project. By the end of 1952, the Community Relations Division approved a Housing Opportunities Program modeled on that in the Chicago Regional Office. Reflecting local conditions, the new HOP would focus on finding "alternate housing for people now living in Richmond war housing, with particular emphasis on equal opportunities for Negroes." To do this, the HOP staff would work on creating a welcoming climate for Blacks in white neighborhoods, investigate new ways to build and finance housing for middle-class African Americans, and apply pressure for the creation of more public housing units for low-income residents.[26]

In December 1952, the Northern California Regional Office hired Phil Buskirk (fig. 1.2) to run the HOP, the first of nearly a lifetime of positions he would hold for the AFSC. Buskirk had been born in Michigan, but owing to bad health he moved around among relatives in Florida and the rural parts of his home state as a child. At age twelve, he contracted polio and thereafter often used crutches or a cane. After Buskirk's family moved to the West Coast, he enrolled at the University of Southern California, where he experienced and witnessed discrimination—first against himself as an outsider and a disabled person, and then when he learned that his fraternity would not accept a Jewish friend. He regretted not resigning from the fraternity immediately, though he did so after a while. He later recalled that after Hiroshima he "began to consider a commitment to help build peace" and moved his family to San Francisco, where he looked for a job serving others. Buskirk's contact with the Quakers began when a neighbor took his family to the Berkeley Friends Church, where he became a member. Through Friends circles he met Helen Baker, an African American Quaker who worked at Neighborhood

FIGURE 1.2: Phil Buskirk (*left*), Housing Opportunities Program staff for the Northern California Regional Office. Courtesy of the American Friends Service Committee Archives, Philadelphia.

House, a social service center in Richmond. Later, Buskirk credited Baker with showing him "that it is possible to see and communicate with the 'me' in every person regardless of such apparent differences as age, color, and experience." "Knowing her," he continued, "was like having a new light on human relations and a new light on how my experience might help me serve people." Shortly thereafter, he applied for a job with the AFSC. After a round of interviews in San Francisco and Philadelphia, he was selected for the Richmond HOP position.[27]

On the heels of the Richmond HOP, the Community Relations Division launched a housing program for Philadelphia and its suburbs. The Philadelphia HOP was rooted in a sense of impending crisis and a desire to avert it rather than a particular incident of violence. In 1951, United States Steel Corporation had announced plans to build Fairless Steel in the rural farming area around Morrisville, Pennsylvania, about twenty-five miles northeast of Philadelphia along the Delaware River in Bucks County. To accommodate the expected new employees, private housing developers promised new subdivisions, including 10,000 to 16,000 homes to be built by the Levitt and Sons company and 3,000 to 4,000 by the Galbreath Gunnison company, the latter a U.S. Steel subsidiary. AFSC leaders immediately began to strategize with representatives of the Philadelphia Housing Association, the NAACP, and the National Committee against

Discrimination in Housing about how to ensure that these communities would be open to all. They were not encouraged when the heads of both development companies announced their policy of no direct sales to African Americans.[28]

In March 1952, the Community Relations Division staff in the AFSC's headquarters in Philadelphia formalized the concern about segregation in the new outlying suburbs by forming a local HOP and asking the Field Foundation to fund it. In its proposal to Field, the CRD argued that the Philadelphia region had a shortage of decent housing for African Americans, which pushed Black families to seek homes in formerly all-white neighborhoods. Those new areas quickly transitioned to majority and then solely Black. The Philadelphia HOP would work to open the suburbs to Black residents by educating white neighbors and developers about "democratic living" while helping stabilize in-town neighborhoods after the first African Americans moved in by encouraging whites to stay. The AFSC was suited to take on this work, because its "reconciliatory" approach was appropriate for such a potentially volatile project. Moreover, program supporters argued that Philadelphia was a good location, because it had "no tradition of using violence as a technique to maintain segregated housing"—either forgetting or unaware of a history of whites' attacks on Blacks who moved into their city neighborhoods stretching back to the early years of the Great Migration. Focusing on more outlying areas, CRD leaders added that there were many Quakers in the suburbs who could be counted on for support. In addition to Jane Reinheimer, the AFSC hired African American activist Jacques Wilmore to work on the housing initiatives. Wilmore had become acquainted with Quakers while a student in the late 1940s at Lincoln University, just forty miles from Philadelphia. While there he had led NAACP demonstrations against discrimination at lunch counters, and local Quakers had supported the protests. Their cooperation inspired Wilmore to get a master's degree from Haverford and the AFSC to give him a job with the CRD.[29]

The Chicago, Richmond, and Philadelphia HOPs were the first of what would eventually be thirty AFSC housing programs nationwide committed to the broad goal of changing "the pattern of American community life from segregation to integration." The initial emphasis of the HOPs drew from the "Quaker conviction that evil is effectively overcome only when the mind and heart of the evil doer is changed."[30] Thus Buskirk, Reinheimer, Wilmore, and James Cassels began meeting with civic and business leaders to induce people in power to support equal housing opportunity. Through 1953 and into 1954, they each spent a large portion of their time conferring with city officials, real estate professionals, bankers, developers, housing advocates, and civil rights leaders. Through this they got acquainted with the local context, assessed what was both needed and possible, and tried persuading people to cooperate in bringing about a change in housing patterns. In Chicago and Richmond, the HOP worked on both urban housing and new suburban developments, while in the Philadelphia region the focus was almost exclusively on the communities springing up in the formerly rural areas around the city. In all three areas, however, the HOP staff quickly got a clear view of how difficult their quest for housing integration would be.

Integrating Urban Public Housing

RICHMOND

In Richmond, for example, despite four years of his persistent presence at public meetings and his hounding of officials charged with housing and development decision-making, Phil Buskirk made almost no headway in securing public housing for the African American families displaced by the closing of temporary wartime units. It wasn't for lack of trying. After attending a hearing on the Richmond Redevelopment Agency's plans for the area, at which "not much was said about permanent housing developments for the people who must be relocated," Buskirk said he planned "to attend every open meeting." In the interest of maintaining relations with all sides in housing conflicts, initially he tried to stick just to raising questions, but he admitted he could not help showing his opposition to some policies and hoped his "presence and action do in fact influence decisions and approaches." The first project slated for demolition was Harbor Gate, where Wilbur and Borece Gary had lived. After several meetings, Buskirk concluded that Richmond Redevelopment Agency director George Tobin was "committed to demolition" and not at all interested in integration or new public housing. After learning about an unpublicized hearing to discuss the sale of the Harbor Gate land, Buskirk—one of only two community group representatives who found the meeting— criticized officials for failing to inform residents that they had the right to relocation help. Next, he organized a group of Black and white Harbor Gate residents to pressure the Richmond Housing Authority (RHA) to be more open about its plans. He also tried to persuade the developer of a subdivision of one thousand homes five miles from Richmond, who was marketing his houses to white Harbor Gate residents, to sell to African Americans. The builder refused and, though he briefly considered building a separate new neighborhood for Black buyers, eventually dropped that plan. Buskirk's efforts came to naught. In 1955, Harbor Gate was knocked down and replaced with a Safeway supermarket complex. The only silver lining he could point to was that at least the Black tenants had gained organizing experience.[31]

Buskirk took a different approach when he learned in June 1953 that the federal Housing and Home Finance Agency, which controlled the war housing properties, intended to sell Atchison Village, a project of 550 apartments, to a private owner. Given the shortage of residential options for those being evicted from other projects, especially low-income families, the Housing Opportunities Program argued that the RHA should take control of the property and convert it into public housing. However, a Citizens Committee of Atchison Village, made up of white residents of the community, protested the move. Atchison had begun as an all-white development and, although a few Black families had lived there since the war, in 1953 was once again homogenous. The residents feared that if it became public housing, it would be "overrun by a 'certain group'"—that is, the African Americans being displaced from other war housing projects. Moreover, the city council, Redevelopment Agency, and Chamber of Commerce all lobbied federal officials to leave Atchison Village the way it was. Buskirk briefly investigated a suggestion that the AFSC buy Atchison Village and convert it into a cooperative, to keep it relatively low cost. But he figured out that not enough of the white residents would leave to open the community to integration. Moreover, cooperative management was, ironically, one of the remaining legal ways to maintain housing segregation, because the residents got to choose the new members. Convinced that their goals would be thwarted by helping the community become a co-op, AFSC leaders decided not to pursue that option. Ultimately, the Atchison Village residents bought the property themselves and converted it into a cooperative, making it one of the few Lanham Act housing projects in Richmond not demolished after the war. Eventually, African Americans moved into Atchison Village, though their numbers never matched those in the surrounding community.[32]

The final war housing demolition to draw the HOP's attention was Codornices Village, just to the south in Berkeley. The units housed over eighteen hundred families, about 88 percent of which included a serviceman or veteran. The project was never segregated, which was a "matter of pride to the residents as well as to the management," though over time it had become majority Black. When all the families were ordered to leave by July 1, 1956, and city officials displayed "disrespect for the dignity of individual human beings" living in the complex, the AFSC organized a meeting to ask "the moral question" of whether "the people of Berkeley" were ready to help these families stay in their community. A committee of local Quakers helped the HOP, which was undergoing a change in leadership, as Buskirk was reassigned to Santa Clara County just to the south of

San Francisco. They considered it a breakthrough when the city council hired a social worker to help the tenants find new homes, though it likely did so as a way of "easing the remaining tenants out of Berkeley." In the end, the City of Berkeley knocked down Codornices Village in 1955–56 and did not build any low-rent public housing to replace it.[33]

In setting out to change the hearts of movers and shakers in Richmond, Buskirk encountered only rigid opposition and hostility. Some men were quite frank about their "dislike for dark-skinned people" and the residents of the temporary war housing. W. W. Henry, chair of the Chamber of Commerce housing committee, told Buskirk that "he does not believe Negroes possess the full capabilities of other people." And Dana Murdock, local Republican Party leader and attorney for the Richmond Housing Authority, explained that the shipyard workers had come from "the jails and relief rolls of cities of the South and Southwest." By bringing "their culture" to Richmond, he continued, they placed an "unfair burden" on the community. In general, Buskirk noted, the position of most of the local industry leaders seemed to be that the city should "sweep all of public housing into the Bay." To his dismay, he also reported "no disagreement" at an RHA meeting when the leader of the local Council of Industries declared, "The people in the housing should be thrown out with the housing."[34]

Facing such comments in public meetings or one-on-one conversations could be dispiriting. In keeping with their goal of reconciliation and their belief in seeing the Inner Light in all people, Buskirk and other AFSC staff struggled to be politically neutral and try to understand the viewpoint of all sides in a conflict. But the strain of doing so sometimes showed. Buskirk recalled that when he heard the Council of Industries spokesman dismiss the lives of the temporary housing residents and no one objected, he was rendered speechless and his Quaker commitment to peace tested. As he put it mildly in his report of the event, "Not finding any words of a reconciliatory nature to say, I kept silent and the meeting was adjourned." But at other times, Buskirk pressed officials to consider the rights of the displaced people and African Americans in particular, as when he challenged Republican leader Murdock to name what his party or Chamber of Commerce had "ever actually done to improve conditions or work toward equality." Buskirk admitted that this made some members of the RHA suspicious of him, and that as a result, he and the Chamber of Commerce were "not mutual admirers." His replacement as head of the HOP, Martin White, noted in his first weeks that as he got to know some of the city's leaders, he, too, struggled "to avoid a most un-Quakerly and un-realistic separation into 'bad guys and good guys.'" By all evidence, the HOP had failed to change many hearts among the civic leaders in Richmond. Nevertheless, Buskirk argued that the HOP work there should continue, and he expressed hope that the "general community will learn that tolerating" the discriminatory policies of the housing authority "is dangerous to us all.[35]"

The national AFSC leadership recognized the toll such work in the field could take on individuals and consequently supported them in any way possible. AFSC administrators acknowledged that Housing Opportunities Program jobs were among the most demanding, that staff might suffer "an attitude of pessimism and negativism," and that the challenges in Richmond specifically were "perhaps more deadly to the staff person than in any other place." Not just anyone could spiritually survive such work. It required "people motivated by a belief in the capacities of the most under privileged and in the creative power of the Lord." Sometimes the "sustaining power of the Spirit" could be lost and staff members had to be replaced. But, as Community Relations Division secretary Richard Bennett put it, "We have a responsibility to treat each other with as much dignity and affection as we would treat those people in 'the opposition.'" Supervisors could not expect staff to be "saints or Gods" when they were "fairly normal, average human beings and subject to the discouragement of other humans." In other words, sometimes people had to be cut a break. Staff were expected to do the best they could, motivated by a "belief in the potential of people," and to hold on to a "common set of objectives, standards and approaches." Most important, they were expected to care for one another.[36]

Barbara Moffett, who replaced Bennett as head of the CRD, set the tone from the top for how to do that. Moffett was not a Friend but had gone to the Moorestown (NJ) Friends School and married Quaker Timothy Haworth, who had served with the Friends Ambulance Unit in the Chinese Revolution. She was a journalist for the *Philadelphia Record* and shop steward for the American Newspaper Guild. When her paper went on strike in 1947, she took a temporary assignment for the AFSC in the publicity department; she never left. After moving to the CRD in 1954, Moffett became its head in 1956 and remained so for the rest of her life. Though not a Friend, she embodied a Quaker tradition of showing "tender concern for one another" and "mutual support." Colleagues later remembered her as a mentor whom staff working in "sometimes dangerous conditions around the country" could call "any time of the day or night if frightened or discouraged." To provide space for sharing insights, recouping energy and inspiration, and just supporting one another, Moffett and the AFSC leadership held regular "roundups," as they called their staff retreats, and paid for people to attend. At one roundup, community relations staff from around the country shared how they kept "going forward" with work that "often makes heavy demands on the individual." Some mentioned finding solace in their relationship with God, or in art and literature. But for most, their main resource was their "relationship to other human beings." As Colin Bell, a Quaker who would lead the AFSC in the 1960s put it, being a part of a community seeking answers to social evils can have a "transcendent and liberating quality." Realizing they were not alone in that searching provided staff members with the strength to continue experimenting in fields where obstacles could seem unsurmountable.[37]

CHICAGO

While Phil Buskirk struggled to find homes for Black families displaced from temporary war housing in the Bay Area, James Cassels and other Chicago HOP staff strove to nurture an embattled effort to desegregate public housing in the Windy City. Although the Chicago Housing Authority (CHA) had a nondiscrimination policy, it continued to ban African Americans in four of its public housing projects, including Trumbull Park in the South Deering neighborhood. In July 1953, "exceptionally fairskinned" Betty Howard applied in person for an apartment in Trumbull Park, and the CHA staff person, not realizing she was African American, accepted her application. Betty and Donald Howard and their family moved in on July 30. By the end of their first week, their neighbors discovered that the project had been integrated. On August 5, approximately fifty white teenagers attacked the Howards' apartment with bricks, stones, and firecrackers. By August 10, the crowd grew to a thousand. When the police blocked off access to the project, the mob spilled onto nearby streets, where it attacked cars and pedestrians. Two-hundred and fifty police officers patrolled around the clock and struggled to keep order throughout the month of August. Despite their efforts, six teenagers attacked Donald Howard on August 23, and residents of the South Deering neighborhood set off "aerial bombs" nightly, a harassment tactic that would continue for the rest of the decade. Defying this resistance, CHA head Elizabeth Wood pressed forward with the integration of Trumbull Park by admitting three more Black families in October and more in early 1954. The rising number of Black families made white neighbors in South Deering, organized in the South Deering Improvement Association, even more determined to make life so miserable for them that they would move out on their own.[38]

While many civil rights groups cooperated to quell the violence, the HOP staff considered it their unique role to pursue reconciliation in the area. To accomplish that, for nearly five years women volunteers and staff members, including Yvonne Priest, Joan Seever, Mary Berger, Judy Miller, and Jane Weston, visited the community at least weekly, trying to get to know Black families and respond to their needs, reach out to the white ones, and establish connections between them. Over coffee and in the middle of housework, the women talked with the mothers in the project and sometimes with couples together. They asked how they and their families were, what they needed, and how the AFSC could support them; most important, they gave them a chance to express their frustrations and fears. The AFSC women also knocked on the doors of white families in Trumbull Park, trying to get them to accept and even befriend their new neighbors. The reports of these visits record small steps toward neighborliness and a normal life. In one of her first accounts, Yvonne Priest noted that three white families had begun visiting with African Americans, and two of the latter attended meetings sponsored by the Tenants Council. About a year later, Joan Seever noted that Frank Brown, one of the Black residents, was editing the Trumbull Park newsletter. The high point of social contact achieved between the project's Black and white families was a weeklong family camp the AFSC organized in 1957, which attracted sixty-seven African Americans and thirty-three whites. Compared with the amount of time invested, the signs of acceptance and positive relationships were slight. But the visits gave the women staff and volunteers a concrete way to act on their concern about racial discrimination and provided some solace for the Black families. Moreover, the practice foreshadowed the person-to-person organizing that HOP staff would do to create a climate of welcome for African Americans in the new suburbs.[39]

Although Judy Miller had hoped the 1957 weeklong camp would encourage some interracial connections, what the event mainly did was "give Black families some breathing room." By then they needed it. Just as CRD leaders recognized how difficult working for open housing could be for the staff, so Miller and the other women worried about the emotional toll that integrating public housing and being the target of white resistance was taking on the African American families. Nearly every chat included a story about an act of violence, vandalism, or lack of help from authorities, including the police. Anonymous vandals threw bricks at Gretchen and Phil Anderson's car and set a neighbor's on fire. Black women in Trumbull Park reported that it was "rare for anyone to walk into the project without meeting some form of vilification or abuse." The worst was the harassment of their children. White teenagers threw rocks from a water tower at the Black youngsters playing below. Bullies teased and threatened the children on their way home from school and in the park. Mrs. Brown sent her child to live with relatives in the Hyde

Park neighborhood during the week, while Gretchen Anderson made her sons run over to school at the last minute and encouraged them to rush home right afterward. In 1957, riots in nearby Calumet Park spilled over into Trumbull Park, with gangs attacking men on the streets, tearing up first-floor apartments, and destroying cars. Thereafter, the level of tension increased as families witnessed police just sitting by as people were attacked by stone-throwing gangs. Throughout this turmoil, the Black residents rarely reported such incidents to the Chicago Housing Authority, because when they did, they were "questioned like criminals."[40]

Housing Opportunities Program volunteer Mary Berger observed in 1956 that even when there were no "dramatic acts of violence," the "steady drip-drip of tension [was] very wearing," and its impact on the families was increasingly evident. The O'Bannons were "disgusted with the authorities" and felt that not being able to walk safely on public streets was "a disgrace." In the first few years, police escorted residents to and from public transportation in squad cars, which was "humiliating," not to mention inconvenient when the escort car failed to show up. Other Trumbull Park residents suffered from the isolation. They had few white friends, because white families feared retaliation if they should socialize openly with African Americans. When the number of Black families was at its peak of thirty, the camaraderie among them helped. But by the end of the decade, the CHA encouraged Black families to leave and did not replace them, leaving those hanging on even lonelier. Mrs. Brown admitted she felt "hemmed in and extremely nervous"—a change, Berger noted, from two years before, when she "was quite cheerful." Moreover, the nightly bombs rattled her nerves, and she felt cut off from her neighbors. Mrs. Young described South Deering's harassment of the Trumbull Park residents as being like "a dull tooth-ache—not violent, but never ending." For her part, Mrs. Page was disturbed that outside do-gooders played down the extent of the trouble, and she said that she herself "never will get used to it." In fact, she was soon moving out. By the end of the decade, many of the families had done likewise, creating what Judy Miller called "a crisis less dramatic than the riots of this past summer but much more likely to negate all the hardships and courage of the past four years": the exodus of Trumbull Park's Black families, leaving the experiment in integration in tatters.[41]

In the summer of 1957, as strain within Trumbull Park and hostility in the surrounding community seemed to be reaching a boiling point, AFSC staff and some of the African American residents debated how to respond. Specifically, what role should nonviolence, made famous by the recent Montgomery bus boycott and Martin Luther King Jr., play? By then it was clear that some of the Black families had had enough.

When Gretchen and Phil Anderson's car was hit by a brick, Mr. Anderson confronted the boys who had done it. Judy Miller warned that although "Phil is not confrontational," "even he is reaching his limit." Rev. David Fison, the white minister of the South Deering Methodist Church who was sympathetic toward integration, suggested that one way to prevent an escalation of violence was to host "a talk on nonviolence as a technique, preferably by a Negro with experience in these situations." Gretchen Anderson, who believed whites were trying to "provoke us into behaving like their stereotypes of Negroes," agreed that a workshop on nonviolence was a good idea. Ed Holmgren, a white Chicagoan who had worked for the housing authority before replacing James Cassels as HOP head, wrote to King, telling him about the Trumbull Park families' "growing impatience with non-retaliation" and urging him to come to Chicago to share his "nonviolent philosophy." At that point, King was unable to accept the invitation, however. Nevertheless, the HOP held an Institute on Nonviolence and Reconciliation in December 1957, with Gretchen Anderson rather than King as one of the speakers.[42]

By that time, the Chicago HOP staff, despairing over their lack of progress in Trumbull Park, called for reinforcements. Admitting that "we [in Chicago] have been so close to the situation we feel we've lost perspective and need some fresh eyes and views," they asked the national AFSC Board of Directors to organize a Quaker mission—a delegation of "weighty" Friends from around the country—to visit Trumbull Park and suggest new tactics. The AFSC had a history of sending teams of Friends into situations of international tension to speak with those involved in the conflict, develop suggestions for resolving it, and "bear witness to [the] belief in the power of reconciliation." Indeed, the proposal for the Trumbull Park mission compared it to AFSC cofounder Rufus Jones's visit with Nazi officials on the eve of World War II or the groups of Friends who traveled to the Soviet Union in the 1950s. The goal was to engage in "honest and humble searching" through one-on-one conversation and to connect with all parties, in keeping with the idea that there was "that of God in every man." Three Philadelphia and three local Quakers met with families, city officials, members of the Catholic Interracial Council, and African American business and civil rights leaders. They tried to talk with members of the South Deering Improvement Association but were rebuffed. Black Trumbull Park families were more welcoming, though they were clearly afraid. At each visit, the family pulled the shades and talked about their mistrust of the police. Still, the delegation came away inspired by the "patience, the persistent good will, and the bravery of the Negro families." It did not, however, come up with many new suggestions but rather endorsed the AFSC continuing to pay a community organizer to work with the families in Trumbull Park.[43]

The fact that the AFSC had sponsored the mission illustrated the priority both the national Community Relations Division and the local regional office leaders placed on the integration of Trumbull Park and the resolution of the conflict there. The goal of the Chicago HOP was to "eliminate those practices in housing which tend to impair and scar human personalities" and which "encourage hatred and violence in Chicago." The Trumbull Park conflict, which caused such hurt to the Black families and convinced "those who sought to prevent the forward march toward freedom" that intimidation and fear were legitimate and effective weapons, stood out as an obstacle to achieving that end. Indeed, in 1956 Holmgren argued that "all other attempts at achieving integration in housing" were futile if the tension in Trumbull Park continued. In the wake of *Brown v. Board of Education* and the Montgomery bus boycott, national AFSC leaders connected the problem of housing segregation in the North to Jim Crow in the South and called them both "domestic critical situations" that required as much attention as international conflict.[44]

Despite its pronouncements about the importance of housing work in general and Trumbull Park in particular, however, the Chicago HOP always struggled for funding and repeatedly nearly closed. In 1954, when the original funding ran out, the Fund for the Republic, which provided money for the CRD program, explicitly rejected the request for future funds for housing work. At the same time, Alphonse Miller, who directed the fund-raising for the national AFSC office, took a "dim view" of the Housing Opportunities Programs, hinting that there was too little to show for too much money invested. He also regarded assisting the southern freedom struggle as more important. There is evidence his view was shared in the national office, as the AFSC launched new projects to assist in the school desegregation crisis in that region. Responding to this attitude, housing staff in Chicago and elsewhere argued that the controversial goals of the program made local fund-raising nearly impossible; if they were forced to rely on such donations, they would likely have to fold up shop. To keep the HOP limping along, the Chicago Regional Office diverted funds to it from its general operating budget. But this meant finding small pockets of money to extend the work for a couple months at a time, causing anxiety and exhaustion for the staff. As Judy Miller complained in 1958, "We've been weathering one crisis after another since I came on the staff two years ago and every time it seems that we might have clear sailing to work on accomplishing something, another crisis is thrown in our way." While she promised to "battle to the bitter end to keep things going," she also pinned the blame for the lack of support for the HOP on influential Friends who lived in the suburbs and were "embarrassed" by the program.[45]

For all their persistent nurturing of the experiment in integration at Trumbull Park, by the end of the 1950s Miller and the rest of the Chicago HOP staff watched as the fruits of their efforts withered. The surge of violence after the Calumet riot in the summer of 1957 broke the spirit of many of the Black families and triggered rapid departures. In just four months nine families relocated, with more following them over the next two years. In the fall of 1957, Alvin Rose replaced Elizabeth Wood as head of the Chicago Housing Authority and made it clear that he would not increase the number of African Americans in Trumbull Park. He claimed that Blacks did not want to live there, it was dangerous to place African American families with teenagers in the project, and he was trying to avoid another "flare up" that would further damage the reputation of public housing. By 1959, the number of Black households had dropped from thirty to twenty. Those losses and the apparent cap on Black occupation at 5 percent further demoralized the remaining Black families, who began keeping to themselves. Meanwhile, the AFSC staff heard rumors that whites in South Deering "think they've won and they just need to wait it out" while the numbers of African Americans dropped to token levels. Worse, the white resisters were convinced that "their violent tactics worked." In the most basic sense, there was integration in Trumbull Park, as some African Americans continued to live there. But there was no acceptance, no sense of community, and certainly no reconciliation between South Deering and its Black neighbors.[46] Ultimately, the lesson the Chicago HOP staff learned from the withering of their hope for integration in Trumbull Park was that the opening of public housing would not happen without pressure on local government to force and protect it.

Stabilizing Integration in "Transitional" Urban Neighborhoods

Briefly in the 1950s, the AFSC also tried to achieve integration in private urban housing by helping residents of transitional neighborhoods who wanted to welcome Black neighbors and prevent white flight. In Chicago, the HOP had barely opened for business when white Friend Julia Abrahamson suggested that James Cassels assist the Hyde Park-Kenwood Community Conference (HPKCC), which had formed two years earlier to stop panic selling in the neighborhood as African Americans began moving in. The members of the HPKCC wanted to find a way to provide welcome and housing in the area to African Americans but not lose white residents in the process. In short, they wanted a balanced population. Cassels investigated ways to accomplish this by building modestly priced apartments in the neighborhood and by influencing redevelopment plans around the University of Chicago. But his enthusiasm for making Hyde Park-Kenwood a priority was never high. The HOP committee, formed to advise the program staff and comprising Friends and housing experts, warned that without integration in the suburbs, neighborhoods like Hyde Park-Kenwood would have trouble resisting becoming all or majority Black. African Americans simply needed the housing and would move into any attractive urban neighborhood they could. The HOP staff noted this was particularly true in Chicago, where areas sometimes converted from all white to all or majority Black in as little as two years—too quickly to organize to do much to keep them more evenly mixed. Thereafter, the Chicago HOP decided not to get involved with what it called neighborhood stabilization. Ironically, largely due to a redevelopment program that removed low-income housing and to the influence of the University of Chicago, Hyde Park became an integrated middle-class and professional neighborhood.[47]

Similarly, very soon after the launch of the HOP in Philadelphia, Jane Reinheimer started advising residents in neighborhoods in the northwestern part of the city that were facing transition as upwardly mobile African Americans searched for better houses. Reinheimer engaged in grassroots organizing on a block-by-block basis, meeting with white residents gathered in living rooms to talk about how to prepare for the expected arrival of Black neighbors. The Germantown Human Relations Committee sponsored the meetings and asked Reinheimer, who had grown up in the neighborhood, to help. At these and similar meetings, Reinheimer presented the positive side of living interracially, circulating promotional literature that debunked common myths about residential integration (fig. 1.3). She also dealt with vocal hostility. In one gathering, she moderated a heated exchange as a young man suggested the residents buy all the houses for sale on the block and make sure they went to white families. That idea melted away when it was discovered how much it would cost. More commonly, the attendees promised not to move and to resist efforts by real estate agents to encourage panic selling. When opposing panic selling didn't seem to be enough, the Germantown Human Relations Committee asked Reinheimer to urge salesmen to show houses in all areas without regard to race. In 1956, residents formed the Germantown Neighborhood Conference to coordinate block-level activities in the hope of "maintaining high standard neighborhoods and developing racial integration," and Reinheimer ceased her direct involvement. Two

FIGURE 1.3: *They Say That You Say*, 1955. Example of literature produced and distributed by the Housing Opportunities Programs to promote residential integration. Courtesy of the American Friends Service Committee Archives, Philadelphia.

years later, a progress report concluded that the neighborhood organizing had slowed down the transition, but by that time Germantown was already majority Black.[48]

In 1953, white residents of West Mount Airy, on the northern edge of Germantown, also began congregating to plan for incoming African American families and to discuss how to sustain a racially mixed neighborhood. Aided by Reinheimer, George Schermer of the Philadelphia Human Relations Committee, and members of the Germantown group, they researched precedents and outlined possible strategies to other residents, who agreed to form West Mount Airy Neighbors (WMAN). To prevent panic selling, WMAN made sure there was a person on every block responsible for countering misinformation and urging acceptance of change. Reinheimer's involvement ended in the spring of 1955, when it was clear the organization was off to a good start. WMAN circulated brochures to about seven hundred households and saw its membership climb to five hundred people by 1960. It emphasized not just ensuring stability but creating a true interracial community that was welcoming and cosmopolitan. The group lasted into the succeeding decades, weathering debates about Black consciousness and racial identity. Like Hyde Park, West Mount Airy remained a racially mixed community made up of mostly highly educated professionals, earning a reputation as one of the most successful efforts at neighborhood stabilization in the country.[49]

The Hyde Park-Kenwood Community Conference and West Mount Airy Neighbors achieved at least some of their goal of keeping their neighborhoods integrated and a desirable place to live. Similar organizations arose around the country in the late 1950s and early 1960s, some of which likewise could sustain a balance of white and Black families. These efforts reveal that there were middle-class whites who were willing to accept integration out of their own economic, social, or personal interest in maintaining their neighborhood. But the HOP staff in both Chicago and Philadelphia never gave precedence to urban neighborhood stabilization and withdrew from such work by the end of the 1950s. In part, the AFSC had a common practice of encouraging independent, indigenous groups to pursue goals on their own, and these neighborhood organizations no longer seemed to need its help. But the HOP staff and committee members also were convinced that stabilization of in-town neighborhoods would not succeed in the long run on any large scale. As long as whites could move out to the suburbs and African Americans lacked that option, Blacks would flock to attractive urban neighborhoods to which they had access and fill them. Only concerted campaigns to prevent sales in such areas would stop a rapid turnover. And every time a white family decided not to move, a Black family had one less option for a pleasant home. Thus, the AFSC's housing advocates ultimately concluded that defending a mixed urban neighborhood was neither ethical nor practical while the suburbs were closed to African Americans. Thereafter, the staff focused their attention on opening the new suburban communities that were rapidly growing around the regional office cities.[50]

Persuading Those in Power to Make Change

To accomplish that form of integration, the directors of the Housing Opportunities Programs tried an approach grounded in Quaker tradition: using personal persuasion to change the hearts and minds of those in power in order to bring it about. In Chicago, that mover and shaker was Philip Klutznick, president of American Community Builders (ACB), which created Park Forest, the first postwar planned suburb in Chicago and one of the first in the nation. The son of Jewish immigrants, Klutznick had experienced and witnessed acts of anti-Semitism as a child and from a young age declared his determination to fight prejudice. After getting his start working for the New Deal, during World War II he had been assistant administrator of the National Housing Agency in charge of defense housing. In that capacity, he had fought to protect the rights of Black workers. He had also gotten to know many builders. After the war, when Chicagoans Carroll Sweet and Nathan Manilow sought his advice for building a "GI town" to house returning veterans in rental units and single-family homes, he joined them as partners. In 1946, they announced their intention to create Park Forest on the southwestern edge of Chicago. Klutznick had an idealistic vision for the new suburb and consciously sought to balance its population among Protestants, Catholics, and Jews, laying out the welcome mat for the latter at a time when other development companies restricted them. The first residents arrived in August 1948, and Park Forest incorporated as a village in February 1949. By 1950, the development had three thousand families in residence, many of whom shared the builder's pride in the openness and tolerance of the community. There was one line that ACB would not cross, however: it would not sell homes to African Americans.[51]

After the Cicero riot in 1951, the village Board of Trustees formed the Park Forest Human Relations Commission (PFHRC) "to do something in Park Forest to make sure that doesn't happen here." A year later, the commission contacted Jim Cassels for help. In June 1952, he and Tom Colgan, a Philadelphia Friend who had moved to Chicago to work for the Job Opportunities Program and who resided in Park Forest, met with the commissioners and promised to find an African American family to apply for a home in the rental units. In September, Cassels informed the PFHRC that Royal and Sara Spurlack were interested. Both the members of the commission and Cassels wanted to give Klutznick the opportunity to approve the integration of Park Forest, based on his reputation as a leader in interreligious social justice work and his upcoming presidency of the national B'nai B'rith, because they believed his leadership would make a move-in go more smoothly. Their reaching out to him also reflected Friends' belief in the Inner Light in everyone, along with the possibilities of appealing to conscience and of reconciliation of parties with different interests. When they contacted him, however, negotiations quickly became rancorous.[52]

For months, Cassels attempted to persuade Klutznick to sell to African Americans but received only increasingly hostile rebuffs. In September 1952, Klutznick called Cassels to check a rumor that the AFSC was trying to place a Black family in Park Forest. At their first meeting, Cassels told him about the Spurlacks' desire for an apartment, but Klutznick was non-committal. When PFHRC members met with him to ask him to accept Black applicants, Klutznick argued that admitting African Americans would hurt the long-term economic well-being of the community and of ACB. Instead, he offered to build a separate integrated section of the suburb on its northern edge, across the railroad tracks. Cassels responded that such a move would likely create a second-class neighborhood for open occupancy. He did, however, ask the national AFSC board to seek foundations or insurance companies that would underwrite ACB's financial risk resulting from integration. The board quickly rejected that idea. In the meantime, Cassels tried to contact other leaders of ACB. The combination of that and the AFSC board rejection angered Klutznick, who accused Cassels of going behind his back and threatened to cut off contact. At a meeting between Cassels, Klutznick, and Frank Horne of the Federal Housing Administration, Klutznick wondered out loud whether the agency would continue to loan to ACB if it integrated Park Forest. When Cassels got a ruling from a local FHA administrator that the agency would finance open occupancy developments, Klutznick rebuked him for gathering evidence from "officialdom" for his own position and ended negotiations. Thereafter, the AFSC concluded that Klutznick was avoiding taking a public position and unfairly blaming Cassels for undermining the relationship. In March 1953, Cassels reported he had tried to coax Klutznick for eleven months and failed. Moral persuasion had not worked. Cassels concluded from the exchange that the only way to integrate Park Forest was to encourage white homeowners to sell to African Americans.[53]

Jane Reinheimer and Jacques Wilmore reached the same conclusion in Bucks County, Pennsylvania, at almost the same time. The Philadelphia HOP had formed with the primary goal of forestalling segregation in the county's rapidly growing residential communities. The largest of those promised to be the Pennsylvania Levittown, built by William Levitt of the construction company Levitt and Sons. Levitt had formed the company in 1929 with his father Abraham and brother Alfred and had some mild success during the 1930s. At the end of the war, he bet that returning veterans would soon be swamping the housing market in search of new homes. To tap that demand, the company bought land on Long Island to build simple, identical houses with mass-produced prefabricated parts. Levittown, New York, as the Levitts named the community, started with rental units and then added homes for sale; what it did not and would not include as long as Levitt had his way was nonwhite families. Indeed, the rental contract initially contained a clause that tenants could not allow non-Caucasians to use the property. After the *Shelley v. Kraemer* decision, that clause was dropped; but despite a pressure campaign from local civil rights organizations, Levitt did not budge from his adamant position that as a private business, Levitt and Sons could choose to whom it would rent or sell and that the presence of Black residents would hurt sales in the community. When the company chose to build on land in Bucks County near Philadelphia, the policy of restricting sales to white buyers was imported along with the mass-production construction technique.[54]

Soon after the announcement of the new residential developments for Bucks County, a coalition of many organizations, including the NAACP, Women's International League for Peace and Freedom, and local unions, began pressing Levitt and other builders to sell to Black families. They tried persuasion first. After a very early meeting between company officials and representatives of housing and civil rights groups, Wilmore recalled that Levitt's attitude was "almost belligerent at first" as he questioned the group's right even to talk with him about integrated housing. The Bucks County branch of the NAACP tried again and hosted a meeting between Levitt and representatives of local liberal groups. Levitt did propose building a separate interracial unit, but that suggestion was rejected as supporting segregation. The NAACP also gathered much the same group to meet with officials of U.S. Steel, who bragged about the company being a friend to African Americans but declined to make a statement in favor of open housing. Wilmore and Reinheimer attended these meetings and through the end of 1953 continued to negotiate with business leaders and builders; they continued to receive negative responses.[55] They also tried legal action. In 1954 and 1955, the AFSC lined up potential plaintiffs for an NAACP lawsuit to force Levitt to open his community. A judge quickly dismissed the case, however, accepting Levitt's argument that he was a private businessman and no law mandated nondiscrimination in housing by nongovernmental entities. The NAACP did not appeal. The joint efforts by the AFSC and civil rights organizations had failed to persuade the major builders to change their policies.[56]

Building Your Own

If open housing advocates could neither sway nor legally coerce leading businessmen to sell to African Americans, perhaps the Housing
Opportunities Program staff could find and support those who would.
In the mid-1950s, AFSC housing directors sought open-minded developers who might build integrated suburbs; coordinated communication
and negotiations between individuals and groups interested in funding
such developments; and promised to help advertise the homes and do
community relations work to head off negative reactions. These efforts
required a lot of daily time and effort, but most often they led to dead
ends or disappointing results. For example, Phil Buskirk spent half of
1953 negotiating with John Tolan and John Melville, who owned two hundred acres outside San Francisco and wanted to build an open occupancy
development of up to one thousand homes. He helped them apply for
financing from mortgage providers and prevailed upon the Philadelphia
office to help as well. Once Tolan and Melville indicated they would not
advertise the suburb's inclusive nature for fear of alienating white customers, the HOP backed off. Around the same time, Charlotte Mack, a
wealthy white widow, approached Buskirk with the offer of $150,000 to
put toward a housing experiment that would demonstrate "how people of
different kinds can plan together, build together, and live together" while
still yielding a profit on the investment. Buskirk tried unsuccessfully for
several months to secure mortgage financing. At that point he gave up
and suggested to Mack that she hire a firm to build as many houses as her
money alone would cover, at most fifteen to twenty, admitting that this
would not make much impact on the need or provide incentive to other
investors to follow her open occupancy example. In Philadelphia, Jane
Reinheimer spent four years helping Betty Jacob, a Friend and wife of
an AFSC board member, sponsor a small integrated development. Jacob
initially wanted to build in Swarthmore but was rebuffed by opposition
there. Although difficulty finding financing and getting city government
permits to build continued to thwart her vision, in the end she put up sixteen houses in nearby Cheyney, of which eight were occupied by African
Americans. The collaboration with these potential builders convinced
Buskirk and Reinheimer that there were sympathetic white individuals
willing to risk an investment in integrated housing, giving them hope.
But the experiences also exposed the obstacles that stood in their way,
including mortgage company resistance, construction firm reluctance,
planning official denials, and neighborhood opposition.[57]

But sometimes those obstacles could be surmounted. By the end of the
1950s, the AFSC housing programs had helped successful interracial com-

munities take root in the suburbs of Philadelphia and San Francisco. In 1952, Reinheimer and Wilmore began assisting Morris Milgram in finding mortgage financing and potential buyers for an interracial development in Bucks County. Milgram was a Jewish social activist turned builder with a long history of engagement in labor and civil rights causes and experience in his father-in-law's construction company. As he was learning the business, he put up white-only developments like most other companies. But by the early 1950s, he decided that his "conscience hurt" and started looking for funds to build and sell houses without discrimination. Twenty mortgage companies turned him down. Wilmore and Richard Bennett contacted Frank Horne, head of the race relations advisory service of the FHA, for help getting mortgage insurance for Milgram's project. Other Philadelphia-area Quakers also stepped up to finance the venture. Most important, George Otto, a builder from a prominent Quaker family who had connections to other wealthy Friends, formed a corporation with Milgram that sold stock and raised $150,000. Otto and Milgram's first project was Concord Park.[58]

The Philadelphia AFSC also recruited residents for Milgram's development. Beginning in the summer of 1952, even before land was selected or financing arranged, Reinheimer started "spreading the word" to people who might be interested in living in "an interracial environment." She approached people individually and reached out to Jewish and Quaker organizations, two groups that had by this time demonstrated their interest in fighting prejudice and in supporting housing opportunity. She also hosted meetings, such as one for thirty people at Fellowship Farm, a training center and retreat for civil and human rights activists. By the end of the summer, she reported that seven white Jewish and two African American families had expressed interest. At the end of 1954, a groundbreaking ceremony at Concord Park attracted over two hundred people, about half of them white. But at that point, of the nearly seventy houses presold, only ten were going to white couples. One of those was bought by George and Eunice Grier, sociologists whom the AFSC paid to do some research so that they would have the down payment for their Concord Park home; another was purchased by Bob Lyon, a Service Committee staff member. Worried that the point of the project would be lost if it became a majority or all-Black subdivision, Milgram established a quota for Concord Park residents of 45 percent Black and 55 percent white. Attracting the white families remained a problem throughout the selling phase of the development, but by the time all houses were built and occupied, the ratio held.[59]

When Concord Park opened, the press hailed it as "America's first single home development built by private enterprise with the firm intent to find both white and Negro buyers—and to keep the place integrated." Built on fifty acres just ten miles from the all-white Levittown in Bucks County, the suburb of 139 moderately priced homes was designed as a counterexample to that more famous community to show that it was possible to make money while building for interracial occupancy. Unlike the scenes of violence and harassment confronting Black families who moved into white suburbs elsewhere, there was no organized opposition to the opening of Concord Park, although Milgram had done nothing to hide his intention that it be integrated. As historian Thomas Sugrue has argued, that lack of trouble was likely due to the careful selection of a location adjacent to an existing Black community and cut off from white areas by a railroad, turnpike, and cemetery. Research conducted by the Institute of Urban Studies in 1958, however, revealed a high level of satisfaction among the white residents. Seventy-five percent of them expressed "unqualified" approval of their neighbors, extolled the sense of community where "people who don't even know you wave, because you live here too," and admitted that meeting African American families had challenged their own prejudices. One African American resident recalled years later, "That was the point of Concord Park. You learned how to be tolerant. You absorbed each person individually"—an observation that would have pleased Friends who saw housing integration as a way to honor the dignity of every person.[60]

But the balance of Black and white families in Concord Park did not last. Subject to the same pressures that caused attractive urban neighborhoods to convert to all or majority Black, that suburb similarly lost its white population, though at a slower pace. Milgram had written into the purchase contracts a stipulation that the initial owners must offer their homes for resale first to his company, so that he could monitor and control the changeover in population. The first family to move out was African American, and they sold their home to a white family. But because most other developments were still closed to Black buyers, in the 1960s, when white families were moving out, African Americans snapped up the available homes. Then, as Sugrue argues, by the 1970s the young liberal whites that Concord Park had been depending on to keep the community integrated were losing interest in the "ticky tacky" houses of the suburbs, and those in Milgram's project were becoming older and less attractive. Moreover, most whites still did not want to live in integrated communities. On September 15, 2000, the last of the original white residents, Warren and Betsy Swartzbeck, moved out.[61]

The AFSC was more directly responsible for the development of Sunnyhills, an integrated, partly cooperative housing development in Milpitas, California, cosponsored with the United Auto Workers (UAW) union but largely midwifed by HOP director Phil Buskirk. In 1954, the Ford Motor Company announced it was moving its Richmond, California, plant fifty-five miles south to Milpitas, in rapidly expanding Santa Clara County. The fourteen hundred Ford workers, of whom about 15 percent were African Americans, would transfer to the new facility and thus need new homes. In response to this news, the AFSC Northern California office formed the Santa Clara County Community Relations Program. By getting in "on the ground floor," the new program sought to prevent segregation in the housing quickly being constructed to accommodate the new population. Buskirk moved from the Richmond HOP to the Santa Clara County office. At the same time, the leaders of the local UAW, which had negotiated the transfer rights for the employees, began looking for housing for its members.[62]

At first separately and then together, the AFSC and the UAW searched for land, a developer, and financing to build integrated housing near the new plant. Buskirk initially worked with John Reardon, who had options on a couple plots of land and was willing to build for open occupancy. But various government bodies made zoning changes or denied permits, stalling him four times, and in late 1954 he gave up. Meanwhile, the UAW had connected with developer Joseph Kaufman, who had assurances from local agents of the FHA that it was financially safe to build for open occupancy in the area. The fact that the UAW would help recruit its members as buyers, and thus guarantee a customer base, also nudged Kaufman to agree to build. Buskirk then secured a promise of mortgage financing from Metropolitan Life Insurance in New York, the same company that had given Concord Park its loan. In March 1955, the UAW found a construction company and signed contracts with it and with Kaufman on prices and specifications for houses in a range affordable by factory workers. Over two hundred couples expressed willingness to buy in the Kaufman development, now called Rancho Agua Caliente. In April, the *Daily Palo Alto Times* announced the pouring of the first foundation and praised the development as "the culmination of a visionary ideal and a 'long tough fight.'" UAW leader Arnold Callan added that it was "made possible by the cooperation of the union" and the AFSC. In thanks, several streets would be named for union leaders and one for the AFSC's Buskirk.[63]

Unsurprisingly, given their experience with building integrated housing so far, the AFSC and the UAW ran into opposition, which slowed down the project. The roadblocks Reardon had encountered signaled the extent of bureaucratic resistance. Around the same time that Reardon gave up his plans, Buskirk attended a meeting of the Milpitas city council and received a blasting. Councilors criticized the AFSC for having taken "upon itself the task of helping Milpitas solve its problems." One member added that in fact, there was no race relations problem in Milpitas because there was no Black population. He was a real estate man, and he assured Buskirk his Black clients did not want to go "where they [were] not wanted." He offered to introduce him to people who could praise the accepting climate in the community. Finally, as Buskirk recalled, the councilor suggested that the AFSC might be "happier if we confined our efforts to communities other than Milpitas." Despite this hostility, in March 1955 the county Planning and Engineering Departments approved the subdivision contingent on the provision of a drainage plan.[64]

That drainage plan became an expensive problem, which exemplified the kinds of policies that could be manipulated to block integrated housing. Under local rules, if a developer built a sewer and drainage system, any new subdivision that connected to it had to reimburse that developer one hundred dollars per acre of the new suburb. Kaufman's Rancho Agua Caliente land adjoined Sunnyhills, a development by San Lorenzo Homes, which had installed a sewer and drainage system. Under the existing law, the UAW/AFSC project anticipated paying $5,500 to San Lorenzo Homes and included that in the financing plan. But the managers of San Lorenzo Homes feared that the presence of an integrated subdivision on their border would prevent them from finding buyers for their sixty-three unsold houses. To stop the UAW project, they pressed members of the Sanitation District Board for more money for the connection to the sewer system and the board obliged, changing the reimbursement rate so that Rancho Agua Caliente now owed $60,000. The UAW protested the decision and asked for an exception, given that their proposal had already been approved for financing, to no avail. Two months later, the matter was still at a standstill, although pressures on all sides were mounting. San Lorenzo was still not selling its last houses and was losing money. Joseph Kaufman wanted out completely. The UAW workers, now commuting over a hundred miles a day to their new workplace from Richmond, were exhausted. To speed things along, the UAW agreed to pay the high sewer fees and absorb the cost. Ultimately, a new developer, the Corporation for the 20th Century, bought both the Kaufman and the San Lorenzo properties and merged them into one large community, keeping the name Sunnyhills and dropping the maybe too prophetic Agua Caliente, or "hot water."[65]

The next step was to sell the houses. In addition to marketing by the developer and UAW's recruitment of its members, the AFSC and the Santa Clara County Council of Churches started a direct mail campaign and called prospective home buyers.[66] Sales were sluggish, however. Throughout 1956, several factors conspired to cause turmoil in the project. The fact that the subdivision was open to African Americans likely contributed, but none of the parties involved pointed to it as a major factor at the time or in retrospect. As sales and move-ins did happen, African Americans comprised only a small percentage of the buyers, ranging from approximately 10 to 14 percent—just under their proportion of the Ford workforce. Moreover, their homes were scattered throughout the subdivision. Instead, the project sponsors noted increased competition from other developments as the building boom in Milpitas continued. To attract more customers, AFSC and union leaders persuaded the Corporation for the 20th Century's sales agents to reduce closing costs and allow veterans to move into a new home after only a token down payment. For a short time, this helped make Sunnyhills one of the fastest-selling communities in the area. But over the summer, management shakeups left construction and sales in limbo. The Corporation for the 20th Century pulled out and collapsed. A new construction company was brought in, but after starting fifteen houses it just stopped building. Stone Enterprises took over the management but failed to do any significant advertising for months. Then its assets got tied up when the owner was sued for divorce. Because Wells Fargo had loaned money to the company, it took over management of the development. Despite the turnover, Buskirk remained optimistic about the "magnificent" promise of Sunnyhills, if a "competent and trust-worthy developer" could be found.[67]

In early 1957, Buskirk and the UAW officials agreed that the competitiveness that had hurt sales at Sunnyhills only involved houses selling at prices above the reach of the typical factory worker. If they could find a way to keep home costs more modest, they could tap into a market of both white and Black families not being served by the area's construction boom. Buskirk argued that the way to do that was by making at least some of the community into a cooperative. Responding to public pressure for alternative means to produce modest-income housing, section 213 of the 1949 Housing Act allowed the FHA to insure forty-year mortgages with a 3 percent down payment on houses in developments that were cooperatively owned and managed by a nonprofit corporation. When 140 union members answered a survey saying they would be interested in acquiring a home in a co-op, the FHA approved Buskirk's proposal. A new building firm, Kavanaugh Construction, built the first section of the cooperative, which included seventy-eight homes. This seemed to break the sales logjam, as by early 1958 there were plans for over five hundred additional homes to be built on a cooperative basis, and the first section of them sold out in advance. Though the number of African Americans in the community remained relatively low at about

15 percent, the AFSC concluded that "already Sunnyhills is one of the largest racially integrated subdivisions in the United States."[68]

As the Sunnyhills community continued to grow, it experienced additional problems. Not long after the launch of the cooperative program, UAW officials and Buskirk learned that real estate agents were trying to scare off white owners and buyers with warnings about a Black invasion. Buskirk confronted one realty company, and the UAW wrote to others and to the state Commissioner of Real Estate to protest. The practice died down, and Buskirk later noted that some of the people who had left later wished they hadn't. Still, there was a lot of turnover in the cooperative sections of the community. In some cases, the Kavanaugh firm had sold to families who did not have the financial wherewithal to make the payments. While some left voluntarily, others had to be evicted. In addition, there remained a lot of new houses for sale with tempting terms in the area, and it was relatively easy for homeowners in Sunnyhills to leave by simply turning their home over to the cooperative rather than having to find a buyer. Finally, many of the people who bought in the newer sections did so because the costs were low rather than out of any philosophical commitment to cooperative principles.[69]

Despite these glitches, Sunnyhills provided housing for Ford and other industrial workers and exemplified integrated suburban living. The proportion of African Americans there remained at approximately 15 percent, and a 1966 report on the area noted that other subdivisions in Milpitas included Black families and experienced no incidents of violence to a family moving into a majority white neighborhood. Sponsors and residents of Sunnyhills noted that "the integration aspect" had never disturbed white buyers or caused conflict in the community. As one salesman put it, "Every white prospect asked about Negroes," and then "they went ahead and bought anyway." United Auto Workers leaders at the time and sociologists George and Eunice Grier in retrospect argued that this response was because the low prices and cooperative financing appealed to low- to middle-income factory workers, who could not afford most of the other homes in the local market. While approximately 40 percent of the residents in the cooperative sections of the development worked at Ford, Sunnyhills also became home to employees of other manufacturers that had located in the county, including the new "space and missile" industries. In their study of Sunnyhills, the Griers argued that the one thing the residents had in common was "they could not have afforded to purchase comparable housing anywhere else within convenient range of their jobs." The desire for a home helped white working-class families accept the integration at Sunnyhills, because, as Walter Reuther, national president of the UAW, concluded, "people will move into an attractive home, at prices they can afford to pay, regardless of prejudice."[70]

Just as the AFSC in Santa Clara was wrapping up its work in Sunnyhills, the Chicago Housing Opportunities Program backed a proposal to build an open occupancy development in the upper-middle-class suburbs on the North Shore; it met with far less success. In 1955 and 1957, Morris Milgram had visited Chicago and attended lunches organized by the AFSC with area builders to promote the idea of a Concord Park for that city.[71] A year later, a group of local businessmen formed Progress Development Corporation (PDC) and became a subsidiary of Milgram's Modern Community Developers. In late 1959, PDC purchased land on the North Shore to build fifty-one homes in the $27,000–$40,000 price range, a relatively high sum attributable to the cost of land in the area and the size of homes in competing subdivisions. Officers of PDC then asked the AFSC for staff assistance, office space, and help in assessing how much resistance the open occupancy development could expect. Before the staff could answer, news of the planned community leaked out. Some members of the PDC board had talked with people in the area about the intent to integrate, and word had circulated through the village of Deerfield, which adjoined PDC's property.[72]

White residents of Deerfield reacted swiftly and virulently against PDC's plans. One hundred people attended a meeting between Milgram and village officials to decry the secrecy of the planning and accuse PDC and the AFSC of forcing integration on an unsuspecting populous. At a meeting with thirty local people, Jane Weston, who had just become the new Chicago HOP director in September 1959, fended off anti-Semitic attacks on Milgram and red-baiting of the AFSC. Then on November 24, a "meeting of over 600 residents of Deerfield" "was the most bitter and violent expression of racial animosities" that had broken out in the Chicago area since Trumbull Park. By the end of 1959, this opposition had spawned the North Shore Residents Association to stop the integration of Deerfield and keep African Americans out of the northern suburbs. After it formed, the more "raucous" behavior at public meetings died down, but white residents remained committed to forcing the Progress Development Corporation to drop its plans.[73]

Although almost drowned out by the naysayers, a smaller but still vocal group of Deerfield residents welcomed the PDC proposal and volunteered to help achieve the peaceful integration of the North Shore. When news of the proposed interracial subdivision leaked, the HOP office immediately released a public statement endorsing private enterprise efforts to challenge segregation by building homes for all. Once its name was positively associated with the PDC plan, the AFSC office began getting phone calls, many negative but some from people offering to help. On November 22, six white residents formed the Deerfield Citizens Committee for Human Rights. Within a month, it had more than one hundred members and had hosted two public forums. After that, it looked to the AFSC for help figuring out what to do next. The HOP encouraged the committee's members to reach out to their own neighbors to try to change minds. Meanwhile, an older organization, the North Shore Human Relations Committee, asked the AFSC for help gathering signatures on an open occupancy pledge by which residents could publicly declare that they would welcome Black neighbors; it planned on publishing the results. Weston wasn't sure how much would come of the specific plans, but she saw the fact that these groups were talking and strategizing as an important first step for a long-term organizing effort on the North Shore. Though smaller than the opposition movement, the pro-integration forces gave the Chicago Regional Office staff "new hope that a way to a solution [to housing segregation] in Chicago may be found," because "a new interest and more important a deepening of concern" in the metropolitan area was evident. Amid the conflict in Deerfield, this new hope encouraged the HOP staff to propose shifting their energy to nurturing human relations activity in the suburbs.[74]

While the public debate raged, the Deerfield Village Park Board filed a condemnation suit in county court to seize PDC's land and use it as a park. Despite campaigning by the Deerfield Citizens Committee for Human Rights against it, on December 21 local citizens voted to approve a bond issue to pay for the Park Board's acquisition of the land. Milgram and Modern Community Developers filed a federal lawsuit seeking an injunction against the condemnation and claiming that the Park Board's actions discriminated against the company because it was planning to sell to African Americans. In March 1960, the local federal district judge ruled against Milgram, who appealed the decision, intending to take it to the Supreme Court if necessary. In the meantime, the Park Board won its condemnation suit in county court. Milgram asked the AFSC to intervene with an amicus curiae brief in the federal case. The HOP staff argued for doing so, because they feared that a legal victory for the opposition would provide a playbook for any suburban officials wanting to stop an integrated subdivision. But the national board refrained. Quaker lawyers argued that it would be hard to dispute the Park Board's legal right to condemn the land and to prove that it did so to prevent the integration of the community. It took several years for the case to complete its passage through the federal courts, but ultimately the Supreme Court would not hear the appeal. Milgram's North Shore development hopes died.[75]

In shutting down Milgram's plan for a Concord Park on the North

Shore, the uproar in Deerfield illustrated both the hostility against open housing subdivisions in the white suburbs and the tactics available to stop them. By the start of the new decade, the AFSC's HOP staff had decided that the time and effort required to sponsor the construction of open occupancy developments was not worth it, because in most cases—Sunnyhills being an exception—they did not lead to integration in the surrounding communities. But the turmoil in Deerfield had a silver lining for the AFSC's housing program. The first weeks of the crisis convinced the staff of a possibility of nurturing a more welcoming instinct among white suburbanites than what appeared on the surface. They were shocked by the level of resistance but also encouraged by the small pockets of organized sympathy. Perhaps more people were beginning to see that the suburbs could not stay segregated forever and were willing to figure out how integration could happen peacefully, even if only to protect the good name of their neighborhood. In retrospect, the AFSC credited the Deerfield crisis with inspiring the formation of forty suburban human relations groups on the North Shore, with approximately one hundred members each.[76] Over the next few years, organizing such groups and working with them to recruit and support Black "pioneer" families—the movement's term for the first African American family in a white neighborhood—became the AFSC's primary strategy to integrate the suburbs, one that would lead it to direct action on the North Shore and ultimately to cooperation with the Chicago Freedom Movement.

·

By the time of the Deerfield conflict, lessons learned in the early years of the Housing Opportunities Programs had informed decisions about what strategies to pursue and which to leave behind or at least minimize. At a 1957 meeting to review the HOPs, community relations staff concluded, with some understatement, that "attempts to persuade builders and Realtors to change housing patterns have not been hopeful in very many places" and instead had only revealed "the extent of blocks in the way." By that time, Jane Reinheimer had "really given up work with the industry."[77] While HOP advisory committees never completely abandoned the hope for changing the hearts of the movers and shakers, the staff greatly reduced time spent trying to achieve it. They also began to recognize how government policies, and the inclinations of the individuals charged with implementing them, limited what could be accomplished in housing integration. The byzantine system of mortgage and construction approvals necessary to build a new development could be manipulated by the opposition at any step, as Morris Milgram and other open-minded developers discovered while trying to launch suburban interracial subdivisions. And city government decisions to curb the number of Black families in Trumbull Park or not build public housing at all reinforced segregation in urban housing. Though initially hesitant to engage in direct political agitation, the AFSC's Community Relations Division and housing staff eventually decided that integration depended in part on challenging the housing industry and changing laws. Finally, Quaker ideals of honoring the light in every person and promoting mutual understanding had led the initial HOP directors to pursue reconciliation between parties in housing conflicts. That meant reaching out both to Black families struggling to obtain new homes and to white families to ameliorate their fears and help them adjust to integration. But it was hard to bring people together when confronted with a wall of hostility such as that in South Deering or Deerfield.

The clearest lesson AFSC workers drew from the early years of the HOPs was that despite the frustrations and failures, they needed to persevere in the pursuit of housing integration as well as draw from new resources and hone new strategies for doing so. By the late 1950s as the southern freedom struggle was getting under way, CRD leaders warned that residential segregation would "nullify progress in other areas of race relations" and that the United States was at a "crossroads" between integration and the "crystallization of existing patterns." Nudging the country in the more moral direction would require tireless effort to find and sustain Black families who wanted to pioneer in new neighborhoods, and the long slow work of community organizing would be needed to create a welcoming environment for them there. The key resource would be longtime staff like Phil Buskirk, Jane Reinheimer and Jacques Wilmore, Jane Weston, and others, who each day would try to knock more holes in the wall of hostility. But the HOPs' early efforts also introduced the staff to potential allies in local civic, church, and civil rights groups in each of the three cities where the programs launched. They collaborated with the UAW in Milpitas and the NAACP in both Trumbull Park and Bucks County. In addition, they had seen liberal-minded whites in small, grassroots groups like the Germantown Human Relations Committee, the Santa Clara County Council of Churches, and the Deerfield Citizens Committee for Human Rights act in favor of integration. In the quest to open the suburbs, the HOPs would collaborate with local civil rights organizations to connect with potential Black homeowners, and they would seek out sympathetic whites, organize them in fair housing organizations, and facilitate their efforts to change their own neighborhoods.

2. Organizing the Suburbs

White Fair Housers and Black Pioneers

In August 1957, William and Daisy Myers and their children became the first African American family to buy a home in Levittown, Pennsylvania. Their move and the violence that greeted it became national news, with popular mass media articles covering their story and a sensationalistic half-hour television program bringing it into living rooms around the country. In the months that followed, Philadelphia Housing Opportunities Program staff member Thelma Babbitt pursued two related tasks that received significantly less attention. She immediately set to work finding other Black families to move to Levittown so that the Myerses would not be lone tokens. To do so, she met with middle-class African Americans in their churches, the NAACP, and women's organizations in Philadelphia and Trenton. Working with a Quaker real estate agent, Babbitt showed families around Levittown to allay their concerns about possible negative reactions and introduce them to the Myerses and to sympathetic whites. After many false starts, she helped Kenneth and Julia Mosby move to Levittown and monitored the community response. Meanwhile, Babbitt responded to a request for help from Friends in nearby Burlington County, New Jersey, who wanted to ensure that minorities could move into real estate developer William Levitt's new suburb there. She set out to "develop a group of citizens who will work on their own to 'open up housing opportunities for Negroes'" and found "enthusiasm among a surprising number of people for seeking ways of making some impact" on segregation. In organizing the Burlington County Human Relations Council, she was not interested in the "professional liberals" but in recruiting sympathetic people who "have not been especially active before so they can take some leadership." Moved by the "new spirit" of the civil rights movement, in the early 1960s the council became an independent entity with its own outreach programs to Black home seekers and a model for organizing "fair housers" in California, Chicago, and elsewhere.[1]

Coming in the wake of the bus boycott in Montgomery, Alabama, and the school desegregation crisis in Little Rock, Arkansas, the Myerses' move into Levittown and the confrontation it sparked there drew attention to racism in the North and located the battle against it in the rapidly expanding suburbs. To join that battle, the AFSC shifted strategy away from lobbying civic officials and major builders. Still guided by Quaker principles of moral persuasion, reconciliation, and the cultivation of the potential of every person, the staff simultaneously worked with individual Black families to help them move to previously closed suburbs and created fair housing councils made up primarily of middle-class whites who would welcome the newcomers into their neighborhoods. The latter task was relatively more successful. The fair housing councils briefly became a popular outlet through which earnest white liberals could respond to the civil rights movement and act on their desire to do something about discrimination in their own corners of the world. Members of these groups ran open housing pledge campaigns, hosted educational forums, maintained lists of available housing, helped Black families negotiate purchases, and defended homes against vandalism and violence. By nurturing the fair housing councils, the AFSC staff sought not only to create a welcoming climate in the suburbs but also to develop independent leadership among the residents there. Internal and external problems, including classist assumptions about who pioneers should be, hostility from local officials and residents, discriminatory federal policies, and ambivalence among middle-class African Americans, limited the councils' effectiveness and kept the actual amount of integration accomplished low. But their experiences in that effort and the lessons learned from it contributed to the Community Relations Division's shift toward grassroots organizing to stimulate local people to take action on their own. Because it was one of the few national organizations with staff devoted to nurturing these community-based organizations, the AFSC's experience with the fair housing councils illuminates how and why they grew, their activities and impact, and the reasons why they stalled in so many places.

The Postwar Human Relations Movement

The fair housing councils had their roots in the post–World War II proliferation of public and private human relations organizations. During the war, mass mobility, dislocation, and competition for jobs and housing had sparked racial conflicts in the form of hate strikes, violence at the site of integrated defense industry worker housing projects, and riots in major urban centers, most significantly in Los Angeles and Detroit in 1943. This climate inspired a concern about race relations among religious groups, including among some of the AFSC's longtime partners. In response to the wartime crises, over one hundred secular interracial relations committees also "sprung up" around the country, the majority of which were private, community-based, and dedicated primarily to reducing "any likelihood of similar trouble" close to home. After the war, revelations of Nazi persecution and mass murder of the Jews demonstrated the horrific result of bigotry, triggering calls for tolerance and attacks on the "race problem." At the end of the decade, the *Journal of Negro Education* reported that there were more than one thousand local human relations committees. Some were state or city government agencies empowered by governors and mayors to investigate problems and lobby for legislation. But over six hundred were grassroots citizen efforts or, as Lester Granger of the Urban League called them, "spontaneous gatherings of people." With a few exceptions, these groups emphasized education and persuasion as they published pamphlets, sponsored mass meetings, presented radio dramas, and circulated literature with the goal of challenging stereotypes about African Americans and changing white racial attitudes and practices.[2]

The postwar human relations committees' strategies reflected an embrace of contemporary social science theories about the nature of racial prejudice and its elimination. The most widely known and influential example of that work was Swedish sociologist Gunnar Myrdal's *An American Dilemma: The Negro Problem and Modern Democracy*, commissioned by the Carnegie Corporation in 1937 and published in 1944. Most readers likely did not digest the over one thousand pages of text stuffed with charts and graphs, but Myrdal summarized his conclusions in a concise introduction, and reviews and commentaries in the mainstream press popularized his argument. In brief, although the study exhaustively documented the social, economic, and legal barriers set up against African Americans, Myrdal characterized the dilemma of race as a moral conflict between professed American ideals and the reality of the Black experience. More specifically, the problem was seated in white hearts and minds. Myrdal believed that white racial animus could be changed, and indeed it was on the verge of changing because of the combination of the war and advances in knowledge. He, like other social scientists at the time and members of the human relations movement who were inspired by them, trusted that white Americans only needed to have their eyes opened to see their own prejudices, recognize discrimination's pernicious effect, and embrace equal opportunity. Like the national Jewish agencies and interfaith groups such as the National Council for Christians and Jews, the AFSC embraced this social science–based racial liberalism, which was not that far from Quakers' belief that people could be persuaded to see the Inner Light in everyone and accept the inherent equality of all.[3]

In the public imagination, the 1950s were a time of conformity and social and political repression. Scholars have characterized the postwar suburbs, where residents organized through their Parent Teacher Associations, coffee klatches, churches, and social networks against both communist threats and Black neighbors, as the birthplace of the modern New Right.[4] But other historians have demonstrated the extent of Cold War–era progressive social activism and organizational life, particularly among women.[5] Indeed, despite the hardening grip of McCarthyite conservatism, the human relations movement persisted in the suburbs throughout the decade. The AFSC staff met and collaborated with people in that movement from the beginning of the organization's Housing Opportunities Programs. In Chicago, one of James Cassels's first contacts in 1952 was with the North Shore Citizens Committee, which presented informal and didactic skits about potential African American move-ins. In the Philadelphia area, the Women's International League for Peace and Freedom helped launch a human relations committee in Bucks County while the League of Women Voters surveyed housing conditions for Blacks in the mainline suburbs. The AFSC's organizers in the Northern California Regional Office in San Francisco encountered so many county and city branches of the Council for Civic Unity and the Fair Play Council that they mainly spent their time coordinating the cooperation among these groups. The AFSC naturally found support in Friends Meetings and Quaker organizations, but other religious organizations and individuals, from the Bucks County YMCA to the Santa Clara Council of Churches, Chicago Catholic Interracial Council, American Jewish Committee and B'nai B'rith chapters in several communities, and the Unitarian Service Committee of Chicago, provided opportunities for faith-based progressive social action. In its fair housing organizing, the AFSC tapped into these existing networks and tried to direct the energy of liberal suburbanites toward welcoming Black families into their neighborhoods.

Integrating the Iconic Suburbs: Park Forest and Levittown

The experience in Levittown, Pennsylvania; Park Forest, Illinois; and Richmond, California had taught HOP directors that they could not achieve much integration by asking builders, real estate agents, or other business leaders to change their policies. In 1953, the staff began to seek alternatives, trying a bottom-up approach of finding white owners willing to sell their house to a Black family, then helping that family move in. The idea of helping a Black pioneer take up residence in an all-white suburb drew from Quaker ideals of moral enlightenment; the hope was that once a Black family was in their midst, the white neighbors would accept and even value interracial living. But national housing experts and advocates also agreed that organizing white resales to African Americans was a strategy worth trying. In late 1952, Robert Weaver, former member of Franklin Roosevelt's Black Cabinet group of advisors who still had close ties to Washington, warned that the Eisenhower administration was not interested in fair housing, and little could be accomplished by pursuing change through top-down government action. The AFSC and other groups, he encouraged, would do better by working through private channels. More specifically, housing expert Charles Abrams suggested to Jane Reinheimer that if done openly, perhaps transfer of a white owner's home into the hands of a Black buyer would teach even William Levitt "the error of his ways." Hortense Gabel of the National Committee against Discrimination in Housing added that she thought this strategy would be "more meaningful" than any other, because it would bring African Americans directly into the community. The bottom line was because builders continued to resist any other strategies, the only way to open the new suburban communities was through the resale of a house to a Black family.[6] The first move-ins to Park Forest and the Pennsylvania Levittown illustrate how AFSC staff and volunteers collaborated with sympathetic residents in these communities to find homes for sale, recruit Black buyers, prepare for the move, and respond to the trouble that greeted it.

After having failed to persuade developer Philip Klutznick to integrate Park Forest in 1952, the Chicago HOP staff began cooperating with residents of the suburb to try again in 1956. In June, new HOP director Ed Holmgren met with a group of families affiliated with the Unitarian Church who were still interested in bringing in Black neighbors. They solicited statements of support for integration from clergymen for release during Brotherhood Week, an annual time set aside nationally since the 1930s for sermons on race relations and exchanges between white and Black churches. Harry Teshima, a Japanese American veteran of both the internment camps and the United States Army, led the Unitarian group and joined the Chicago HOP advisory committee. He pushed the Park Forest group to take more assertive action, saying that "the way to have integration is to integrate," and began searching for houses whose owners would sell without prejudice and for Black pioneers interested in the community.[7] By early 1957, he had identified three potential houses but failed to locate a pioneer buyer for them before they were sold to whites. Then in the spring of 1958, he found an interested Black family. The Unitarian group got their hopes up and asked the AFSC for help preparing for the family's arrival. But no house was available, and again nothing happened. To give the group something to do while he tried to arrange a resale, and to persuade more neighbors to support the effort, Teshima organized a community education program. His hopes dimmed when in the summer of 1959 a white owner listed his house with a Black real estate broker, and belying the community's open-minded self-image, a mob gathered and engaged in a shouting match with the seller. Klutznick's American Community Builders used the incident as an excuse to resist opening the suburb to African Americans even more firmly.[8]

When a Black family finally purchased a house in Park Forest, the pro-integrationists sprang into action to head off any negative reaction. Charles Wilson was an assistant professor in the School of Commerce at DePaul University in Chicago. He was acquainted with some of the whites in Teshima's group and "was intensely interested in breaking the racial barrier at Park Forest." In advance of his family moving in, members of the village board and the Park Forest Human Relations Commission visited the homes near Wilson's to let people know what was happening, encourage neighborliness, and identify potential resistance. The local press cooperated by not publicizing the move. In addition, Wilson followed the AFSC's suggestion to move in quickly, not leave the house unoccupied, and get an unlisted phone number. He and his wife and children moved into their house just after Christmas, 1959. There were no incidents of violence or harassment. According to national media reports, Klutznick's wife, Ethel, even sent a cake with the inscription "Welcome to the Wilsons to Park Forest—The Klutznicks." Village President Robert Dinerstein, who had supported the move-in, recalled sardonically that the cake was real but delivered by the chauffer, and the story helped Klutznick, who had "done absolutely nothing to help this," come out "smelling like a rose."[9]

The absence of violence did not signal an absence of opposition. In the days between the visits to neighbors by human relations commissioners and trustees and the Wilsons' move-in, rumors swirled rapidly through the community, metastasizing to some extreme lengths. Dinerstein recalled hearing stories that five Black families were planning to move in and that some residents held the absolute conviction that one hundred new houses were being sold to African Americans. Village officials got so caught up dealing with the flood of complaints during the first twenty-four hours after the move-in that they forgot to call the Wilsons to make sure the family was alright. When they did, they discovered Wilson's biggest trouble was that he could not hook up his dryer. Over the weekend, holiday cocktail parties became incubators for anxiety. On Sunday night, Dinerstein attended a gathering of about forty people who had "whipped themselves up into a state of excitement and fury" and greeted him with a barrage of questions about whether more African Americans were moving in and what would happen to property values. Dinerstein, who had come armed with folders full of research on the latter question, talked them down. He confronted one man who shouted, "But I don't like it" with "Who's asking you to like it?" The tensions in this self-proclaimed liberal community demonstrated the underlying resistance that would make effective fair housing action difficult in the years to come. Still, whether anyone welcomed or befriended the Wilsons, the police and village trustees promised to maintain law and order.[10]

The Wilsons' arrival also elicited enough support—or at least tolerance—that the AFSC thereafter invoked it as exemplifying the results of community education and careful preparation. Wilson told a reporter: "I have met a lot of interesting people in Park Forest. And for every crackpot, there are many high-class people taking just the opposite tack." Indeed, the family received dozens of visits and friendly welcomes. In the aftermath, human relations commissioners and village officials began receiving invitations to conferences and speaking engagements, although Dinerstein said they turned them down because they were just doing their jobs and did not want the publicity. Some of the HOP staff felt that the trustees would not make the best ambassadors for integration precisely because they valued maintaining order and community reputation but not necessarily interracial living. Moreover, further integration of the suburb came slowly: the next African Americans arrived in 1962, after the Wilsons had moved away, and by 1965 there were only thirty Black families in the community. Nevertheless, the Chicago AFSC office continued to employ the Park Forest story as a positive example of what happens when an organized community works for the acceptance of Black neighbors. Because of its timing, the very month that the Deerfield crisis erupted on the North Shore, the Wilson move-in with its lack of furor was held up as a hopeful sign that "ignorance, hate, and violence . . . are not inevitable."[11]

Meanwhile in Bucks County, Pennsylvania, Jane Reinheimer and Jacques Wilmore, along with a handful of sympathetic residents and members of liberal organizations, undertook the task of trying to match up white sellers and Black buyers in the Levittown subdivision. In July 1953, Reinheimer and Joan Paubionsky, a white resident of Bucks County who wanted to see the area integrated, began visiting families who had listed their property to see whether they would be willing to sell to African Americans. As in Park Forest, a few were eager to cooperate. Barry and Betty Nemcoff, who were moving and had about two months either to sell their house or find renters, agreed to have Reinheimer look for an African American family to move in. In late spring of 1954, Lorraine Cleveland, who was an AFSC staff member, bought a house in Levittown specifically to rent to African Americans. Making these contacts took a lot of time and often did not yield any practical benefit. In one case, Reinheimer visited a couple who were getting ready to move out and had declared their opposition to discrimination at a public meeting. But when Reinheimer privately asked whether they would sell their house on the open market, the wife strongly objected, admitting that "morally" her position was not "highly defensible." As Reinheimer reported it, the visit was a "waste of time." HOP staff also fielded calls from potential sellers who had heard they were helping to broker contact with African American buyers. In those instances, they had to investigate whether the caller actually wanted to arrange a "spite" sale meant to get back at white neighbors for some slight or simply to secure a higher price from desperate Black customers, neither of which the AFSC wanted to facilitate. In some cases, the departing Levittowners were apparently sincere in their effort to sell without discrimination, but they simply could not wait long enough for the AFSC to locate a Black family whose needs matched the house. Lorraine Cleveland, for example, had to care for the house and lawn herself while waiting for a renter, and when it became too much for her, she hired a real estate company to manage and sell the property.[12]

Meanwhile, Reinheimer and Wilmore tried to recruit a Black couple to buy one of the houses available in Levittown. In early 1953 and again in the spring of 1954, Reinheimer asked local labor unions and the Bucks County and Philadelphia branches of the NAACP for names of Black families who might be interested in a Levittown home. The Philadelphia NAACP president provided her with a list of those who had come to the organization after being turned down by Levitt's sales staff. Barry Nemcoff worked for the *Levittown Times* and had access to names of people who wrote in response to articles about segregation in the community. The *Philadelphia Independent*, an African American newspaper, also carried stories about the Housing Opportunities Program effort. Reinheimer met with some Black women who were potential home buyers. Although none of them were interested in Levittown, they encouraged her to keep a list of home seekers and their needs so that when a house became available, she could quickly contact people. Keeping such a list, with a matching one of houses available, became a common function of HOP programs and their allies around the country. More often, however, Reinheimer and Wilmore sought out individuals or responded to calls and visited one-on-one to determine what the home seeker wanted and needed and could afford. That effort, like that expended on finding nondiscriminatory white sellers, consumed much of their days but often led them to dead ends.[13]

When Reinheimer and Wilmore met with potential Black home buyers, at some point they raised the question of how the purchase would be financed. In a few cases, sympathetic individuals or organizations offered help in making the down payment, but more often the family had to meet the cost of the home on their own. Prices in Levittown thus limited potential pioneers to those with stable middle-class jobs. The couples Reinheimer and Wilmore cultivated consequently included a postal worker, a chemist, and a minister, as well as teachers, social service workers, and quite a few military personnel stationed at Fort Dix, which was just over twenty miles away in New Jersey. In short, they were looking for African Americans whose occupation, class, and financial wherewithal would match those of the whites to whom communities like Levittown were marketed.[14]

Yet to Reinheimer and Wilmore, more important than whether the buyer/renter family could afford to move to Levittown was the question of whether they were "willing and able to be a pioneer." To some extent that meant identifying African American couples who would be "as nonthreatening" to whites as possible, as historian Thomas Sugrue put it, and who were "middle class with normative families." Pioneers would ideally be married with children, churchgoers, and occupied in white-collar professions. Preferably, the husband would be the breadwinner and the wife would stay home. Veteran or active-duty soldier status was a plus. This set of qualifications resembled the screening process in the Job Opportunities Programs, in which the AFSC sought African Americans of "superior quality" who could smoothly fit into an integrated situation and "adjust easily in social relationships."[15] Nearly every potential pioneer couple had some of these characteristics. Moreover, Reinheimer praised would-be buyers who were "attractive, well-educated, gentle people." She interviewed only one single woman, but she was a widow and a US Army captain whose "personality and uniform" were sure to win over her neighbors. Wilmore reflected on the problematic nature of their screening bias. After concluding that one young couple was not "what we would consider ideal pioneers" because they lacked the "smoothness, sophistication or intellectual development which might be desirable in this case," he went on to admit, "I know I sound like a snob and I hate myself for it and maybe I am making too many concessions to the prejudice of others." Indeed, if the couple wanted to move forward with a purchase, Wilmore concluded, "we ought to accept them with open arms." Ultimately, the couple declined for financial and other reasons.[16]

Being a good pioneer also meant being willing and able to take the pressure of being first and to stand up to any negative reaction. In her meetings with home seekers, Reinheimer talked with them about what might occur and what their concerns might be. From the start, her contacts cited specific cases of violence both near and far as a reason not to move to the white suburbs in general or Levittown specifically. In late 1952, a Black family who had moved into Broomhall, just forty miles from

Levittown, suffered harassment and vandalism, which weighed on the minds of the first group of women with whom Reinheimer met. The trouble in Chicago's Trumbull Park public housing came up as well. But she also met other candidates, especially those associated with the military, who asserted their willingness to be "guinea pigs." As Sargent Clifton Lee explained, he had been the first before, had faced discrimination, and was quite capable of "dealing with the pioneering aspects of the situation." George and Hope Haley likewise told Reinheimer they were used to challenging discrimination because she had worked for the Philadelphia Fair Employment Practices Commission and he was in the Air Force. In her notes, Reinheimer praised the bravery of those who might not fit the stereotypical middle-class suburban image but were "calm about pioneering." She also, however, expressed regret for pushing people to make a choice for which they were not quite ready. For instance, when a young mother-to-be changed her mind at the last minute about moving into the house Lorraine Cleveland had purchased, Reinheimer took the blame: "I now think it was a mistake to consider them. . . . Her passivity and lack of interest should have warned me," she wrote.[17] Despite their steadfast efforts and judgment that most of the couples they interviewed would be good pioneers, by the summer of 1957 Jane Reinheimer and Jacques Wilmore had yet to help a Black family move into Levittown.

The Myers Family Integrates Levittown

In late July 1957, Peter von Blum, a Quaker living in Levittown, contacted the AFSC Philadelphia headquarters and asked for help with the anticipated mid-August arrival of William and Daisy Myers. The Myerses fit the HOP's bill for pioneers. William Myers was a veteran, a college graduate, and a skilled tradesman working in refrigeration. Daisy was a teacher and caretaker for their three children, including a newborn. The family lived in a semidetached house in Bloomsdale, a "small black enclave" of two hundred homes in nearby Bristol Township. With the new child, they wanted a bigger house and yard, sharing the suburban dream with increasing numbers of both white and Black middle-class families. Daisy Myers was active in the Levittown League of Women Voters. Both she and William participated in a discussion group hosted by the William Penn Center nearby, and as a result had gotten to know liberal whites in the suburb. From people at the center, they heard about a house that had been for sale for two years at the corner of Daffodil and Deepgreen Streets in the Dogwood neighborhood, and they weighed the possibility of buying it. When they bought the home, they decided not to contact neighbors or do any community preparation but simply to move in as normally as possible. The couple scheduled their moving trucks for August 13 and got to work transferring boxes to their new home, with the intention of sleeping in Bloomsdale for a week while waiting for an oil tank to be repaired at the new place.[18]

Although the Myerses were aware of both the failed campaign to get William Levitt to sell to African Americans and the possibility of trouble, they did not anticipate the extent of the violence and harassment that greeted them in the first weeks and even months of living in their new home. As they unpacked on the first day, they noticed small gatherings of two or three people on nearby lawns and sidewalks, and one man walking through the neighborhood with a piece of paper. Then in the late afternoon, the local daily newspaper reported that a Black family had moved into Levittown. By evening, cars were inching bumper to bumper past their house and a crowd of approximately two hundred had formed, with the police doing little about it. The Myerses left as planned to spend the night in Bloomsdale. Only the next morning did they encounter the broken glass and garbage left behind by the mob. During the first week, while the family sought refuge at night with relatives in York, Pennsylvania, or at their old Bloomsdale house, the harassment escalated. The Levittown Betterment Association formed, led by James Newell of the local Veterans of Foreign Wars, and its members set up a headquarters they named Confederate House in a home behind the Myerses' property. While pledging not to be violent, the Betterment Association members declared that it was their intention and their right to protect their children, their property values, and their status as a white community.[19]

The nightly mob actions climaxed on August 19 and 20, the first two nights after the Myers family moved permanently into their home (fig. 2.1). By that time, William Myers had secured a promise from Pennsylvania Attorney General Thomas McBride to send state police to Levittown to reinforce local law enforcement. On Monday the nineteenth, the state troopers ordered the crowd to move away from the house. Someone in the crowd threw a stone at them, whereupon the commander gave the mob ten minutes to disperse. When people failed to move, the police pushed them back and skirmishes broke out, but the mob was forced two blocks away. The next night, the mob charged the police line and a rock hit Sergeant Thomas Stewart, knocking him unconscious. Although incidents continued, including crosses burned and KKK graffiti painted at the homes of the family's supporters, Daisy Myers recalled that the injuring of a police officer seemed to have deflated the opposition.[20] Daily strain continued, however, as the Myerses dealt with verbal abuse, delivery company boycotts, and harangues against them at public rallies and in the press. The family did not really begin a normal life in Levittown

FIGURE 2.1: Large crowd gathering near the Myerses' home in Levittown, Pennsylvania, on August 19, 1957. Photograph by Jack Tinney. Courtesy of Special Collections Research Center, Temple University Libraries, Philadelphia.

until December, when the attorney general secured an injunction barring leaders of the opposition from harassing acts and when two men were found guilty of burning crosses.

At the same time, the Myerses were almost literally overwhelmed by the support they received from individuals and organizations in Levittown and beyond. Expressions of encouragement started coming as the family cleaned up the mess from the first night of vandalism—so many that the William Penn Center sent teams of volunteers to the house to receive telegrams and take messages. Over the next couple weeks, the Myerses received 150 messages of support just from people in Levittown, along with stacks of letters from outside the community and as far away as Australia. Neighbors arrived to mow the lawn, hang curtains, bring gifts and food, or simply pay a visit. On one particularly busy day in the second week, Daisy Myers recalled, "At times during the day, I thought I would go mad with the telephone, Lynda [her infant daughter] crying, telegrams arriving, and friends coming and going."[21] Meanwhile, sympathizers began organizing within existing liberal groups and in new support committees to issue statements, reinforce the family, and sway public opinion. In addition to this grassroots backing, Governor George

M. Leader denounced the rioters and invoked Pennsylvania's tradition of tolerance, asserting that any family had the right to live wherever it could buy a house.

This conglomeration of defenders was a heterogeneous bunch whose reasons for reaching out to or speaking up for the family varied. In her memoir of her time in Levittown, Daisy Myers criticized the local liberal committees and spokespeople for taking limited and tepid positions and for refusing to endorse her family's right to live in Levittown. The Levittown Citizens Committee, for example, released a "Declaration of Conscience" that seemed only to deplore "all actions of violence and intimidation" and call for "the maintenance of law and order." For many people, the problem was limited to the black eye the Myerses' ordeal gave the Levittown community and their desire to distance themselves from the ugly racism demonstrated by the rioters, which was associated with the South and the contemporaneous Little Rock school desegregation crisis. Moreover, Cold War anticommunism remained a stifling force, and the timidity of some parts of the community, including Catholic Church leaders, resulted from rumors that the Myerses and their neighbors the Wechslers might be subversives. That faintheartedness caused Mrs. Myers to dismiss the Levittown Citizens Committee, saying it was "too busy arguing among themselves and conducting loyalty checks on innocent people" to give her family support when they needed it most.[22]

But at times, individuals and both religious and secular organizations explicitly critiqued discrimination and affirmed the Myerses' move to Levittown. Daisy Myers was grateful for letters that wished her well, declared support for the family, and urged them to stick up for themselves in the face of the mob. Specifically, writers from Levittown welcomed them to the community and hoped they would remain; as one writer put it, "Please stay and fight for what is rightly yours—the right to live where you please." Established liberal organizations were among the first to speak up for the family's right to the home. The Women's International League for Peace and Freedom, which had called for integration in Bucks County as early as 1951, released a statement saying that unless principles such as "all men are created equal" were "put into practice in community patterns of living, they have little worth." Also employing patriotic rhetoric, the steelworkers' union announced that as "an American citizen" and veteran, William Myers had the right to be free from bigoted attacks and to live in the home he "worked and saved to buy." Correspondingly, the Bucks County chapter of the Americans for Democratic Action asserted that the right to choose where to live is a "basic American tradition," and the Myerses should be "treated as any other new residents." Among the religious groups, the Jewish and Quaker communities were the most outspoken in welcoming the Myerses and integration in general. Within days of the move-in, the Bucks County chapter of the American Jewish Congress voiced its unequivocal support, and the Friends Service Association, which ran the William Penn Center, declared that every person was entitled to equal treatment before the law and by his neighbors, regardless of creed, color, or national origin. For its part, in the days after the move-in the AFSC circulated a press release declaring its support for integrated communities in which all Americans "live side-by-side in a peaceful, democratic way."[23] These voices expressed the views of a minority of whites in the community and were nearly drowned out by the opposition, but they were not absent. The support offered to the Myers family reflected the impact of the postwar human relations movement and gave Housing Opportunities Program staff hope that they could organize a pro-integration force in the suburbs.

Although the AFSC as an organization had not helped William and Daisy Myers find their house, the staff quickly became involved in providing protection, service, and friendship to the couple during the crisis that followed their arrival in Levittown. On August 15 Tom Colgan, who had worked in Chicago on the Park Forest situation and in the summer of 1957 joined the Philadelphia AFSC headquarters office, went to Levittown to see how the service committee could help. He moved in with the Myers family and stayed with them for three weeks, and then through the end of the year devoted several days a week to the crisis. During that time, he worked mainly behind the scenes to help the Myerses with safety and financial problems. He and Steve Remsen of the Jewish Labor Committee made sure there was always somebody in the house, recruited and coordinated friendly visitors, and organized a citizen guard for when the police were not doing an adequate job or during times of anticipated trouble, such as Halloween night. Colgan went with William Myers to the local police chief and the state attorney general to argue for better protection, failing in the first case and succeeding in the second. When the family's bills started mounting because of property damage and travel expenses during the crisis, Colgan secured financial assistance from the AFSC's Right of Conscience Fund, which had been set up to supply small grants to people being persecuted for their political beliefs or actions. Finally, when the Myerses' insurance company canceled their policy, he procured new coverage through Quaker business contacts.[24]

Colgan also spent his time in the first months after the Myers move-in prodding white residents of Levittown and the vicinity to take a positive stand. Daisy Myers recalled that at the start of the crisis, the opposition got organized quickly, while sympathizers took longer to mobilize and had to be prompted to do so. Colgan worked with staff from the Friends Service Association and recruited people into the Levittown Citizens Committee as a counterweight to the Levittown Betterment Association. But after the Citizens Committee circulated a Declaration of Conscience and published it with five hundred signatures, it withdrew from the controversy. Colgan also tried to recruit ministers to take the lead, but he could not get Catholic clergy on board because of the charges of communism. In October, he solicited help from John McDermott, the local field worker of the National Council for Christians and Jews, who held a series of meetings for about a dozen families called the Dogwood Hollow Neighbors, named for the Myerses' neighborhood. He also reached out to the B'nai B'rith and American Jewish Congress to coordinate their similar efforts. At that point, Colgan concluded that the HOP work could not be just reactive, nor could it depend on the one-on-one work of lone organizers. At the end of the year, he proposed to the AFSC that while he continued to help the Myers family deal with the fallout of the crisis, the HOPs should nurture integration by arranging more move-ins and organizing white neighbors in the new suburbs to welcome and even facilitate desegregation.[25]

Organizing "Fair Housers" in the Philadelphia Suburbs

For the next several years, AFSC housing activists did as Colgan suggested, expending considerable energy reaching out to suburban whites to cultivate, amplify, and channel support for integration. The HOP staff attended meetings in churches and homes to discuss open neighborhoods and encourage those who indicated sympathy to form general human relations or specific fair housing groups. Then they provided guidance about how to formalize and run an organization and how to fight housing segregation, along with moral and logistical support. The latter could mean anything from recruiting members to writing bylaws, calling meetings, or nudging people toward more assertive action. The aim was to create a cadre in the suburbs that would find houses for sale, use social networks to educate their neighbors about the value of integration, and most important befriend Black families once they arrived. HOP staff planned to devolve such groups—that is, set them up as independent organizations—when they became self-sufficient so that they could carry on the work on their own. The process of nurturing local leadership and helping people make change in their own neighborhoods drew from Quaker ideals about person-to-person persuasion and developing the potential in every person. It was also akin to the community organizing strategies that would be common in the AFSC's Community Relations

Division programs over the next decade as well as in other contemporaneous social movements. Ultimately, the goal was both to increase the number of African Americans living in previously all-white suburbs and to change the climate in those areas to make them more closely represent the Friends' vision of a democratic community.

By this time, both local crises and national events were pricking the consciences of some white residents and officials around the country. In the wake of the attacks on William and Daisy Myers, an expanded Philadelphia HOP staff tapped a network of concerned individuals who hoped to forestall similar violence in Levitt's next project across the river in New Jersey. Similarly, after the integration crisis in suburban Deerfield, human relations groups sprang to life along the North Shore of Chicago and called out for help. In California, the HOP staff had already encountered fair housing and human relations groups, and events in the state would soon inspire the formation of many more. More generally, the Montgomery bus boycott, the Little Rock confrontation, and the sit-in campaign dramatically called attention to the problem of racial inequality and discrimination as well as to inspirational efforts to overcome it. In response, the AFSC planned a major "civil rights thrust" in both the North and the South. In the South, the organization would support school desegregation and provide aid to the direct-action movement, while in the North, housing integration became its top priority. In naming that priority, the national AFSC Community Relations Committee acknowledged that residential segregation was more "deeply rooted and resistant to change than any other form of racial discrimination." But the members hoped that national dialogue on civil rights would "direct attention" to the problem. Signs of that happening came quickly; by January 1961, seven of the eleven AFSC regional offices had asked for help launching a housing program.[26]

Acting on Tom Colgan's recommendations, the AFSC augmented the Philadelphia housing staff to organize and serve human relations groups in a wider area, stretching from just outside the city across the Delaware River to southern New Jersey. In 1957, Thelma Babbitt became director of the newly renamed Metropolitan Philadelphia HOP. Babbitt (fig. 2.2) was a Methodist from Massachusetts who in 1952 became director of the Job Opportunities Program in Columbus, Ohio, the first woman in such a position. During her training for the job, Babbitt immersed herself in Friends theology and practice and discovered she was "ready for Quakerism," with its "principle of love expressed through creative action." Turned off by the size and segregation of Methodist churches in Columbus, she started attending a Friends Meeting to "recharge (her) batteries." The JOP position was her first encounter with African Americans

FIGURE 2.2: Metropolitan Philadelphia HOP staff member Thelma Babbitt and her children, 1956. Courtesy of the Harris Center, Hancock, NH.

and with prejudice based on skin color. She later recalled drawing from lessons her father taught her about eschewing intolerance and from role models among the other Quaker staff for controlling her temper in the face of discrimination. When Babbitt moved to Philadelphia to become coordinator of the employment program, she lived in the Germantown neighborhood and witnessed its transition from white to mixed to primarily Black. She knew that when she took the job with the HOP, she was going to be dealing with people like her white neighbors, who had fled for communities like Levittown. Soon after she took the job, she gained an assistant: Richard Taylor, a Philadelphia-area Friend and graduate of Haverford College who started as an intern, became assistant director, and then took over for Babbitt in 1959 when she moved to an AFSC position in Little Rock, Arkansas.[27]

In her time with the Philadelphia HOP, Babbitt formed a human relations council in Burlington County, New Jersey, that would serve as a model for other AFSC offices working to organize suburban communities. Early in her tenure, she met Kent Larrabee, a Friend who had helped form a short-lived and ultimately ineffective human relations council in Bucks County. Disappointed by that failure and keeping an eye on William Levitt's plans for a new development across the river in southern New Jersey, in February 1958 he suggested that Babbitt organize to ensure that this new suburb would be integrated from the start. Levitt planned to build five thousand homes in the township of Willing Borough, and he had announced he would refuse to sell to African Americans and would eschew Federal Housing Administration or Veterans Administration money to avoid antidiscrimination charges. Babbitt investigated the extent of support for integration of the development, meeting with local people already publicly engaged in social causes—the "professional liberals," as she called them—as well as seeking out African American leaders. In July she hosted two public meetings; at the second, thirty people agreed to set up the Burlington County Human Relations Council. While the group would be generally concerned with human relations, the primary focus and the task of its largest committee would be housing integration.[28]

The newly expanded Metropolitan Philadelphia HOP's first annual report noted that organizing in the suburbs demanded "slow and careful movement." During her year in the program, Babbitt submitted logs which detailed her activities. These logs reveal the day-to-day process of making personal contacts across the region—from Bucks County, Pennsylvania, to Burlington County, New Jersey, which was sixty-two miles to the southeast across the Delaware River—and engaging strangers in conversation about one of the most controversial issues of the day. On one day, May 27, 1958, Babbitt drove to Burlington and met with Dr. Preston Wiles, an Episcopal priest whom she found "to be fairly well informed on race relations though admitting his church had taken no particular leadership in solving racial problems." Nevertheless, she thought he might be willing to be involved in a human relations group as an individual. She next stopped by to see Henry Albertson, a "well known Quaker farmer" who was "quite elderly himself but expressed the hope that he could do something to relieve the rigid pattern of discrimination in housing." He expressed guilt over missing an opportunity to sell land to African Americans, and thus in the future he would be "glad to make available" an apartment in his house for a Black family, should the opportunity arise. Later the same day, Babbitt spoke with Emerson Darnell, a Quaker lawyer who said he would be willing to join a human relations group, and then with Sidonie Schafer and Shirley Kaplan, who had gathered some people interested in hearing about how to form such a group. Two days later, she was back in Levittown, Pennsylvania, talking to Rev. Fred Manthey about his efforts to organize ministers to prevent violence when the next Black family moved in, then off across the river to a meeting with John Milligan of the New Jersey Division against Discrimination, who was "very anxious to maintain a list of bona fide Negro buyers" interested in Levittown, and who discussed options for legal recourse against Levitt's decision to sell only to whites in his new development.[29]

In some weeks, Babbitt bubbled with optimism about the prospects in Burlington County. New Jersey state law already prohibited discrimination in housing that received any public support. There were also several Friends Meetings in the area, with individuals willing to help. On the advice that she seek out other supporters because Quakers already had the reputation of involvement in liberal causes, she attended meetings of the Joint Committee on Employment and Housing in Moorestown, which was dedicated to doing something about jobs and housing for African Americans in the area. She also allied with J. Tabor Bolden, who led a group of Black executives and engineers who were looking for housing. Some of them would accept segregated housing, but the others were willing to cooperate with white residents to bring about integration. And, given their professional status, Babbitt believed they would make exceptionally good pioneers. Indeed, she concluded that "Burlington County, New Jersey is proving to be a fruitful place to work on housing." In retrospect, Babbitt considered the high point of her work to be when she arranged for Eleanor Roosevelt, who was "an extremely dedicated and inspiring speaker," to address a public meeting in Burlington. The event was a "huge success" that led to several Black families coming forward to apply to Levittown for homes. Even better, a series of "neighborhood meetings with friendly people" were held to welcome them.[30]

Like Phil Buskirk in California, Babbitt encountered nearly daily frustrations as well. Over the course of a couple days, she met a Methodist minister who said that because he was new in his church, he could not risk taking leadership; members of a Friends Meeting who argued that trying to change Levitt's mind was hopeless; and the Quaker mayor of Moorestown, New Jersey, who claimed to oppose every form of segregation but told her he had "to search his conscience and determine the extent to which he had the courage to stand up and be counted and actually work to eliminate this evil." Plus he was busy; she would have to get back to him. After a long conversation with a Baptist minister, who was "rather outspoken in his criticism of Negroes" and who told her "they really were much happier by themselves," Babbitt could only conclude that "I did not get far in this conference" and "it was a most painful and unhappy experience all around I am afraid." Later, she learned that a builder who hoped to develop a separate Black subdivision was circulating the complaint that "Quakers were meddling in this controversial field," and she suffered through a conference with members of a local Meeting who chided her for "jeopardizing the respectability of the Society of Friends by becoming involved in such a controversial issue." Finally, another builder opened the "flood gates" and unleashed on her a torrent of charges that integrated housing would damage property values and rob white residents of "their right to choose their own neighbors." With an almost audible sigh, Babbitt concluded her notes on this encounter: "This is one of those cases where there is little hope of our making very much impression."[31]

Babbitt was used to running into hostility or indifference from her days with the Job Opportunities Program in Columbus. In that position, there were times she "really lost control, of my disposition" and realized it meant she missed any opportunity for real effect. She recalled later that she dealt with it by reminding herself of the paraphrase from 1 Corinthians, "There but for the grace of God, go I," and the Quaker principle that "there is that of God within each person." She added, "Sometimes that quality is overlaid with all kinds of fear and hatred," so to "really speak to the person," you had to dig beyond that. She admitted that sometimes that was hard to do. When facing Friends who were skeptical of the Housing Opportunities Program, Babbitt reminded them that Quakers had always challenged "practices which violated the basic dignity and worth of the individual." With real estate men she "made the point as forcibly as I could" that Black families should have their "choice of the kind of house they wanted in the place they wanted to live." To overcome resistance to the HOP's activities, she told opponents that "we are as concerned for the person who discriminates as for the victim of his discriminatory practice." She believed that "by engaging in unjust practices," a builder was "not living up to that of God within himself." With this, she did persuade the mayor of Moorestown to pledge police protection for Black families who might move in, and one builder to sell to both whites and Blacks. But that approach did not work on many people in high places. Reluctantly, she gave up on some of her most vocal critics.[32]

Despite the opposition Babbitt encountered, by the end of the summer of 1958 the Burlington County Human Relations Council (BCHRC) had been established, and its housing committee had gotten to work. Members of that committee sent letters to area organizations soliciting help in identifying potential Black pioneers, and they educated themselves about the barriers to housing integration. At the start of the new year, the committee launched its first major effort: an open covenant campaign in which residents signed a pledge not to discriminate in selling their house and to welcome Black neighbors. Open covenant campaigns would become a common tactic used by fair housing groups around the country to identify sympathizers and demonstrate public support for integration. The BCHRC gathered 826 signatures by the end of July and raised the funds to publish the covenant and the signees in local newspapers. Meanwhile, subcommittees researched houses for sale in the county to see whether they were available to African Americans, and they followed up on leads for potential pioneers. In the spring, the BCHRC formalized this work by setting up a registry of homes for sale and African American families looking to move, referred to in fair housing circles as a listing service. Meanwhile, Thelma Babbitt and Richard Taylor worked with individual Black families as they negotiated the labyrinth of obstacles to buying a house in Burlington County and vicinity. A few families did move in, but the pace continued to be slow, and the New Jersey Levittown itself continued to be closed to African Americans.[33]

Legal action against Levitt eventually forced him to sell directly to African Americans. In June 1958, he had applied for FHA and VA financing for his New Jersey development, but at the same time he announced it would be white only. This direct violation of state law incensed the civil rights forces. The governor pledged to prevent discrimination, and legal action began against the company. As a lawsuit against Levitt wound its way through the state courts, the BCHRC tracked its progress while working independently on resales and lining up future African American purchasers. At the end of the year, the New Jersey Supreme Court ordered Levitt to integrate by April 15, 1959, but he appealed the case and got a stay of the decision. In the meantime, HOP staff member Richard Taylor arranged a meeting with Levitt's lawyer about how the BCHRC could help integration go smoothly. Finally, Levitt announced in April that he would sell to African Americans in the New Jersey Levittown development. Charles and Vera Williams moved in at the end of July. Other African American families soon followed, and the BCHRC turned its attention to other developments in the area. Although acknowledging that "no one thinks the housing problem in the county is solved," the AFSC proposed beginning the process of making the BCHRC independent and passing to it the task of coordinating further pioneer move-ins in the area.[34]

When forming groups like the BCHRC, the AFSC's intention was always to create a local group, nurture it, and leave it to operate on its own when it was strong enough. In this case, the timing was also good because of the BCHRC's shift in emphasis after the victory against Levitt and because Taylor was leaving at the end of the year. Only one staff person, Charlotte Meacham, a Quaker who had joined the Metropolitan Philadelphia HOP staff in 1959, would be left working on outreach to suburbanites in the area. At the same time, the HOP and the Community Relations Division staff wanted to make sure that the parting was amicable and went smoothly. Meacham especially wanted to make sure that the council's Black members, who were mostly either pioneers in Levittown and elsewhere in the county or people who wanted to be, would feel welcome and be well established in the group hierarchy before the AFSC staff departed. She feared that the white members might find the housing work too hard without professional help, and the BCHRC would thus become a general interest group without an aggressive position on residential integration. She believed that the Black members, who had more at stake, would keep the group "honest" and focused on housing. In August 1961, the Dolfinger-McMahon Foundation gave the AFSC a three-year grant to wrap up its work in Burlington County. With the money, the AFSC hired and trained a staff person, who would then work under the direction of the council. In 1964, the devolution concluded with BCHRC becoming completely independent.[35]

The AFSC considered the Burlington County Human Relations Council to be a model for organizing suburban fair housing groups. From the start, the HOP staff asserted that the success of their program would be measured in the "extent to which local people are involved directly in the work and in the extent to which they take responsibility for the program." At early meetings, Thelma Babbitt would tell people that progress "comes from the combined efforts of individuals who undertake creative action in a spirit of good will and persistence." Such an approach could be vexing for locals and organizers alike. When the work was going slowly, Babbitt noted that people had to take time both to learn and to reflect on their own motivation and firmness of commitment when they confronted the extent of hostility to their goals. Groups might have difficulty agreeing on methods, even if they agree on principles. The staff had to let them figure it out themselves and make mistakes, and they had to avoid rushing in the "anxiousness to get something done," thereby alienating people by getting out too far ahead of them. Most important, Babbitt strove to make sure that African Americans took some of the leadership. In general, Babbitt, Taylor, and Meacham considered their work in Burlington a success, and even invited staff from the Chicago HOP to come to study the council as a model. One example Meacham gave was that during the devolvement process, members of the BCHRC stepped up to handle a contentious move-in by organizing a vigil, contacting local ministers, arranging the family's utilities, and working with local authorities. In a final review of the program, however, Taylor noted that the AFSC could improve by giving local people specific tasks more quickly so that they did not come to rely on staff.[36]

Spreading the Fair Housing Council Model

In the early 1960s, the AFSC employed the strategy used in Burlington County in its housing programs and regional offices elsewhere in the country to nurture support for residential integration in the suburbs. During that period, the CRD devoted staff time to fair housing councils in Boston, Hartford, a wide territory surrounding New York City, Chicago, Northern and Southern California, and a group of small cities in Ohio and Indiana. In 1962, the national board signaled its prioritization of such work by creating the position of National Housing Secretary—held first by Charlotte Meacham—and allocating $25,000 to launch a Housing Opportunities Program in the nation's capital. The choice of Washington, DC, symbolized the national nature of the problem of housing discrimination and was intended to draw the attention of federal government officials. But other housing programs in that area also attracted the AFSC. Between 1956 and 1959, the Urban League had run a Three Year Project in Housing in the capital, which engaged in many of the same activities as the HOPs, and in 1963 its local leaders consulted with the AFSC about their shared interest in suburban work. In 1961, the Catholic Interracial Council had conducted a fair housing pledge drive in and around the district and gathered over five thousand signatures, an unusually high number at that time. Finally, friends of the AFSC were already engaged in stabilizing integration in communities within and just outside the district through Neighbors, Inc. The overall goal of the Metropolitan Washington Housing Opportunities Program (MWHOP), then, was to break the "white noose" surrounding the city by promoting fair housing and laying the groundwork for the peaceful acceptance of Black neighbors, as well as to "create community, moving beyond the temporary tensions caused by change to a recognition of the positive values that flow from the practice of democracy." African American Quaker and longtime AFSC worker Helen Baker launched the program. Over time, the staff included white Quakers Dan Safran and Merlin Myers, and James Harvey, an African American pioneer and BCHRC member from Moorestown, New Jersey.[37]

The MWHOP shared many of the goals and strategies of the other regional HOPs, but the staff focused on establishing fair housing groups on the Burlington County Human Relations Council model in Montgomery and Prince George's Counties, Maryland, Northern Virginia, and eventually in the district itself. Initially, it seemed the AFSC would once again confront William Levitt, who was building a new Levittown near Belair in Prince George's County and refused to sell to an African American applicant in July 1963. The Congress of Racial Equality stepped into the situation, however, threatening Levitt and other builders with demonstrations. The AFSC chose to offer support but allow the young activists in that civil rights organization to take the lead there. Instead, its staff began reaching out to people in other suburbs around the city. Merlin Myers told interested residents he could provide staff time, operate a central list of homes for sale, arrange speakers, distribute literature, help with clerical tasks, make initial contacts in the African American community, assist people in filing discrimination complaints, and teach residents how to respond to emergencies that might arise around a Black family's move into their community. In Maryland, the staff built on existing networks of integrationists in Montgomery County to promote arrivals of middle-class Black pioneers in private homes; in Northern Virginia they focused on apartments and on employees of federal government agencies and military bases.[38]

In the fall of 1964, the Washington program staff surveyed their progress and expressed a qualified optimism. Noting that "one measure of our work is the stimulation of local leadership and the growth" of fair housing groups, they bragged that at that point there were eighteen hundred members of such organizations in the metropolitan area, with up to five thousand more sympathizers reachable through their mailing lists. The largest and most successful group was Southern Montgomery Fair Housing, which had 385 members and in one year had held thirty-five neighborhood meetings to spread the open housing message. That effort paid off when its summer 1964 open housing pledge campaign netted fifteen thousand signatures. Progress in organizing residents came a little more slowly in Prince George's County, where the housing picture was complicated by the conflict over Levitt and other builders, and in Northern Virginia, where the desegregation of public accommodations competed for attention and an organized group of "antis" attended meetings to cause disruption. Nevertheless, in April 1965, Northern Virginia Fair Housing conducted an open housing pledge campaign netting forty thousand signatures, with over three thousand volunteers participating in the drive. These numbers prompted the AFSC staff to conclude proudly that the "quality of citizen involvement and leadership has exceeded expectation." In turn, Safran, Myers, and Harvey had the confidence to begin devolving the local groups, preparing them for independence by establishing an umbrella organization for communication, coordination, and cooperation.[39]

The AFSC staff boasted of the African American moves to white neighborhoods that resulted from this organizing and sympathy. In two years, Southern Montgomery Fair Housing had organized thirteen such moves to Montgomery County, where there had been only seven Black families in the previous seventeen years. In the fall of 1964, the MWHOP staff counted eighty Black families now living in white areas, with sixty-five of them being on the Maryland side of the district. Acknowledging that "this seems small," the report noted that "on the other hand between the end of World War II and fall 1962 only ten Black families are known" to have made that move. In 1965, a UPI report gave a more generous count, crediting the AFSC program with 120 integration moves since its launch.

Over time, African Americans would comprise significant percentages of the population in Prince George's and Montgomery Counties, even a majority in the former case. In the mid-1960s, however, though they pointed with optimism to the signs of change, Myers and Meacham were dismayed that they had not accomplished more, and that housing discrimination was still "the most ubiquitous and deeply rooted civil rights problem in America." Thus, as they were beginning to devolve the program, the AFSC staff regarded its impact with some ambivalence. They were proud that white suburbanites were beginning to get involved and were committed to facilitating local leadership to continue the effort. But they had no illusions the problem was solved. Indeed, they worried about the fair housing councils' ability to inspire more African American buyers and make more of a dent in segregation.[40]

As in Metro Washington, the California HOPs increasingly focused on serving local human relations and fair housing groups. But the Northern and Southern California Regional Offices' programs, in San Francisco and Pasadena, respectively, followed different timelines reflecting different influences and conditions. Like Metro Washington, the San Francisco region of the AFSC was widely spread out. But rather than focusing on a ring around a single major urban center, it was composed of many small cities with their own identities spread out around the Bay area and through San Mateo and Santa Clara Counties. When Phil Buskirk, Martin White, Leonard Menand, and Norman Goerlich, the successive leaders of the open housing work for the Northern California Regional Office, traveled around in the mid- and late 1950s, they encountered a number of existing groups, including the San Mateo Housing Council, the Santa Clara Council of Churches, the Fair Play Council, and city branches of the Council for Civic Unity, that had begun during the postwar enthusiasm for human relations. Indeed, by 1959 there were eleven fair housing groups in San Francisco and the immediate vicinity alone. By 1963, that number had increased to twenty. These groups circulated fair housing pledges, helped African Americans and other minorities find homes in white areas, and maintained lists of available houses. In most cases these were small volunteer operations, often with one couple or woman doing all the work. Goerlich incorporated some of these in the area south of San Francisco into the Valley Committee for Open Housing, gave the group space in the AFSC office, and set up its listing service. Thus, instead of doing pioneer placement work themselves, the AFSC staff in Northern California coordinated the work of other, smaller groups.[41]

The Southern California Regional Office in Pasadena got started on housing work a little later, but because it was one of the first and for a long time the only major organization in the field in that area, its staff person had primary responsibility for nurturing the fair housing movement there. As a later report recalled, in 1958 "there were practically no groups with a concern for fair housing in southern California." In 1959, the AFSC received $1,000 from a foundation to set up a Fair Housing Committee of Pasadena, which held a pledge drive and gathered seven hundred signatures. In January 1960, the office started a housing program and hired Curt Moody as its full-time director in January 1962. In February, he hosted a conference on open housing and within a month was working with neighborhood people to start human relations councils. Beginning in April 1962, he published a newsletter about the work of fair housing committees, which were springing up "practically every week," providing a forum for communication between them.[42] In 1964, the members of these small local groups were a source of opposition to a referendum seeking to prohibit fair housing laws in the state.

Despite being relatively smaller and less cohesive, the fair housing movement in the North Shore suburbs of Chicago would play a key role in changing the nature of the open housing movement. In the early years of the Chicago Regional Office Housing Opportunities Program, the staff received calls for help from interracial or human relations committees such as the Evanston Interracial Fellowship, North Shore Citizens Committee, and La Grange Interracial Fellowship, which had sprung up as part of the postwar human rights movement. In the wake of the violence in suburban Cicero and Chicago's Trumbull Park public housing apartments, members of these groups worried about housing conflicts arising in their own communities. Although they were removed from the likelihood of large numbers of move-ins by their geographic distance and by the cost of their homes, they looked for guidance in promoting better human relations and fighting housing discrimination. As elsewhere, initial actions by these groups included circulating open occupancy pledges, researching real estate practices, and holding public discussions. After the Deerfield crisis, existing groups like the North Shore Human Relations Committee or new ones like the Deerfield Citizens Committee for Human Rights were energized and eager for help. As the HOP's new assistant director, Al Eichholz, noted, white suburbanites in these northern edge communities were anxious to avoid the notoriety of Deerfield and ready to show they could do better. His job was to help them find a way to do so. To help him accomplish that, the Field Foundation gave the Chicago Regional Office a grant of $65,000 to organize human relations groups in the white suburbs.[43]

Eichholz, a white Chicagoan who had worked for both the YMCA and Hull House, spent most of 1961 and 1962 getting to know people on the North Shore, responding to calls for help from fledgling human relations groups, hosting meetings about neighborhood integration, and organizing public lobbying efforts in favor of a fair housing bill introduced into the Illinois state legislature. Like Thelma Babbitt in the Philadelphia metropolitan region, he sometimes met frustration and resistance. North Shore residents were broken up into many communities, each with their own character and conditions. As a result, many of the groups Eichholz and HOP director Jane Weston encountered were small, and they found it difficult to meld them into a regionwide organization or program. Moreover, when Eichholz talked with ministers or other leaders, they consistently told him that although residents were concerned about discrimination and would do the right thing if a move-in occurred, there was insufficient support for proactive moves to encourage or prepare for it. Moreover, the clergymen themselves quite often declined to take a public position unless their congregation specifically asked them to do so.[44]

But there were more signs of a grassroots desire to confront segregation than what these ostensible community leaders indicated. In Des Plaines, a woman identified as Mrs. Courteol offered to sell her house to an African American physician after the local hospital started hiring minority medical professionals. Inspired by a National Council for Christians and Jews workshop, she became the center of a Des Plaines human relations group, which had seventy-five people attend its first public meeting. A Quaker couple led a discussion at the Barrington Methodist Church about finding ways to end discrimination, ministers in Elk Grove issued a joint public statement, and a group of clergymen in Mt. Prospect planned a joint response to a move-in. In 1962, the number of these small, informal gatherings of people professing an interest in ending housing discrimination slowly grew, and by June 1963 the HOP reported it had helped organize ten human relations committees and six official human relations commissions on the North Shore since the 1960–61 Deerfield integration crisis.[45]

The Work of the Fair Housing Councils

With growing public attention to southern civil rights demonstrations, the question for many of the suburban fair housers was how to move beyond talk to action. As Weston observed when she gave a workshop on open housing at the North Shore Women's Conference outside Chicago in the fall of 1962, there was a "feeling of frustration on the part of a number of women . . . that little action resulted from conferences of this type." At that point, most groups focused on community preparation, such as when the North Shore Human Relations Committee trained suburbanites what to do in the event of a move-in to their neighborhood. At the conference, Weston met five participants who wanted to go further than that, to persuade the North Shore Real Estate Board to prohibit discrimination by its members. They also volunteered to host Black families for a visitation day, during which potential home buyers could observe life in the suburbs. A year later, such visits began as the first step in a program of bringing Black home seekers into direct contact with North Shore communities and real estate agents.[46]

One function served by suburbanites eager to help integrate their communities was putting home buyers and sellers in touch with each other through listing services. One of the more extensive and long running of such efforts was Home Opportunities Made Equal (HOME) in Chicago, launched by a group of white fair housing enthusiasts just before the Deerfield controversy broke out. Searching for a way to do something more than talk about the problem of segregation in suburban communities, these individuals briefly considered starting their own real estate firm but decided that was too costly. Instead, they compiled lists of homes for sale and of Black families seeking houses. Their main targets were stable communities in the far suburbs rather than the already transitioning urban neighborhoods. HOME's first successes came with Black families moving into Deerfield, Skokie, and Park Forest. The AFSC provided the organization with office space, and the HOP staff and volunteers devoted much time to distributing information about the organization's program in the Black community, screening calls (including hate-filled ones), identifying potential pioneers, and showing them houses. In 1963, because of trouble fund-raising for it as a separate entity, HOME became a program "affiliated" with the Chicago AFSC. Listing services like HOME proved popular with fair housing groups through the mid-1960s, because they provided volunteers with something concrete to do: researching houses on the market and ascertaining whether they would be for sale on an open basis, meeting with Black families, and giving support when they moved in.[47]

The point of all the listing services, and the fair housing organizing more generally, was to facilitate those move-ins. In the late 1950s when move-ins happened, the HOP staff had reached out themselves to local officials and sympathizers, monitored the community for signs of trouble, and helped in times of crisis, even staying with families for several days to make sure someone was on hand in case of an emergency. For example, not only had Thelma Babbitt helped Kenneth and Julia Mosby find a house in the Pennsylvania Levittown, she also surveyed local ministers, asking whether they and their congregations would welcome the family. Once the Mosbys decided on a house, she quietly reached out to local officials to alert them. When rumors about the move-in started circulating among the nearby residents, she gave information about the family to church and civic organizations. At the last minute, she even helped negotiate the date of the move and set up a support system in case of trouble. The night before the move, the AFSC hosted a meeting of thirty-five religious, civic, and educational leaders who agreed to ensure a peaceable welcome. The family settled in without incident, which Babbitt attributed both to preparation and to the desire on the Levittown residents' part to avoid the turmoil and embarrassment of the conflict when William and Daisy Myers arrived.[48]

But in the early years of the new decade, HOP staff withdrew from such direct involvement in move-ins, because they wanted neighborhood people and organizations to take on the task of cultivating local support. In early 1961, a Black couple moved into Skokie in the northern suburbs of Chicago.[49] A few days before the move, the North Shore Human Relations Committee met with residents and representatives of the AFSC, the Illinois Commission on Human Relations, and the Catholic Interracial Council. A small delegation then visited the village manager and trustees, persuading the latter to make a statement supporting the rights of all residents of Skokie, "old and new." After a milling crowd broke windows in the couple's house, police dispersed onlookers, and clergymen and real estate agents held a meeting to assure neighbors that there was no threat to their property values. The family experienced no further trouble. Nearby in Deerfield just a few months later, HOME helped a Black Presbyterian minister find a house and connected him with a white dentist who had volunteered to provide mortgage financing. Pam Coe, a new staff member of the AFSC, and Ed Holmgren, now with HOME, met with some of the neighbors, and moving day went without incident; indeed, the seller arranged a party to greet the new family. By this time, Richard Taylor and Charlotte Meacham in the Philadelphia office had begun advising that advance dialogue and preparation could attract "unwanted notoriety" and was not necessary. Not long after, Jane Weston in Chicago concurred, arguing that the AFSC's role should be to investigate quietly and alert the Illinois Commission on Human Relations, then let that agency and local fair housing councils take the lead.[50]

As regional offices began passing the job of facilitating pioneer move-ins to local groups, one of the AFSC's last major contributions to the fair housing council movement was to codify lessons learned. In 1965, Meacham cowrote *Fair Housing Handbook* with Margaret Fisher of the National Committee against Discrimination in Housing. The guide was aimed at people in suburban communities or transitional neighborhoods who wanted to start fair housing councils, of which there were well above one thousand nationwide. The authors began with detailed instructions on how to get started, emphasizing in point number one that groups be "interracial and interfaith," even if organizers had to seek out minority group members through civil rights agencies to accomplish that. Later chapters included step-by-step procedures for surveying local opinion on housing issues, soliciting potential council members, writing invitations to join, hosting informational meetings—including such party planning advice as "It sets a pleasant atmosphere if the persons who signed the letter of invitation greet those attending as they arrive"—electing officers, writing a mission statement, and setting up subcommittees assigned with specific tasks. The introduction to the guide referred to the fair housing council as the "classic example of grassroots initiative formed by residents of the locality in which it is working." Indeed, the *Handbook* can be read as a manual for community organizing, even if in a relatively privileged middle-class setting rather than among a marginalized and disempowered group. The section on good-neighbor pledges, for example, included advice on how to line up and use neighborhood captains, track signers on a map, and canvass in potentially hostile blocks. The *Handbook* exemplified the AFSC practice of creating a model or a technique for accomplishing a change and then hoping that others would learn from their experience and employ it independently. Not only did the *Handbook* reflect the cumulative experience of HOP staff who had been doing this day-to-day organizing work since the late 1950s, but it also echoed the direction in which they were moving by 1965. Under the heading "If Available Housing Is Denied," it advised testing resistant real estate agents and landlords and conducting direct-action protests to secure a change in their practices.[51]

By the time the publication appeared, however, the strategy of integrating the suburbs by helping Black families move to them had about run its course. Open housing leaders could point to signs of welcome and reasons to be optimistic. Social science survey researcher Paul Sheatsley found that in 1963, 70 percent of whites claimed they would accept a Black neighbor who shared their class and education level, a statistic closely matching the 63 percent who said they supported integrated schools. In 1965, one of the open housing pledge drives conducted by fair housing groups on the North Shore of Chicago netted thousands of signatures in Deerfield—suggesting at least a partial change of heart in that once hostile community. In the same year, sociologists George and Eunice Grier examined the experience of Black pioneer families in New York State and found that few of them had significant conflict with their new neighbors. Although white residents vented their anger at the sellers or real estate agents, they were "very friendly" to the newcomers, even showing up with

Welcome Wagon gifts from local businesses. More generally, the early southern freedom movement's quest for national civil rights legislation was reaching fruition, and majorities of Americans told Gallup pollsters they supported both the 1964 Civil Rights Act and the 1965 Voting Rights Act. If the goal had been to change white hearts, nurture opposition to overt discrimination, cultivate leadership among residents of segregated suburban neighborhoods, and lay the groundwork for an expanded and more inclusive community there, the Housing Opportunities Programs could claim evidence of some success. How extensive that change of heart was, how deep the commitment to achieving true integration ran, and to what extent would white actions uphold these attitudes were more difficult questions, especially when many white Americans were also telling pollsters that change was happening too quickly.[52]

The problem remained, however, that there just weren't many newcomers to welcome—only eleven of the Griers' interviewees, for example, ended up living in previously all-white suburbs. Though HOP staff often put a positive spin on reports of the number of move-ins by comparing the rate with the trickle that preceded their efforts, by mid-decade they had to admit that "the tight noose around the city has not been broken." The eighty Black families HOME had helped buy houses in the suburbs of Chicago had not made much impact on residential segregation. As African American staffer Bert Ransom, hired in 1964, put it, "It would take fifty to one hundred years to have enough Black move-ins to create real change." Watching polarized residential patterns solidify—and threaten integration of the schools and other civil rights goals—while worrying that the slow pace of change would undercut what progress had been made in nudging white attitudes, the HOPs analyzed the reasons for the failures of the fair housing councils and ultimately debated new strategies that might bring about a more wholesale change.[53]

Where Are the Pioneers?

From the beginning of the fair housing organizing, the problem that surprised, dismayed, and stymied equal housing advocates the most was the ambivalence of middle-income African Americans about making a move to the white suburbs. The HOP staff had always encountered individuals who were eager to break barriers. James Harvey, an African American staff member of the Metropolitan Washington HOP, had moved his family into several formerly all-white areas with the help and support of Quakers. He later told his son that "the only way that people would change is that we had to break stereotypes," and living in integrated neighborhoods was one way to do that. He understood there would be opposition and even danger but declared "somebody had to do it." "We were that somebody," his son added. Moreover, when Jane Reinheimer and Jacques Wilmore interviewed candidates for Levittown, they met several couples who proudly asserted their qualifications for and interest in being pioneers. But Reinheimer had also met with Black women who bluntly informed her that they wanted new homes, but interracial living was only a secondary goal. Indeed, most of them did not want to be pioneers, especially after they heard about nearby violence. The Griers found much the same attitude when they surveyed Black scientists and engineers seeking housing in Upstate New York; they were interested in good schools, space for their children, and middle-class neighbors. They did not care if the neighborhood was all-Black or integrated, only that it was "decent."[54]

In their efforts to promote integration, HOP staff had gained insight into Black families' concerns and began to understand why pioneers might be in short supply. While some of the couples Reinheimer and Wilmore interviewed about moving to Levittown refused owing to financial constraints, more often they chose not to move to the community for other reasons. One Black chemist did not want to put undue "psychological or emotional burden" on his pregnant wife, for example. Several candidates worried they would not be able to get a new job near the community, and the distance from their current employer was too far. In a couple cases, the wife would not have had access to transportation. Moreover, some of the women did not want to be so far from Philadelphia or "so isolated from a Negro community." They especially did not want to put their children into schools where they would be the only Black student. By 1957, a frustrated Tom Colgan concluded that "it should be perfectly obvious to all of us by now that Negroes are not making any great rush into the suburban areas." Although these families specifically rejected Levittown, their reasons reflected the ambivalence the HOPs would encounter among middle-class African Americans regarding moves to white suburbs more generally over the next several years.[55]

In responding to African Americans' resistance to the idea of pioneering, the AFSC staff in Philadelphia and elsewhere questioned their own assumptions and strategies. In the spring of 1958, Thelma Babbitt made a round of visits to African American organizations, trying to find families that could help advance integration, and was surprised by the lack of interest and even hostility. She was one of the few whites to attend an NAACP meeting on housing and noted "a very definite overall belligerence that I've never seen before," which made her uncomfortable. But, she concluded, it was an "unusually good opportunity for me to have a chance to hear first-hand what kind of thinking is going on in the

Negro community." One African American in attendance summed up his main concern by saying, "We are not going to be forced out of the city to the suburbs now that we have established political strength in the city. White people created the situation by moving out and we are not going to be pressured into dissipating our strength by isolating ourselves in the suburbs." What the NAACP members wanted was "free choice" and "no discrimination" as well as better schools, "but not necessarily integrated ones."[56] Leonard Menard of the San Mateo County AFSC program reported around the same time that the West Coasters were having difficulty as well, because the "'better class'" of African Americans "doesn't seem anxious to become pioneers—perhaps they feel they are being used by starry-eyed integrationists." Babbitt wondered whether the HOPs had underestimated the "education job needed in the minority community and the time required to raise aspirations for free choice in housing." More colorfully, but with the same hint of paternalistic thinking plus perhaps a touch of sarcasm, Colgan said that fair housers needed to reach out to African Americans to "stimulate a desire for that rose covered cottage in suburbia." By the end of the decade, the HOP staff worried that they did not have an answer for African Americans' concerns, a strategy for how to integrate the suburbs without sufficient pioneers, or much of an idea how to recruit them.[57]

In 1960, one of the first Black families in the New Jersey Levittown had a suggestion for recruiting pioneers. Bernice and Willie James moved into the community in the summer and joined the Burlington County Human Relations Council. At a fall meeting of the group, they suggested holding workshops to provide Black families looking for housing with a "sense of the situations they will meet" in the suburbs and to "help them navigate the process" of moving to new communities. At a workshop, Black families already residing in the county would reassure prospective home buyers by talking about their own experience and about New Jersey fair housing laws. The organizers also planned to use role playing to encourage people to apply to new developments, prepare them for what they might encounter, and nudge them toward filing a complaint if they were rejected. The first workshop was planned for February, though a blizzard forced it to be postponed until April. Approximately one hundred people attended the event. The AFSC considered it a success, because a few families applied for houses in new suburban developments over the next couple weeks, and other county and city human relations groups asked to collaborate on similar workshops. To meet this new interest, the BCHRC prepared kits to help educate groups of possible buyers and laid plans for aiming a future session specifically at African American civic leaders. Progress on the workshops was sporadic, however, because the devolvement process to separate the BCHRC from the AFSC had begun, and it absorbed much of the energy of both organizations.[58]

HOP staff members' enthusiasm for the workshop reflected the impact of the southern freedom struggle on their thinking about how to work for integration and with African Americans. A report on the workshops and their place in the Housing Opportunities Program called them an example of a "new spirit" in the BCHRC. In spring 1961, the organization was half African American, and the Black families not only coordinated the home seeker workshop and led council meetings but also worked with the AFSC's southern school desegregation efforts. Most important, they provided the BCHRC with "not only time but knowledge, understanding of the Negro community, and creative ideas." This new spirit was not confined to Burlington County, New Jersey. A year into the direct-action protests of the southern freedom movement, Charlotte Meacham noted that the white staff of the HOP was taking to heart the message of Martin Luther King and Philadelphia civil rights leader Rev. Leon Sullivan: "The Negro is on his way. If white people want to join in, fine, we're glad to have them. But we aren't waiting around until they make up their minds and the initiative lies with us." For the white staffers in the HOP, that meant "not cramming our methods down their throats; we are the facilitators of social change, not the instigators, and we have as much to learn as to give in our new relationship."[59]

The "new spirit" also persuaded the HOP staff in Chicago to develop new means for reaching out to African Americans both to understand their concerns about pioneering and to figure out better ways of cooperating. Indeed, in February 1961 Al Eichholz suggested copying the Burlington home seeker workshops. A few months later, Jane Weston attended a meeting of Home Opportunities Made Equal at which African American buyers discussed their concerns to "help us understand the reasons Negroes are not interested in moving out" to the suburbs. In response to what she heard there, Weston asked national AFSC leaders for permission to hire a staff person to work specifically in the Black community. In their reply, Philadelphia office staff noted that it was "almost hard to believe" that when the Chicagoans had asked for money in February 1960, in their naïveté they had not mentioned "working with the Negro community" at all. A year and a half later, they were rushing to catch up with the times and had already "learned so much" about incorporating more African American input into their housing work.[60]

While waiting for the funding and searching for a permanent staff member to do outreach in the Black community, the Chicago office got started on that project by inviting African American Quaker Helen Baker to spend several weeks making contacts and assessing the level of interest in pioneering in the city. In Chicago, there was a history dating to the early years of the Great Migration of upwardly mobile Black families striving to move to less crowded neighborhoods.[61] Baker met with forty Black leaders and several small groups to assess whether substantial numbers of people still held that desire. Leading with the positive, HOP leaders reported that "her work confirmed our belief that there is a potential market among the Negro middle-class for houses in new areas." But Baker also gleaned some discouraging insights into the mood in the early 1960s. A member of the NAACP told her he saw housing as a "personal goal" and not something "related to any group action." Other contacts warned her not to expect much interest among professionals, who would not want to move away from the Black community, or among mothers, who feared their children would be "spiritually hurt" in the suburban schools. Most disconcerting, Edwin Berry of the Urban League bluntly informed Baker that "the community was more or less unaware of the existence of the program of the AFSC." The new staff member would have an uphill battle.[62]

Weston had hoped to hire an African American to do that outreach work, and to make "our housing program staff an interracial team." But after failing to secure her first choice, a Black woman named Marian Gray, she hired a white applicant, Bill Moyer. Moyer had been born and raised in Philadelphia and had graduated with a degree in industrial engineering from Pennsylvania State University. After a brief career in that profession, however, he "walked out of his Philadelphia-based Presbyterian church, where he was a deacon, when it excluded Negroes," and became a Quaker. At a Friends' Meeting he met an older couple who taught him about nonviolence and, as he later recalled, set him on the path to his "new profession as a full-time activist." With his newfound interest in social activism, he went to Bryn Mawr for a master's in social work, writing a thesis on Black housing choices in Philadelphia. Despite "what might be a barrier of race," Community Relations Division head Barbara Moffett recommended him to Weston for the Chicago Regional Office position because of his "extensive interracial experience," including working in a settlement house and at previous AFSC jobs, and his "skill in communicating with the minority community."[63]

Beginning in 1962, Moyer launched an ambitious program to publicize HOME in the Black community. He wrote new promotional literature and prepared a slide show of suburban communities and Black pioneer families. He persuaded the *Chicago Defender* to run articles on HOME's services and launched an advertising campaign, including mass mailings to Black fraternal, civic, alumni, and church organizations. Moyer's weekly reports reveal hours spent meeting with Black ministers and other leaders and attending small group discussions about housing. He also continued to respond to calls for help from Black families looking for housing and white families interested in contributing to integration by selling their home on the open market. In addition to HOME listings, he took potential pioneers to visit properties available through FHA and VA repossession and sale, which were supposed to be covered by President Kennedy's executive order banning discrimination in federally supported housing. Also, like his HOP predecessors, Moyer supported families through difficult move-ins, including in one case staying with the sellers in their last few days in their home to protect them from their angry neighbors. In late 1963, he followed the BCHRC home seeker workshop model and organized an AFSC/HOME conference intended to reach out to a broader cross section of African Americans.[64]

By that time, Moyer and the whole HOP were working in a rapidly changing environment. There was an "increasing impatience on the part of Negroes in Chicago to achieve equal rights now" due to events in the South. Especially after the Birmingham demonstrations in the spring of 1963, several staff members both in Chicago and in the national office recognized a new mood affecting their work. Charlotte Meacham noted that since the "divide of Birmingham the pace of everything has accelerated," with many housing groups around the country dropping listing services as no longer sufficient. In Chicago, Moyer worried that Black frustration could lead to tension, and that if more integration did not happen in the suburbs soon it would be too late to change hardened patterns. Moreover, despite the relative lack of progress up to that point, open resistance to civil rights was increasing, including a backlash against any possible changes in housing or neighborhood school policies and a campaign by real estate agents and white residents for a public vote against fair housing legislation.[65]

In response, the Chicago HOP expanded its staff to support a more intensified effort to reach out to Black communities and promote suburban moves. It hired Bert Ransom, an African American intern, to contribute to the work—finally fulfilling Weston's hope of integrating the housing staff. Ransom had been born in Jackson, Mississippi, and had moved to Montgomery to attend Alabama State College, just in time to participate in the bus boycott. After graduating from Xavier University in New Orleans, he moved to Chicago to be a music teacher. He began his internship in September 1964 and easily slipped into the duties formerly carried out by Moyer, who had been promoted to assistant director of the HOP. He revised and expanded the slide show and took it to twenty-two meetings, organized a citywide open housing conference, and revamped HOME's lists and practices. He believed that personal visits remained the best way to circulate information and recruit potential buyers and sellers, so he continued the one-on-one visiting with and helping pioneers, meeting with twenty individuals or couples in one two-month period in the winter of 1965, for example. Over the course of his internship, he did some lobbying for legislation as well. When Jane Weston left the Chicago Regional Office and Moyer became HOP director, Ransom became the assistant director for the program.[66]

During his tenure, Ransom saw the dwindling of the Chicago HOP's efforts to recruit individual pioneer families for move-ins. Despite his and Moyer's intensive efforts, the integration of suburban communities failed to catch the attention of large numbers of African Americans, including in activist groups. Ransom noted that in human relations conferences and meetings, he was often one of few Black attendees. In November 1964, after participating in a citywide housing conference of 250 attendees sponsored by thirteen public and private organizations, he mused that either the cold, rainy weather or many years of restrictions had dampened enthusiasm for the meeting. Whatever the reason, the small proportion of African Americans "left much to be desired with regard to a good cross section of discussion." The meeting took place at a time in Chicago of increasing agitation about educational inequality and attention to the civil rights movement in the South, so potential African American interest in housing was shifting to other issues. Ransom ultimately concluded that housing "as an emotional issue" had not reached the "full concern" of the community. Moreover, in his own one-on-one contacts with potential Black home seekers, he encountered hostility to the idea of relocating outside the city. In late 1965, he tried to organize a "buyers' committee" of potential pioneers who would visit real estate offices on the North Shore and ask to be shown listings in their price range, but he had trouble recruiting enough participants. That convinced him that although the HOP program needed to continue to work on integrating suburban communities, and that "all sensible approaches should be exhausted" to accomplish that, "the Negro we've been working with is trying to tell us something, and we are failing to hear it."[67]

Other Limitations of the Fair Housing Councils

Besides the quandary of how to proceed with only a "trickle" of Black suburban home seekers, by the mid-1960s the Housing Opportunities Programs continued to struggle with external barriers to integration and internal weaknesses in both the pioneer move in approach and the fair housing councils themselves. As the *Wall Street Journal* reported, despite the encouraging numbers of people joining local human rights commit-tees or signing pledges, the majority of whites demonstrated their op-position to housing integration by voting for anti-fair-housing measures. Moreover, Moyer and Ransom continued to encounter public hostility, so much so that they seemed to get used to it. Ransom calmly tried to see the silver lining in some of the harassment, reporting that dealing with the nasty crank calls "goes into the development of my personal-ity as an intergroup worker." After one particularly rough encounter, he praised Moyer's ability to control a volatile debate at an open housing meeting in a white area, later mentioning offhandedly, "oh and my car was taken apart during my stay" at the event. Moreover, there had been little change at the federal level as agents of the FHA and VA employed a variety of practices for barring African American families from buying repossessed properties at all, let alone in white neighborhoods. Finally, in their study of Black pioneer families in New York State in 1965, George and Eunice Grier documented the "widespread discrimination by indi-vidual property owners and real estate agents" that kept their subjects from finding homes in previously white suburbs. The tactics real estate agents used cost the home-seeking couple not only the failure to find a house, or the prolonged delay in doing so, but also the wasted time and energy as well as battered dignity as they were confronted by dubious excuses again and again. Organizing a friendly reception in the suburbs through a fair housing council did not help much if the African American buyers could not secure a house in the first place.[68]

Although aware that the fair housing movement faced these obstacles, impeding the securing of move-ins and the achievement of even token integration of white suburban communities, over time the HOP staff grew increasingly disenchanted with the councils themselves as agents of change. As Richard Taylor in the Philadelphia office understood it, the HOP staff member's job was to "strengthen local initiative" by stimulat-ing interest, nurturing leadership, and providing assistance as people formed groups, set the agenda, developed a program, and took action. In the early 1960s as the fair housing councils became a central part of the HOP work, the staff had been optimistic that their job was succeeding. But at times, Taylor admitted, they did too much themselves and failed to give "people the opportunity to be involved" and learn skills. More im-portant, members of the councils looked to the HOP too much for guid-ance and to do the day-to-day grunt work of typing up minutes and mak-ing calls. In some cases, local people developed workshops for pioneers or coordinated move-ins. But too often, fair housing efforts faltered when volunteers did not step up, or when prolonged periods between move-ins caused their enthusiasm to dissipate. Then the burden of keeping the program going fell solely on the shoulders of the HOP staff members.[69]

When the HOP staff withdrew, leaving the local organizations to act independently without the help of full-time field workers, these groups' weaknesses became more obvious. In 1966, Barbara Krasner of the Metropolitan Philadelphia program estimated that only about eight of the thirty "so called fair housing councils" in the area were "viable." In those eight, she noted, until very recently not one person had seen "it as their task to go into Negro communities to offer their services." The regional listing service could not get enough volunteers to keep the office open five days a week, and no one in the fair housing movement was willing to serve as a "front"—that is, purchase a house and transfer the property title to a Black family. Putting it bluntly, she concluded "we're losing the open housing fight," at least in part because of the inaction and timidity of fair housing councils. The situation in California was similar. By then the Southern California Regional Office in Pasadena had nurtured and supported 110 fair housing or human relations councils, many of them formed in reaction to the southern civil rights movement or to a referendum campaign led by real estate agents to overturn state open housing legislation. But only about one-third of them were really working on housing, and even then they moved "slowly and cautiously" for fear of conservative backlash.[70]

The classism of the fair housing organizing in the suburbs also limited its effectiveness. As Jacques Wilmore had admitted in the early efforts to facilitate a pioneer move-in to the Pennsylvania Levittown, the strategy of opening the new white suburbs to African American families who could afford to move there was inherently class biased, or in his terms snobbish. The Griers found in their interviews with Black professionals that they shared the expectation that a "good neighborhood" had "congenial neighbors of roughly equivalent income and educational background." According to social scientists George B. Nesbitt and Elfriede Hoeber, fair housers' classism was so pervasive that "nonwhites of lower status are rarely seen to offer any potential for successful pioneering occupancy." Instead, the suburbanites organized in the fair housing councils expected that middle- and upper-middle-class African Americans would have an income sufficient to make payments on a new suburban home, maintain the property, and share a lifestyle with their white neighbors. Most important, perhaps, was the hope that there would be few enough Black buyers in that income range to prevent their "inundation" into any one community. In their 1965 critique of the fair housing committees, Nesbitt and Hoeber argued that these assumptions limited the open housing movement to focusing only on single-family homes for sale, ignoring the needs of moderate- and low-income minorities. By then, HOP staff in offices from Boston to Pasadena had agreed with that assessment. Disenchanted with the fair housing councils and the drive to integrate the middle-class suburbs, they began to turn their attention to the low-income minorities being displaced from their inner-city homes by urban renewal with nowhere else to go.[71]

•

As HOPs nationwide began to lay down or transform the suburban housing work, they developed different answers to the question, If not fair housing councils and pioneer move-ins, then what would bring about more equal housing and integrated communities? AFSC Community Relations Committee members in Boston and Pasadena called for more attention to the housing problems of the urban poor—those who could not afford to move to the suburbs even if they were open—launching new initiatives that would be models for other regional offices over the course of the 1960s. Meanwhile, the Chicago and Metropolitan Philadelphia HOPs devised their own answers. In Philadelphia, housing staff planned what would be their last initiative: an investigation into discrimination by the FHA and VA aimed at providing the evidence to challenge agency administrators to uphold Kennedy's executive order banning unequal treatment in federally supported housing. Meanwhile, rather than educating whites and helping "a few Blacks bypass" the obstacles to a free and fair housing choice, the AFSC staff in Chicago decided to launch an assault on those obstacles and a campaign against the "real gatekeepers" upholding neighborhood segregation—local, state, and federal authorities, and the real estate companies that controlled the housing market. Drawing from the inspiration and model of the nonviolent movement against the Jim Crow system in the South, Bill Moyer began to argue for and experiment with direct-action tactics that would open those gates.[72]

3. Direct Action

Battering the Gates, Nonviolently

In the spring of 1965, Bill Moyer announced the launch of the North Shore Summer Project, a campaign of testing real estate offices, canvassing white residents, and standing vigil for equal and open housing in the Chicago area. "If the term, 'summer project,' rings a bell, it is meant to do so," Moyer explained. "Many of us who live here have expressed our deep concern and indignation about events in Alabama and Mississippi. We condemn these closed societies—closed to Negroes, that is—yet we ourselves live in a closed community. . . . For three years North Shore fair housing committees have helped Black families look at the few houses opened to them. Now Negroes are being asked to be served like first class citizens . . . and Negroes are being turned away, just as they are at the courthouses in the South."[1] By this time, the Congress of Racial Equality had picketed in Chicago's Hyde Park neighborhood, Black families had conducted look-ins—organized groups visiting a neighborhood to view homes for sale—in suburban neighborhoods, and members of fair housing committees had demonstrated outside real estate offices in the North Shore suburbs. As Moyer's words hint, these actions and his proposed North Shore Summer Project sought to transplant to the North the sit-ins and other nonviolent direct-action tactics being used in the southern campaign against Jim Crow and adapt them for use against housing segregation. These early actions contributed to Martin Luther King's decision to bring the Southern Christian Leadership Conference to Chicago, the choice of housing discrimination as the organization's main target, and the strategies it would use in the 1966 Chicago Freedom Summer campaign. Moyer and other AFSC regional office staff would play key roles in formulating those strategies and organizing the movement at the grassroots.

The involvement of AFSC program staff in direct-action protests in Chicago and elsewhere marked a significant change in the organization's strategies for bringing about open housing. HOP staff and committee members now saw their previous methods as "inadequate to the demands of the times for equality and justice." Influenced by the civil rights movement's attack on systemic discrimination, they concluded that the "question is not whether one qualified minority person can break a barrier, but whether a whole group of people can be accepted as having equal opportunity." Invoking a treasured memory of Quaker antiracism, the Chicago HOP staff asserted, "Helping nice Negro families move to all-white suburbs in 1966 without directly challenging the real estate system's discriminatory practices was like working in the underground railroad in 1846 without, at the same time, working to abolish slavery." In short, changing the hearts of housing industry leaders or white neighbors was not enough; fair housing would only be achieved with a broad challenge to the system that undergirded residential segregation. But how to make that challenge while remaining true to historic Quaker values of reconciliation, respect for the human dignity of your adversaries, and the avoidance of violence, even in spirit? Inspired by the direct-action campaign against Jim Crow in the South, AFSC personnel debated what nonviolence meant in practice, reconciled the new tactics of the Black freedom struggle with their own values, and most important developed strategies for employing direct action against housing discrimination. In the process, they forged a partnership with the civil rights movement, especially the Southern Christian Leadership Conference, and together generated pressure on the gatekeepers to open the doors to equal housing opportunity.

The Roots of Modern Nonviolent Resistance in the United States

Although it had nineteenth-century precursors, modern nonviolent resistance in the United States grew out of the confluence of pacifism, the labor movement, and the African American struggle against racism in the 1930s and 1940s. In the wake of the calamity of World War I, pacifists searched for active ways to do something about sources of conflict at home, including both industrial conditions and racial discrimination. For the early AFSC, that meant sponsoring interracial work camps and race relations institutes. For some radicals like A. J. Muste and others in the Fellowship of Reconciliation (FOR), that search led to involvement in the labor movement, where they encountered and admired the "sit-down" strikes, in which workers remained inside the factories but refused to work. But the most significant inspiration for the turn toward "resisting evil nonviolently" came from the Gandhian movement in India, which demonstrated the moral power of peaceful noncooperation with an oppressive state. Gandhi aroused American sympathies, attracted social justice activists, and ignited a debate among African American leaders about the applicability of his methods in the battle against racial oppression in the United States. Then in 1934, Richard Gregg, a labor lawyer who was living in India, wrote *The Power of Nonviolence*, which explained Gandhi's *satyagraha* (meaning truth, or love, force) and proposed pragmatic methods for applying nonviolence to social conflicts. American pacifists immediately embraced the book, which one of them called the "'Bible' of nonviolence," and Gregg became a sought-after speaker including for the AFSC. With his work still freshly published, in 1935 he served as an instructor for the summer Institute on Race Relations, at which he presented nonviolence as "one method of attempting to settle questions growing out of racial conflict." He also spent time visiting AFSC work camps to talk about employing the power of pacifism to create social change. In addition, individual Quakers and other pacifists associated with the AFSC read the book "avidly" and referred to it in their peace work in the late 1930s.[2]

During and immediately after World War II, white and Black pacifists and nonpacifist African American leaders began experimenting with putting nonviolence in practice against Jim Crow. Gregg's book, and conversations about his methods, circulated among the men in the Civilian Public Service camps, which had been established during the war to house conscientious objectors (COs). These conversations led to direct actions, often aiming to integrate the camps themselves. Meanwhile, the FOR and A. Philip Randolph's March on Washington Movement conducted a series of "nonviolent institutes" around the country, with the intent of creating cells of activists and sparking local demonstrations against Jim Crow in public accommodations. In Indianapolis in 1942, a group of AFSC work campers attended a similar workshop, this one organized by the NAACP and featuring African American Quaker and CO Bayard Rustin. In his presentation, "Nonviolent Direct Action in Areas of Racial Tension," Rustin stressed that the technique depended on recognizing the "something of God" in every man, which appealed to the young Friends in the group. After the session, the NAACP planned an integrated "theater party" to see *Mrs. Miniver*, which the work campers agreed individuals could join according to their own conscience's lead. Perhaps most important, the Chicago FOR's actions led to the founding of the Congress of Racial Equality, an interracial pacifist organization devoted to using direct action to end racial discrimination. CORE formed local affiliates, which used sit-downs and other nonviolent protest tactics to target segregation in public facilities, jobs, and, in a few cases, housing. In its early years, however, the hesitancy to use direct action in the South, public apathy, and the anticommunist crusade limited CORE's effectiveness and ability to gain attention.[3]

Nonviolent direct action as a weapon against Jim Crow burst into national awareness in 1956 when the Black community of Montgomery, Alabama, peacefully protested segregation on the city buses through a mass boycott. Soon after the boycott began, Bayard Rustin and Glenn Smiley of the FOR traveled to the city to lend advice from a pacifist perspective. Smiley brought with him *The Power of Nonviolence* and introduced it to the new leader of the Montgomery Improvement Association, the Reverend Martin Luther King Jr., who was so "deeply affected" that he wrote Gregg to thank him for giving nonviolence a "realistic and depthful interpretation." The AFSC also sent people to Montgomery, including executive secretary Clarence Pickett, to give moral support to this example of nonviolence and express sympathy for the goal of equal citizenship. In the wake of the boycott, the staff of the AFSC's Community Relations Division hailed the action as an example of the "social power within the Negro community" and warmly endorsed the use of such tactics. The boycott's impact as a demonstration of peaceful direct action resonated with African American leaders far and wide—all the way to Nagpur, India, where an African American Methodist missionary named James Lawson heard about it and was inspired to return to the United States to be an activist minister. After a few detours, Lawson arrived back home and began to teach his strategies of nonviolent direct action, culled from Gandhi, Gregg, and Montgomery, to African American students in Nashville.[4]

The AFSC's Response to Nonviolent Direct Action

When the Montgomery bus boycott demonstrated the possibility of a mass nonviolent attack on racial discrimination, the community relations staff pondered what role they, as a majority white middle-class pacifist organization, could play in the drive against Jim Crow. Up to this point, while supportive of African Americans' embrace of nonviolence, the consensus in the AFSC was that individuals could follow their own conscience in taking an action, but in doing so they did not represent the organization. Now, with the prospect of more widespread demonstrations across the South and the likelihood of a violent reaction, Community Relations Division staff strove to square their own traditional values and practices with the new tactics of nonviolent direct action. How could they be both a "stirrer of conscience" and "a reconciler of sharply conflicting groups"? As much as they wanted to "be a bridge" between adversarial groups, they would always be on the side of integration. And if they were going to engage in actions to bring that about, they would necessarily contribute to tension. In a May 1958 essay, Judy Miller, who had seen firsthand how desegregating public housing created conflict in Chicago's Trumbull Park public housing apartments, challenged her coworkers to clarify their intent when they talked about "reconciliation as the goal; love, nonviolence and understanding as the means." Referencing the work of Dan Dodson, sociologist at New York University and prolific antiracist writer, Miller argued that "love thy neighbor" was "meaningless if it remains sheerly verbal." True love meant taking actions to "make it possible for the minority individual to be seen and judged without prejudice or stereotype." Making a point that would be echoed in the southern struggle, Miller asserted that the AFSC needed to accept conflict "because sometimes it can be creative." More pointedly, she concluded that if the AFSC priority was reducing tension, organization members would become "placators [sic]" who kept "change from happening" and "relations from being restructured."[5]

As concerns like Miller's bubbled up from the field staff, the national Community Relations Committee asked the Representative Council, a board of Quakers charged with overseeing and guiding the whole of the AFSC program, "What are the responsibilities of an organization, concerned about peace making and reconciliation, in situations of racial injustice?" In February 1959, the council responded with a ringing endorsement of nonviolent direct action. The goal of the community relations program was to "strive to achieve justice for individuals in situations in which it has been denied." Doing so required a challenge to the deniers, and that would create conflict. But the real source of tension was injustice, not the effort to overcome it. Indeed, tension did not need to lead to violence but rather could be a source of "growth and constructive change." Members of the council went on to emphasize the religious underpinnings of how AFSC staff should proceed. Reminding people that "our work in this difficult field has its justification in a religious conviction that each man is a child of God," they urged that all community relations actions be "characterized by humility, compassion, and openness to communication." The goal was still reconciliation, which was "neither the avoidance of all tension, nor a compromise of good and evil," but rather "an experience between man and God in the process of which men are drawn closer to one another." The council's report, which circulated widely over the next year, effectively approved AFSC participation in nonviolent direct action if it was done in a spirit of love, with pure motives, and with integrity.[6]

Over the next several years, community relations staff debated what that meant in practice and how they could incorporate nonviolent direct action into their strategies for change in housing and other division concerns. At the spring 1959 CRD staff retreat, or roundup, the attendees had a wide-ranging conversation about specific tactics that might or might not be used in the spirit of love. Without coming to any conclusions, the participants hashed out the pros and cons of accepting police protection and the difference between doing so on a picket line versus during a pioneer move-in; whether using government complaint processes or the courts was a sign of the failure of moral persuasion and an inappropriate reliance on state coercion; and whether it was acceptable to boycott before negotiating. After the start of the spring 1960 sit-ins, some members of the Southern Program, which had been launched in 1957 and largely focused on school desegregation, expressed discomfort with civil disobedience. Jean Fairfax, an African American woman who had worked for the AFSC for ten years and had been appointed to head the new program, warned that to many southern whites, the civil rights movement was "coercive." She laid out specific criteria by which any nonviolent direct action should be measured: the presence of concern for one's opponent, including a "real respect for him and a willingness to listen to him," a "willingness to suffer" (that is, go to jail), a "genuine willingness to forgive," and the "discipline and restraint" to stop short of the full goal in order that a "spirit of reconciliation can have a chance to take hold." At the conclusion of that debate, the national AFSC office issued a declaration endorsing the sit-ins. Moreover, over the succeeding years the Representative Council rearticulated its endorsement of staff participation in direct action, calling civil disobedience a moral "individual act of conscience."[7]

Training for Nonviolent Direct Action

Amid the AFSC's organization-wide conversation about nonviolence, some in the field offices began hosting workshops to teach people what it was and how to use it. In doing so, they joined a long tradition dating back to the early diffusion of Richard Gregg's work in the 1930s, the Fellowship of Reconciliation/March on Washington Movement wartime institutes, and CORE's postwar use of workshops to promote local activism. In the wake of the bus boycott, Martin Luther King's Montgomery Improvement Association used CORE's model to teach African Americans how to respond nonviolently to attacks on the now desegregated buses; and its successor organization, the Southern Christian Leadership Conference, hired James Lawson to demonstrate nonviolent direct-action techniques. Lawson's workshops in Nashville, along with the ongoing efforts of CORE, laid the groundwork for the mass demonstrations to come. These workshops followed a similar format regardless of decade or sponsor; they included lectures, discussions, and sociodramas—exercises in which participants played the part of demonstrator or mob and experienced what it was like both to act nonviolently and to be confronted with a person who refused to cooperate with evil. Historian

Anthony Siracusa has called the FOR/MOWM institutes sites of "collective learning"; the description was apt for workshops in general, which provided opportunities for whites and Blacks, pacifists or not, to come together to exchange ideas, practice and experience nonviolence, and disseminate practical applications of that idea. As a result, nonviolence workshops created a shared social justice movement practice, which the AFSC adopted and sought to apply to housing.[8]

The AFSC began to sponsor nonviolence training in Chicago in 1957. Inspired by the Montgomery bus boycott and the crisis in Trumbull Park, the Chicago Regional Office and the FOR cohosted an Institute in Non-Violent Methods. Fifty people attended the event, which covered the background and techniques of nonviolence and discussed ways of using them for the "peaceful integration of our city." The organizers invited King to speak, but he could not attend. In his stead, participants heard Glenn Smiley, a number of local ministers, and Gretchen Anderson, resident of Trumbull Park, who testified about what it was like to react nonviolently to the attacks against her and her family. To make the connection with the rising southern movement, in the afternoon the attendees watched the film *Walk to Freedom* about the bus boycott. The event ended with sociodramas to bring the lessons home. The organizers considered the event a success, and while it was not repeated in the short term, it planted the seed for later work in the Chicago office.[9]

Once the sit-ins were in full swing, other programs and offices of the AFSC organized their own study of and training in nonviolence. In the thick of the action, regional office staff in Texas and North Carolina hosted workshops on how to protest nonviolently. Then in September 1961, Lawrence Aspey of the Peace Education Division proposed a program of seminars about how to use nonviolence to provide protection for the Freedom Riders or for young people integrating schools. Turning to issues in the urban North and West, he also suggested developing nonviolent ways to "police a slum area or forestall violence between juvenile and other gangs." Although most of the Peace Education Division ultimately focused on using nonviolence against militarism, the Peace Education Committee of the Northeast Regional Office in Cambridge, Massachusetts, developed an outline for eight weekly two-hour sessions on the theory, method, history, and practical applications of nonviolence, with advice on adapting these lessons for one's own community; the syllabus was then used in Chicago and other regional offices. Meanwhile, on the West Coast the Northern California Regional Office worked with the Berkeley Friends Meeting to sponsor the conference Nonviolence in Public Demonstrations in June 1964, at which about 150 people heard about "religiously oriented nonviolence" and were encouraged to make personal witnesses.[10] These and other workshops demonstrated the thirst in the AFSC constituency for instruction on how to engage in the movements of the time in ways that accorded with their pacifist principles.

Although regional office HOP staff in other communities led and participated in demonstrations, the AFSC's most extensive employ of nonviolent direct action for open housing occurred in Chicago.[11] In 1963, local events inspired the regional office staff to host more workshops and use them to build cooperation with the city's civil rights movement. By that time, the Birmingham campaign had garnered attention and sympathy in Chicago, exemplified by a benefit for the Southern Christian Leadership Conference presided over by a beaming Mayor Richard J. Daley. Plans for demonstrations closer to home were also circulating. The relatively new Coordinating Council of Community Organizations was gearing up for school desegregation protests. In addition, the Chicago affiliates of the Congress of Racial Equality and the Student Nonviolent Coordinating Committee (SNCC) were looking for ways to use direct action against housing discrimination. Finally, the Chicago City Council had adopted a fair housing ordinance, meaning demonstrations could call for enforcement of an existing law. After broaching the idea of workshops with some AFSC staff and civil rights supporters, Bill Moyer organized a "leadership consultation"—a meeting for area activists to discuss whether there was a need or desire for such training and whether the AFSC should provide it. The meeting was held on July 14 and attended by thirty-five people representing CORE, SNCC, the West Side Christian Parish, the Presbyterian Interracial Council, and others. Bayard Rustin and J. Metz Rollins Jr., who had been active in the Nashville sit-ins and the Freedom Rides, chaired the meeting. The participants had a wide-ranging discussion of how to work with allies who did not embrace nonviolence, whether it was okay for people to defend their homes, how nonviolence could address economic inequality, and how to engage white citizens in the movement. In the end, the group asked the AFSC to plan training sessions and hire a staff member to run them.[12]

With that vote of confidence, the Chicago Regional Office staff proceeded to host workshops on nonviolence. They held the first training in the "philosophy and practice of nonviolent direct action" in November 1963, but it fell short of expectations. The organizers had found it difficult to line up speakers with direct personal experience, and the audience was small. In spring 1964, the regional office organized a stronger panel of speakers and held four more events in April and May. Attendance peaked at eighty people in one session, evenly divided between whites and Blacks. Participants included regional staff and committee members, along with young people from SNCC, CORE, area high school Black history clubs, and Lake Forest College. Discussion leaders in these sessions included national pacifist leader A. J. Muste; Bob Gore of CORE; Charles McDew, formerly of SNCC; and other peace activists. Representing the AFSC was Tony Henry. Henry was an African American who had grown up in Houston and got acquainted with Quakers in 1957 when he was a student civil rights activist at the University of Texas. In 1961, he started working for the AFSC in a foreign service program in Tanzania before transferring to Chicago in 1963 to run a program for high school students. Henry would stay in the regional office until 1968 and continue to work for and with the AFSC long afterward.[13]

While the regional office organized and sponsored these sessions, executive director Kale Williams pursued hiring a staff member who could take over the nonviolence training and engage with the local civil rights struggle. A Navy veteran turned "militant pacifist," Williams came home from the Pacific theater of the war and became a Quaker before joining the AFSC as a staff member in the early 1950s. Excited about the prospect of expanding the social justice work of the office and marrying it to pacifist action techniques, he asked the national AFSC Board of Directors to fund a three-year program "to relate the insights and resources of Friends in conflict resolution and non-violent challenge to injustice to the civil rights movement in Illinois and Wisconsin." Citing the fear that demonstrations might turn aggressive or be motivated by "violent attitudes," the Chicago office wanted to hire a staff person who could encourage civil rights activists toward a philosophical commitment to nonviolence. But the proposal went further. The regional office staff, led by Williams, wanted to begin to tackle poverty in addition to inequalities in education and housing. To do so, they suggested creating a program that would focus on problems in low-income, minority, inner-city communities.[14]

In May 1964, having secured permission from the national board, Williams hired Bernard Lafayette to lead nonviolence workshops and head a new Urban Affairs Program. Lafayette was an African American activist who had been involved with civil rights work since his days as a teenage member of the Tampa, Florida, NAACP Youth Council. As a student at the American Baptist Theological Seminary in Nashville, he and his roommate, John Lewis, had attended James Lawson's workshops on nonviolence. Lafayette recalled that those experiences taught him how "moral behavior could be a force for change," to "embrace others as human beings" and to use that "moral force" to change an "entire community." During this time, he also encountered the Society of Friends through attending conversation meetings with other students at the home of Nelson Fuson, a Quaker physics professor at Fisk University. Lafayette employed the lessons he had learned in the Nashville sit-ins and as one of the first Freedom Riders. Now fully part of the new southern movement, he went with SNCC to do voter registration work in Selma, Alabama, in 1962 and 1963 before returning briefly to Nashville as a student at Fisk University. By that time, he was married to his wife, Colia, and in early 1964 they had their first child. That change in life circumstances convinced Lafayette that he needed a more full-time job, though, he hoped, one still engaged in civil rights work. Rev. Lawson and Glenn Smiley recommended him to Kale Williams for the AFSC's new staff position. In reminiscing about his decision to move to Chicago, Lafayette credited a philosophical sympathy with Quaker pacifism and the fact that the job came with hospitalization, paternity leave, and retirement benefits. His decision to stick with the AFSC for years despite Martin Luther King's invitations to join the Southern Christian Leadership Conference, he later joked, was in part because "there were no benefits in the movement."[15]

Lafayette exemplified a tendency in the Community Relations Division to hire people who had experience in social action organizations and/or some expertise in the subject at hand but were not themselves Quakers, though they shared basic values with the Society of Friends. This practice was not new in the 1960s. From the beginning, the AFSC had recruited people with needed skills for foreign service work even if they weren't Friends. Moreover, while many of the leaders of the domestic programs in the 1930s through 1950s had been Friends who had worked in other areas of the AFSC or men who had been in the Civilian Public Service camps, from the start the Race Relations Committee and then the CRD had cast a wide net, beginning with hiring African American G. James Fleming as the committee's first executive secretary. Overall, by 1947 only 32 percent of the AFSC staff was Quaker.[16] In the Housing Opportunities Programs, some of the key figures were birthright or convinced Friends, while others were not, including Jane Reinheimer and Judy Miller, both of whom were Jewish. The more important qualification, rather than religious affiliation, was shared values. In 1961, a study of fifty-three previous and current CRD field workers revealed that while they were not all Quakers, they shared a "religious commitment to the worth of the individual," "a cherishing of the concept of a free and equal society," and a "willingness to put belief to action." Moreover, as the division's engagement with the civil rights movement increased and as it began to participate in the new War on Poverty, the leadership found it was competing with more service agencies to hire qualified staff. Consequently, it began to emphasize developing "local talent" from among the populations with whom the programs worked. This, plus the goal of diversifying the staff, led to the hiring of people like Lafayette, Bert Ransom of the HOP, Tony Henry of the youth programs, and Jerry Davis, an African American from New York City who had graduated from Fisk, started with the Chicago youth program, and went on to be the AFSC's contact person with the Oakland Black Power movement.[17] Eventually, the shift toward a majority non-Quaker staff would cause tension within the AFSC and between it and Friends Meetings, but in the meantime the more activist- and issue-oriented employees helped the CRD build bridges to the civil rights movement.[18]

That bridge-building task was the first Lafayette turned to in the summer and early fall of 1964. In his first few months, he expanded the AFSC's ties with the movement both near and far and laid the groundwork for stepped-up direct action. He moved into Project House, an AFSC facility in the East Garfield Park neighborhood on Chicago's West Side, and used it as his base of operations. Project House also hosted the youth program run by Henry, which facilitated cooperation between the two men from the start. Lafayette gave nonviolence workshops to constituencies ranging from Friends Meetings to the shop stewards of the Amalgamated Clothing Workers Union to young people associated with the gangs of the West Side. During one of Lafayette's meetings with the youth, they challenged him to join them at a protest the next day, saying, "'We've never done this before, and so we want you to go with us.'" Lafayette couldn't say no, as he recalled: "Well, okay, alright. You can't train somebody else to go, but you're not going to go." Just to be sure, he cleared his participation with Kale Williams, who gave him a day's leave of absence so that he could go and get arrested. Besides leading to acts of protest, some of the workshops produced grassroots groups committed to persistent direct action, including the Evanston Nonviolent Action Council and the Englewood Christian Leadership Conference. Lafayette also brought the AFSC into the Coordinating Council of Community Organizations and strengthened the regional office's relationship with the Student Nonviolent Coordinating Committee. After October 1964, he began to focus his time on building the Urban Affairs Program.[19]

Early Direct Action on Housing in Chicago

By that time, several groups in the Chicago area had begun using direct action on housing issues, often with support, coordination, and advice from Bill Moyer. The Congress of Racial Equality took the lead. In the postwar era, CORE chapters around the country had tried to attack residential discrimination, including in San Francisco, where it sent testers and pickets to segregated apartment buildings, and in suburban

Maryland, where the group led demonstrations against Levitt and other big developers. In January 1962, young people in the Windy City chapter started to address the issue by protesting the University of Chicago real estate office's role in keeping Hyde Park segregated. The next spring, the group campaigned to get the Veterans Administration to make sure that its repossessed homes were sold on the open market. Moyer also met with the Chicago SNCC affiliate to talk about how it might apply direct action to housing in the suburbs. Finally, he advised smaller local efforts, such as look-in campaigns led by a Black minister and by the Organization of Southwest Communities. In the summer of 1963, in response to the growing local interest in civil rights at Friends Meetings, Williams advised area Quakers to make a public witness by joining in some of these ongoing protests.[20]

In 1964, protests increasingly targeted real estate offices as the gatekeepers to homes in the suburbs. Moyer approached the HOP advisory committee with the idea of focusing on real estate companies in May. At that time, he suggested picketing and boycotting those having a large Black clientele in the city but discriminating against them in the suburbs, pressuring them to change the latter practice. The committee rejected the idea as impractical, however, and suggested that Moyer find a more positive approach to the brokers.[21] But grassroots enthusiasm for direct action against a clear target quickly overrode that resistance as North Shore community organizations started a campaign against realty firms in Evanston, "protesting their practices" and their opposition to fair housing legislation. As the summer wore on, the North Shore Coordinating Council held a march of several hundred people, mostly whites, against the Evanston and North Shore Suburban Real Estate Boards. More than thirty people were arrested when CORE launched sit-ins in four offices in Evanston. Shortly thereafter, a group of high school and college students in the Evanston Nonviolent Action Council picketed real estate offices. Moyer reported that like a leader running to catch up to the start of the parade, he participated in some of these demonstrations but not in the initial planning. By the end of the summer, he did nudge the young people a bit on tactics. Responding to the HOP committee's concern for a more reconciliatory approach to complement the street demonstrations, he met with liberal and moderate real estate agents to try to see things from their perspective and figure out how to get them to follow their better instincts. He also suggested conducting a pledge campaign that would indicate the extent of community support for open housing and prove to the agents that they would not necessarily lose business by adopting a nondiscriminatory policy.[22]

The North Shore Summer Project

Moyer's suggested pledge campaign soon became one of the core components of an expanded and more coordinated direct-action effort on the North Shore. In January 1965, he called a meeting of representatives of North Shore fair housing groups and presented an idea for an intensive summer push to support integration in their communities. North Shore activists by this time had shared the HOP staff's conclusion that on their own, pioneer move-ins facilitated by fair housing groups would not make a dent in the patterns of segregation developing in American suburbs. While they helped individual families achieve their goal of new housing and had some educational impact on white neighbors, the move-ins were simply too sporadic. Instead, as the choice to target real estate offices indicates, the suburban activists were looking for ways to challenge the system that kept African American families out of their communities and were eager for a direct-action method for doing that. Moyer proposed that they cooperate on a North Shore Summer Project (NSSP), which would involve local people and college students in door-to-door canvassing of neighbors to solicit support for open sales, negotiations with area real estate boards, and sit-ins and pickets at real estate offices. The fair housing representatives agreed and began fund-raising. Moyer would be the main organizer and the AFSC the fiscal agent and lead sponsor, but local people would make decisions, raise the estimated $12,000 needed for the project, and run the "freedom centers," community-based movement headquarters, in each suburb.[23]

From the beginning, Moyer and others linked the NSSP rhetorically and structurally to the southern civil rights movement in general and the recent Mississippi Freedom Summer specifically. As early as 1963, Moyer had been making an analogy comparing a house to a cup of coffee and the real estate office to the southern lunch counters, emphasizing the role of the businesses as the primary site of discrimination. Now he expanded on the connections between the movement in North and South, equating Chicago's closed neighborhoods with Mississippi's "closed society." Whereas in the Delta the Klan burned churches, in Chicago segregationists burned Black families' homes. He pointed out that although from "nowhere has come more support for COFO [Council of Federated Organizations], SNCC, and CORE than . . . Chicago," if "a Black man from there moved here he could not get a house on the North Shore." Indeed, of the two thousand homes for sale in the area, only five were available to African American families. Moyer argued that the consciences of people in those communities had been pricked by events in the South, and they were now ready to take action at home: "Many North Shore residents feel that they cannot in good conscience be active in supporting the summer projects in the South in 1965 unless they also are working just as hard, or harder, to remove the barriers of injustice in their own community."[24]

Drawing further from the analogy, the tactics employed by the NSSP were modeled on the Mississippi Freedom Summer Project. Just as students in the South went door-to-door on Delta backroads to talk with people about registering to vote, so college students would canvass on the North Shore, asking people to "register"—sign a pledge—to sell their home on a nondiscriminatory basis. These pledges would be used to negotiate with real estate agents to persuade them to treat African American customers equally. As Moyer put it, Black families were "tired of using the back door of the fair housing committees," like their southern counterparts begging for coffee and crumbs from the rear of the restaurant. Now they were going to go to the front door—the real estate office—to demand equal service. If they were denied, like the civil rights activists in Selma, Alabama, and Greenwood, Mississippi, waiting at the courthouse door to register to vote, they would line up outside the real estate office until served. Over the course of the summer, the NSSP would also hold vigils and rallies along with mass marches to the Board of Realtors' headquarters, by now familiar tactics people had seen in the South. Again, Moyer pointed out that white residents of Chicago had supported the southern civil rights movement, including by going to Selma, Montgomery, and Mississippi. Now it was "time to do something about our own hometown."[25]

That spring there was a flurry of organizing to get ready for the June launch of the project. Committees reporting to program coordinator Carol Kleiman and chairman Rev. Emory Davis worked on recruiting students, lining up sponsorships, fund-raising, and arranging publicity. By May, ten North Shore suburban communities had committees working on the NSSP. Freedom centers were set up in a second-floor office in Evanston's business district and in the police station in Kenilworth, with the headquarters in Winnetka. The list of sponsors included human relations and fair housing committees, the North Side Veterans Club, the American Jewish Committee, the Chicago Conference on Religion and Race, over one hundred clergymen, and four state representatives. Black home seekers, armed with a script from Moyer addressing what questions to ask and how to document their experience, began approaching real estate offices; volunteers also started circulating petitions. In June, college students underwent a week of training on housing, nonviolence, and interview techniques. With an inaugural rally on June 26 for the project volunteers, the NSSP was ready to go.[26]

In publicity and in reports over the course of the summer, NSSP organizers emphasized signs of support for both the project and open housing. At first, the grassroots work of young people talking with residents at their doorways seemed to yield hopeful results. Over one hundred Black and white students interviewed people whose homes were listed for sale, asking them whether they would accept Black buyers, while adult volunteers invited their neighbors to pledge to welcome them or donate to the project. The summer newsletter carried regular quotes from the students about the welcome they received, and halfway through the campaign Rev. Davis declared that 55 percent of people surveyed said they would sell to African Americans and 85 percent said they would not mind Black neighbors. A final report indicated that 673 home sellers were interviewed, and most said they assumed their house was being sold on the open market, that they had not requested an "owner reserves the right to refuse" clause, and that they would accept Black neighbors. Meanwhile, 12,059 people signed open housing petitions, 1,617 people sponsored the NSSP, and "hundreds" donated. Finally, a "mostly white" crowd of ten thousand people attended a rally with Martin Luther King on the Winnetka village green to call for open housing (fig. 3.1). Conceding that not enough African Americans had been involved, Charlotte Meacham argued that the "strength of the project" had been its impact on North Shore residents, especially "the learning process they went through about the real estate industry, the challenge to the Realtors, the linkage between the movement and housing . . . and the reaction and enthusiasm of white students and suburbanites."[27]

Belying this optimism, however, the NSSP made little headway with Realtors, represented by the Evanston-North Shore Real Estate Board (ENSREB) and its president, Lou Pfaff. On May 7, representatives of the NSSP met with the officials of the ENSREB and asked them to adopt a policy of nondiscrimination in showing, selling, and renting houses; ask all members to give equal service to all home seekers; and encourage all home sellers to sell on the open market. Ultimately, the NSSP wanted the Realtors to refuse to sell a home if the owner asked for a restricted sale. The requests met a wall of silence. By late June, the board had not even made a reply. When pressed, Pfaff wrote Rev. Davis to say that the board would not adopt a nondiscrimination policy. Meanwhile, some individual firms simply refused to negotiate. By the end of the summer, Pfaff conceded that member agents would show houses to African Americans if the sellers requested it, but that fell short of the NSSP goal of equal service. Meanwhile, the NSSP shared another trait with the Mississippi Freedom Project: a relative lack of measurable results toward the main goal. Just as the latter did not boost African American voter registration much, not many Black families moved into new suburban homes.[28]

FIGURE 3.1: North Shore Summer Project flyer for Martin Luther King Jr. rally, 1965. Courtesy of the American Friends Service Committee Archives, Philadelphia.

The recalcitrance of the Realtors led to more demonstrations on the North Shore. After the ENSREB rejected its requests, the NSSP began daily silent vigils in front of the board's offices, expanding them to real estate offices refusing to negotiate. Before these events, participants had received nonviolence training and had been instructed to refrain from smoking or talking during a vigil and to hand out a statement to anyone inquiring about its purpose. The text reflected the values that undergirded the AFSC's work, moving beyond blame and welcoming people into a shared project of liberation. "We stand here today in our own villages and towns to bear witness to the fact that we who live here—not just the Realtors—are responsible for the serious social evil of discrimination in housing," the statement read. "We stand here not just for the freedom of a specific race or religious group to be able to have equal access to all homes on the market, but for the freedom of all North Shore residents. We stand here because we are not free." At the end of the summer, seeking to complete the project on a dramatic note, the organizers sponsored a march from the NSSP headquarters to the Evanston office of the ENSREB; this was followed by an all-night vigil, after which Rev. Davis presented a report of the canvass's findings to the board president. Moyer predicted that because of the negative response, direct action would go on.[29]

Bill Moyer's prediction turned out to be correct. As the North Shore Summer Project wrapped up, the student workers formed FREE (For Real Estate Equality) to continue to challenge real estate agents. First, Moyer and then new HOP assistant director Jerry Davis advised the group. Following a common pattern by this point in the civil rights movement, the young people started with nonviolence workshops and held educational forums. Then they focused on opening apartments in Evanston, which already had a substantial African American population. In the fall of 1965, when the Evanston City Council closed the Veterans Administration World War II housing project for Blacks, FREE helped the affected families find new housing. Still angry and frustrated over the Board of Realtors' refusal to meet with the NSSP, they also strategized how to confront the broader real estate system. During one training session in October, looking for new tactics to supplement public demonstrations, Moyer counseled the students, who were "all but out the door with their picket signs," to use the real estate offices as classrooms and combine direct help for individual Black home seekers with community education and persuasion. To do that, the group would accompany Black couples as they sought service from Baird and Warner, one of the largest landlords in the area; observe and document the "discrimination in action"; and use that evidence to negotiate, publicize the problem, and garner public support for change.[30]

Laying the Groundwork for an AFSC-SCLC Partnership

In the fall of 1965, the prospects for more extensive direct action increased when the Southern Christian Leadership Conference (SCLC) chose Chicago as its first northern target. In the wake of its Selma campaign and the passage of the Voting Rights Act, the SCLC was debating its next move, and Rev. Martin Luther King Jr. was anxious to move into the North. James Bevel, who once worked with the SCLC in the South, had recently relocated to Chicago. He had served as a speaker at the AFSC's local and regional workshops on nonviolence in 1964 and 1965. Then he became the program director for the West Side Christian Parish on the

Near West Side and settled in the city. Already friends, he and Bernard Lafayette further developed their relationship as both men served the same part of the city in their jobs. According to Andrew Young, the two young activists urged King to come to Chicago, saying, "You have to prove that nonviolence will work in the North." Chicago was also attractive to King because he knew people in the movement there, and he had other friends and associates in the area. Moreover, the Coordinating Council of Community Organizations was organizing a citywide civil rights network. The result was that by the end of September, Bevel had become director of a Chicago project, and ten SCLC staff members were assigned to the city, moving into the West Side Parish Project House and apartments in the surrounding neighborhoods.[31]

Bevel drew from community organizing traditions and precedents in the southern movement to lay the groundwork for what would become the Chicago Freedom Movement. First, he held a five-day retreat in late September to "create an atmosphere of mutual trust and a sense of federated unity" among the city's civil rights organizations, although, as AFSC staffer Jerry Davis pointed out, the NAACP, the Urban League, and "nationalists" were not invited. During the retreat the participants, including Davis and Moyer, discussed how to cooperate and participated in nonviolence workshops. Afterward, Bevel hosted twice-weekly meetings for representatives of different community organizations to plan the movement. At these meetings, attendees listed the many problems confronting Black Chicagoans, including weaknesses in the welfare system, the grip of Mayor Daley's political machine, and above all the lack of access to good housing. For his part, Bevel articulated a broad vision for the movement's goals, which were to create brotherhood and community and model the "beloved society." The immediate task was not to focus on specific problems but to "develop grassroots people" so that by the spring a cadre of local leaders would be ready to take responsibility for teaching their neighbors about nonviolence and the interconnectedness of the issues. From the start, the AFSC was recognized as a key player in this process because of the community organizing approach employed by both the HOP under Moyer and the Urban Affairs Program under Lafayette, and because of the latter's ties to the SCLC and friendship with Bevel.[32] The AFSC also influenced the decision to make housing the central theme in the Chicago Freedom Movement.

During these preparatory months, Moyer and others elaborated on the relation of nonviolence and direct action to the problem of housing discrimination, and how it could reflect Quaker values. The HOP's position was that "no business whose doors are open to the public and which is licensed by the state should be able to treat customers differently by race." Just as southern segregated restaurants were forced open by a nonviolent witness, so, too, could the real estate offices be. Adhering to the spirit behind nonviolence, Moyer noted that the real estate agent was not "a villain" but rather someone "caught in a dilemma that encourages hanging on to the status quo. The heart of nonviolent resistance," he continued, "is to fight the antagonism, not the antagonist." The goal was to "create a climate" in which "new ideas can confront old ideas." Thus, in addition to picketing, the movement would take positive actions that might persuade real estate salesmen to change their ways. In this way, the direct action would not be coercive but rather a means for helping the real estate agents recognize the light within themselves and others.[33]

Although by this time HOP advisory committee members had agreed on the need for direct action, some continued to express discomfort with specific tactics. To some extent, their concerns grew from their responsibility to protect the legal and financial well-being of the AFSC. In mid-April 1966, Moyer proposed to have concerned people call the office of the Baird and Warner real estate firm to ask whether they served Black home seekers equally. One committee member wondered whether the phone company would consider this harassment and cut off the AFSC's service. Others asked whether such actions were truly in keeping with pacifist, nonviolent, and Quaker principles. As member Alice Walton reminded, "Under nonviolence, actions should not be undertaken which will inflict hurt on others." Harassing phone calls would inflict "hurt on our antagonist instead of ourselves." Focusing on one company could create a climate of hostility that would be detrimental to reconciliation, and going into an action expecting discrimination did not reveal much good faith. Moyer agreed to check with the phone company but defended the use of testers. He also pointed out that the day-to-day decisions on tactics were made by the people working on an action, and in the interest of developing local leaders and of nonintrusive collaboration, "we can't tell them what not to do." Once the mass demonstrations for open housing began, events overtook these discussions; but as they reveal, in their approach to direct-action protest tactics, AFSC program staff strove to balance their support for grassroots decision-making and their understanding of appropriate and peaceful Quaker practice.[34]

Beginning in the spring of 1966, Jerry Davis and Bill Moyer organized weekly actions foreshadowing the mass movement that would follow. In February, Davis went with eleven Black families to the near western suburb of Oak Park to ask its real estate offices for services. Oak Park would later develop a national reputation for the success of open housing forces in balancing the population there in the 1970s and onward. But at this point, real estate agents had shown only one of the families a house, and it was in an already integrated neighborhood. For the next sixteen weeks, testers went into other offices, focusing on Baird and Warner; over time the numbers grew, so that up to thirty-five families were accompanied by supporters and observers. In March, a coalition of the HOP, the Urban Affairs Program, and the SCLC christened the effort Project Open Communities and expanded to other areas while Davis continued to focus on Oak Park. Over time, Project Open Communities included other forms of action besides testing. Moyer reported that five hundred sympathizers did indeed call Baird and Warner. In mid-May, instead of leaving after being refused service at a real estate agency, the families held a sit-in. Clergymen supported them by standing outside and trying to talk with the agents. On another occasion, a group of clergy marched to the Oak Park Baird and Warner office, followed two weeks later by a larger group of 350 people. Meanwhile, there was a rally in nearby Stevenson Park of five hundred people. For two weeks in late June, Moyer organized about forty people to attend open houses. Half of them picketed outside with sandwich-board signs while the others went inside to document what happened. These small demonstrations modeled tactics that would be used by a coalition of local civil rights groups and the SCLC in the Chicago Freedom Summer. They also convinced the members of the HOP advisory committee of the value of nonviolent direct action; the committee now agreed that the pickets "should be kept up."[35]

The Chicago Freedom Summer Open Housing Campaign

LAUNCH

While AFSC staff, especially Moyer and Davis, were experimenting with direct-action tactics against housing discrimination, James Bevel and the SCLC began calling for an "end to the slums." But how to accomplish that? In February 1966, Moyer suggested an answer. First, he prepared a report, System of Housing Negroes in Chicago, and educated SCLC staffers on the connection between the barriers to free housing choice and the conditions in low-income neighborhoods. A month later, he wrote Prospectus for a Nonviolent Project to Achieve Open Occupancy throughout the Chicago Area, summarizing his arguments for direct action against real estate offices using the southern movement analogy. The examples of direct action on the North Shore, in Project Open Communities, in Evanston, and in Oak Park illustrated how that project could work. Bevel later recalled, "You can't have some obscure issue that is cloudy in the minds of people. Should a man have a right to rent and buy a house in the city if he works or lives in that city and he is a citizen of that city? You have to pick a target." Moyer showed how real estate offices, as licensed businesses open to the public, could be that target and thus both helped persuade the SCLC to focus on housing discrimination and provided the blueprint for using direct action to attack it. To launch Moyer's suggested strategies, in June the SCLC sent eight people to Chicago to cooperate with the HOP in documenting two hundred cases of discrimination by real estate agencies.[36]

The Chicago Freedom Summer open housing campaign was formally kicked off by a rally and march on Sunday, July 10. On that day, despite oppressive heat, thirty thousand people packed into Soldier Field stadium on the shore of Lake Michigan for a chance to hear Martin Luther King. The AFSC regional office staff did their part to get people there. Bernard Lafayette's Urban Affairs Program raised money and rented three buses to transport people from East Garfield Park. The College Program meanwhile trained students to be nonviolent marshals and ushers for the rally. Kale Williams remembered that as "the numbers swelled, the spirit was buoyant, cheerful, with a sense of movement and purpose." A diverse range of speakers addressed the crowd, reflecting the coalition nature of the movement. The rally came just after the Meredith March in Mississippi, and some young people in the crowd waved Black Power banners, testimony to the division in movement forces that was growing that summer. After King's address, the rally became a march that surged through Grant Park and the Loop. At City Hall, King fastened a list of the movement's demands to the door, mimicking the action of his namesake and officially launching the summer's mass open housing campaign.[37]

The open housing demonstrations in Chicago in 1966, certainly the largest and best-known nonviolent direct actions focusing on that issue during the civil rights era, were organized and led by a partnership of the Southern Christian Leadership Conference and the Coordinating Council of Community Organizations, with AFSC staff members playing key roles in both policy- and action-oriented bodies. In early 1966, the SCLC-CCCO had established an Agenda Committee of twelve people from some of the most involved organizations and charged it with making overall policy decisions about the movement. Over the course of the summer, Williams, Lafayette, Bert Ransom, and Moyer participated in the Agenda Committee, including when it represented the movement in negotiations with city officials in August. Then, just before the Soldier Field rally, King and Bevel appointed an Action Committee of fifteen people from different organizations to decide on direct-action strategy. According to one observer, Lafayette, Moyer, Ransom, and to a lesser extent Davis "carried a large part of the burden of the detailed work and planning required to see that marches came off as planned." Because they expected the movement to be large and diffuse, leaders also established Action Centers on the city's South and West Sides. Located in churches, the centers were places where people who were interested in participating could come to learn what they could do. The "nerve center" of the movement, they provided meeting spaces for planning, training, and rallies as well as jumping-off points for demonstrations. Bert Ransom ran the more successful South Side Action Center with the help of a group of volunteers. Jerry Davis briefly led the West Side Action Center before two SCLC staffers took over, though neither he nor they could get as much activity off the ground. Through these positions, the AFSC staff brought their understanding of housing issues and the expertise they had gained in direct action as tools for addressing them to the larger, broader movement.[38]

Two days after the Soldier Field rally, an outbreak of riots on the West Side threatened to disrupt the momentum of the movement. Tuesday, July 12, was another scorching day, and young people were in the streets looking for relief. When police tried to close an open fire hydrant, African American teenagers using it to cool off pushed back. Violence quickly spread through the neighborhood. That evening, King spoke to a rally at the Shiloh Baptist Church, calling for nonviolence, but got a muted response from the crowd. The next day was quieter, until officials closed all the hydrants. On Thursday, violence escalated and spread to Lawndale and East and West Garfield Park. On Friday, Mayor Daley asked the governor to call in the National Guard to stop the unrest. During that week, Bernard Lafayette organized a group of about fifteen SCLC and Urban Affairs Program staff and East Garfield Park residents into a "peace patrol" to go out into the streets and encourage people to go home—an example of what historian Amanda Seligman calls "counter-rioter" practice that the AFSC and other organizations and individuals employed during the long, hot summers of the 1960s. King and other SCLC leadership likewise tried to quell the unrest. That did not stop Daley from blaming King and Bevel for causing the riots. The *Chicago Defender* did not go that far but did hint that the Chicago Freedom Movement was going in the wrong direction, because King failed to heed local leaders' advice. The episode did not derail the incipient open housing campaign, but it did raise questions about the SCLC's influence in the community.[39]

DEMONSTRATIONS

Despite the riots, the Chicago Freedom Movement open housing campaign successfully launched using tactics developed by the North Shore Summer Project and Project Open Communities: the testing of real estate offices with accompanying support actions. One difference was that movement organizers, following Ransom's advice, decided to target real estate offices in city neighborhoods that were white-only but moderately priced rather than those in the costlier and more distant suburbs that had been so much the focus of earlier HOP activity. The first such community was Gage Park, a neighborhood of small brick homes on the Near Southwest Side that was several blocks from the nearest Black population and thus not yet in transition. On Monday, July 11, approximately five hundred people attended an evening mass meeting, and Lafayette gave workshops on how to test and behave nonviolently. On Tuesday, the same day the riots broke out, small groups of Blacks and whites started visiting Gage Park's real estate offices to ask for service. On Thursday, a mixed group of about one hundred walked through the business district and tested two companies, one of which closed its doors. On Saturday about two hundred people, both Black and white, picnicked in the park and shopped at the stores. On Sunday, sixty African Americans visited local churches, largely without incident, and then had a prayer meeting in Marquette Park, which was just south of the neighborhood. While Black participants used the community facilities and visited real estate offices, white organizers developed plans for how to establish contact with the residents and encourage more whites into the movement.[40]

During the rest of July, the number of actions and their participants grew. Testers continued to go to Gage Park, attempting to visit twenty-three different real estate offices. None of them served the Black testers, and three offices closed and did not reopen. The movement also arranged different forms of public witness in the area, including picnics, all-night vigils, mass marches, and a rally at a local Catholic church. Meanwhile, organizers added two target communities. In the first week, they started sending people to test in Belmont Cragin, a similar community to Gage Park, on the Near Northwest Side of the city. One hundred people, approximately half Blacks and half whites, visited eleven real estate offices during the week and conducted mass testing of one office on Saturday, followed by a picnic for 150 people in Reese Park. The following week, testers went into the Logan Square community area. Organizers chose it because they had heard from sympathetic whites in the area that if there was resistance, neighbors would turn out to help. African American teenagers organized in the Student Organization for Urban Leadership tried to reach out to white youth in the area. On Friday night, after a week of small actions in the neighborhood, Lafayette led a rally at Saint Philomena's Church in Logan Square (fig. 3.2). Meanwhile, the Action Centers held mass meetings to mobilize people in the southern and western sections of the city to join the demonstrations.[41]

By the second week of demonstrations, hostility against the move-

FIGURE 3.2: Martin Luther King Jr. and Bernard Lafayette (*at microphone*) at street rally during Chicago Freedom Summer, CULR_04_0120_1892_003, Chicago Urban League digital image collection. Courtesy of Special Collections and University Archives, University of Illinois Chicago.

ment began to escalate. At first, white civic leaders tried to encourage a "sensible" reaction, hoping not to prolong the civil rights actions in their neighborhoods. During the first week, residents offered little response, but that did not last. By this time, whites on the Southwest Side had already expressed their opposition to Black incursion into their streets and institutions. Although the area had long seemed unaffected by tensions over housing, in 1963 Black families moved into the communities of West Englewood and Englewood—sparking a riot in the latter case—making adjacent Gage Park next in line. Around the same time, Southwest Siders had resisted the integration of their schools and harassed their alderman after he supported the relatively toothless Chicago fair housing ordinance adopted in 1963. Now they stirred to resist direct-action strategies aimed at making that law effective. On the second weekend of the open housing testing, picnickers were met by "jeers and comments" in Gage Park, and an unknown assailant shot at a car carrying demonstrators. The next day at a church rally, hecklers jeered and threw eggs at Kale Williams and Jesse Jackson, a young minister just getting his start as a civil rights leader, and their assembled followers. In Belmont Cragin, someone vandalized cars belonging to the picnickers, breaking windows and pouring sand in the gas tanks. Bernard Lafayette also encountered hectoring and shouting at his rally at Saint Philomena's in Logan Square.[42]

Things got worse in the third week of the campaign. Frustrated with the lack of media coverage of the testing and other actions, King and other SCLC leaders felt the need to step up demonstrations and increase the likelihood of a confrontation that would draw attention. At a rally on the Southwest Side on Thursday, July 28, King announced plans for an all-night vigil for the next evening. On Friday, a group of about forty people began standing in silence outside a real estate office in Gage Park. By nine o'clock, a crowd of approximately one thousand whites began to harass and threaten the group. Greatly outnumbered and fearing violence, the demonstrators returned to the South Side Action Center to plan their next move. The next day, demonstrators marched from Marquette Park to a local real estate office. A white mob followed them, chanting and carrying signs supporting George Wallace and "White Power." When the marchers passed in front of a brick wall of a Jewish temple, they were "suddenly showered by shattered glass and pop bottles [which] were hurled at the wall and broken above their heads." The group hurried back to the park, where cars from the action center met them and whisked them away, under police protection.[43]

On Sunday, about four hundred marchers returned to Marquette Park and began walking to a Methodist church to pray for a change in the hearts of local real estate agents. A mob of whites met them, dogging the demonstrators the entire route and throwing rocks, bottles, and firecrackers at them. "Youthful hooligans" chanted and sang about lynching Blacks while middle-aged couples joined in the taunting and violence. Facing a level of fury they had not seen before, march leaders turned back to the park. When the protesters reached it, they found their car windows smashed, tires slashed, whole vehicles burned, and a couple of cars pushed into the park's pond. More than fifty participants sustained injuries, including Kale Williams, who suffered a cut on the head that required stitches. He was okay, he later reported, just tired "from a reaction to the hostility and fear involved in the march." He added that "he had never been in the midst of such anger and hostility" as when "the crowd of white people descended upon the marchers," who were "simply abandoned by the police and were at the mercy of the mob." A week later, the scene repeated when King led a march through Marquette Park and the Chicago Lawn neighborhood and was himself struck on the head by a rock. Like Williams, King later remarked that he had "never seen as much hatred and hostility on the part of so many people."[44]

During the height of the demonstrations, the AFSC in Chicago got swept up in a movement aimed at housing integration, the goal long pursued by the HOP—but the tactics deployed by the Chicago Freedom Summer campaign were more confrontational than any the organization had yet pursued. The vicious response to the demonstrations revived questions about whether nonviolent direct action, at least as practiced by the Southern Christian Leadership Conference and the Coordinating Council of Community Organizations, contradicted Quaker values. Williams called King's strategy "coercive nonviolence," because it relied on white hostility and the resulting massive disruption to pressure city officials. King's willingness to provoke confrontation to win support and put pressure on authorities had been criticized by moderates and conservatives before. Now, like many pacifists, Williams questioned whether asking for or accepting police protection in such circumstances was true to the spirit of Quaker peace-building. Would it not be more "redemptive" to "take more of the violence upon ourselves," he asked, rather than seeking protection? Al Raby and other CCCO leaders, however, chose to make police protection for the marchers a major movement demand. In addition, several people, including Lafayette, expressed doubts that southern-style nonviolence could be accomplished in the North, and they worried that young Black men attracted to the new philosophy of Black Power might be repelled by that strategy's seeming passivity. Those fears did not come to fruition, however. Acknowledging that nonviolence was not a "way of life" for many of the foot soldiers of the demonstrations, the AFSC report on the summer's events noted that "teenagers from active gangs, impatient and frustrated young adults, and people from the most brutalizing areas of the city" had successfully adopted a modified, "situational" nonviolence as they "walked silently and nonviolently, some perhaps even with love, through jeering, rock-throwing mobs." Although they may have disagreed on the fine points of nonviolence theory, the Friends in the AFSC accommodated themselves to the SCLC approach to direct action for the purposes of unity in the open housing campaign.[45]

The SCLC's top-down style rankled and caused tensions in the partnership throughout the summer, however. In their previous efforts to change housing patterns through the fair housing councils, the AFSC staff had stressed organizing residents to integrate their own communities, believed in the educational value of person-to-person contact, and used consensus decision-making while increasingly deferring authority to the local people. Moreover, Bernard Lafayette, whose job in the Urban Affairs Program aimed to mobilize and empower inner-city residents, wanted community organizations to benefit from the energy of the direct-action campaign. He advocated for neighborhood groups to spend five days a week on their own local problems and two days on testing and open housing activity in other parts of the city. His vision was overridden, however, when King and SCLC leaders decided to hold mass demonstrations in "hot areas" where they could be sure there would be resistance. Once demonstrations and confrontations in such areas heated up, all the staff and volunteers were needed, and they had little time to cultivate or support grassroots programs. As a result, organizing local communities was neglected. Lafayette, Bert Ransom, and Bill Moyer resented the directives coming from the SCLC leadership. As Ransom put it, unilaterally scrapping plans made by people in the neighborhoods indicated a "lack of faith in them" that was "an affront to their dignity." Yet for the duration of the open housing campaign, AFSC staff maintained a close relationship with the SCLC and worked to support its program because of their own commitment to housing integration. Moreover, they recognized that the SCLC would eventually be gone, and they would be responsible for the more long-term work of securing whatever results the movement achieved. That would require their own forms of "nonviolent organization for radical social change."[46]

Indeed, while helping organize and participating in the SCLC-CCCO open housing demonstrations, the regional office staff continued to work in their own ways on their own priorities. Although Lafayette was central to the Action Committee and the planning of the direct action, he kept away from most of the marches themselves so that he could concentrate on the grassroots community organizing in East Garfield Park that he had been hired by the Urban Affairs Program to do. As head of the regional office, Williams spoke for the AFSC on the Agenda Committee and as an individual participated in marches. But he also reached out to religious leaders during the peak of the campaign and participated in negotiations with public officials, reflecting the HOP tradition of persuasion of those at the top. During the summer and into the fall, Ransom squeezed in time between his South Side Action Center duties to monitor move-ins and to advise suburban groups trying to welcome Black neighbors. Pioneer move-ins had slowed down substantially, he reported, because the mortgage market was tight. But he continued to gather evidence for complaints against discriminatory real estate agents. Each of these tracks—urban community organizing, negotiating with leaders, and helping individual Black families—was based on long-standing AFSC values and persisted independently during the summer of 1966 and long after the SCLC summer campaign concluded.[47]

One of the AFSC's most important ideals in its open housing work had always been interracial contact and action. For years, Bill Moyer had worked in suburban communities cultivating sympathy for open housing among white residents there and encouraging them to take action. Alongside his role in the direct action, he and a group of young volunteers working with the AFSC for the summer of 1966 strove to make the Chicago open housing movement interracial by developing opportunities for white participation of different kinds. Moyer continued to advise the North Suburban Organization for Fair Housing, which was the new name for the coalition that had formed during the North Shore Summer Project, as the members initiated their own direct action in Oak Park. The White Participation Arm meanwhile sought to cultivate whites in the target urban neighborhoods, though Kale Williams reported it was "hard to make any headway" at the peak of the summer tension. Nevertheless, the AFSC staff and volunteers held meetings at churches, connected with local clergy, and organized whites and Blacks to visit each other in their homes. On the South Shore, a Mrs. Farrara hosted about forty participants in a series of weekly meetings for about a month. In addition to producing a brochure about open housing that a local priest offered to pay for and distribute, her group raised money and placed an ad in a local paper expressing solidarity for the marches. The ad generated some calls expressing interest and support, but in general it was difficult to get people to make a stand beyond calling for the end of violence. In addition, Moyer focused on getting more liberal and already convinced whites to test real estate offices, escort Black families looking for real estate services, and join marches. Finally, acting on the traditional person-to-person approach, the HOP staff formed Women Mobilized for Change, which consisted of Black and white housewives in the city and suburbs who exchanged visits in the effort to increase understanding and introduce the African American women to welcoming communities. Observers at the time and historians since have noted the relatively high level of white participation in the Chicago Freedom Movement. It was not due just to AFSC involvement. But at a time when African Americans were starting to question whether whites could play an appropriate role in a movement for Black freedom, and when a white backlash against civil rights and fair housing was building, the organization enlisted some white residents from the North Shore to the South Side in the movement for residential integration.[48]

Over the first two weeks of August, the number and size of demonstrations and the response to them intensified. Al Raby of the CCCO and Rev. Jesse Jackson of the SCLC kicked off the month with a Monday, August 1, rally. Mass testing occupied the movement on Tuesday and Wednesday, with three hundred people going to the real estate offices in Belmont Cragin. Then Martin Luther King returned to town on Thursday, August 4, for a rousing mass meeting of two thousand at Friendship Baptist Church. As Lafayette reported, "The air was electric with the spirit and conviction of the Movement as Dr. King declared an end must be put to virtual slavery in the United States" and called on "white brothers and sisters" to "join the freedom fight." The next day was the mass march that began with King being struck on the head by a rock. The demonstration culminated in a prayer vigil at Halvorson's Realty. Threatening mobs followed the march each step of the way, with hundreds of whites being chased away by police, only to reassemble and continue to throw rocks, bottles, and other projectiles. The assault on King and the growing boldness of resistance prompted both additional commitment to the marches, as more people turned out for those on the weekend, and more of a police response. On Sunday, August 7, fifteen hundred people marched through Belmont Cragin and visited a church and a real estate office. Rain kept the usual opposition crowds at bay, as did the fact that "almost as many policemen as demonstrators lined the march."[49]

In the next week, movement leaders applied more pressure to the city by striking multiple targets at once. The goal was to show that the housing problem was not confined to particular areas but affected the entire city. The protesters would "hit" previous target areas to "let them know you haven't forgotten them," move into new neighborhoods to attract press coverage, and shift from place to place to keep ahead of the mobs. On Sunday, August 14, marches and vigils were held in three communities. Al Raby and Andrew Young returned to Gage Park with five hundred people. James Bevel led four hundred to Jefferson Park, a new target. Bill Moyer, Bert Ransom, and AFSC staffers Carl Zietlow of the College Program and Maria Pappalardo, who had been sent by the Philadelphia headquarters to help the local office, joined a march to Bogan Park led by Bernard Lafayette and Jesse Jackson. In kicking off the demonstrations, Jackson declared that "anyone who can't be nonviolent shouldn't be in the march" and "we're going out there to educate these people." Pappalardo recorded what happened next. At first there were "small crowds on corners or in yards doing a little yelling and muttering." The movement folks "marched two across on the sidewalk. There were marshals along our lines, keeping discipline, passing information, scooping up stuff that might get thrown." There were also "police about one for every ten marchers" in a line formation. After visiting some real estate offices, the marchers followed police advice that they turn off the business street to avoid a large crowd of opponents. But in the residential area the mob grew. "Young white boys started throwing rocks, bottles, firecrackers from behind the houses." To reach safety, the marchers circled back and ended up having to walk under a railroad bridge. The embankment "was lined by hundreds of white residents." Rocks continually "whizzed overhead." To break up the mob and give the marchers a chance to get through, the police charged, scattering the people on the hill. The marchers ran for their cars, into which the women were hastily loaded, with men to follow.[50]

SUMMIT NEGOTIATIONS AND AGREEMENT

By this time, the pressure on city leaders to bring some resolution to the housing discrimination crisis, or at least end the daily demonstrations, was mounting. Various officials began making statements aimed at undermining the moral authority of the Chicago Freedom Summer movement and de-escalating the crisis by moving it out of the streets and to the conference table. Ed Marciniak of the Chicago Commission on Human Relations complained that activists had not given the discrimination complaint process outlined in a 1963 city housing ordinance time to work before protesting. Moreover, the chief of police denounced movement leaders for not informing law enforcement of their plans, hampering police ability to keep the peace. On August 4, a group of Black aldermen talked with civil rights leaders at a meeting that began with some tension but ended with general agreement on the goals of the movement, though without any commitment to doing much about them. Other potential or seeming allies of the open housing campaign began to call for a peaceful solution, meaning a moratorium on direct actions. Local media declared that the marchers had "made their point" and should act to avoid "more bloodshed," putting the responsibility for the violence on the civil rights leaders rather than on the perpetrators. Labor leaders met with Mayor Daley and agreed it was time to "resolve the problem without more violence" by negotiating. And "with a heavy heart," archbishop John Cody, a liberal leader of the Chicago Archdiocese, asked the movement to end the demonstrations. According to Kale Williams, rumors were in the air that soon open housing advocates would be invited to sit down with representatives of the real estate boards and city agencies. That call eventually came from the head of the Chicago Conference on Religion and Race—at the urging of city human relations commissioners, who wanted a seemingly more neutral and morally compelling host for a summit meeting.[51]

The first meeting between city officials and movement leaders took place on August 17, 1966, in the parish house of St. James Episcopal Church. Arranged around a U-shaped set of tables were movement representatives, led by King and including Kale Williams of the AFSC, and city officials, including Mayor Richard J. Daley. A representative of the Commission on Human Relations opened with the city's plan to end the crisis, which included a moratorium on marches and a series of pledges from city agencies to implement open housing. Raby then presented the movement's demands. Though generally calling for the city to enforce its open housing ordinance, the list also included much more specific, concrete, and measurable steps to be taken by its agencies, such as the human relations commission, the housing authority, and the public aid department, to bring about equal housing. Moreover, the movement asked private entities to do their part, including banks, labor unions, churches, and the Association of Commerce and Industry. Tensions arose at the summit meeting, which lasted from ten-thirty in the morning until eight at night, over whether the Chicago Real Estate Board could or would promise nondiscrimination on behalf of its members. When it became clear that no agreement would be reached before this initial session ended, Mayor Daley pressed for a suspension of demonstrations during the negotiations. King firmly demurred, saying, "We have only our bodies and you are asking us to give up the one thing that we have when you say, 'Don't March!'" The meeting closed with the establishment of a subcommittee to work on an agreement, with Williams as a member, and a clear implication that the movement would keep up the pressure through continued demonstrations.[52]

The movement leaders' determination to keep protesting and Daley's desire to stop them soon clashed. Over the next few days, organizers discussed plans to use small marches and visits to real estate offices to "test the good intentions declared at the summit meeting" and "keep pressure on in advance of the next summit meeting." But then Daley requested and obtained an injunction ordering no more than one demonstration per day with no more than five hundred people participating. Moreover, marches could not be held at night or during rush hour, and they could not obstruct either vehicular or pedestrian traffic. The mayor justified this request by citing strain on the police trying to keep order. The injunction sparked debate among already frustrated and tired movement leaders. King called the mayor's move "immoral and probably unconstitutional," but he said the campaign would not seek to violate it and instead would begin to look at other strategies while building up strength. As in other movement locales, younger leaders chafed at King's direction. Jesse Jackson wanted to violate the injunction. He declared that "because it is a sign of lack of good faith on the part of the city," the movement "should not return to the negotiating table as long as it is in order." Bevel agreed and called for more sit-ins in real estate offices to keep the attention on the problem of denial of service, not on confrontations between marchers and mobs. In the end, organizers decided to follow the injunction by leading one march in the city in the South Deering neighborhood but holding others simultaneously in communities just outside the city limits. A heavy rainstorm helped keep the number of white antiprotesters in check. But on the same day, white nationalists held a rally in Marquette Park, foreboding even more violence and open racism. Meanwhile, King announced an upcoming march in Cicero, a well-known site of resolute segregation and the white suburb where attacks on Black newcomers in 1951 had led to the creation of the Housing Opportunities Program.[53]

In this atmosphere, the negotiating subcommittee struggled to come up with a plan before disorder could get worse. Kale Williams reported that a spokesman for the mayor had urged him and Bevel to come up with a proposal by Monday the twenty-second, with promises that he could secure approval from Daley, which would bring other parties into line. Debate on the subcommittee dragged into the next week, however. Williams believed that movement leaders were going to have to "tell people in the city how to go about desegregating," because they had the experience with housing. The goal, he reported, was to "tie the city down to enforcing what laws exist." One stumbling block was how specific to get: should the subcommittee write into the agreement some specific number of Black families arriving in white communities as a measure of success? The debate over a "quota" to demonstrate progress reflected a shift in approach to civil rights enforcement in the country at the time as well as the affirmative action practices being outlined by the Johnson administration. Indeed, in its report to the summit group, the subcommittee called for "affirmative measures to attack the problems of discrimination in housing." The members backed off from indicating a specific target number, however, emphasizing vaguer goals instead. But they did insist on the establishment of a watchdog group that would track the city's progress on promises it made.[54]

On August 26, the subcommittee delivered its recommendations to the summit participants, asking each to agree to a list of promises of action. Most important and coming first in the list, the Chicago Commission on Human Relations would step up efforts to enforce existing legislation through the prompt processing of discrimination complaints. The agreement also called on urban renewal and public aid officials to help displaced families find new homes without regard to racial restrictions, and the Chicago Housing Authority to end policies that reinforced segregation and instead affirmatively seek integration through the selection of families for its units. In a major concession reflecting the direct-action campaign's focus on the real estate industry, the Chicago Board of Realtors would drop its opposition to state fair housing legislation and call on its members to provide service without discrimination. The plan asked church groups to take concrete steps to persuade their members to accept open housing and to prepare white communities to welcome Black families, via strategies that mimicked the fair housing council organizing. One particularly specific request was that within thirty days, the members of the Chicago Conference on Religion and Race would set up fair housing centers to counsel Black home seekers and help them find homes in white areas. Finally, that organization would also establish a permanent group that would take responsibility for seeing the agreement fulfilled.[55]

Acceptance of the agreement was neither immediate nor without hesitation. Al Raby stood almost immediately to question whether there was a personal commitment from everyone in the room to see that the provisions were swiftly acted on. The summit participants gave speeches endorsing the agreement and pledging their constituency's action, but as one observer friendly to the movement put it, these were "statements of good will and good faith but nobody was really throwing anything into the pot, saying 'and to demonstrate our commitment we will do this or we will do that.'" Having been burned by the weakness of such negotiated solutions in southern crises, King and others pushed for guarantees, while local leaders wondered how they would sell the summit agreement to the movement rank and file. The civil rights side then took a recess to debate whether to accept, and although opinion was split, they came back to the room to declare they were almost ready to finalize the agreement. But King raised one more question: Would Mayor Daley withdraw the injunction as a sign of good faith? This set off a last-minute flurry of strained discussion, which left several in the room worried that the whole thing might break down. In the end, the activists and the civic leaders agreed to put off that issue to separate negotiations and voted to accept the summit agreement unanimously.[56]

The vote on the summit agreement, and the agreement itself, did not please all the leaders involved, including those affiliated with the AFSC. Bill Moyer felt that the movement "should have held off longer, a week or so." "Words are only words," he said, and there were not enough specific directives pushing real estate agents to do away with discriminatory listings. For example, the agreement lacked either benchmarks or timetables. Specifically, Moyer argued that the Commission on Human Relations should be responsible for conducting a set number of tests per week of real estate offices to determine whether they were providing equal service and for actively investigating discrimination instead of waiting for complaints. In addition, the commission should follow up with Black families after the complaint process to ensure that they got housing. Jerry Davis and Bert Ransom were similarly frustrated. Ransom felt that the summit had "produced no real dialogue" and that there was "no real response" to the housing problem from city leaders on a "moral level." Williams did not really defend the agreement he helped write, except to point out that a watchdog group was being set up to monitor compliance. Beyond that, he admitted the outcome was "far short of the ultimate revolution which must take place if basic structures are to be changed and the basic thinking of people is to be changed." Under pressure to restore public order, civic leaders may have reached an agreement on actions, but there had been no reconciling of the white power structure to integration. Williams blamed this in part on the movement itself, saying that by "continuing the marches" in the face of violence, "perhaps we had stopped generating spiritual power and [had] begun generating political power." What resulted was a "political solution to the problem of open housing," with few hearts being genuinely changed.[57]

Moving On from Direct Action

In the wake of the summit agreement, which formally ended the direct-action campaign for open housing in Chicago and triggered the departure of Martin Luther King and most of the Southern Christian Leadership Conference forces, HOP committee members and staff considered what to do next. The consensus was to keep the pressure on; to continue to utilize some of the direct-action strategies that had been developed, such as the testing of real estate offices; to participate in monitoring the summit agreement; and to return to their traditional approach of helping Black families find housing. Almost immediately, the HOP staff focused on ensuring that the Chicago Commission on Human Relations (CCHR) enforced open housing and that the relocation services of the urban renewal program practiced integration in placing families. Ransom coordinated sending teams of Black and white checkers to test whether real estate offices were following the agreement, and to file complaints with the CCHR as needed. By mid-September 1966, four offices had failed the test. Soon thereafter, he tried to help 158 Black families being displaced by an urban renewal project in Englewood. His efforts continued the longtime strategy of working with individual families to obtain housing. But the AFSC stressed that this project was not just an attempt to place pioneers in white neighborhoods, which everyone by this point had agreed was not enough. In addition to helping families, the goal was to generate evidence of violations of the Chicago open housing ordinance to pressure the CCHR to act against recalcitrant real estate agents. Meanwhile, Moyer became chair of a committee investigating the extent to which city departments were upholding their part of the bargain. In that position, he was charged with making sure that laws and policies meant to bring about open housing were indeed being enforced and acted on.[58]

•

In the early and mid-1960s, AFSC personnel had used strategies inspired by and modeled on the southern direct-action campaign against Jim Crow to pressure real estate businesses and public officials to change practices and commit to affirmative actions that would end systemic discrimination in housing. This effort required a consideration of the relationship between those tactics and the values of reconciliation and nonaggression. In short, as many pacifists asked about nonviolent resistance: Was it nonviolent enough? Discomfort with the coercive nature of some of the mass protests existed among the HOP staff from the early encounters with nonviolence, and it never completely went away. Yet their support for the goal of open housing and their desire to collaborate as respectful and equal partners with African Americans led most of them to look past their differences in order to participate in a cooperative campaign. In doing so, they honed techniques—such as testing and canvassing—that corresponded well to their Quaker values. More generally, the experiences of individuals who participated in mass direct action persuaded national leaders of the organization to give regional office and program staff the freedom to engage in local struggles as they saw fit. Meanwhile, the commitment of people like Bill Moyer and Kale Williams in Chicago and their willingness to join the fight in the trenches strengthened the relationship between the AFSC and the civil rights movement, which would continue throughout the decade. Hiring African American veterans of that movement, like Bernard Lafayette, Jerry Davis, and Tony Henry, diversified the AFSC staff and brought fresh perspectives and connections to Black communities that would shape new grassroots empowerment strategies for addressing housing problems in low-income neighborhoods. The HOP staff in Chicago and AFSC members elsewhere had seen in nonviolent direct action a strategy for education, persuasion, and bringing pressure on the gatekeepers who sustained segregation in neighborhoods. In the end, nonviolent direct action had not changed the hearts of many real estate agents; but HOP staff had learned that direct action could also aim for, indeed go hand in hand with, changes to and aggressive implementation of law and policy.

4. Speaking Truth to Power

*Using the Power of Government
to Integrate Housing*

In 1954 Richard Bennett, secretary of the AFSC's Community Relations Division, went to the top level of government to lobby personally for aggressive policy on behalf of integrated housing. Along with Henry Patterson, a Philadelphia Quaker and longtime Republican, he visited Dwight Eisenhower's advisor Maxwell Rabb to convince him that the president could act on his conscience and address housing discrimination without having to go through Congress. Rabb encouraged the AFSC to prepare a list of proposals for such action, though the resulting report ultimately languished, unattended to. Ten years later, AFSC program staff in both the Northern and Southern California Regional Offices drew from years of experience organizing fair housing councils to coordinate a grassroots campaign to stop Proposition 14, a referendum sponsored by real estate organizations that would nullify statewide legislation against housing discrimination. In the short term the campaign failed, but the California courts soon overturned Proposition 14 and upheld the state's fair housing laws. At the same time, on the East Coast the Metropolitan Philadelphia Housing Opportunities Program embarked on a program of real estate office testing aimed at pressuring officials to enforce John F. Kennedy's executive order banning discrimination in federally supported housing—an initiative that produced evidence strong enough to persuade congressmen to support more aggressive national fair housing legislation. In each case, the AFSC acted on a long Quaker tradition of speaking truth to power as a means for bringing the organization's values to bear on public policy.

The nature of the housing market in mid-twentieth-century America meant that eventually, any effort to alter residential patterns would require engagement with government entities. Initially, HOP staff were unsure whether government officials were potential allies in, or obstacles to, the quest for equal housing, and some advisory committee members insisted that the AFSC programs be educational and persuasive only. But over time, even those who at first focused purely on changing the minds of individuals overcame their qualms and endorsed lobbying for government action against discrimination. In part, they recognized that appeals to voluntarism simply did not work. More important, they understood that government was responsible for segregation—indeed, that all levels of government enabled and protected all-white neighborhoods—and consequently must be part of the solution for ending it. Finally, the AFSC's new strategic course paralleled the trajectory of the civil rights movement, which by mid-decade advocated "affirmative action" to ensure a systemic response to persistent racial inequality. Efforts to enlist the power of government to integrate housing did not necessitate a break from the organization's other practices or values, however. Rather, while the community relations leaders understood that fair housing would require the muscle of the state to overcome resistance in both public agencies and private businesses, they would work for government action in ways that paralleled their other approaches: persuasion of those at the top, because they believed that individual change must still accompany and reinforce policy change; community organizing and cultivation of public sympathy; and, ultimately, direct action to apply pressure on government entities for enforcement of law.

Roots of AFSC Political Lobbying

In 1682 William Penn, the revered early leader of the Society of Friends, wrote, "True godliness don't [sic] turn men out of the world, but enables them to live better in it and excites their endeavours to mend it."[1] Quakers have long differed in interpreting what Penn's words meant in practice. In its early history, the Society of Friends went through a period of "quietism," defined as a spiritual and communal looking inward. As individuals, Quakers attended to an indwelling divine guidance through introspection and meditative silence. As a community, they kept themselves apart from their neighbors through their rules about simple living and withdrew from the "compromise and corruption of political life." Yet alongside this quietism from the start and becoming more characteristic of the Society of Friends in the United States over time was the practice of making a personal witness to those in power to try to make the world a better place. Since the nineteenth century, making that witness has taken the form of "long and persistent" campaigns to protect pacifists' right to conscientious objection in times of war, improve treatment of Native Americans, abolish slavery, and guarantee the equal citizenship of African Americans. In 1955, the AFSC published *Speak Truth to Power*, which called on Friends to confront those in "high places in our national life" with their vision of a better world, their analysis of social problems, and their proposed solutions to those problems. Focusing on international relations, the pamphlet advised practical nonviolence as a tactic for resolving conflict. For Friends and others in the AFSC Community Relations Division, speaking truth to power manifested in political action on the causes of tension at home, whether by engaging in street demonstrations or lobbying Congress on a wide variety of domestic issues.[2]

From its very inception, the AFSC used the levers of governmental power to secure its goals as members alternately partnered with and challenged local, state, and federal officials and laws. The inaugural project of the organization, sending volunteers to Europe during World War I to perform acts of service to people of war-torn countries, required the AFSC leaders to negotiate a furlough for each man with his local draft board. Often, "wires flew back and forth" between the headquarters in Philadelphia and the Selective Service in Washington, DC, as the organization fought for the exemptions from military service supposedly guaranteed under law. The contributions the AFSC made in the postwar reconstruction effort later inspired President Herbert Hoover, himself a Quaker, to ask the organization to run a feeding program for children in mining communities devastated by the onset of the Great Depression. Its work in the Appalachian coalfields in turn led to a partnership with the Subsistence Homestead Division of the New Deal, which sought to build houses for displaced miners. The closeness between AFSC chairman Clarence Pickett and those allied with the New Deal administration, especially Eleanor Roosevelt, plus the respect Quakers and the AFSC had earned for their service, helped establish relationships that the Community Relations Division would draw from in the early years of its race relations and housing programs.[3]

In the first decade of the HOPs, however, both philosophical ambivalence and practical questions arose about using the power of the government to secure residential integration. In Chicago, advisory committee members emphasized that "the AFSC approach would distinctly be a quiet, consultative and educational program rather than the legal action and pressure" tactics of other agencies, "which we cannot use." Around the country, the HOPs did not rely on appeals to the courts very much. Although they sometimes helped with funding or with research and advance preparation, AFSC leaders tended to regard lawsuits as the bailiwick of the NAACP and left such challenges to that venerable civil rights organization. Moreover, in the early years of the housing program, advisors questioned whether it was worth putting much effort into national legislation that was unlikely to pass anyway. Even when more liberal states like New Jersey adopted civil rights laws that applied to housing, as late as 1957 and 1958 some community relations staff argued that while such legislation might help, it "does not replace community acceptance and the individual's sense of responsibility to help bring about democratic communities." In short, government action might help, but by itself it was not enough.[4]

In the post–World War II period, another reason the housing advocates in the AFSC did not focus on legislation, particularly at the national level, was that the job belonged to someone else: the Friends Committee on National Legislation (FCNL). In 1939, Quakers in the Philadelphia area had established a War Problems Committee, which successfully lobbied to create conscientious objector status under the new selective service laws. At the height of the war, looking to the future, leaders of that committee and members of the AFSC Peace Section argued for a more permanent body to work in Washington to present Friends' views on the draft and militarism to legislators. In 1943, the FCNL became the first Protestant church lobby in the nation's capital. Headed by AFSC Peace Section staffer E. Raymond Wilson, the organization was guided by a General Committee composed of representatives from Yearly Meetings. Its first task was countering Cold War–era proposals to expand requirements for military service, but its goals expanded over time to include supporting legislation on civil rights, prisoners' rights, and immigration. The FCNL's first statement on legislative policy laid out its distinctive Quaker approach, saying that its staff would avoid "political pressure methods" and instead meet with members of Congress and the administration to persuade them at an individual moral level.[5]

Appealing to the Heart: Personal Lobbying

Over the life of the Housing Opportunities Programs, every strategy the staff at each location employed contained an element of speaking truth to power. In the early years, they first sought government intervention for open occupancy through personal lobbying of officials at all levels, seeing it as an extension of traditional Quaker practices of convincement, the slow unfolding of understanding through appeals to conscience. Indeed, in their cooperation with other civil rights organizations in the 1950s, they considered their role to be conveying the human values involved in the housing issue directly to government officials, with the goal of encouraging them to take moral action. The HOPs could pursue this one-on-one dialogue because of the AFSC's prior partnerships with the federal government and the high standing of many Friends in their communities. By the late 1940s, the AFSC had earned a strong reputation—and a Nobel Peace Prize—for its effective humanitarianism in post–World War I reconstruction, Depression-era feeding programs, New Deal homestead projects, aid to victims of World War II, and record of working for both domestic and international peace. In addition, the housing committees in the regional offices included Quaker business-men, real estate agents, bankers, lawyers, political party activists, and heads of nonprofit reform organizations whose prominence in their fields gave them high-level contacts. Finally, as one of the few organizations with paid staff working in the housing field in cities across the country, the AFSC became a respected source of expertise on the issue. The combination of these factors gave AFSC personnel access to government leaders and created a two-way conversation about housing policies. For example, as soon as the Philadelphia HOP was launched, both Flora Hatcher, who handled public relations for the Federal Housing Administration, and Frank Horne of the Housing and Home Finance Agency met with staff and committee members to suggest possible avenues of approach for the new program. For their part, community relations and housing staff were not shy about writing letters to FHA officials or even President Eisenhower himself with advice about how the administration could ensure integration in federally supported housing.[6]

One such missive led to the hopeful yet confidential negotiations between White House staff and the AFSC over what Eisenhower could do to promote housing integration. In April 1954, when Henry Patterson reached out to Maxwell Rabb, he cited his friendship with Navy Undersecretary Thomas Gates Jr. and his credentials as both a loyal Republican and an anticommunist. He went on to argue that the best way to defeat communists was to deny them their "only solid piece of propaganda"— racial segregation and discrimination—by "putting an end to second-class citizenship in the United States." Doing so, he added, would benefit the Republican Party and honor the moral example present at its founding. The letter resulted in an invitation, and one month later Richard Bennett and Patterson headed to the White House for a chance to "make clear the basic principle of integration" to someone having the president's ear. Rabb, a white Jew regarded as liberal on race issues, was Eisenhower's point person on minority affairs charged with "trouble shooting" and responding to complaints. Although some of the meeting was spent in "simple political talk," by the end he asked the AFSC to "quietly examine all of the legal, sociological, etc ramifications of the problem and also set down the various practical steps which might be taken by the White House." Though it would "be a lone wolf, quiet, no-credit project," Bennett eagerly jumped at the chance to be part of something that "could result in some directives or policy decisions which might have a tremendous effect within a few years."[7]

Over the next couple months, a flurry of conversations between open housing advocates and Rabb took place, all kept out of the public eye. Allies in the National Committee against Discrimination in Housing and the Fund for the Republic agreed with Bennett that this was the time to explain why voluntary measures were not enough and that there needed to be a "general policy" giving support to those who wanted to integrate. HOP staff submitted specific lists of recommendations for what such a policy might look like. Jane Reinheimer, for example, called for an "equity formula," under which builders could not get FHA or Veterans Administration mortgage insurance without demonstrating that their previous projects were open to nonwhites, and for a clause written into FHA and VA forms prohibiting builders who relied on the government programs from discriminating. Jim Cassels suggested a tax write-off for producers of interracial housing projects, perhaps recalling home builder Philip Klutznick's concern about losing business if he integrated. With Chicago's Trumbull Park also likely on his mind, Cassels asked in addition for a presidential order that "no one can be barred from government-aided housing because of race, with a grievance procedure." In their recommendations, both Reinheimer and Cassels combined fairly aggressive—for their time—policy solutions with strategies reflecting a more consultative approach, including a White House conference with leaders in banking and building and the appointment of a national committee on segregation and housing. On July 1, 1954, Bennett sent Rabb a memo outlining what he called these "practical realistic recommendations" and awaited a response.[8]

That response was slow in coming, deflating the hopes of Bennett and others in the open housing community for imminent White House action. In mid-July, Hortense Gabel of the National Committee against Discrimination in Housing met with Rabb, but in their two-hour conversation he never mentioned the AFSC memo or its suggestions. Instead, he criticized the NAACP for calling for a law against government assistance to segregated housing and said that Eisenhower would not host a meeting on the issue. Moreover, when Gabel suggested opening all federally owned housing without regard to race, Rabb recoiled, crying that such a measure was "too drastic." He said he would consider prohibiting federal aid to "self-contained cities such as Levittown," but given his overall demeanor Gabel doubted he was serious. By September, the AFSC still had not heard from Rabb, and Bennett noted that in the meantime Albert Cole, head of the FHA, had made it clear that the White House had "made a policy decision not to do any of the things we suggest." Though he was "not giving up hope," Bennett concluded that "the White House [was] going to fumble the ball again"; this was a "very grave error," he added, because the idea that housing integration would somehow "work out" on its own without "fairly direct action on the part of the Administration" was a pipe dream.[9]

The disappointing result of the conference with Rabb reflected the resistance in the Eisenhower White House and the federal bureaucracy to residential integration. As historian Arnold Hirsch and others have argued, under the Truman administration and in the immediate aftermath of the *Shelley v. Kraemer* decision, some officials within housing bureaucracies used their positions to nudge federal policy away from supporting segregation. The early HOPs had worked with some of these individuals in the Race Relations Service, local FHA offices, and in Chicago in the local public housing authority. Those contacts, plus a Quaker predisposition to see the potential for moral action in anyone, contributed to the AFSC's hopefulness. But during the Eisenhower administration, particularly after the *Brown v. Board of Education* ruling in 1954, such people were marginalized as conservative Republicans took steps to minimize the likelihood of racial change in housing. Eisenhower himself set the tone. He believed that change in race relations should come from education and persuasion, and he explicitly stated a preference for state-level laws and an opposition to using the federal government as a "coercive instrument." More specifically, as former FDR advisor Robert Weaver warned Jane Reinheimer right at the start of the Eisenhower administration, the president simply wasn't interested in housing. He showed little understanding of the nature and extent of residential segregation and left the problem in the hands of pro-business appointees. Indeed, perhaps the clearest indicator of Eisenhower's position was his choice of Albert Cole, who was hostile to public housing, allied with real estate interests, and openly declared that the federal government had no role in securing integration, to head the Housing and Home Finance Agency.[10]

After the White House rebuff, rather than dropping the lobbying effort, in early 1955 the AFSC's community relations program released the report it had prepared on the causes of and possible solutions to housing segregation and distributed five hundred copies to government officials, members of the housing industry, and other interested organizations. While giving an overview of both private and public actions that contributed to the spread of housing segregation in the postwar period, the report emphasized the role of the FHA and the VA in providing mortgage insurance for large suburban developments despite the builders' openly declared policies of discrimination. These agencies were "instrumentalities of the Federal government dispensing a government benefit," the report asserted. Invoking Supreme Court decisions on civil rights and housing, it stated that the government could not "pass racial zoning ordinances," "operate racially segregated schools" or housing projects, or enforce "race restrictive covenants." Moreover, it was clear by this point that the VA and FHA would not "come to grips" with the problem on their own, nor had private business shown any inclination to act without government prodding. Thus the AFSC, speaking for the broader open housing community, called on the president to issue an executive order forbidding discrimination or segregation in federally supported housing, including homes "receiving mortgage insurance or guarantees" by a federal agency.[11] This goal would not be accomplished until Kennedy's Executive Order 11063 in 1962, which prohibited discrimination in housing owned or funded by the federal government.

Meanwhile, the HOP activists in the regional offices employed one-on-one personal outreach to local officials to address segregation in their communities, likewise focusing on government-supported housing. In 1951, the federal government declared Bucks County, Pennsylvania, a "critical defense area," because the new industries being planned there would be producing military materials. Consequently, as soon as it became clear that new housing would spring up around those factories, Reinheimer and Jacques Wilmore looked for ways to have the federal government lean on the real estate developers Levitt and Sons and Galbreath Gunnison to sell to African Americans. Frank Horne, in his capacity as the minority groups consultant for the Housing and Home Finance Administration, advised them to secure a memo from Neal Hardy, head of defense housing for the FHA, promising that his department would give preference to builders who practice open occupancy. With Horne's introduction, Wilmore was able to meet with Hardy and secured his statement in writing, an example of support from individuals within the housing bureaucracies. This seeming coup had limited impact, however, and reinforced the HOP staff's growing conviction that relying on such individuals was ineffective in the long run. Though he had been sympathetic, Hardy was replaced two months later by Charles Dougherty, whose priority was getting some housing for minorities built, even if it was segregated. Moreover, when Wilmore visited regional administrators of the FHA to talk about Hardy's memo, they had neither seen nor heard of it; indeed, one of them got quite "defensive," insisted it would be a "waste of time" for the FHA to endorse open occupancy to the builders, and refused to call a meeting to discuss Hardy's memo or any policy of encouraging nondiscrimination.[12] Getting no more help from federal officials than from the private builders influenced Reinheimer and Wilmore's decision by the mid-1950s to turn to a more grassroots program of working with pioneers to secure housing.

While Reinheimer and Wilmore strove unsuccessfully to secure federal pressure on Bucks County builders to integrate, Phil Buskirk tirelessly urged Bay Area officials to guarantee African Americans displaced from decommissioned wartime projects equal access to new housing. Even more than in the other early HOPs in Philadelphia and Chicago, Buskirk dedicated much of his day-to-day activity to attending local government agency hearings and buttonholing politicians and bureaucrats, pressing the case for more, and for integrated, public housing. But he also went to the top. In May 1954, he presented a detailed analysis of the problems with Lanham Act housing in the San Francisco Bay area and proposed solutions to Albert Cole at the FHA. In that report, he chronicled the imminent threat to up to ninety thousand people in temporary wartime and defense industry housing projects who faced deadlines for eviction. In addition, he demonstrated that private business was not inclined to do anything to provide new homes for them, least of all the large proportion who were minorities. Moreover, local governments had balked at providing public housing options. Only the federal government, he concluded, could force a regionwide solution to the problem. Unsurprisingly given Cole's stated positions, Buskirk had no more success with him than he had with San Francisco and Berkeley civic leaders. Indeed, Buskirk's experience highlights the limitations of personal lobbying as a strategy for influencing policy makers in an overtly hostile climate for either low-income or mixed-race housing. His frustration with dealing with obstinate personalities in both local government and federal agencies likely shaped his response to Richard Bennett's memo to Maxwell Rabb. When asked what could be accomplished by policy change, unlike Reinheimer and Jim Cassels, he submitted no proposals.[13]

In Chicago, the HOP waged a persistent campaign throughout the mid- to late 1950s to protect and extend equal opportunity in public housing. In addition to supporting the Black families in the Trumbull Park housing project and working for reconciliation between them and their white neighbors, people in the regional office tried to persuade city and federal officials to use the power of their office to halt the violence there and spread integration to other projects. In 1955, Ed Holmgren went with members of the local NAACP to visit Mayor Richard J. Daley about the crisis in the Trumbull Park public housing apartments. They found him surprisingly "sincere but naïve" about how to reach "the eventual day when Negroes could seek housing in any community . . . without fear of violence." Still, Holmgren was hopeful enough to formulate a list of recommendations from the AFSC for specific actions Daley might take, including declaring a "city policy about the rights of all Chicago's residents to live in neighborhoods of their choosing" and hosting a conference on equal housing with white residents near Trumbull Park. Daley responded that he had already made a speech announcing such a policy, and thus a conference was not necessary. Six months later, the Quaker mission headed by Clarence Pickett studied the crisis. Although most of their recommendations focused on private efforts at reconciliation, they, too, recommended that the mayor take assertive action by appointing a special liaison to work on the Trumbull Park problem. Once again, Daley declined.[14]

The HOP's interactions with leaders of the Chicago Housing Authority, like Wilmore's experience in Bucks County, revealed how volatile cooperating with government bureaucrats could be, when sympathetic officials could be replaced with hostile ones at any time. At the beginning of the Trumbull Park crisis, the CHA was headed by Elizabeth Wood. In 1950, it had adopted a resolution against segregation and discrimination in tenant placement in its public housing and reaffirmed that position in 1952. But informal directives to preserve neighborhood composition kept four older projects, including Trumbull Park, all white. Wood had persistently campaigned for the integration of these last holdouts, even against the wishes of the CHA governing board. In the wake of the first attacks on the Howard family after they arrived at Trumbull Park, she affirmed a policy of no discrimination, and additional Black families began moving in. The organized resistance in South Deering caused an abrupt reversal of both her efforts and the CHA's nondiscrimination policy. Wood was fired in 1954, and Daley became mayor in 1955. In 1958 the new CHA executive director, Alvin Rose, departed from his predecessor's approach, declaring, "We are not going to use public housing as a wedge" to integrate neighborhoods. When Kale Williams tried to meet with Rose about the attrition of Black families in Trumbull Park, he explained that he considered it his job to protect public housing by not adopting politically unpopular positions, least of all integration.[15]

In retrospect, the AFSC housing staff's hopes for a positive response in these cases may seem naïve; but from the perspective of 1954 and 1955, their call for government agencies to enforce nondiscrimination drew from recent precedents and successful rhetorical and legal strategies. *Brown v. Board of Education*, with its declaration that separate was in fact unequal and its proscription against governments practicing discrimination in education, struck civil rights advocates as the death knell for state-sponsored segregation, leading them almost immediately to push for the logic of the case to be applied to other public spaces, including parks, universities, government buildings, and housing. Meanwhile, civil rights organizations were making the case that government could also not facilitate, and indeed could prohibit, discrimination by private entities. During the war, the federal government had prohibited discrimination in employment in private business with defense contracts. *Shelley v. Kraemer* declared that the courts could not enforce private acts of discrimination. Likewise, in its inter- and intrastate transportation decisions the Supreme Court ruled that private buses or trains could not segregate. Civil rights advocates in the NAACP, the Fund for the Republic, and the National Committee against Discrimination in Housing joined the AFSC staff in connecting the dots and making the argument that local authorities could not segregate public housing, and that federal agencies could not facilitate or acquiesce to discrimination on the part of builders. Yet the national leaders of these organizations agreed that at this time, a federal law to that effect could not pass Congress because of southern opposition—though it would likely not only be the South resisting—so they attempted other means of securing open housing through policy: by recommending a presidential executive order, through NAACP court cases, and through persuasion of bureaucrats in a position to act.

But the brick wall of resistance the HOP staff kept hitting ultimately convinced them that their top-down persuasion strategy with government leaders, like their efforts with builders, simply did not work. Despite the respect for Friends in high levels of government, in the 1950s neither the AFSC nor the open housing movement had the power to overcome business and grassroots white resistance and political pressure to motivate government leaders to cooperate in integration. Thus, although housing personnel would continue to cultivate relationships with sympathetic federal officials and press for a presidential order against discrimination, they needed to employ other strategies to secure pro-integration policies and enforce them.

Campaigns for Open Housing Legislation

After 1961, the outbreak of the southern direct-action demonstrations, the growing fair housing council movement in the North and West, and the passage of civil rights laws at a local and state level seemed to create a window for generating mass pressure for governmental intervention. Increasingly, regional office HOP staff began to testify, lobby, and organize grassroots campaigns for open housing legislation. State-level committees often invited HOP directors to hearings because of their expertise on housing issues. They willingly agreed to speak because they saw it as a chance both to "educate people about legislation" and, just as important, to "testify about moral aspects" of such policies. In these opportunities they drew from their own publications, including the 1955 report *Equal Opportunity in Housing*, and the work of scholars who had debunked myths about the results of housing integration. They described the "turn-down and run-around and . . . buying out" that prevented African Americans from securing "a good home in a good neighborhood," and they argued that "public opinion is readier to accept and abide" fair housing legislation than ever before. Most important, they documented how government agency practices had buttressed discrimination. Since "law in times past has been used to enforce segregation," they concluded that it was time now to use legislation "to promote equal opportunity."[16]

In their testimony, the AFSC representatives explained the connection between personal and policy change. They understood that legislation was not a "panacea." As "practitioners of convincement and persuasion," they believed that an education program such as theirs would need to complement government action. But at the same time, "persuasion and voluntary efforts [were] not enough" to solve housing segregation. The force of law was needed to "break such rigid and large-scale patterns as exist." As Jane Weston put it, "Laws not only caution and restrain those who would do wrong; they lend support to those who want to do the right thing but are afraid." Legislation would create a climate in which nondiscrimination is the norm and provide a recourse against those who would act on their prejudice. Changing the latter's behavior, Weston and Charlotte Meacham both argued, would eventually change attitudes. In the meantime, the law would ensure that people were not denied the "right to live where they please."[17]

Although spending a lot of time tracking and working behind the scenes to nurture potential legislation, housing activists were realistic about the obstacles they faced in securing it. In 1958, white Democratic alderman Leon Despres, who represented the Hyde Park area, introduced an open housing ordinance to the Chicago City Council, cosponsored initially by Black alderman Claude Holman. Ed Holmgren "attended virtually every meeting on the proposed" ordinance, though he was not "overly sanguine about the prospect of success." His doubts were confirmed when the proposal did not get far. In 1961, Jane Weston reported that Despres was trying again, this time with no Black support on the council. But while there was "a bit more enthusiasm than in the past," she, too, was "not hopeful." Indeed, councilman Holman himself raised the question of whether the council "even had the power to adopt such an ordinance." In the end, the city government punted the issue upward, requesting that the Illinois state legislature pass a statewide fair housing law. In June 1961, that bill failed even to pass the house, much less make it through the senate "graveyard of civil rights legislation." Weston pronounced, "We're not surprised." At this stage, HOP staff may have come to see the value of legislation but, putting it mildly, had little optimism that policy makers had done so.[18]

The Deerfield integration crisis of 1959–60 seemed to create an opening for hope, as the reaction to it signaled possible public sympathy in the Chicago suburbs for either local or state legislation against residential discrimination. Fair housing sympathizers on the North Shore were anxious to do something concrete in the wake of the hostility over that conflict. Thus, HOP staff member Al Eichholz cooperated with other groups to create and nurture the Freedom of Residence Committee (FRC) to lobby for a state law. In October 1962, the AFSC, the FRC, and others cosponsored a meeting on the North Shore to rally for legislation, at which approximately one thousand people heard from Martin Luther King Jr. Like other efforts since 1957, this campaign for a state fair housing policy was opposed by the housing industry in general and the Chicago Real Estate Board in particular; indeed, even some of the real estate agents friendly to the AFSC came out against this attempt at "forced" housing. The bill once again failed.[19]

Then, amid heightened attention to civil rights nationally, the Chicago City Council adopted a fair housing ordinance, somewhat suddenly and apparently with little public organizing on the part of the AFSC or its allies. On September 11, 1963, after three hours of "heated debate," council members voted 30 to 16 to prohibit discrimination in the sale, rental, or lease of any housing and ban the practices commonly referred to as block-busting. The job of enforcing the new law was given to the Chicago Commission on Human Relations. Mayor Daley himself had endorsed the measure, saying, "I believe it is the right of all people to be treated with respect and dignity." But public opposition and resistance emerged from the start. As the aldermen were voting, a "throng" of thousands marched outside, protesting the new law and demanding their "constitutional rights" to exclusion. In the weeks after the vote, alderman James J. Murray from the Gage Park community on the city's Southwest Side was ostracized and harassed, and ultimately driven from office. He had helped marshal the bill through the council. Finally, the Chicago Real Estate Board filed a legal challenge against the new law, which was still pending during the 1966 Chicago Freedom Movement demonstrations. The lack of enthusiasm on the part of the Commission on Human Relations and other agencies for enforcing the ordinance became one of the central complaints and sticking points in that movement as well as the summit negotiations that concluded it.[20]

As the state legislative session of 1964 approached, housing advocates in the Chicago region found themselves gearing up to fight two simultaneous battles. In June, the AFSC was one of two hundred sponsors of the Illinois Rally for Civil Rights, which initially was planned to support the proposed federal civil rights bill. After that bill passed, the AFSC, the FRC, and others decided to keep the momentum going by focusing on a campaign for a state fair housing bill. Jane Weston set up a professional office to coordinate the lobbying efforts of the various groups involved.

Her work was interrupted when the Chicago Real Estate Board started to collect signatures for a statewide referendum against any open housing measures. Weston then worked with the Catholic and Presbyterian Interracial Councils to put together the ad hoc Interfaith Organizations for Fair Housing specifically to fight such a referendum. She also recruited some sympathetic real estate agents to sign an ad opposing the measure that ran in the local papers. The real estate board had trouble getting enough signatures for its referendum, however, so the state election board did not put the measure on the ballot. Though open housing advocates avoided that setback, they had little success pushing for a proactive measure in the legislature. Weston reported that Interfaith Organizations for Fair Housing approached the platform committees for both political parties about including a promise for a fair housing bill. Democrats refused to put anything in their platform on fair housing at all. For their part, "Republicans were sort of nasty," because they "then included a plank specifically against fair housing."[21] Engaged thereafter in the direct-action movement to secure enforcement of open housing in the city, the HOP spent little energy in subsequent sessions of the Illinois state legislature.

Meanwhile, the community relations staff in California's Bay Area did "steady unreported" organizing for city fair housing ordinances as a way of "laying the groundwork" for a statewide law. In late 1961 the Catholic Interracial Council, which had partnered with the AFSC on fair housing for years and was one of the most active groups on the issue throughout the Bay Area, asked the San Jose City Council for an open housing ordinance. The council passed a resolution approving the idea in principle and gave the job of researching and writing one to the city's human relations commission. The AFSC assigned HOP staff member Norman Goerlich to devote as much time as necessary in helping the commission write the bill and, more important, strategizing a public campaign to lobby for its passage. Goerlich himself gave testimony to the council on the issue, but the climax of his efforts was a public hearing at which thirty people representing twenty-one organizations spoke in favor of open housing, dwarfing the handful of representatives from the housing industry who opposed it. Nevertheless, in early 1963 the San Jose City Council turned down the bill by a 5–2 vote. A similar measure lost in San Francisco. Nearby in Berkeley, a fair housing ordinance was adopted in January 1963. But almost immediately, white conservatives, real estate agents, and apartment owners, led by a group called Berkeley Citizens United, secured enough signatures to call for a repeal, and in April 1963 local voters overturned the fair housing law by a margin of 22,750 to 20,456—close, but still a defeat for residential integration in a liberal bastion. After the Berkeley vote, Stephen Thiermann, executive secretary of the Northern California Regional Office, reported that this "failure of the proposed fair housing ordinance has intensified Negro and White extremism." The disappointment was fueling "anti-white feeling" and "Negro nationalism," as some African Americans took the defeat as a signal to give up on "interracial efforts." Fair housing opponents saw it as evidence of the political power of white homeowners to turn back antidiscrimination laws.[22]

By that time, the state legislature had passed three measures that made California a leader in housing opportunity and seemed to promise a firm government hand in ensuring minorities had equal access to homes of their choice. In 1959, lawmakers adopted the Unruh Act, which broadly prohibited unequal service by businesses, and a quick legal challenge led to a court decision confirming that builders and real estate offices were covered by the law. The same year, Augustus Hawkins, African American assemblyman from Los Angeles, successfully sponsored a law banning discrimination in publicly assisted housing. Civil rights advocates quickly pressed for more aggressive legislation, however, as both new laws put the burden on minorities to file civil suits to get their rights enforced. In June 1963, seeking stronger legal protections and taking advantage of the sympathy for civil rights generated by the Birmingham crisis, William Rumford, a Black legislator from Berkeley, secured passage of an eponymous state law to outlaw discrimination based on race, creed, or national origin in the sale and rental of private housing. With the Berkeley repeal fresh in the news, however, opponents of open housing led by the California Real Estate Association, the John Birch Society, and state Republicans began pushing Proposition 14, a referendum calling for an amendment to the state constitution to prohibit any state or local government action that limited the absolute free choice of an owner or landlord to sell or lease; in other words, it would outlaw open housing laws and nullify the Rumford Act.[23]

The AFSC's local and national housing and community relations staffs immediately saw the need to defend the Rumford Act and fight the proposed amendment, which they believed would "freeze into law permission to practice racial discrimination in housing." Not only California was at stake, Charlotte Meacham pointed out. People all around the country were awaiting the outcome of the Proposition 14 ballot. If it passed, she feared it would open a "Pandora's box of ugly hatreds" and inspire copycat actions in other states while damaging the chance for national fair housing legislation. Colleagues in the fair housing and human relations movements requested that the AFSC help organize and fund a cooperative statewide effort to fight Proposition 14. After securing reassurance from its lawyers that the AFSC's tax-exempt status would not be threatened by devoting time to that effort, community relations leaders gave the green light for major commitments from the regional office staff.[24]

To gear up for a battle against the proposition, the AFSC helped set up the staff and the infrastructure for a grassroots campaign. The Northern California Regional Office hired Frank Quinn, the longtime leader of the San Francisco Council for Civil Unity, as temporary associate community relations secretary. In that capacity, he was to reach out to pro-integration real estate agents and circulate information on Proposition 14. In addition, the Southern California Regional Office in Pasadena assigned staff person Isabel Gehr to work full-time on the issue. After the formation of Californians for Fair Housing as the statewide coordinator of all efforts in support of open housing, the AFSC paid the salaries of one staff person and the secretary. Meanwhile, mimicking the Freedom Summer campaign going on at the same time in Mississippi, the Northern California Regional Office's College Committee organized students to go door-to-door to talk with people about the initiative and urge voter registration. The College Committee held training workshops for the students, teaching them how to respond to potentially hostile residents, talk with people about Proposition 14, and follow up with registered voters in the fall.[25]

Much of the work of the AFSC staff members assigned to the campaign to defeat Proposition 14 involved coordinating the myriad activities of the "spontaneous citizen committees" that arose to defeat the referendum, as well as the work of existing fair housing and human relations groups that now turned their invigorated attention to the battle (fig. 4.1). In Pasadena, Gehr started a fair housing newsletter and collected and promulgated evidence of what different groups were doing, both to encourage people and to demonstrate the popular opposition to the initiative. Across the state, those activities reflected the tactics the HOPs had used in the pioneer placement and fair housing council organizing, such as hosting debates, interracial conversations, and coffees among neighbors; preparing and circulating literature; and arranging cross-race home visits. In addition, the AFSC sponsored a high school essay contest to encourage teenagers to speak out, and it directed people to resources including a calendar of events and "defeat the initiative" workshops by the American Civil Liberties Union. The clearinghouse role demonstrated how the grassroots fair housing council organizing flowed into and supported lobbying for government action. Community groups opposed to Proposition 14 contacted Gehr for help attracting African American families to move to their neighborhood and for information about how to facilitate that move; meanwhile, she forwarded clippings, newsletters,

FIGURE 4.1: Members of CORE picket real estate offices to protest Proposition 14 on January 13, 1964. Photograph by Bob Martin. Valley Times Collection. Courtesy of the Los Angeles Public Library.

and other evidence of grassroots activities to Friends who were lobbying legislators and opinion-makers.[26]

Despite these efforts and voices of opposition, Proposition 14 succeeded at the polls. Although the United States Supreme Court declared the proposition unconstitutional in 1967 and thus restored and affirmed the state's fair housing legislation, by then the movement to defeat open housing had had its impact. The swell of public hostility to open housing evidenced by the passing of Proposition 14 dealt a blow to the momentum of the national civil rights movement and was a harbinger of vocal white resistance to further change in race relations outside the South. The victory emboldened reactionary groups in California and increased open housers' anxiety about attacks by the John Birch Society on civil rights legislation in general and housing integration specifically. Yet the campaign against the proposition also sparked the formation of more fair housing and human relations groups and networks, strengthening that movement and leading the AFSC to devolve the administration of it to local groups. Soon after the defeat, the Northern California Regional Office paired with the Council on Civil Unity to launch a new Central Housing List Service, and the new AFSC community relations secretary for the region, Carl Ulrich, put together the Bay Area Fair Housing Council, which united over twenty-four local organizations. In the southern region, Isabel Gehr reported a blooming of the fair housing council movement, which produced 110 local organizations. With the growth in the number and coordination of local groups in the wake of the campaign against Proposition 14, both California regional offices increasingly left the suburban work and lobbying for further legislation in the hands of umbrella fair housing council organizations. Instead, they took up new work, focusing on the problems of minorities in low-income urban housing.[27]

Pressing for Enforcement of Local Government Policies: Chicago

Though some cities and states were beginning to adopt laws that directly or indirectly prohibited discrimination in housing, these policies mattered little if they were not enforced vigorously enough to change either the culture of the housing industry or the residential patterns in neighborhoods. In the wake of the Civil Rights Act (1964), activists became increasingly frustrated with systems of enforcement that relied on conciliation of individual complaints rather than proactive investigations and punishments that held serial discriminators accountable. Through the mid-1960s, they began pressing President Lyndon Johnson to develop an affirmative action program that would give government agencies more authority to seek out discrimination and develop mass solutions to it. Members of the AFSC Housing Opportunities Program moved in the same direction at this time. In their work with pioneers, the staff had learned that it was simply too difficult, even with private agency support, for a lone Black family to navigate the myriad forms of exclusion and obtain legal redress for housing discrimination that violated the new laws. Local, state, and federal government agents needed to use their policy leverage, punish lawbreakers, and develop practices that affirmatively integrated housing. In the mid-1960s, the AFSC housing program staff around the country devoted significant energy to using a variety of means to pressure officials to enact these measures, including monitoring, testing, filing complaints, documenting persistent discrimination, and participating in direct-action demonstrations. Indeed, while they often left lawsuits to other groups, especially the NAACP, and lobbying to either the Friends Committee on National Legislation or local fair housing groups, housing activists in the AFSC pursued both top-down and grassroots efforts to press government to enforce equal housing laws.[28]

In Chicago, the housing staff documented the ineffectiveness of executive orders and laws at the city, state, and local levels. In June 1963, they collaborated with the Congress of Racial Equality to research local Veterans Administration and Federal Housing Administration practices and concluded that President Kennedy's executive order on federally supported housing "has had no real impact on the Chicago area," and that "there is confusion about what it covers and if and how it will be enforced." Passage of the city ordinance in September 1963 was a coup for the open housing movement, but the Chicago Commission on Human Relations took a passive approach of responding to individual complaints rather than trying to change real estate practices. By the first anniversary of the law, forty-seven such complaints had been filed, but not even one real estate business had been punished; two years later, still not a single person had lost his or her license for discriminating.[29]

Caught up in the same emotional response to the southern civil rights movement that had led to the adoption of Chicago's municipal ordinance, in July 1963 Illinois governor Otto Kerner had issued a Code of Fair Practices, which forbade racial discrimination by state-licensed entities. The AFSC regional office called for it to apply to real estate agents, with little evident success. Then, just as the Chicago Freedom Movement was launching its summer campaign in July 1966, Kerner issued a specific order against discrimination in housing. However, a cumbersome enforcement procedure required the home buyer to file a complaint, which would then be the subject of an investigation and a public hearing before any relief could be granted. Moreover, staff member Maria Pappalardo reported that "spies" friendly to the HOP had attended a private meeting at which a representative of the governor reassured real estate agents that the procedure would take "six months to a year and in any eventuality no licenses will be revoked." This pattern of anemic attention by authorities to policies on the books led the Chicago Freedom Movement to make aggressive enforcement of open housing by city and federal authorities central to its demands.[30]

Indeed, during the summer 1966 campaign, testers visited real estate offices not only to draw attention to discrimination and put moral pressure on individual businesses to serve Black families, but also to document how those businesses were flouting the city law and Kerner's order. In the spring, in advance of the launch of demonstrations, the AFSC worked with the SCLC to "organize 200–250 cases of discrimination in housing" to prepare for a lawsuit. At first, some members of the HOP advisory committee objected to this form of testing, warning that the volunteers should be bona fide home seekers to avoid accusations of harassment and to ensure the cases were strong if the complaints did lead to a lawsuit. Bert Ransom assured them that the Black families seeking service were "lookers"—that is, people "in need of housing who may not have the money right now." Throughout the summer, testers approached real estate offices in the targeted neighborhoods, asking for service and documenting their experience. By mid-August, they had filed seventy-two complaints of discrimination with the Chicago Commission on Human Relations.[31]

The summit agreement that signaled the end of the Chicago Freedom Summer demonstrations secured promises from various city agencies for affirmative actions to combat residential discrimination. Open housing advocates and the HOP staff, however, did not trust that those promises would be kept without vigilant monitoring. Almost immediately after the summit agreement was signed and announced, Bill Moyer, skeptical about the intentions of the public agencies, called together representatives of civil rights groups to form a watchdog group. The group, which included Bert Ransom, met every other Wednesday at the AFSC offices to share information about what the covered agencies were doing and whether their actions matched the "word and spirit" of the agreement, with the intent to report their findings to local civil rights organizations. Moyer led the group, while Ransom kept watch over the CCHR to make sure it was upholding its promise to increase enforcement of the open housing ordinance. The HOP staff considered the latter job particularly important, explaining that "we put a lot of energy here because as more laws pass it's important to document enforcement procedures and develop ways for them to be effective." In that spirit, Ransom continued to train and send testers to real estate offices, helped them file complaints with the CCHR, and then kept track of how the commission handled the cases.[32]

In October 1966, Moyer presented a scathing report from the watchdog committee to a Coordinating Council of Community Organizations delegates' retreat. The watchers had found that Chicago's urban renewal program, even with pressure from Ransom, failed to relocate African American families to formerly white areas and concluded that "there is no indication the Department of Urban Renewal is following its promise to help create an open city." Further, the Chicago Housing Authority had not yet integrated its senior citizen apartments or ended the separate white and Black waiting lists for units. Moreover, the CHA had proposed eleven new sites for public housing, all in Black areas. As for the Department of Public Aid, the report was unequivocal: there had been "no change from past practices." Special attention was reserved for the CCHR, which according to Moyer "as of today" had not "met any of its commitments." Indeed, the commissioners had decided they could not do their own testing, because that might be "entrapment," and they continued to resist reform in real estate practices. Five months later, Moyer and Ransom went more public with the report and, according to press reports, accused the CCHR of "'flagrantly' breaking the Summit Agreement." They argued that the commission had not kept any of its four promises and that despite one hundred cases of discrimination being reported, there had been "to our knowledge no hearings or reprimands."[33]

The AFSC staff in the Chicago Regional Office continued to press the CCHR through testing programs until early 1969. By that time, the HOP had become the Open Communities program under the direction of Jim Reedy. Bert Ransom had moved to Washington, DC, to work for urban renewal and eventually became a pastor in Alexandria, Virginia. Moyer, too, left Chicago but remained an activist, opposing the Vietnam War and the expansion of nuclear power, supporting the American Indian Movement, and training peace activists around the world through the Movement for a New Society. His enduring legacy for social justice work includes his translation of his experiences in nonviolent direct action into a "Movement Action Plan," which was used to train future activists in a number of progressive causes, and his coauthorship of a how-to book for social movements, *Doing Democracy*, shortly before his death in 2002. Reedy pointed out that by 1968, the context for the AFSC housing work had changed. Chicago had extended its open housing ordinance to cover owners' sales, the state and federal fair housing laws had passed, and other local entities were working on enforcement and public education. The final testing program provided evidence for lawyers attempting to prove that the enforcement of the Chicago ordinance did not meet standards established under the federal law, so complaints of discrimination could henceforth be turned over to the Chicago office of the US Department of Housing and Urban Development (HUD) instead of languishing at the CCHR. With that, Reedy concluded that the "loose ends of past efforts have been tied up," and, with others pursuing further enforcement, the regional office could lay down its housing integration efforts per se and focus on other concerns.[34]

The main organization taking up the housing integration work was the Metropolitan Leadership Council for Open Housing, which grew out of a promise stated in the summit agreement. The last point in that agreement had called on the Chicago Conference on Religion and Race to form a "separate, continuing body" made up of representatives of religious, civic, and civil rights organizations to coordinate future programs aimed at achieving fair housing. The Leadership Council's task was to promote public education on the issue, draft fair housing laws and ordinances, create fair housing centers to do the work of listing services like Home Opportunities Made Equal, and "regularly review the performance" and undertakings of governmental and nongovernmental actors toward enforcing the law. Ed Holmgren, former head of the Chicago HOP, became the first executive director. Kale Williams served on the initial board and then took over as the organization's executive director from 1972 to 1991. Hardly a radical group by any means, and indeed accused of selling out more militant open housing advocates in the interest of mollifying the real estate industry representatives on its board, the Leadership Council struggled for the first few years to get organized, decide on a program, and figure out how to adapt the goals of a movement into the procedures of a private bureaucracy with little real political power. Its first major initiative came in 1976, when HUD contracted with the Leadership Council to help seventy-five hundred minority families find housing in formerly white neighborhoods in the metropolitan area. This arrangement came about under the auspices of the Gautreaux Program, which originated from a court order to the Chicago Housing Authority to provide housing for Black applicants outside segregated areas. Ironically, in this program the Leadership Council's role resembled the pioneer work of the early HOPs, as the members worked with individuals seeking and moving into new homes. More generally, reflecting the conviction that real estate practices remained the main culprit blocking equal housing opportunity, during the time of Williams's leadership the council continued tactics used by the Congress of Racial Equality, the AFSC, and the Chicago Freedom Movement: testing real estate offices, monitoring the practices of the mortgage and real estate industries, and providing documentation to support more than fifteen hundred lawsuits against discriminatory firms.[35]

Pressing for Enforcement of Federal Policies: Philadelphia

While in Chicago the AFSC focused on getting a recalcitrant private real estate industry to follow state and city fair housing policies, the Metropolitan Philadelphia Housing Opportunities Program (MPHOP) organized a campaign to pressure federal government agencies to follow their own rules. What started as a plan for collaborative partnership between a private agency and government authorities quickly became the basis for AFSC accusations of discrimination by the Federal Housing Administration and the Veterans Administration, generating nationwide publicity as well as congressional pressure for enforcement of existing policies and enactment of new federal legislation. In 1963 and 1964, FHA officials met with private and state housing agencies and representatives of the President's Committee on Equal Housing Opportunity to talk about how to cooperate. Not long after, the FHA asked the AFSC to develop a model for how private housing advocates could help government agencies promote suburban integration. The AFSC initially suggested that fair housing councils work with local FHA staff to make sure that Black buyers had equal access to sales of homes repossessed by the FHA and the VA. The FHA considered both Chicago and Philadelphia as potential pilot locations for testing this model. Chicago had a low volume of repossessions, however. On the other hand, Philadelphia had the advantage of a long and relatively positive history of over two hundred Black pioneer move-ins to suburban communities. In addition, certain state laws in both Pennsylvania and New Jersey could strengthen the hand of integrators. Because the fair housing councils were weaker in the Philadelphia area, however, the AFSC took this project on as its own and decided to devote the last eighteen months of the MPHOP to accomplishing it. Both the housing staff and the Community Relations Division leadership regarded this effort as a promising opportunity to "work with federal agencies to develop ways to make a more affirmative action rather than complaint reaction policy."[36]

Initially, the planning for the pilot project focused on developing mechanisms by which Black buyers could gain access to repossessed FHA and VA homes—homes whose mortgages had been foreclosed and were now back in the hands of the federal agencies and put up for resale. From the start, the AFSC made it clear that it expected the FHA to cooperate by providing the resources essential for that access to happen. The agency needed to send a list of available properties to area fair housing councils and to real estate agents, both Black and white, who had signed a pledge not to discriminate. In addition, representatives from fair housing groups would be given keys or codes to lockboxes so that they could access and inspect the repossessed properties in advance of advertising them for sale. Beyond that, the AFSC asked FHA officials to demonstrate their commitment to the success of the project and to affirmative practices by publicly stating their commitment to equal opportunity, supplying buyer education materials, helping educate the real estate industry, providing advice about finances and application procedures, and in general "promoting a positive climate" for the effort, both within and outside the agency. For its part, the AFSC would publicize the availability of FHA and VA homes; recruit potential buyers; work with individual families as they viewed and made offers for homes; meet with area real estate salesmen; monitor the sales of repossessed homes to make sure there was no pattern of continued discrimination; prepare neighborhoods for move-ins and respond to repercussions; file complaints on behalf of families who experienced discrimination; and document the project's results with an eye toward replicating the pilot elsewhere. To undertake these tasks, the AFSC hired Nathan Greene as director and Barbara Krasner and Julia Robinson as field workers.[37]

The project got off to a rocky start when Greene encountered hostility and resistance from local FHA officials almost immediately. He had to get FHA commissioner Philip Brownstein to intervene before the Philadelphia insuring office director, Tom Gallagher, would even meet with him. When the meeting did happen, "the atmosphere was icy." Throughout Greene's presentation of the MPHOP's plans, he recalled, "faces were frozen and most of the men stared at the table before them." Eventually a representative from the Camden, New Jersey, FHA office bragged that his group had sold repossessed properties to nonwhites, and Gallagher added that at least 45 percent of sales were to minorities. When asked why none of those sales were in the suburbs, one man retorted that "'they' like to live together." Greene then criticized the FHA practice of designating a "management broker" to oversee the sale of each property. These men were often real estate agents with records of discrimination, and in practice they froze fair housing brokers out of the sales from the start. In a later meeting, both Brownstein and Gallagher denied that the management brokers had any advantage, and then they claimed that they could not try to "even the playing field" between them and non-discriminatory brokers, because that would be "partial." Moreover, both men refused even to discuss broadening the pilot project to include new homes insured by the FHA instead of just repossessions, leaving out large numbers of homes that should have been covered by Kennedy's 1962 executive order or by state law.[38]

Despite getting little encouragement or cooperation from the FHA, the MPHOP staff set to work on their part of the project. In late 1965 and early 1966, Krasner and Robinson began the slow process of reaching out to Black leaders and organizations to lay the groundwork for buyer education and recruitment. Krasner (fig. 4.2) was a white Jew who later recalled being influenced by her Russian immigrant grandfather and by feeling like an outsider growing up in a Catholic neighborhood in West

FIGURE 4.2: Barbara Krasner (*center*) meets with Germantown residents at the Germantown Center, November 12, 1967. Photograph by George Nelson. Courtesy of Special Collections Research Center, Temple University Libraries, Philadelphia.

Philadelphia. She had gotten involved in sit-ins as a young mother and then started a fair housing group when she moved to King of Prussia, a suburb northwest of Philadelphia. Through that work she met Richard Taylor of the MPHOP and got acquainted with the AFSC. When Robinson, who was African American, moved in about a block away from Krasner's home, she, too, joined the group, so that the pair were not only friends but also experienced in grassroots fair housing work before joining the AFSC. Indeed, their daily tasks in the FHA pilot project resembled those pioneer placement efforts, which involved daily meetings and phone calls and driving back and forth between Philadelphia, its suburbs, and nearby New Jersey communities. They encountered enthusiasm and a willingness to partner from civil rights leader Rev. Leon Sullivan, but some hostility from a Black real estate man who came to a meeting with "two six shooters drawn"—figuratively—and didn't want to hear about the program and its potential competition with his business. More generally, Krasner reported there was "lots of uncertainty and suspicion in the black community" about pursuing FHA-owned properties in the white suburbs.[39]

By the end of the spring of 1966, moving on from research and community education, the Philadelphia housing staff began planning the direct-action step of testing brokers who were dealing in the FHA homes in order to document and report discriminatory practices. Greene suggested recruiting five Black and five white couples from suburban fair housing groups to test real estate offices without worrying about whether they were bona fide buyers. But when the process of identifying these volunteers went slowly at the start of the summer, Krasner and Robinson decided to start the testing themselves. Greene's direction to them was to visit brokers and inquire about FHA-acquired properties, which under Kennedy's executive order had to be available on a nondiscriminatory basis; assess the "general manner" of the real estate agents as well as "specific information" provided; and, more generally, record "what differences in service did you receive."[40]

By the end of June 1966, Krasner and Robinson had tested nine real estate firms in three counties. In total they visited ten: five that were management brokers for FHA properties and five others selected at random. The encounters proved emotionally trying, as they "encountered discrimination which ranged from subtle to crude in all cases"; indeed, "in not one of the ten offices visited was equal service offered." Krasner described herself as having the relatively easier job of going into the office to determine whether properties were available. Robinson's experience was harder. She reported that "most of the brokers, salespeople and secretaries" were nervous from the moment she entered the office. One time, the real estate salesman "never even asked me to be seated. He talked with me standing in the middle of the floor." In some cases, Krasner and Robinson did not even get as far as the door because of the real estate agents' suspicions and their own fear of the consequences. Early in the process they set out for Delaware County but turned back when Robinson pointed out that "they're still lynching Negroes" there; they mutually decided to skip that area. Robinson caught brokers making repeated and poorly concealed lies and providing different treatment from what Krasner received. In one case, the salesman at least seemed upset about "the system," but another followed her out the door and stood watching, evidently to "catch" her driving off with Krasner to prove that they were from some "human relations committee." She was so frightened that when she got in Krasner's car, she urged her to "speed away immediately."[41]

Robinson reported one detailed, representative story in the program's final report. In this instance, Krasner visited an office that had advertised serving as the broker for the FHA in the area and had listed three dozen homes as available. Though she did not have an appointment, she received "solicitous" service. While the agent steered her away from properties "near projects," he offered to show her houses seven days a week and gave her information about financing options. Then Robinson entered the office five minutes after Krasner left, with an appointment to see Mr. S——. When she walked into the lobby no one greeted her, but she found two men in an inner office. They did not identify themselves but insisted that Mr. S—— was down the street at lunch. She sat down to wait. Later, a secretary curtly told her Mr. S—— had been detained. She encouraged Robinson to leave, but she refused. Then one of the men left. Still waiting, Robinson asked the remaining broker to serve her, and he refused, saying he wasn't a salesman. He took a call and told her that it was Mr. S—— saying he would not be back, so Robinson left. On a whim, she decided to return half an hour later and found the same man sitting at the desk, who now identified himself as Mr. S——. Apparently, he did not recognize her or remember his attempted ruse. Robinson chose not to point it out to avoid the mutual embarrassment. At this point, Mr. S—— took her into a back room and showed her a book of listings that did not include FHA properties. He did not provide any information about financing options and made no effort to set up a time to show her homes until she pressed him into an appointment. On the selected day, Mr. S—— called her to cancel the showings. Experiences like this made Krasner, Greene, and Robinson glad they had used staff as testers and not real buyers, because they had avoided subjecting others to the "indignities and dehumanizing assault of discrimination."[42]

After wrapping up their testing, the staff of the Metropolitan Philadelphia Housing Opportunities Program moved to the next step: speaking truth to power by presenting their findings to the leadership of the FHA. Harkening back to their traditional goals of reconciliation and persuasion, the staff initially wrote to and met with the FHA representatives quietly and privately. Their desire for reconciliation, however, did not mean they would not "confront the FHA with the findings to show without question that the FHA is contributing to segregation at the same time the government says there is no discrimination in their programs." Charlotte Meacham, the national housing program secretary, told Tom Gallagher that Barbara Krasner and Julia Robinson had "uncovered outright discrimination" and "inequities born of long and deeply rooted practices." Put bluntly, she concluded that FHA officials and those in the real estate industry with whom they worked were "violating their obligations under federal rules" not to discriminate. In a fuller report, the Philadelphia office staff argued that the federal housing agency had "heavy moral and legal responsibility to affirmatively pursue the reality of equal opportunity," in part at least because of its long history in aiding and abetting segregation.[43]

In its interim report to the heads of the Philadelphia and Camden, New Jersey, FHA insuring offices, the AFSC called for aggressive action by the agency to ensure compliance with Kennedy's executive order and listed specific steps in that direction. In a preamble, the report detailed how the FHA had historically promoted segregation, concluding that "for more than twenty-five years, the FHA had not only told Philadelphians and other Americans that they had a right to discriminate, but it assured them that the government supported that right." The result was a culture in which the expectation was that such patterns of behavior could continue unchecked. In addition, the AFSC found that no Black firms were invited to submit applications for management broker contracts. White management brokers regularly allowed friendly real estate firms—that is, other white-only discriminatory firms—to preview houses before they were listed as available on the open market. They then accepted buyers' offers on a first-come, first-served basis, privileging white clients. The AFSC recommended that the five management brokers found to have provided unequal service be fired and that a new open bidding process for the contracts be started to allow Black firms to compete for the position. Moreover, it requested a daily public listing of all properties, and it asked that all houses be listed four weeks before offers could be made on them. Perhaps most important, it argued that in the case of competing offers for a house, the property should go to "those previously excluded by discriminatory policies and practices." In short, the AFSC sought an explicit affirmative action policy in the sale of FHA properties.[44]

One week after submitting that report, representatives of the AFSC met with agents of the FHA to discuss it. After a short presentation by Robinson, Gallagher responded. He insisted that the FHA "does not permit discrimination," but also defensively evaded responsibility. He could not "be continually on top of the situation everywhere at all hours of the day"; moreover, policies were set in Washington, and he did not know what more could be done locally. The issue was not that significant anyway, because FHA-insured and -repossessed homes were a "shrinking part of the market." He took the names of the five management brokers who during testing had discriminated against Robinson, but he also insisted that he had acted on this issue before "it became popular." The AFSC attendees thought perhaps that the "FHA had been shaken" by the report, but none of them "were feeling sanguine" about the likelihood of any changes in practice. As Robinson pointed out, Gallagher seemed to be "measuring equal opportunity by dollar signs," and an MPHOP advisory committee member who attended the meeting added that the FHA would continue to operate as always unless there was pressure from Congress or a lawsuit. Nathan Greene tried to reach out to Gallagher again three weeks later to ask about progress on the complaints against the five management brokers. Instead, he got twenty-five minutes of the "most acrimonious and offensive statements I have ever heard from an official at such a level of responsibility." After accusing the AFSC of sending the testers to trap the FHA, Gallagher defended the management brokers, insisting to Greene, who was white and Jewish, that he had done more "'for the Negroes'" than Greene ever would "'sitting behind your desk and shooting your mouth off.'" Gallagher ended the conversation by saying that he would be taking no further action on the report because it was the responsibility of the FHA's Washington, DC, headquarters.[45]

Meanwhile, people associated with the AFSC testing program began investigating other ways to force the FHA to act on their findings. The staff discussed whether it would be a good idea to get groups in other cities to "'go after'" their local officials to build cumulative pressure. Greene planned to coordinate with the Philadelphia Human Relations Commission to track any complaints the FHA reported to it, though he doubted there would be any. Arthur Levin of the Potomac Institute pushed for a lawsuit against the federal agency and offered to pay legal expenses. In July 1966, a lawyer named John Silard seconded that recommendation but suggested that the AFSC line up bona fide home seekers and not rely on evidence collected by the testers. Although the MPHOP advisory committee was sympathetic to the prospect of establishing a legal precedent preventing the FHA from continuing to support discrimination, Greene noted the difficulty of lining up home seekers to do additional testing and the ethical questions about putting them through that humiliation. He also worried that the legal route would require staying quiet about Krasner and Robinson's experiences; he thought that publicizing their results would have a greater impact. He suggested instead that the AFSC pressure federal officials by going to the press with their findings, and indeed threatened Philip Brownstein with such a course of action if the FHA did not respond by October 1966.[46]

The FHA took some measures in the fall, but they failed to satisfy the AFSC's concern. Instead, the agency demonstrated that it still did not take equal housing opportunity seriously. In August, Gallagher had written to brokers who handled FHA repossessed properties sales, reminding them that they could not show such properties before listing them for sale. He added a new practice: any offer received within seven days of listing was considered simultaneous, and the buyer with the best combination of payment, credit, and mortgage terms would get the sale. In cases of equal offers, the broker would determine the "winner" by a random drawing; in short, there would be no preference for low-income buyers or those in groups that had historically experienced discrimination. Greene was angered to discover that despite this ray of hope for change, the FHA had rejected the discrimination complaints against the five management brokers, and he despaired that the "system is basically unchanged." Brownstein did promise to hold meetings with area brokers to reaffirm the antidiscrimination intent of Kennedy's executive order and to announce the FHA's commitment to enforce it. But as of December, no member of a fair housing group was notified about or invited to such a meeting. When Greene and former pioneer James Harvey, who had helped integrate Burlington County, New Jersey, and now worked for the AFSC, finally did attend a meeting in February 1967, they came away disgusted. FHA officials presented the executive order as if it were new and meant to give "low- and modest-income people a 'fair shake.'" They also treated racial discrimination as a joke and Gallagher insisted that federal policy did not require "preferential treatment." Greene and Harvey came away concluding that brokers dealing in FHA properties had no reason to believe that the agency was any more serious about preventing discrimination. As Greene closed his description of the meeting, "If this is an equal opportunity meeting then I am George Wallace."[47]

Shortly before this low point, the housing program staff stopped making appeals directly to the FHA leadership and began to focus on generating public pressure. In November 1966, they carried out their threat to Brownstein by holding a press conference to publicize their report about the MPHOP's testing of the management brokers' practices. But only one television station covered it, and no radio stations did. Only two newspapers were present, although they did report the story positively. In May 1967, the AFSC was ready for a larger publicity campaign. At that time, it released *A Report to the President: AFSC Experience and Recommendations re: Executive Order 11063 on Equal Opportunity in Housing*. This report painstakingly documented how employees of the Federal Housing Administration and the Veterans Administration, as well as brokers contracted by them, perpetuated a dual housing market and denied minorities equal access to federally supported housing, violating Kennedy's executive order. In it, the AFSC presented detailed recommendations covering both new and repossessed homes and everything from advertising and buyer education to the handling of discrimination complaints. Fully half the document consisted of thirteen case studies not only from the Philadelphia testing program but also from Chicago, San Francisco, and Washington. This time, the AFSC's efforts drew more attention. The organization circulated over twenty-five hundred copies to President Johnson, cabinet secretaries, members of Congress, and people in the fair housing movement. Eighteen television and radio stations and thirty-three newspapers and magazines, including a long essay in *Jet* magazine, reported on the conference and the content of the report. Media coverage and queries continued through November.[48]

Slowly, political pressure on the FHA and the VA began to build in response to what one civil rights leader called "the best critique of the federal role or non-role in equal opportunity in housing that has been done." After the press conference, Congressman William Fitts Ryan of New York organized a meeting of some of his colleagues, FHA representatives, and the AFSC. The AFSC was represented by James Harvey and William Cameron, former MPHOP advisory committee member and current head of the Fair Housing Council of Delaware Valley. Not long after Brownstein began to speak, Congressman Hawkins of California interrupted him, and "the fireworks had now begun." Hawkins and others peppered Brownstein with questions about what was being done about discriminatory practices, but he only wanted to talk about the FHA's new effort to counsel low-income and minority buyers on purchasing an FHA-insured home. In the wake of the meeting, eight congressmen signed a letter that said, "Our conclusion is that the picture portrayed by the AFSC report is substantially accurate." Specifically, they criticized the FHA's failure to adopt an affirmative posture on enforcement, instead leaving "those aggrieved to pursue complicated complaints on their own." Most important, they agreed on the need for more federal legislation. In the meantime, they would hold the FHA accountable and demand enforcement of policies already on the books. Later that summer, the report got additional attention from legislators, who cited it several times in hearings about the fair housing bill of 1967.[49]

In February 1968, the AFSC's national housing staff prepared a summary of the response to *A Report to the President* that served as a sort of swan song for their residential integration program. After a summer of "rather disappointing" meetings with government officials in the wake of the confrontation between the congressmen and the FHA, housing advocates began to see some small actions. In August 1967, the Department of Housing and Urban Development launched a free Housing Counseling Service in fifteen cities for helping minorities, low-income families, servicemen, and veterans find suitable homes. Brownstein became more vocal about enforcing the executive order, telling his staff that "you should work at this task as though your job depended on it—because it may!" And the FHA and HUD requested the AFSC's help in promoting apartment integration in the national capital region. None of these measures went far enough in the eyes of the housing staff at the AFSC, however. Moreover, as the summary concluded, "We've worked with HUD for years and have learned the need for follow through and keeping the pressure on so that promises are kept, changes made, and guidelines enforced."[50]

•

That statement could serve as a digest of the lessons learned by the AFSC from its whole history of engagement with government agencies on housing policy. The long study of housing patterns produced by its staff had taught them that government had been both the font and the enabler of discriminatory and segregationist practices at the local and national levels; ironically, however, their experience in seeking integration had also taught them that the power of government would be necessary to overcome resistance from the real estate industry and achieve a systemic solution to the problem. But, as community relations staffers had worried in 1957, legislation alone was not enough. Supporters of open housing needed to make constant efforts to educate and persuade those in government to support fair housing, and they needed to maintain persistent vigilance and pressure to make sure the officials enforced it. The path to equal housing was neither changing the minds of people in power nor enacting policies to attack systemic discrimination. Rather, it required a multipronged movement that combined speaking truth to power, grassroots lobbying, and direct action to hold officials' feet to the fire.

Two months after the AFSC released its summary, housing advocates received extra backup and a stronger weapon for fighting segregation when Congress passed the Fair Housing Act, which was signed into law by President Johnson in April 1968. Although the AFSC celebrated the new law and immediately called for its "vigorous enforcement," the organization had not actively engaged in securing its passage, leaving that job largely to the Friends Committee on National Legislation. By that time, the AFSC's regional offices and local programs either had already closed or were in the process of closing their HOPs, moving away from seeking integration and toward addressing the housing problems of low-income families. As the Metro Washington staff put it in their final report, the "pioneering work" in housing integration practices in the urban North had been done. It was time to pass the reins to local fair housing councils and move the AFSC's energies to other problems. Acting on that admonition, the Washington program folded in early 1967, with the new Metropolitan Washington Fair Housing Council picking up the cause. Likewise, as part of a regional office reorganization, the Philadelphia program shuttered and was succeeded by the Fair Housing Council of Delaware Valley. On the West Coast, the Northern California Regional Office staff helped create the East Bay Housing Office, which took over pursuing FHA/VA complaints, advised people looking for homes or apartments, and coordinated the activities of twenty fair housing groups under the umbrella of the Housing Opportunities Committee of the Council on Civil Unity. By this time, with the explosion of small fair housing groups after the Proposition 14 fight and the creation of a Housing Information Service in conjunction with the local group Altadena Neighbors, the Southern California regional program had laid down its housing integration work and turned its attention to the problems of low-income people in the immediate vicinity of its office.[51] Finally, in Chicago, while the oldest HOP loaned its top staff to the job of monitoring the city government's equal housing opportunity promises, others in the regional office pioneered community organizing strategies aimed at empowering low-income minority residents to address their own housing problems.

5. Community Organizing

"A People Program in a Housing Context"

In February 1969, Barbara Moffett, secretary of the AFSC's Community Relations Division, wrote to Jane Weston in Chicago: "We're all breathless, but bright-eyed and eager to get moving on what seems to us here to be one of the more exciting programs to facilitate change that the AFSC has been able to apply itself to in a while." She was referring to the organization's decision to pay Tony Henry to create and direct the National Tenant Organization (NTO), a move reflecting division leaders' convictions that "tenants' rights were an idea whose time had come," and that tenant unions "offered a real key to a nationwide attack on the problems of the quality and supply of low-income housing." The AFSC's support for the NTO marked the culmination of its transition in focus away from helping middle-class African Americans move to previously white suburban neighborhoods and toward addressing the housing needs of low-income inner-city minorities.[1]

In the early 1960s, Housing Opportunities Program staff in the regional offices realized that even with an open real estate market, many minority families would not be financially able to move. Influenced by a national conversation about poverty, they and their CRD colleagues began to explore how economic inequality hamstrung their programs. Increasingly, they saw community organizing—which drew from both their traditional beliefs and approaches and new methodologies around them, including those employed in the War on Poverty—as an effective way to address that inequality. In addition, at mid-decade the Black Power movement's demands for indigenous leadership and control challenged the AFSC to reconceptualize its role in the urban minority community. The organization did not give up on integration, so it continued to provide support to grassroots efforts to implement the Fair Housing Act; but in response to Black Power, it began to focus more on empowering local people to improve their own living conditions. While redirecting their housing work, AFSC staff explored ways to expand the supply of low- and moderately priced housing through cooperatives and other models, and they pressured local governments to enforce housing codes. Ultimately, however, organizing tenants to demand repairs and decent treatment emerged as the strategy that both promised concrete results and, as important, best reconciled long-held Friends and AFSC values with the social justice organizing of the era.

Roots of AFSC Community Organizing with the Poor

By the early 1960s, the AFSC's CRD and its regional office programs had been working with the poor and marginalized for a decade. In that time, its grassroots programs around the country had created a citizenship preparation course for Latinos in Texas and built water systems for migrant workers in California. The Indian Program staff had set up a center to aid young Native Americans adjusting to urban life in Los Angeles, helped the Maricopa people in Arizona establish farm cooperatives and increase tillable land, and did housing repair and small business development on New England reservations. Like the work for school desegregation, housing integration, and job opportunities for African Americans, these programs were motivated by a common belief "in the worth of the individual and his right to grow up in a social environment in which he can freely develop his God-given potential to the fullest." Over the 1950s, the programs had shifted away from a charitable service model and toward a collaborative strategy of working with rather than for minorities and the poor. Despite these efforts, at an AFSC roundup in the spring of 1957, staff and committee members from around the country realized they had not gone far enough. One-third of the nation remained "ill-clothed, ill-housed and ill-fed," and community relations programs had only made "it possible for a few gifted people to enter into middle-class prosperity" while leaving "unshaken the economic order which condemns many to poverty." To understand better how to shake that order, those assembled launched an exploration into how poverty undermined their goals.[2]

In early 1963, the CRD reported on the results of that investigation. In California, volunteers in the migrant labor program warned that changes in agriculture made it difficult for farmworkers and their families to sustain themselves with work in the fields; civil rights workers in the Mississippi Delta argued that for African Americans, the intersection of race and poverty was a barrier to progress toward full citizenship. In the Housing Opportunities Programs, staff had seen how urban renewal caused further segregation by limiting the housing options of low-income minorities. Moreover, members of community relations committees from around the country concluded that "if we eliminated housing discrimination completely, Blacks would still not get homes because their incomes are too low." But better jobs depended on better education, they argued, which in turn was limited by the lack of resources at schools in poor neighborhoods. In short, problems in all areas of community relations were inseparable from economic inequality. To address that root problem, members of the CRD, including in the HOPs, began to work alongside low-income minorities to "break the cycle of poverty."[3]

The AFSC's internal dialogue about economic inequality took place at a time of growing national awareness of poverty's persistence amid affluence. Left-wing, minority rights, and faith-based organizations had never completely abandoned concern for the poor after World War II. The Catholic Worker movement aimed to alleviate hunger and homelessness in urban areas, for example. Liberal Protestants in mainline denominations began to turn their attention to racial and economic problems in the city, seeking a "renewal" of the churches' missions there and foreshadowing their support for War on Poverty programs. Meanwhile, the National Council of Churches Migrant Ministry, the Catholic Rural Life Conference, and the AFSC itself—comprising what journalist Ernesto Galarza called the "liberal conscience" of the nation—worked to improve living conditions in rural communities.[4] But for much of the 1950s, the problem of poverty had receded from the national consciousness, absent from the mainstream press and political debate due to a consensus that the New Deal and the postwar consumer boom had solved structural economic problems. Indeed, when John Kenneth Galbraith published *The Affluent Society* in 1958, the title caught on as a way to describe the "genius and bounty" of the American economy, despite the fact that the book demonstrated that "poverty does survive" and called for the provision of additional resources to the public sphere.[5]

In the years after Galbraith's book, however, several events brought more attention to the remaining poverty and to the estimated one-fifth to one-quarter of the population excluded from American affluence. In the spring of 1960, Senator John Kennedy visited West Virginia during the presidential primary campaign and attracted attention to the squalor in the state's coalfields. On the day after Thanksgiving that year, CBS broadcast *The Harvest of Shame*, showcasing the destitution of farmworkers to middle-class Americans still digesting their holiday feasts. Over the next few years, the civil rights movement brought to the rural South journalists with television cameras who broadcast images of sharecropper shacks and stories of desperate inequality to the rest of the country. Meanwhile, critics of Galbraith's book began writing exposés on the nature and extent of American poverty, including the young writer and social activist Michael Harrington, hired by *Commentary* magazine to produce a series on the subject. In 1962, Harrington published his essay collection as *The Other America*. The book, which presented a stark, blunt view of the lives of the poor, received critical acclaim, including a fifty-page review in the *New Yorker*. Harrington's role in shaping the national conversation about poverty received a boost when Kennedy aide Walter Heller recommended the book to the president as a source of "facts and figures" on the problem. Moreover, the book sold seventy thousand copies in hardcover and went through five reprintings in paperback by 1965, demonstrating a substantial public impact.[6] The nation's awareness of poverty had been raised.

Concern about the "other Americans," a ripening spirit of reform fostered by the civil rights movement, and increasing confidence in the ability of government to solve social problems, created the climate for both Kennedy's and Lyndon Johnson's policy responses to economic inequality. Inspired by his visit to West Virginia and by Harrington's book, Kennedy promised to do something about the conditions he witnessed in the coal regions and started to build the federal government's mechanisms for overcoming poverty. While he launched a pilot food stamp program in Appalachia and initiated education, job training, and juvenile delinquency programs, he did not live to see much of his promise fulfilled. After Kennedy's assassination, President Johnson took up the crusade with fervor, declaring an "unconditional war on poverty" in January 1964 and using his considerable political skills to pass the Economic Opportunity Act (EOA) a few months later. The EOA established the Office of Economic Opportunity to wage a multipronged battle, which included job training, youth employment, adult education, economic development for distressed areas, and aid to the rural poor. For the AFSC's urban housing efforts, the most important component of the War on Poverty was the Community Action Program (CAP), which created local community action agencies for coordinating ventures to address the needs of low-income residents in their areas. These agencies were required to include the "maximum feasible participation" of the poor in the planning and implementation of their programs, an effort to make sure that local elites did not bypass minorities. Although hampered by political opposition from the start, the CAP provided funding and a framework for grassroots community organizing for empowering the poor to address their own conditions.[7]

Grassroots community organizing had a long history in modern American social movements. The twentieth-century origins of community organizing against poverty lay in the social work of the settlement houses during the Progressive Era, when young women went into poor and immigrant neighborhoods to assess needs and deliver services. Working in the blue-collar neighborhoods of Chicago in the 1930s, Saul Alinsky developed the democratic potential of community organizing. Alinsky's method emphasized reaching out to people through local institutions and nurturing their leadership by teaching them to name their own goals and use their collective power to achieve them. In the 1950s in Tennessee, Myles Horton developed a model of adult education at Highlander Folk School that strove to prepare people for direct participation in democracy in ways that challenged the social structure. His students then fanned out across the South to organize the incipient struggle against Jim Crow. The bottom-up and collaborative approach of organizing in that struggle and in social movements in the mid-1960s was perhaps best conveyed by Bob Moses of the Student Nonviolent Coordinating Committee, who said, "The organizer does not have the complete answer in advance . . . the organizer wants to construct a solution with the community." By the mid-1960s, this grassroots community organizing had spread to the Black freedom struggle, student antipoverty work, and campaigns by women and minorities for equality and self-determination.[8]

By the early 1960s, the AFSC Community Relations Division shared with contemporary social justice movements and the War on Poverty's CAPs the belief that the most effective way to attack economic injustice and inequality was from the bottom up through community organizing. The role of a "small group like ours" in this "seemingly overwhelming problem," its Executive Committee argued, was to "inspire the poor themselves to participate in the development and implementation of programs" and to "develop among the presently inarticulate . . . the power to voice their own demands" and the "capacity for . . . constructive participation in the decision-making processes of their communities." AFSC staff who had worked in housing or other regional office community relations programs for the past decade or more found little new about this approach. In testifying before Congress in favor of the EOA, Helen Baker argued that the AFSC's "fifty years of working with the poor in this country and around the world" had taught the organization the importance of participation of the poor people themselves, the flexibility to try "experimentation" and "imaginative approaches," and the patience to allow people to "try things for themselves."[9]

One example of early CRD grassroots work illustrates the connection between Quaker beliefs and community organizing, and the CRD's early application of community organizing to low-income housing—albeit in a rural, not an urban, setting. In 1955, the Northern California Regional Office sent Quaker Bard McAllister to live and work among the farmworkers of the San Joaquin Valley, where he spent "about six months getting acquainted and finding out what was going on" in the community. He hired himself out as a laborer and did odd jobs such as hanging doors, fixing windows, and hammering shingles. He also spent a lot of time listening. McAllister did not have a plan from the outset, he explained, because "community development is an effort both to enrich community life and to spark confidence and initiative in individuals and an understanding of their role as children of God." Foreshadowing Moses's approach, he added, "If you come in with your mind already made up, no one else is inspired to make up his mind." Launching a concrete project to improve living conditions through community organizing could take a long time, and progress would be slow. But in the end, the local people's accomplishment would be "genuinely theirs" and not something they owed to an outside group. Around the same time, Thelma Babbitt was using much the same language to describe the work of organizing the Burlington County Human Relations Council and other similar groups in the Philadelphia suburbs.[10]

In his earliest visits in the San Joaquin Valley, McAllister found that "almost every seasonal laborer I talk with expresses a desire for a little piece of land. They want to settle down." But land uncontrolled by ranchers was expensive or simply unavailable, and banks would not extend credit to workers because of their insecure employment. Reaching back to models from the organization's early history, McAllister suggested that "one of the greatest contributions the AFSC can make in the area of the 'migrant'" would be to launch a Penn-Craft style self-help housing program to enable the farmworkers to build their own homes for their families (fig. 5.1).[11] Although HOP staff no longer regarded self-help housing as a promising way to provide housing or integrate neighborhoods in cities, the leaders of the regional office's migrant labor program enthusiastically endorsed McAllister's proposal. With guidance from AFSC staff members, in 1962 six families formed a cooperative housing association, the Casa de Mañana. Using their labor, or "sweat equity," as a down payment, they applied for loans for property and supplies from the federal Farmer's Home Administration (FmHA) under new provisions allowing mortgage insurance for farmworkers. Next, they built their homes with help from construction supervisors paid for by the AFSC. After finishing the homes and moving in, the families became the best advertisement for the program, spreading word of it to eager friends and relations. The AFSC self-help housing program quickly became popular in the San Joaquin Valley as well as with the War on Poverty's Migrant Section as a way to use grassroots organizing to provide housing to one of the lowest-income and most in need populations in the country.[12]

McAllister's community organizing process in California, like Babbitt's in the suburbs of Philadelphia, reflected Friends principles and

FIGURE 5.1: Self-help housing project, San Joaquin Valley, California, 1965. Courtesy of the American Friends Service Committee Archives, Philadelphia.

paralleled approaches being used in other contemporary social movements. Their work was based on the idea that given space for learning and reflection, people will make up their minds by drawing from their conscience, or, in Friends terms, attending to their Inner Light. But the CRD's small-scale, person-to-person approach; encouragement of local leadership and control; insistence on listening to people on all sides of a conflict; and tradition of inclusive decision-making also resembled strategies being employed by Ella Baker, the Student Nonviolent Coordinating Committee, the Economic Research and Action Projects of Students for a Democratic Society, and other groups that promoted participatory democracy. Going forward, the community relations programs in general and in housing specifically increasingly combined these time-tested AFSC approaches with ideas from contemporaneous models of community organizing to address problems of low-income peoples.

Community Organizing for Low-Income Housing: Boston

The staff of the Northeast Regional Office (NERO) in Cambridge, Massachusetts, which served Boston as well as the wider New England area, led the way in employing community organizing to tackle the housing problems of low-income inner-city residents. They had launched their community relations program in 1958 in response to a concern among local Friends about housing for African Americans. In its early years, the program had only a half-time secretary and a group of volunteers. Nevertheless, they engaged in many of the same fair housing council strategies seen in the outskirts of Philadelphia, in the Washington, DC, metropolitan area, and in the North Shore suburbs of Chicago. They encouraged the development of thirty fair housing groups, ran workshops for suburban leaders, held group meetings for Black home seekers, lobbied for antidiscrimination legislation, and in emergencies rushed to defend African American families in their new homes. As elsewhere, however, other groups were taking over many of these tasks by 1962. A federation of fair housing committees began serving as an information clearinghouse, and a new Massachusetts Committee against Discrimination was developing a more activist and legislative agenda. Feeling like other local people and groups were meeting their goals, the NERO Community Relations Committee began seeking a new direction.[13]

A new concern arose when Boston officials launched an urban renewal drive in several low-income neighborhoods. It quickly became clear that the city planned to get rid of substandard housing without an adequate plan to rehouse the families who would be displaced. Moreover, Boston already had a shortage of both public and private low- and moderate-cost rental units. In response, the NERO Community Relations Committee proposed looking for ways to increase the supply of nondiscriminatory low-income housing. Reflecting the AFSC's awareness of how the civil rights movement was shifting relationships between well-meaning whites and African Americans, the committee members argued they did not want to start a charitable effort but instead sought to work "with the minority group to help them speak out for themselves and to represent themselves." This would include providing community education, forming neighborhood committees, collaborating with Black leaders, reaching out to landlords, and organizing in the working-class areas to which displaced African Americans might move.[14]

Committee members thought Boston would be a good place to start working on low-income housing and thus create a model for other regional offices for several reasons. Historically, the city had a relatively good climate for fair housing and civil rights in general, though the drafters of the proposal recognized how reality did not always match that image. The African American population was relatively low, comprising only 3 percent of the metropolitan area and 9 percent of the city proper. Although 90 percent of Blacks lived in Roxbury, Dorchester, or the South End, the rest were dispersed; indeed, minority families resided in every one of the metropolitan area's census tracts, and relatively little violent resistance to move-ins had occurred, according to local fair housing groups. Some committee members worried that the working-class neighborhoods to which displaced African American families were likely to move would put up more resistance. But a study by George Grier pointed out that most of the people being affected by urban renewal and the shortage of low- and moderate-cost housing were white. African Americans represented only 8 percent of the families with incomes below $4,000. AFSC leaders hoped white families would recognize their shared need for housing and join an interracial campaign for decent shelter for the poor and working-class.[15]

Over time, however, the vision for the new Boston program came to emphasize grassroots community organizing and empowerment specifically in low-income Black neighborhoods. Early in the planning process, Community Relations Committee members debated a range of possible projects, from building new housing to rehabbing older structures to becoming a "pressure group" to get the "powers that be" to enforce housing codes. While they ultimately rejected the first two ideas, they recognized that speaking truth to officials would be required to accomplish their ends. But who would do the speaking? Ultimately, they concluded that their real goal was not to create more or better housing for poor minorities per se but to "support the people in their efforts to secure a radical change in the overall environment in which they and their children now live." Specifically, the new program would seek to establish relationships with low-income families, strengthen local leaders, and help them develop "their own organizations with power to achieve social change." Mary Berger, who worked in the NERO office, acknowledged that in the changing context of race relations, program staff would surely end up working with Black community groups who "may appreciate our help but will not appreciate our directing a program for them." Indeed, this new direction might involve AFSC workers in "militant" situations or partnerships with local organizations who took such positions. As Grier put it, the new low-income housing initiative would require a "top notch community relations worker" who could respond to the fluidity of situations in urban minority neighborhoods. The success of their new program would also require AFSC leaders to allow local staff to ally with and follow the lead of newly empowered residents who challenged the status quo.[16]

The Boston low-income housing program got under way in late 1964 with site selection and the hiring of staff. NERO leaders chose a six-block section of Roxbury, which was plagued by problems in schools, a lack of jobs, police brutality, and impending urban renewal. But it also was home to some whites mixed in with the dominant population of low-income Blacks, offering the opportunity to do at least some cross-race organizing. The NERO leaders wanted at least some of the program staff to have roots in the neighborhood, so they hired local African American Daniel Richardson as a program associate. Richardson had lived his entire twenty-one years in Boston, with thirteen of them spent in public housing. He and his wife, Betty, resided in Roxbury with their two children. The program also hired a Black secretary, Ruby Magee, who had attended college in Mississippi and was a research assistant for the US Department of Justice before moving to Boston. The only Quaker on the staff was Robert Gustafson, who had led Friends work camps in Tennessee in 1963 and in Roxbury in 1964. The leader of the team was James Reeb, a white Unitarian minister who had served a church in Washington, DC, before moving to Boston.[17]

In late 1964, Reeb and his staff set up a storefront office in Roxbury and began getting to know the local people's concerns and figuring out what they could do to help. In conversations with their new neighbors, they found that people felt "trapped and at the mercy of landlords." Bad experiences with public welfare agencies had also built up a feeling of distrust and powerlessness among community residents. To begin to address some of the more specific complaints, the AFSC Roxbury staff started Call for Action (CFA), a program in which residents could report problems with their apartments and then the staff and volunteers would help them find solutions. Then on December 31, an apartment building in the neighborhood burned down, killing four people and leaving thirty homeless. The Roxbury staff worked to make sure that people were rehoused, and they investigated the building conditions that had contributed to the blaze. When Reeb prepared a preliminary report and began to confront public officials with it, one of them warned him not to release the findings. In early March 1965, he put the finishing touches on a more detailed description of the deficiencies in the building and the lack of building code enforcement in the community. Reeb did not have a chance to pursue the issue further, however, because he answered a call from the Southern Christian Leadership Conference for members of the clergy around the country to join the civil rights demonstrations in Selma, Alabama. There, a group of segregationists brutally beat and killed him as he emerged with some companions from an integrated restaurant. Reeb's death set the Roxbury program back; it struggled until early 1966 to get back on its feet.[18]

At a memorial for Reeb on Boston Common, Richardson called on people to honor him by working for the "end to poor, inadequate, expensive housing and the insidious secret covenants and agreements that keep a man from the freedom to live where he pleases."[19] The first and most persistent part of the strategy for doing so was an expanded CFA program. The contacts made on the phone through CFA were the primary way the Roxbury staff got to know their neighbors. Staff and volunteers recruited from the community took the calls and became caseworkers. They met with the caller, and then helped the tenant negotiate with his or her landlord, contacted the city housing inspector, or called a meeting of all the renters affected by the same situation. The AFSC revealed its philosophical approach in two rules for the program: decisions about how to proceed on a complaint should be made by the tenant, not the caseworker, and the process of resolving the issue must include meeting with the landlord to get his or her side of the story. In early 1967, one report estimated that the program had served approximately one thousand people. Regardless of changes to the Roxbury staff and program over the years, CFA remained the centerpiece of the work in the neighborhood.[20]

But, as one staff person put it, responding to individual complaints was "the tip of the iceberg," and the Roxbury program needed to address more systemic problems.[21] Thus, nearly from the beginning, CFA served as the source of broader organizing and challenges to the housing and welfare systems in Boston. Almost right away, staff member Erna Ballantine, an African American woman from the neighborhood, used the records of CFA callers to launch a tenant organizing effort. In January 1966, she sent three hundred letters to people who had called the hotline. Two weeks later, she hosted a meeting for people to discuss their rights and responsibilities as tenants as well as how to use a new law that allowed rent to be withheld and put in escrow if landlords refused to make repairs. That spring, the NERO Community Relations Committee decided to "blitz" two buildings with an intensive organizing effort meant to experiment with methods that could be used elsewhere. One result was the development of a tenant-landlord covenant reflecting the reconciliatory goals of the AFSC, in which the owner promised to maintain the property in good order while the renters agreed to "take reasonably good care of the property and pay the rent on time."[22]

One day in August 1966, George Morrison, a local African American civil engineer who was hired to replace Dan Richardson when he left the staff, took a call that drew the organization into a conflict over public housing tenant rights. A woman from the Bromley Heath public housing complex in Jamaica Plain asked him to help her launch a complaint about mice, lead paint, deteriorating walls, and faulty heat. He called the city's housing inspection agency and was told that it could not inspect a public housing apartment. For six months, he and Bob Gustafson pressed the issue. They tried writing to the mayor and after a "suitable interval" went to the press. Ultimately, the city legal counsel decided that the inspection department did have jurisdiction over all city-owned property, thus helping bring about "enforcement of the sanitary code" in public housing. As Gustafson put it, this was an example of how "a complaint of a single tenant" could lead "to a change that will affect thousands."[23]

Morrison and Gustafson also nudged the city welfare department toward better practices regarding housing conditions for the poor. Morrison quickly realized that 80 percent of the complaints to CFA came from welfare recipients, meaning the city welfare department was paying for "inadequate and unsafe housing." In early 1966, he and Gustafson went with women from Mothers for Adequate Welfare to visit the staff of the Grove Hall Welfare Center, which served about fifteen thousand people in Roxbury and Dorchester. They described the "reception" as "icy," as a Miss Dugan told them that "their clients don't have housing problems." The Mothers for Adequate Welfare representatives begged to differ. By the end of the meeting, Gustafson proposed training welfare department staff about housing codes and how to file an inspection request and complaint. In November, he published a housing manual and distributed it to Grove Hall employees; in early 1967, AFSC staff and volunteers began using it to hold training seminars for social workers. The staff was proud of both their process and their accomplishment. As Gustafson described it, "Before last January, nobody, I repeat, nobody had been able to make a dent in the stone wall of the Welfare Department. We have not only made a dent; we've established a dialogue and have engaged both participation and support of the Welfare Department" in the preparation and use of the manual. He had no illusions that housing problems of those on public assistance would go away, but he felt that the manual was a first step, a catalyst for action toward a "city wide solution" to some of the worst conditions.[24]

Meanwhile, Morrison and Gustafson recognized the need to reach out to small-property owners and work with the "decent landlords" to address their concerns. In the spring of 1966, Morrison later recalled, a "lady came to us who had inherited some property" from her father. The buildings needed repairs and she'd had some problems with renters, but since the "social service agencies and civil rights groups were 'all caught up championing the tenants,'" she asked the Roxbury program for help.

Though not a Friend, Morrison responded in Quaker terms, saying that it made him realize "we need to look at both sides of the coin and try to help both if at all possible." The Roxbury program ran a work camp to fix up one of the woman's buildings, and then it started a property owners' association, ultimately called the Real Estate Owners' Association. From the members, Morrison learned that small owners in poor neighborhoods had trouble getting loans and insurance, plus they had transient tenants who did not take care of the apartments or skipped out without paying rent. Keeping in mind the need not to abuse the low-income people who found themselves in these buildings, he helped the owners learn both their rights and how to collaborate against specific problems like the piling up of garbage. By the summer of 1967, the group was growing and tentatively exploring holding joint meetings with tenant organizations.[25]

Launching the Urban Affairs Programs: Chicago

Nearly simultaneously with the development of the Call for Action and other efforts in Roxbury, the Chicago Regional Office launched the AFSC's first Urban Affairs Program (UAP), whose grassroots work in inner-city neighborhoods put the organization on the path to tenant union organizing. In 1964, in an effort to engage more directly with the local civil rights movement, Kale Williams had hired Bernard Lafayette to do nonviolent direct-action training for local community activists. Reflecting the AFSC's growing concern about the interrelationship of poverty and problems with housing, education, and discrimination in urban minority communities, however, Williams intended to develop a broader program that would "apply Friends testimonies of peace, equality and community to the intense human problems of urban society." The AFSC regional staff and volunteers were concerned about the slow pace of change in race relations, that the "white backlash" was causing the breakdown of communication between Blacks and whites, and that both situations deepened the "alienation of Negroes." Hinting at apprehensions about the budding Black Power movement, Chicago AFSC leaders warned that as a result of that alienation, "leadership dedicated to nonviolence may be supplanted by more militant and less restrained leaders." Since "old patterns for dealing with these problems are proving inadequate," they suggested a two-year effort to expand and combine some of the regional office's housing and youth opportunity work, leaving specifics of the program's tasks open so that Lafayette could discover "new approaches" to urban affairs.[26]

The UAP initially targeted East Garfield Park, a neighborhood located on the western edge of Chicago approximately four miles from the Loop downtown. The area had originally been annexed by the city in 1869 and encompassed the new Central—later Garfield—Park, one of the three large parks on the West Side. To the west lay West Garfield Park and to the south ran Lawndale. Before World War II, the neighborhood's residents were mainly middle-class Irish, German, Italian, and Russian families. But in the 1950s, African Americans displaced by construction of the Congress (later Eisenhower) Expressway began moving in, and by the end of the decade the neighborhood had transitioned from white to Black. Before Lafayette's arrival, the AFSC had cooperated with a local institution, the Warren Avenue Congregational Church, and had located its Project House in the neighborhood. The area was also served by other social service and justice organizations, including the West Side Federation, the West Side Christian Parish, and the Urban Progress Center of the Office of Economic Opportunity. Most pertinent to the AFSC's tenant work, in January 1966 the Southern Christian Leadership Conference also chose East Garfield Park as the center of its community organizing. Although both the AFSC and the SCLC focused on East Garfield Park because of its identity as a "slum," tenant organizing volunteer Herman Jenkins, who had grown up in the neighborhood, later recalled its "many blocks of neat gray stones and sunny, pleasant apartments as well as wide tree-lined boulevards of old mansions, all focused around the emerald-like Garfield Park itself." By the mid-1960s, the physical conditions of those structures had deteriorated because of landlord neglect, but the neighborhood remained home to people like Jenkins who were committed to making it "more livable both materially and spiritually."[27]

In the UAP, Lafayette and his staff pursued goals and used strategies reflecting AFSC and Quaker beliefs. As Colia Lafayette framed it, the program's primary task was "building a self-determining loving community." In AFSC terms, that meant "helping people mutually to recognize their essential worth as human beings" and their ability to work together to seek out "alternative solutions" to their problems. UAP staff were committed to demonstrating the role of nonviolence in community development and talked about creating the "beloved community" in East Garfield Park, by which they meant "a pleasant place to live in and where residents can develop to their full potential"—a vision shared by the early Housing Opportunities Programs. The invocation of the civil rights movement's beloved community as a goal in East Garfield Park illustrated how the UAP in Chicago combined long-standing AFSC values with influences from contemporary social movements. In specific terms, the regional office funded the UAP to work on housing conditions in the neighborhood for three years.[28] But in his first report, Lafayette articulated what he saw as the true spirit of his new position, declaring, "It should be the responsibility of leadership to develop leadership to replace itself."[29]

In his first months in his new job, Lafayette focused on nonviolence training, but in the early winter of 1965 he developed a proposal for a summer Community Organizational Project in collaboration with the regional office's College Program and Youth Opportunities Program. The young volunteers recruited to participate would not do "traditional community service kind of jobs" but instead would canvass the neighborhood "to see what people need and want and help local people develop leadership." Lafayette predicted that some possible outcomes might be a cooperative day care or a tenant council to agitate for improved housing conditions. In day-to-day practice, the project would resemble the community organizing work of the Community Action Projects of the War on Poverty—and indeed would rely on labor from members of the national service group VISTA (Volunteers in Service to America)—or the Economic Research and Action Projects of Students for a Democratic Society. Lafayette's proposal also incorporated Quaker and AFSC concerns when it emphasized "the application of the philosophy of nonviolence and the power of love in an urban community, where too often reliance in human relationships is placed upon physical and mental violence."[30]

Thus in the summer of 1965, at the same time Bill Moyer was leading the North Shore Summer Project for open housing in the suburbs, Bernard Lafayette's young volunteers organized low-income African Americans to press for improvement in inner-city housing. Their first goal was building or reviving block clubs in East Garfield Park and merging them into a United Block Club. Block clubs, which organized neighbors on a street both to socialize and to improve and control their own environment, dated back to the early Great Migration when the Urban League initiated them in response to the flood of newcomers into the city. Located primarily in African American and working- or lower-middle-class neighborhoods that lacked access to power, by the 1960s they had become a fruitful site for community organizing. Lafayette recalled that his team began by launching a recreational program for local kids and through that reaching the parents. They then responded to specific needs such as getting extra police to protect the neighborhood women from street harassment and forcing landlords to do repairs and install window screens. Lafayette argued that such "modest successes" strengthen morale, "bring hope and stretch the imagination," and perhaps most important, "lift the spirits of neighborhood people by demonstrating that a few people can change things." By the end of the project in early August, the volunteers had organized six blocks into clubs, and they planned to fan out to nearby streets.[31]

In late August as the summer project was wrapping up, a family emergency for the secretary of the Maypole Block Club triggered a new campaign. After she missed a meeting, Rachel Howard explained to Lafayette that she had rushed her son and daughter to Presbyterian-St. Luke's Hospital with swollen bellies. There she learned that both her children had lead poisoning from eating peeling paint chips off the walls and ceiling of their apartment. As Howard described the prognosis, Lafayette thought, "She was explaining this as a medical problem, and I thought it was a housing problem. . . . So I said 'that's exactly what we need to be working on.'" In the fall of 1965, he organized the Citizens Committee to End Lead Poisoning to talk with parents about the causes and symptoms of the illness. Dr. David Elwyn, who was associated with the Medical Committee for Human Rights, created a simple test for indicators of lead in the urine, and in the spring of 1966 high school students from the Student Organization for Urban Leadership began canvassing the neighborhood to collect urine samples. They set up a lab in the basement of Project House and ultimately screened over six hundred children. The program encountered some resistance from authorities at first. The Chicago director of health recoiled at the prospect of mass testing, telling Lafayette, "If we had this screening test you're talking about, the hospitals will be full." "So I asked him," Lafayette recalled, "'would you rather for the funeral homes to be full or the hospitals?'" Ultimately, the campaign was able to get Mayor Richard J. Daley to hire summer employees to do the lead testing, and Lafayette gave it some credit for raising the issue of unsafe paint in the Illinois state legislature. For the AFSC work in East Garfield Park, a secondary impact was that the campaign gave organizers an entrée into more homes; the canvassers could point to a specific problem that landlords were not addressing that threatened children.[32]

Meanwhile, a broader organizing effort was under way. In January 1966, the SCLC and the AFSC contacted "every church, block club, social agency, etc." in East Garfield Park and asked them to send representatives to a planning meeting for a communitywide People's Conference. Then, invitations went out to all residents of the neighborhood but no further, as the organizers wanted a "maximum of community people" and a "minimum of habitual meeting-goers." In February, 450 people attended the conference, held at the Mozart Baptist Church, and engaged in workshops on housing, income, and education. The day ended with a speech by Rev. Martin Luther King before an audience of seven hundred. The People's Conference passed resolutions calling on landlords to repair dangerous buildings and end the "color tax" by reducing rents to equal those paid by whites in similar structures. It also demanded that the city enforce building codes, demolish condemned structures quickly, and provide adequate garbage collection. Most important for the long-term trajectory of the AFSC's Urban Affairs and Housing Opportunities Programs, the conference resolved "to organize East Garfield Park on a building-by-building, block-by-block basis, forming a tenant union." The purpose of the union would be to "educate people about the forces that create slums; to process grievances, [and] to work out a strategy for accomplishing the above goals," which might include "appropriate action such as picketing or rent strikes."[33]

The First Target and the First Contract

The idea for a tenant union in East Garfield Park "evolved during months of meetings in Bernard [Lafayette]'s apartment," promoted by him and Tony Henry. United tenant protest had had a long history in major US cities by this point, including a series of rent strikes in Harlem just a few years earlier in 1963 and 1964.[34] Lafayette later recalled that the presence of powerful local labor unions in Chicago had convinced the UAP team that collective bargaining could and should be used to address problems in rental housing. He argued that the root problem causing "cancerous pockets of slums" was an imbalance of power, which allowed landlords to make profits by keeping rents high while spending a minimum on the upkeep of their buildings. The city was not going to do much about that. And as individuals, tenants were powerless to do so. Instead, when they confronted their landlords and asked for basic repairs, they were treated with "gross disrespect." Collective bargaining through a union could correct that imbalance and help residents "demand and expect living quarters fit for human habitation." Moreover, tenant organizing appealed to those searching for a nonviolent way to engender power and self-determination in the inner-city Black community, making it one way to answer the rising calls for Black Power.[35]

In the spring of 1966, the UAP, the SCLC, and other neighborhood organizations formed the East Garfield Park Union to End Slums. The organizers divided the neighborhood into eleven sections, or "locals," borrowing language from the labor movement; the UAP was assigned Local #1, which included a ten-block area housing about seven thousand people. Block clubs organized tenant groups in each building on their street; each group then selected a building steward to represent them on a grievance committee. The eleven locals elected representatives to the union strategy committee to oversee the whole project. To arouse interest, the union printed and circulated a flyer throughout the neighbor-hood explaining that collective bargaining was "the method for introduc-ing the ways of democracy into the landlord tenant relationships." The flyer also described what unions could do with "strength in numbers" and charged that landlords had forced tenants into collective bargaining by refusing to negotiate. Minnie Dunlap, who had moved to East Garfield Park from Mississippi five years earlier, recalled that at first, she just "stepped over" the flyer when it came through her mail slot and put it "in the garbage." But she had a hole in her wall that the landlord refused to fix. When two young people came to her door and said they would get her wall fixed if she would attend a union meeting, she changed her mind. Dunlap went on to become one of the union's key organizers. Af-ter holding meetings in individual buildings, Local #1 held its first mass gathering at the Church of Christ, at which about eighty people sang freedom songs and heard about the purpose and structure of the union.[36]

Throughout the spring and summer of 1966, union organizing took place at a block-by-block, building-by-building, and person-to-person level. To help with the legwork, in April Lafayette secured twenty VISTA volunteers and a grant-funded supervisor, who began arriving in June and going door-to-door to talk with people about the union. Teenagers from the Student Organization for Urban Leadership joined them as the lead poisoning campaign wound down. Their first task was to encourage residents to attend an informational meeting and join the union. Once a majority of the tenants in a building "decide[d] that they [were] tired of letting themselves and their children live in dangerous conditions," together they drew up a list of complaints. Building stewards then pre-sented their grievances to the landlord or management company and awaited a response. If none was forthcoming, tenants launched a rent strike, which the union called "one of the ways to end slums by forcing landlords to repair their buildings and keep them that way." During a strike, residents withheld their rent or gave it to the union to hold until either repairs were made or the landlord agreed to negotiate, with the union representing all the tenants. The union also conducted nonviolent direct action in the form of pickets or sit-ins to pressure the landlords to respond to grievances and, ultimately, sign a tenant-landlord contract.[37]

In the initial months of organizing, the Union to End Slums leaders chose to focus on buildings managed by Condor and Costalis, one of the largest rental management companies on Chicago's West Side. Owned by John Condor and Louis Costalis, the firm managed approximately sixty to eighty buildings in the area in the mid-1960s. In March, the own-ers attended an open forum moderated by Rev. Martin Luther King at which six hundred residents heard testimony about housing conditions on the West Side. At the end, Condor and Costalis pledged to work with tenants to try to improve conditions. Once building-level protests and rent withholding began, however, the firm became less sympathetic. Organizers and residents began to picket the company offices and promised to continue until the officers agreed to negotiate with the union. Some tenants began informally withholding their rent, but the union put off a large-scale rent strike until more buildings had been organized. The company responded by sending eviction notices to the withholding families, whom the union urged to stay in their apartments. Then on June 20, company officials came to a mass meeting and delivered an injunction against four individuals and the union, prohibiting demonstrations in the business offices and banning organizers from entering Condor and Costalis properties for the purpose of talking about the union. The Urban Affairs Program and the union staffs continued to picket, but they talked with people only indirectly about rent strikes. At a hearing on the injunction on June 28, the judge ordered Condor and Costalis to hold at least one negotiating session with the union. On June 30 the tenants, their negotiators, and Condor and Costalis officials met, and the union presented them with a draft contract. Another session was scheduled for early July. In the meantime, two children fell off ramshackle porches in Condor and Costalis buildings and were injured, one fatally. The parents sued the company for negligence in failing to make repairs, thus increasing the pressure on it.[38]

On July 12, 1966, "five men and two women" representing the Union to End Slums "gathered around a scarred wooden table in a faded Chicago Church" and signed a contract with Condor and Costalis. The key element of the agreement was that the company accepted the union as a representative for all tenants. Moreover, the landlord promised to make repairs that were reported through the union. Immediately, the union urged tenants to submit complaints about bugs, lead paint, hallway lighting, janitor service, and other common problems. If repairs were not made, the tenants had the right to pay their rent to a third party, who would hold it in escrow until landlords acted or use the money to do the maintenance required. In return, the union promised that tenants would put their refuse in garbage cans, take care of their apartments, and "cooperate with reasonable rules and regulations." The feeling of victory was expressed by AFSC volunteer Sally Olds, who in an essay for *Christian Century* called the contract the "Magna Carta of the nation's slum tenants," because it gave renters a way to force landlords to fulfill their obligations. Although this was not the first tenant union–landlord contract in Chicago—Jobs or Income Now, a subunit of the local Students for a Democratic Society, had signed a similar agreement a month earlier—the Condor and Costalis agreement went further by including provisions for a rent strike. Condor inspired optimism for the success of the new relationship when at the signing ceremony he declared the contract to be "'an important step for the welfare of the community and for the benefit of his business.'" The next task for the organizers was to get the residents of other buildings managed by Condor and Costalis into the union so that they would be covered by the contract.[39]

Building the Tenant Union Movement

Ignited by the success at Condor and Costalis, union organizers spread out to other neighborhoods and targeted additional rental management companies during the rest of the summer. Thanks in part to the work of VISTA volunteers and to the tenants themselves, mass meetings, rent strikes, and picketing began popping up in buildings in Local #1's territory as well as in nearby Lawndale. Indeed, Bernard Lafayette wrote weekly reports featuring a rapid-fire list of actions. In late July, Local #1 was negotiating with three small landlords in buildings once managed by Condor and Costalis while its compatriots in Lawndale opened negotiations with building owners who wanted to avoid rent strikes. Even some larger companies, including Atlas and Balin, sent feelers to the union about talks, and two others seemed likely to follow. Meanwhile, organizers identified buildings in the worst shape and talked with tenants about joining the union, filing grievances, and backing up complaints with a rent strike. By the first week in August, according to Lafayette, more buildings were "becoming ready to rent strike every few days."[40]

Signs of such grassroots enthusiasm and leadership heartened and inspired the UAP staff. In one incident, while a small group of tenants were meeting in the yard of a building the landlord called the police, who made the gathering break up. The tenants moved to the sidewalk, and then the rest of the residents walked out of the building and straight into the union, signing up for membership on the spot. In another case, when a staff organizer was late for a meeting in one building, the resident steward from next door came over and simply took charge. Very quickly, local African American women stepped up to take leadership positions in the union. In addition to Minnie Dunlap, who was an organizer and the first president of Union to End Slums, Mary Brown became a steward in a Condor and Costalis building. She persuaded people to join the union by pointing out that "When you're born Negro and poor, you're automatically involved." Vernedia White succeeded Dunlap as union president. She also became a cause célèbre when she went through the union's first jury trial, fighting an eviction for rent withholding and winning. Building the union in East Garfield Park was a cooperative effort between such local leaders, the AFSC UAP staff, and VISTA volunteers, but ultimately it depended on the interest and enthusiasm of the tenants.[41]

As union organizing spread through the area, residents and their UAP staff supporters ran into more resistance. Some smaller landlords claimed they could not afford to make the requested repairs, while others justified their opposition in more ideological terms. According to the *Wall Street Journal*, Jacob Sampson, who owned a "decaying four story apartment building 'which has literally been taken over by tenants,'" accused the union of being a "communist conspiracy," while James C. Downs, head of the Real Estate Research Corporation, feared that the tenants' organizations would "thwart the operation of the free market." In short, many a landlord believed he had "the right to keep his property in bad shape and you have the right to leave." Hostile landlords and management companies met rent strikes with eviction notices or simply refused to negotiate at all. For example, the Hanover Equities Corporation, which owned the Old Town Gardens, sent vacate letters to two hundred families and evicted seven of them. The union pushed back, however, launching pickets at the offices of the companies and helping six families move back into Old Town Gardens after their evictions were served. Through the late summer and fall of 1966, East Garfield Park and Lawndale became hotbeds of negotiations, rent strikes, eviction notices and resistance to them, picketing, other direct action, and court appearances for those arrested.[42]

Still, some of the largest property management firms, the peers of Condor and Costalis, stonewalled. At the start of August, it seemed that Atlas and Balin might be cooperative as they approached the union for negotiations. But then relations soured. The East Garfield Park organizers focused on three Balin-managed buildings. Gilbert Balin, who "often articulated the slumlords' position," refused to talk. In late September, after tenants picketed his offices for about a week asking for a meeting, a dozen of them decided to hold a sit-in inside. Balin had the doors locked to block them and they were taken to the police station, though not arrested. The following Saturday, picketing resumed. During one demonstration, Balin stepped outside and agreed to negotiate, but he repeatedly failed to appear at scheduled meetings. In October, the union decided to try another approach and reached out to the building owners instead. When they, too, refused to talk, the tenants began picketing at their homes along with the Balin offices. The impasse broke in late November, when a new owner bought the three buildings, began repairs, dropped the eviction proceedings and the trespassing charges, and promised to meet once a month with a tenant committee about grievances. He also found a new manager to replace Balin, who continued to resist the union by requesting an injunction against picketing at his home office or the buildings he managed. The confrontation had mixed results. The tenants in the three buildings at the center of the conflict won an agreement with the new owner, giving them some protections and a way to improve conditions. But one of the largest management companies in the area never yielded to collective bargaining.[43]

Atlas Realty, another major firm on the West Side, likewise resisted working with the union. Much of the action regarding that company took place next door in Lawndale and with the Lawndale Union to End Slums and its successor, the Lawndale Community Union. As with Balin, the union conducted sit-ins and picketing, and the company responded with evictions. When three union staff moved a family back into their apartment, they were arrested and charged with trespassing. In late September, Atlas agreed to a moratorium on evictions and to negotiate in return for a cessation of direct action. Tensions came to a head, however, when the company violated that agreement by walking out of negotiations. Only after Martin Luther King Jr. began a tour of Atlas-managed buildings in Lawndale, bringing press attention to conditions there, did company representatives agree to settle the cases against nineteen women awaiting hearings on their evictions and to drop other trespass charges. A month later, Atlas signed a contract with the union. But in a last-minute turn of events, the company claimed it could not afford to make the repairs on the Lawndale buildings that were the focus of the conflict, and it said it wanted to sell them. Six months later, the Lawndale Community Union, Atlas Realty, and the Kate Maremont Foundation agreed that foundation would purchase nine Atlas buildings in that neighborhood, rehabilitate them, and convert them into tenant cooperatives.[44]

Similarly, the sale or transfer of buildings was one outcome of a renewed and increasingly tense battle between Condor and Costalis and the Union to End Slums. Just over a month after signing the tenant-landlord contract, a group of stewards representing Condor and Costalis buildings had presented a list of grievances and received promises that improvements would start soon. But by early October 1966, the company still had refused to set up a fact-finding panel or select an escrow party to collect rents. The residents of one building decided to move forward on their own and asked the Chicago Church Federation to act as an escrow agent and collect the rents until repairs were made. That move got a quick response. Claiming that the building owners were operating at a loss, John Condor proposed making repairs but also raising rents. When tenants rejected the proposal and continued the strike, Condor and Costalis served nine eviction notices on strikers. For a time, it looked as though the eviction actions might go to court, serving as a test case for the collective bargaining agreement. But instead, the company agreed to make the repairs without raising rent and the tenants agreed to start paying again once that work had begun. More important, in November Condor and Costalis agreed to sell the building to a nonprofit corporation selected by the union.[45]

A few months later, several other Condor and Costalis buildings prepared to strike because of "overflowing garbage cans, falling plaster and broken mailboxes." Mary Brown, who had persuaded the residents to strike and was now representing them, wrote the company, telling it to "either get out or put money into the building to make necessary repairs." Illustrating the nitty-gritty of negotiations, Brown specified that three-fourths of the submitted grievances be addressed and three-fourths of the apartments be repainted and/or redecorated. The union by this time had collected over $1,000 in rent, and representatives said they would release the money to the company when bills for the repairs and painting were presented. The company agreed to do the repairs but not the repainting. It also issued eviction notices for all the tenants in Brown's building because of their failure to pay rent. The tenants insisted that at least three rooms per apartment be painted, and they voted to extend the rent strike until that was done. Ultimately, the company agreed to paint the rooms and the strike ended. But negotiations over the eviction notices lingered on. Meanwhile, a broken broiler led residents of another building to join the union en masse and launch a strike, and those at still another demanded that the company investigate the myriad maintenance issues or face rent-withdrawals. These conflicts led to Condor and Costalis's decision in late May 1967 to sell one building and turn the mortgage to two others over to the Southern Christian Leadership Foundation to hold until a citywide cooperative association could buy them.[46]

Exploring Tenant Cooperatives

The transfer of properties from Atlas and from Condor and Costalis to nonprofits and activist organizations demonstrated the overlap of union organizing with another strategy to address the housing needs of low-income urban residents: tenant cooperatives. Section 221d3 of the 1961 Housing Act provided long-term mortgages at interest below market rate for nonprofit housing, and it allowed the mortgage to cover part of the purchase and renovation of older buildings or the construction of new ones. In August 1965, the Urban Affairs Committee discussed pursuing such a project for the low-income residents of East Garfield Park, arguing that it could provide decent apartments at lower rents, a model of cooperative ownership, and an "experience of real democracy on a small scale." That fall, Bernard Lafayette, Tony Henry, and program committee member Irwin Kipnis started looking for possible properties for sale in East Garfield Park that could be purchased and developed perhaps in collaboration with the new East Garfield Park Cooperative Association. Early in 1966, Kipnis reported he had identified eighteen such properties.[47]

But the staff of the UAP and the people in the neighborhood debated the wisdom or feasibility of an organization like the AFSC undertaking the development of low-income housing, even with federal funds. In early discussions, some program committee members raised the question of whether the AFSC should support a housing development in East Garfield Park, which would almost certainly be all Black and thus "segregated." In response, one member of the Urban Affairs Committee insisted that "housing has to be improved before there can be integration." More pointedly, the committee maintained that "exploitation is a major prop for prejudice, and that the elimination of exploitation ought therefore to be a prior goal of any action-oriented program."[48] But when Jane Weston researched the question, she found a lack of enthusiasm for cooperatives among urban studies experts in Chicago. More damning, however, AFSC representatives learned at a meeting with the United Block Club members that while local people were interested in ownership, they did not favor cooperative arrangements or large, densely populated units.[49]

Despite these signs of ambivalence, over the next two years the Urban Affairs staff in the Chicago office remained interested in supporting nonprofit community efforts to purchase and rehabilitate housing in East Garfield Park. In addition to lowering rents, cooperative tenant ownership and management seemed to be one way to empower local people to take control of their communities and conditions—goals aligned with the sentiments of the Black Power movement. Moreover, new federal policies as well as local and national nonprofit organizations promised financial support. Finally, six months of experience had taught the union organizers that "when pressured to make repairs to make slum buildings decent, landlords sell because it is no longer profitable for them to operate." A potential solution was for nonprofit organizations in the community to buy those buildings and either run them themselves or turn them over to the tenants to manage or even own.[50]

The possibility of accomplishing this goal increased in late 1966 when the Community Renewal Foundation, formed by the Chicago Missionary Society, received $4 million in mortgage insurance from the Federal Housing Administration to rehabilitate structures on the West Side. The foundation's program reflected mainline liberal Protestants' interest in

urban antipoverty work, which made churches one of the largest financial supporters of nonprofit housing in the nation. Jess Gill, who worked
for both the foundation and the SCLC, began seeking buildings in the
neighborhood to purchase. Meanwhile, in addition to the outcomes of
the Atlas and Condor and Costalis strikes, a few small landlords also
negotiated selling their properties. For the rest of the decade, the Urban Affairs Program continued to monitor and advocate for more such
transfers. The AFSC's role in these cooperative initiatives was not, like
the churches or their foundations, to plan or construct the housing or
operate the buildings but rather to organize and train the residents for
tenant ownership and management.[51]

Meanwhile, as organizing and rent strikes spread throughout East Garfield Park and surrounding neighborhoods, Lafayette and others worked
to bring people into a unified and more influential organization for joint
actions and mutual support. Already by the end of August 1966, there had
been Unions to End Slums in East Garfield Park, Lawndale, and South
Shore, as well as on the Near North Side, where it was called the Tenant
Action Council. Lafayette represented East Garfield Park in a meeting to
form an umbrella group, the City-Wide Tenant Union Federation, which
originally consisted of ten unions from around the poor areas of Chicago. In its first year, the group met with members of the Illinois Housing Commission about legislation that would protect tenant collective
bargaining rights, and it worked with a committee of lawyers to draw up
a model tenant-landlord contract. Lafayette sowed seeds for the group's
later activism when he headed a committee to talk about the city's urban renewal plans and discuss strategies for how to react to them. Approximately a year after the federation formed, however, he resigned from
the UAP and left Chicago to join Boston's Ecumenical Center. His role
there would be to direct a new program combining federal and local government resources with the work of local community organizations for
pursuing a multipronged approach to the problems of the people in the
Roxbury neighborhood. After Lafayette's departure, Tony Henry became
the director of the UAP and assumed leadership of the joint efforts of
tenant unions on the West Side.[52]

The AFSC and the Black Power Movement

Lafayette's move to New England was in part a result of events there
that sparked an AFSC-wide consideration of the relationship between the
organization's Community Relations Division and the Black Power movement. The roots of that movement reached deep into the long century
of struggle for African American self-determination through social soli-

darity, political and economic power, and cultural identity.[53] But in the summer and fall of 1966, the phrase "Black Power" rocketed through the civil rights community after SNCC leader Stokely Carmichael invoked it during a rally in Greenwood, Mississippi. Frustration with the lack of real change in the experience of Black people and the search for new strategies for achieving more genuine liberation and empowerment coalesced into an invigorated and increasingly compelling movement. Responding to what they saw as rising tensions between Blacks and whites over the future of the freedom struggle, in September 1966 members of the AFSC Northeast Regional Office in Cambridge hosted the Conference on the Racial Crisis. The dialogue at that meeting made clear the growing gulf between whites who felt that the civil rights movement and the War on Poverty were doing enough to combat racism and inequality, and African Americans' insistence that much more needed to be done and indeed the job had just begun. The question coming out of the meeting was whether the AFSC, with its "strongly held belief in nonviolence, the dignity of all men, the importance of reconciliation, and the necessity of using just means to attain good ends," could take the radical actions needed to challenge structural inequities. More important, could the majority white AFSC support African Americans as "they develop a sense of pride in themselves and in their race" and engage in the "wholesome process of achieving through organization the political and social strength" that would enable them to determine the future of their communities?[54]

After the Conference on the Racial Crisis, the Northeast Regional Office decided to dedicate its 1967 Avon Institute to seeking answers to those questions. The Avon Institute was an annual summer function begun in 1953 and hosted by the NERO Peace Education Committee. In March, invitations went out for the event, with the message that it would offer an opportunity to "bring together people from low-income inner-city communities with those from peace and civil rights groups in the suburbs to talk about the racial crisis," with the ultimate goal of examining the link between "peace and poverty, at home and abroad." The institute, held July 29 through August 5 at Lake Winnipesaukee in New Hampshire, was attended by approximately three hundred people, including thirty-three African Americans. The other participants were not all Friends but "like minded largely middle-class white suburbanites interested in current issues." Blacks and whites alike came expecting lectures, conversation, and interracial living.[55]

According to George Morrison of the AFSC office in Roxbury, the Avon proceedings "got off to a good start." Bernard Lafayette "hit the nail on the head" with a report on the shifting mood in Chicago, explaining that "Black people are saying that since we could not break out, we are going to stay in the ghetto and own it and control it." The agenda also included Bryant Rollins, a former *Boston Globe* reporter now with the Urban League, who called the AFSC "neo-colonialistic" and "unable to deal with the things out in the streets." Rollins also introduced the Black Power Manifesto that had been produced by a conference in Newark just before Avon. Attendees then heard from Black nationalist Omar Ahmed, who argued that "instead of mouthing rhetoric about brotherhood, white people should begin working among themselves to create the kind of society in which brotherhood may be possible." But speakers then "veered off into international topics," including the war in Southeast Asia, and away from the situation in the inner cities. Frustrated and feeling they were being used "as a crutch," some of the African American participants called for a meeting of a separate Black caucus. A few of the Black attendees hesitated, but in the end they all joined the walkout. After a day of meeting separately, the Black caucus returned to present ten resolutions, and it asked the institute participants to endorse them in their entirety.[56]

The white participants were divided in their response to this turn of events. NERO representatives later recalled that many of the attendees were "paralyzed, very upset"; "they felt alone, deserted, rejected." Some could not overcome their feeling that "the unity of the institute had been destroyed," and they left. Others felt that the resolutions amounted to an ultimatum for the AFSC to change its ways or "get out of the ghetto." But several white attendees embraced the caucus's challenge, seeing it as an opportunity to address the emerging phenomenon of Black Power. Some expressed the urgency of doing so. As one participant in the conversation among whites put it, "Either we accept this and respond to it positively or the society will come crashing down." Fay Knopp, the head of the Avon Institute, argued that African Americans needed time to "help themselves their way," and when whites and Blacks rejoined together it could be from a "different moral premise." More generally, the sympathetic whites discussed the need to "exercise responsible white power" and change attitudes in their own communities. Perhaps most dramatically, Bob Gustafson volunteered to resign from his leadership of the Roxbury program. He followed up a few days later with a formal letter of resignation effective December 1, stating that he wanted to make way for a Black male director for the Roxbury program as a step toward the "jolting" changes the AFSC needed to make. In the end, 100 out of 147 whites remaining for the debate approved the resolutions, 30 more wrote a statement backing them in spirit if not in all the details, and a group of teenagers made their own separate endorsement.[57]

The confrontation at Avon inspired introspection in the Community Relations Division about how its programs might respond, or were

FIGURE 5.2: Barbara Moffett, head of the Community Relations Division. Courtesy of the American Friends Service Committee Archives, Philadelphia.

already responding, to Black Power. In the fall of 1967, division head Barbara Moffett (fig. 5.2) organized a series of meetings at the Philadelphia headquarters and in regional offices in Boston, Oakland, and Baltimore to discuss how "agencies like the AFSC" might restructure their relationship to African American communities and commit resources to addressing urban problems while leaving the "power and responsibility in the hands of Black leadership and groups." She brought to this challenging task what Southern Program activist Connie Curry called her "total clarity on the principles of civil rights and civil liberties" and her reputation for having "understood the importance of empowerment before it became fashionable." Perhaps most important, although she was not a Friend, she had a strong ability to help a group come to consensus. Moffett launched the division's dialogue, stating that she believed that majority white organizations like the AFSC were not being asked to leave inner-city minority communities, but rather that Black militants were saying "do not run away, but stay and be tested. Are you with us in terms of work which will build our strength and power?" She did not expect there would be unanimity on the proper AFSC response. What would unite that response, however, was a shared conviction that "the basic impulse [of Black Power] is that of people wanting the power to make the decisions which affect their lives."[58]

The challenge for the AFSC, as Moffett saw it, was "to sort out which demands of Black Power run counter to [AFSC and Friends] principles" and which run counter only to "habit and convenience." In the discussions trying to sort that out, three key points surfaced consistently. First was the problem of separatism, specifically the demand that AFSC programs in the Black community be led by African American men. Percy Baker, an African American who had worked with the Housing Opportunities Program in Richmond, California, pointed out that satisfying that demand would not be that much of a stretch, because one "AFSC purpose is to discover and develop indigenous leadership." He and others argued, however, that jobs should not be restricted only to African Americans, because the AFSC was "supposed to be color blind and hire on merit," and because it wanted to keep the door open for whites to experience the challenge of working in a Black setting. Baker acknowledged that separatism as a strategy for enhancing "self-direction and self-esteem" was understandable. Other staff members agreed, drawing the comparison to other ethnic and immigrant groups and arguing that African Americans could not really "participate in society on an equal basis without the separate development of the power to do so." But integration remained a priority for the organization, and participants in these debates often voiced the determination to protect it where it was occurring. Moreover, they worried that the "exclusive" nature of the Black Power movement could, in Baker's words, result in "solidifying separateness." Eleanor Eaton, a white Friend and longtime member of the CRD, expressed concern that such separateness required seeing people in starkly divided groups and thus denied "the value of an individual as an individual," which was a basic Quaker and AFSC value. They understood that Black militants saw integration, at least in the short run, as part of the problem, but the AFSC leaders believed that their faith required them to continue to fight for it.[59]

The second and perhaps most obvious key point was that AFSC staff worried about the "contradiction between peace and violence." The rejection of nonviolence in the search for new strategies and even the harshness of Black militants' rhetoric seemed to cut to the core of Quaker and AFSC principles. Compromise on this point was not negotiable. Even before the Avon confrontation, a group of NERO staff drew up a statement in which they affirmed their commitment to "a respectful and loving approach to all men, including those who most vigorously oppose values which the AFSC deems eminently worthwhile." They rejected the idea of working for "social change at any price" if that price included abandoning their principles of nonviolence and reconciliation. In the wake of Avon, Percy Baker seemed to think it not worth even discussing "the avowal of violence as a means of protest by some Black Power elements," because it "is so completely alien to our philosophy." Community relations leaders largely agreed with him, though they tried to see the militants' perspective and to understand that "until the lot of the oppressed minorities in America is objectively better," there would be violence inherent in the status quo. Still, the AFSC's goal was a nonviolent society, its strategy was "honest and creative communication," and its paramount commitment was a rejection of "violence as a means to attaining an end."[60]

Finally, participants in these dialogues complained about the "contradiction between democracy and totalitarianism" in Black Power rhetoric and approach. They recognized that "the demand for greater power to make decisions affecting their own lives is a basically democratic one on the part of Black power advocates." But several people criticized the tendency to issue demands "in the manner of totalitarian leaders." As Irene Osborne of the school desegregation program pointed out, at Black Power conferences, "resolutions were presented as either/or" or with a "take it or leave it attitude." For example, at Avon in 1967 the Black caucus called for an up or down vote on its entire list of demands rather than allow debate on them individually. A year later, militants attending the Avon 1968 meeting gave the AFSC two weeks to decide whether to donate $10,000 to a Black Power conference. Some people reacted negatively just from personal distaste. Baker bluntly said, "I just don't like ultimatums," because they were "a tactic designed to compel confrontation." But such provisos also ran up against the "three centuries" of Quaker tradition and decades of AFSC practice of a "group centered decision-making process" which relied on a "sense of the meeting." These ways were more than just "habit or convenience." They were rooted in beliefs about the value of each individual conscience. They led to a slow national AFSC response to militants' demands and thus exacerbated conflict, but the CRD staff argued that such respect for individual conscience also opened the way for diverse relationships between staff in regional offices and local Black Power leaders.[61]

Despite concerns about these tensions, participants in the AFSC dialogues always couched their discussions about Black Power in terms of a desire to react positively to this new current in the African American community. As members of the CRD Executive Committee determined early, "We are at a desperate point of confrontation and must respond creatively." Barbara Moffett urged people to focus on the positive aspects of Black Power and to see it as a "new assertion from Black communities to take initiative in addressing wrongs, [and] in gaining leadership and control over areas of their lives." The Chicago staff added that this "surge of energy" had "great potential for constructive action." Indeed, the emphases on "self-respect and self-determination" were "congenial" and even fundamental to the AFSC's community relations approach. In describing their urban affairs work, staff proposed that the AFSC was uniquely suited to reaching out to Black militants because the organization had long strived to empower the powerless. The changing context required a "sensitive and understanding cooperation" rather than a "strongly directive program" for successful outreach, but such an approach was already the hallmark of the East Garfield Park program under Bernard Lafayette and Tony Henry. The CRD staff pointed out that other inner-city programs were by that time largely under Black leadership and that white people who worked in those communities had mostly been accepted. Most important, the AFSC's "commitment to radical social change based on the power of love to change people's lives" made it able to work constructively and across racial lines in the "fragile network of interdependence" of the inner city.[62]

In these discussions, AFSC staff struggled to determine how the organization could accommodate the new context and demands, particularly in its Urban Affairs Programs, which had by this point spread to regional offices nationwide. UAP participants proposed serving as fund-raisers for indigenous Black Power organizations and allowing local groups to use office space and the AFSC name as long as they did not violate basic principles. Barbara Moffett believed that one of most important roles for the AFSC was that of a bridge, helping concerned but bewildered whites understand and not be frightened by the demands of Black Power. As noted by Perry Ottenberg, a white Philadelphia psychiatrist who for years had been involved with the Community Relations Executive Committee, the AFSC could help people "deal with their emotional responses in a creative way" by "not getting either immobilized or cancelling themselves out with overwhelming guilt." Reflecting the Black Power demand that whites organize against racism among whites, regional office staff suggested that the AFSC could "engage white and comfortable Americans" to meet the "challenge to share power and to cope with the racism and acceptance of privilege which characterize too many lives and institutions." By early 1968, these discussions had produced a set of "operating principles" for reconciling AFSC values with Black Power ideology, including the need to "provide resources without dominating" and "recognize the validity of group identity." Traditional rhetoric about employing "ways of change which recognize the worth of all people—the powerful and the presently powerless" now appeared alongside calls to help whites learn to "share power" and preserve the "values of diversity." Tensions did not go away, however: for the next two years, national AFSC leaders continued to debate how to respond to Black militants in ways that preserved the organization's commitment to nonviolence. But many of the staff in the regional offices moved forward with making practical efforts to adjust programs to the new climate.[63]

INCORPORATING BLACK POWER INTO
HOUSING WORK: ROXBURY

One successful and enduring example of that adjustment arose from the Northeast Regional Office's response to the Avon conflict. In the fall of 1967, NERO established a Roxbury Community Committee (RCC) with twenty members, including eight public housing tenants and young people. A young African American, Lloyd King, became chair of the RCC and represented it on the executive committee of NERO. The RCC had veto power over hiring staff for the Roxbury work and chose to have George Morrison replace Robert Gustafson as program director in the neighborhood.[64] The committee members, reflecting the spirit of the Black Power movement, insisted that going forward, "power and authority for self-determination must be put into the hands of Blacks who live in urban communities." Thus, over the next six months NERO and the RCC hammered out an agenda and a relationship that reflected these new dynamics in Black-white relations and ongoing concerns about the urban crisis. For its program, the RCC would continue the Call for Action hotline, engage in tenant union organizing, and train community activists.[65]

In the next two years, the RCC reorganized, became more independent, and renamed itself the Roxbury Action Project (RAP). George Morrison continued his role as director, and at first the group's focus remained on tenant organizing through the Call for Action program and sporadic rent withholding to pressure landlords. In 1969, RAP wanted to progress further, toward tenant self-determination over housing. Morrison, King, and others believed that control over resources, especially homeownership, was vital to empowerment of individuals and the Black community as a whole. To accomplish that, they turned to a model of cooperative and/or tenant-controlled housing similar to that experimented with in Chicago after the rent strikes. After a fire destroyed its original office, RAP moved to the Highland Park neighborhood, which had deteriorating but once quality housing stock and a declining population. With help from former AFSC staff person James Morely, who developed a model for financing low-income housing development, and a grant from the Massachusetts Housing Finance Agency, RAP purchased dilapidated buildings in the neighborhood, rehabbed them using local labor, leased the apartments, and with the income reinvested in more buildings and in community organization. The goal was to turn the buildings over slowly to tenant ownership as cooperatives over a five-year period.[66]

Roxbury's African American leaders saw the AFSC's role in all this as purely financial and insisted that "resources must be committed to this process with no strings attached." Local and national AFSC staff endorsed continued monetary support for first the RCC and then RAP based on shared principles of "nonviolence, equality, social justice, and the worth and dignity of the individual," which had been central to the AFSC's community relations mission and housing work from the beginning, and a mutual commitment to "self-determination and development of grassroots leadership," which had increasingly informed its strategies since the early 1960s. When the RCC became RAP, the AFSC promised to provide $46,000 a year for two years to support its program in organizing tenants and improving slum conditions. In September 1969, RAP leaders asked the AFSC national board for $325,000 over the next three years, $25,000 of it immediately so that they could buy more old properties in the Highland Park neighborhood and begin rehabbing them. The national Community Relations Committee, citing other priorities requiring funds—including its efforts against the war in Vietnam—provided the $25,000 and promised to help RAP with fund-raising up to $10,000 a year through 1971. In describing the relationship and promoting donations to the project, NERO leaders argued that "RAP is making the rhetoric of community development a reality, working in a financially feasible way that guarantees community control, organizing for the long-term not the temporary crisis, and getting people training and educating the citizenry." Despite the strain on AFSC resources, they believed that supporting RAP was one way they could respond to Black Power, facilitate the development of low-income housing, and most important, at least indirectly help inner-city residents fulfill their own housing needs.[67]

EMPOWERING BLACK COMMUNITIES FOR BETTER HOUSING: CHICAGO

In Chicago, the Urban Affairs and the Housing Opportunities Program staffs began talking about Black Power almost immediately after Stokely Carmichael's 1966 speech in Greenwood and quickly incorporated some of the new movement's concepts into their work. Indeed, Lafayette and others regarded what they were doing in East Garfield Park as reflecting the same fundamental goals as those of Black Power. Specifically, the community organizing in that neighborhood aimed to "give the residents . . . control over their own destinies." Over the next two years, the AFSC staff articulated two paths for finding creative "ways to respond to the feeling of powerlessness" in the Black community and securing "community involvement in decision making and local self-determination." One emphasized ownership and control of resources in the community through creating "locally controlled democratic enterprises in which management and ownership are in the hands of local people, like cooperative businesses, [and] cooperative and condominium home ownership." The other empowered renters through their numbers and solidarity to stand up to landlords and city housing authorities and improve their living conditions. Both strategies grew out of the expanding membership, goals, and actions of the tenant union.[68]

In the wake of Bernard Lafayette's departure, the City-Wide Tenant Union Federation became the Chicago Tenant Union (CTU), and by the fall of 1968 had five hundred members. The AFSC continued to support the union through the staff time of Tony Henry (fig. 5.3) and Major Beverly, who was hired after Lafayette left, and by turning the Project House over to the CTU to use as its headquarters.[69] The rechristened and expanded CTU gained attention in late 1968 with a new tactic for addressing the housing problems of West Side residents: a "camp-in." On Friday, October 4, four mothers and their children moved into tents in the 172-acre Garfield Park. This protest followed months of complaints that families left homeless by urban renewal had not been relocated. The CTU demanded that the city provide housing by leasing property in vacant buildings, renting apartments, and purchasing mobile homes for those who lost their shelter because of redevelopment/slum clearance, building condemnations resulting from code violations, fires, and even evictions. On Saturday, the Department of Urban Renewal moved the women and their children into mobile homes in the neighborhood. A few weeks later, ten families who faced eviction because their buildings had been condemned moved with their possessions into the mayor's office in City Hall. Daley refused to meet with them, but again officials from the Department of Urban Renewal promised to find them housing. A week later, because those promises had not been kept, seventeen families returned to Daley's office. As the five o'clock deadline for leaving or otherwise facing trespassing charges approached and it became clear that the families would not leave, Charles Swibel, chair of the Chicago Housing Authority, promised to move them into public housing apart-

FIGURE 5.3: Kale Williams (*left*) and Tony Henry (*right*) at a news conference, 1965. Photograph number ST-60003518-0021 in the Chicago Sun-Times Collection. Courtesy of the Chicago History Museum, Chicago.

ments the next day. The protests had worked for these families, but CTU leaders recognized that dramatic and attention-getting direct action did not even put a dent in the lack of decent low-income housing on the West Side, a widespread problem.[70]

Seeking other solutions, the CTU returned to the idea of converting properties into tenant-owned or -managed co-ops to generate more decent affordable housing in poor neighborhoods. Earlier opportunities to do this, when landlords sold or transferred ownership of buildings in the face of rent strikes and direct action, had not often worked out because of the expense of rehabbing the neighborhood's substandard housing stock. But by early 1969, the idea of nonprofit community-driven housing development was gaining ground. Such projects seemed to be one way both to incorporate the "maximum feasible participation" of the poor into the planning and management of new housing and to respond to the Black Power movement's demand for community control of resources. Moreover, by then successful national and local models existed. In New York, the Bedford Stuyvesant Restoration Corporation, the first community development corporation in the country, was up and running; closer to home, the Ecumenical Institute received a grant, became Fifth City, and undertook a project to rehabilitate homes in East Garfield Park. As Herman Jenkins recalled, Fifth City had connections to the tenant union, including Minnie Dunlap, who had left the union to work for the development corporation. With these models, and with the growing size, power, and impact of the union, the CTU leaders looked to undertake their own rehab projects.[71]

A promising opportunity for community ownership and management of low-cost housing arose in February 1969 when the CTU "captured"— Tony Henry's word—a boarded-up former seminary and families moved in to occupy it. The buildings had been converted into senior citizen apartments owned by the Federal Housing Administration but had closed and sat vacant for five years. The East Garfield Cooperative Association had expressed interest in the building as early as September 1966, and the CTU had been pressing the city to do something with the property. In the summer of 1969, the occupying families formed a corporation named Midwest Village, with representatives from several community organizations including the AFSC serving on its board. Major Beverly served as the lead consultant and liaison with government agencies. Midwest Village's goal was to take advantage of federal funds for low-income, nonprofit, and/or cooperative housing through sections 221d3 or 235 of the 1961 Housing Act. Initially, public agencies had been amenable and even supportive. Government officials allowed the families to remain while they decided the future of the property. The Illinois Housing Development Authority provided some interim financing while the CTU prepared a proposal for FHA mortgage insurance, and officials of the latter gave the Midwest Village board the right to administer the property while the application was considered for a nominal fee of a few dollars. Meanwhile, Midwest Village hired an architect and approved plans for the conversion of the former seminary into a mix of apartments of different sizes and price ranges. "Governmental delay and manipulation" as well as "community power plays" allowed the property to deteriorate and the anticipated cost to increase, however. Then in the fall of 1970, the FHA rejected the proposal, calling the Midwest Village plan economically unfeasible. With great disappointment, Kale Williams wrote to the director of the local office, asking for a review of a new proposal or even just the confirmation that the FHA would protect the property until a new plan could be made. But further AFSC or CTU involvement in the buildings ceased.[72]

In the wake of the FHA rejection of mortgage insurance for the Midwest Village, Williams expressed dismay and near hopelessness over the state of low-income housing development. "An assessment of public and private programs to improve or add to the supply of housing for families of low and moderate incomes in the city points to the inescapable conclusion that up to now *no* program has really worked," he wrote to the head of the General Service Foundation, a humanitarian grantmaker. "This is our impression of the situation in Chicago," he continued, "governmental and private efforts, both profit and nonprofit have not succeeded or even held the line." As a result, local people grew frustrated, urban living conditions continued to deteriorate, and neighborhoods were being abandoned. The reason for this failure, Williams argued, was that doing something about such housing required a long time. People needed to get organized, "familiarize themselves with all aspects of the problem," and learn how to access programs to attack it. Moreover, community groups lacked an "independent financial base" and thus needed to depend on foundations for money—which was often sporadic and short term—and on volunteer advice from experts for know-how. Finally, government aid was simply inadequate, always in danger of further cuts, and hostage to the "interminable nature of the bureaucratic process." But in characteristic AFSC fashion, that letter didn't mean that Williams was giving up. Indeed, in the same letter he asked the General Service Foundation for a grant to rehab some older structures in Chicago; that funding appears not to have been forthcoming, however, as the regional office did not engage in such a project. Over the next decades, the nonprofit community development corporation became a more widespread model for securing low-income housing, fueled by both federal funding and national foundation interest. But in Chicago and elsewhere, the AFSC left that work to others, including Fifth City, while focusing on other strategies in the short term and devolving housing work in the long term.[73]

Meanwhile, the Community Relations Division poured its energy into the other strategy arising from the Chicago Urban Affairs Program: collective bargaining on behalf of tenants to empower them to improve their own living conditions. In January 1969, Tony Henry helped convene the National Conference on Tenants Rights and Housing in Chicago, at which two hundred representatives of groups from around the country agreed to start the National Tenant Organization (NTO). The CRD agreed to pay Henry, who would be based out of a new office in Washington, DC, to organize the NTO and get it off the ground. National AFSC leaders' "breathless" and "bright-eyed" eagerness to support his new role, to borrow Barbara Moffett's words, revealed the extent to which tenant unions seemed to resolve the tensions that had been raised by the challenge of Black Power. Calling unions "the most creative response to date" to the new movement, the AFSC formally endorsed the NTO as "a practical means for affording a share of power to the relatively powerless poor, giving men and women more of a say in the immediate circumstances of their lives, and attacking economic inequality and injustice through essentially peaceful means." The endorsement praised unions for increasing the "sense of worth and power of those who have been demeaned by exploitation" while being a "powerful channel for peaceful social change," thus reconciling the AFSC's traditional pacifism with the goal of empowering Black and poor communities. The CRD's enthusiasm for collective bargaining had already led to the spread of Urban Affairs Programs and tenant organizing to other cities, including Elizabeth, New Jersey, and Louisville, Kentucky. Now, the AFSC supported institutionalizing the approach at a national level by giving the NTO $50,000, shifting Henry to the new organization, and promising to raise funds for it through 1971.[74]

For those two years, the AFSC tracked the results of its investment in the NTO, observing and reporting on its work at both the grassroots and the national levels. Henry initially focused on discovering what tenant organizing was going on around the country and finding ways to provide support to build new local groups. Part of that work involved serving as a communication link, putting people in touch so that they could learn from and support each other. Thus, the NTO published a newsletter, provided information and other resources, and hosted regional and national conventions and training seminars at which local organizers could share experiences and gain advice. In addition, Henry and others at the NTO lobbied alongside other organizations for changes from the top. For example, the organization helped get the Brooke Amendment passed, capping public housing rents at 25 percent of income. Together with the National Association of Housing and Redevelopment Officials, it got the US Department of Housing and Urban Development to "prohibit objectionable phrases in public housing leases" and give tenants some rights and an increased role in public housing decision-making. Then in April 1971, the NTO with its 177 affiliates and three hundred thousand members gained an important victory when HUD ordered all public housing authorities to use a model lease and grievance procedure, creating a process for evictions and for challenging them. But, like many of the AFSC's housing initiatives, the NTO met resistance within and outside government; indeed, a study four months after HUD's order showed that only thirty of seventy large city housing authorities were following the new lease and grievance procedure. Nevertheless, the AFSC Community Relations Division considered the NTO a worthy successor to carry its goals forward.[75]

·

By the early 1960s, the people in the CRD had realized that residential integration, whether by persuasion, community organizing, direct action, or implementation of law, would be thwarted by the economic inequality that limited low-income minorities to overcrowded, inadequate housing, and that living conditions in the inner cities were among the most pressing sources of tension and potential violence in American society. Indeed, many in the AFSC had by then come to see the degradation of urban neighborhoods as a form of violence that threatened the humanity of the people living there. In response, regional office staff searched for ways to provide more and better housing to the poor. Early community organizing on the issue led to challenges to authorities to uphold housing codes, and pressure on landlords to make repairs. Responding to new sources of government and foundation funding, the AFSC in both Boston and Chicago also collaborated with community groups seeking to develop nonprofit housing through cooperatives, tenant ownership, rehabilitation, and other models. The empowerment potential of this strategy as envisioned by Black Power advocates and grassroots housing activists—including in the AFSC—was not met. But over time, churches, service agencies, and other groups were able to provide housing with some community control and input through nonprofit housing and community development corporations. AFSC staff and committee members involved in cooperative development became frustrated by the high barriers to building such housing created by local and federal bureaucracy, however. Ultimately, the CRD leadership concluded that as a small group, they could best supply the human resources—staff consultants to provide know-how and organizers to conduct community education—to support and nurture nonprofit housing development by others.

The emphasis on person-to-person organizing and support, summed up by Robert Gustafson's characterization of the AFSC urban affairs work as "a people program in a housing context," manifested most successfully in the tenant organizing that the CRD enthusiastically embraced by the end of the decade. The AFSC put staff on the ground in distressed communities around the country and gave them the time and flexibility to get to know residents and their needs. The staff brought with them traditional Friends and AFSC values and approaches: respect for individual conscience; nurturing of local leadership; creation of structures in which people could reach their full potential; and commitment to nonviolence, participatory decision-making, and reconciliation. They were influenced by the ideas and practices of the War on Poverty and the community organizing strategies of contemporary social movements, especially the emphasis on enabling low-income and marginalized people to make decisions and find solutions of their own. And as a primarily white organization, they were challenged by the Black Power movement to restructure their relationship to the Black community to promote grassroots empowerment and self-determination. The CRD leaders saw tenant organizing as the best expression of these values and goals in the contemporary urban context. It promised results at both a systemic and a local level, influencing national public housing policies and curbing the excesses of landlords in poor urban neighborhoods. But, as Bernard Lafayette put it, the goal of the tenant union was not just securing better housing conditions. The union was also a "vehicle to motivate, organize, educate, train, and develop people." Reflecting long-held AFSC goals and the mission of both the Community Relations Division and the Housing Opportunities Programs, the real "product" of tenant organizing was a "community of people who realize their dignity, self-worth and resources within their persons and groups."[76]

Conclusion

In 1965, the Southeast Regional Office of the AFSC acted on the organization-wide concern about poverty and housing conditions by launching a program to build homes for and with migrant farmworkers in the citrus groves of south-central Florida. Facing resistance from landowners, discrimination by Farmers Home Administration agents, and violence by the Ku Klux Klan, the migrants and staff member Jim Upchurch struggled to construct houses by both hiring contractors and using the self-help model that proved so popular in California's San Joaquin Valley. Despite these obstacles, Upchurch bragged in a 1974 report that they had helped families in six counties build 177 new homes and renovate thirty more. That "may not seem impressive in view of the staggering demand," he concluded. "But compared to what public agencies had done to meet the housing needs of farmworkers it is an important breakthrough." Moreover, most of the new homeowners were African American, and their process of securing land and moving into new houses had "broken a 100 year barrier of segregation."[1] While Upchurch and others in the Community Relations Division took satisfaction in the success of the Florida effort, it also was the last AFSC housing program and soon devolved to a new organization. By then, local groups directed much of the integration work around the country, and the federal government was cutting funding to nearly all programs supporting new low-income housing. Moreover, beginning in 1968 the CRD and the AFSC had begun a process of reevaluating their priorities and methods in light of the changing social, political, and economic context. The reflections of housing program leaders during this process provide a framework for assessing the significance of the AFSC's story in the campaign for integration and contemporary movements for social justice.

·

By the time the National Tenant Organization began its work, Congress had passed the Fair Housing Act (1968), and the political environment for progressive social movements had changed. The assassination of Martin Luther King and the violence that followed saddened and alarmed the members of the AFSC but also drew their attention to police abuse in minority communities, the injustices in the court system, and government repression of activists across social movements. They worried about the polarization of society over the Vietnam War and the need for further radical change in the economic system, and they wondered how to counteract the rising conservative backlash among white Americans. When that backlash helped elect Richard Nixon president, the leaders of the CRD had to learn to work with an administration openly hostile to left-wing activists and willing to cut antipoverty programs and rein in the enforcement of civil rights legislation. Underlying these developments, they concluded, along with the Kerner Report, that poverty and institutional racism continued to divide the nation into two societies and relegate many Americans to a separate and unequal life.[2] The onset of a recession in the early 1970s further exacerbated economic insecurity.

In responding to these new conditions, CRD leaders held a series of dialogues that led to both internal changes and new programs and approaches. The influence of identity-based movements and a feeling of "malaise" in the AFSC prompted the formation of a Women's Working Party and a Third World Coalition of staff people of color to demand more attention to issues of concern to women and minorities. Initially, both groups focused on access to leadership positions within the organization, but over time they sought incorporation of their perspectives into program choices. In the mid-1970s, the negative experience of George Lakey, a prominent Friend who came out as gay, prompted a group of gay and lesbian staff members to call for the AFSC to acknowledge them and address insensitive treatment within the organization. By the end of the decade, the combined efforts of these groups persuaded the AFSC national board to adopt an affirmative action policy which went further at the time than those advocated by the federal or state governments by explicitly including gays and lesbians. Tony Henry, who was involved in the Third World Coalition, later gave credit to these groups for shaping the future nature and direction of the organization, but the new affirmative action policy was and remained controversial among more conservative Friends.[3]

At the same time, the leaders of the CRD searched for productive ways to work for social justice in a changing political environment. In 1971, in response to the persecution of minorities and government crackdown on protests and direct actions, Barbara Moffett proposed a Search for Justice pilot program to monitor police brutality in three cities, initiating a new emphasis on criminal justice that would remain a priority thereafter. In 1973, the CRD expanded the program to more regional offices, gave it the largest share of the community relations budget, and added to it work specifically addressing prisoner rights. As the US military involvement in Vietnam wound down, the AFSC shifted its antiwar activism to fighting militarism at home, an issue that gained even greater significance with the election of Ronald Reagan as president and his revival of the Cold War. As Henry recalled, the internal constituency groups also influenced new programs. The Women's Working Party called for more consideration of problems facing women, which led to an organizing effort in Appalachia to combat gender discrimination in the legal system, health care, and employment. Meanwhile, the Third World Coalition directed the AFSC's attention to the US-Mexico border, prompting work addressing living and working conditions there as well as immigrant rights, which over the succeeding decades became a major center of effort. While the national CRD adopted immigration, antimilitarism, and criminal justice as priorities, the thirty community relations programs nationwide continued to work at a grassroots level on health care, hunger, education, employment, and other local concerns. Often missing, however, was the division's former "major thrust": housing.[4]

Indeed, twenty years after launching the Housing Opportunities Programs, the CRD laid down or devolved to local organizations most of its housing work. After it completed and publicized the report on FHA and VA discrimination, the Metropolitan Philadelphia Housing Opportunities Program closed because of a reorganization that moved all local community relations work out of Philadelphia to a new Mid Atlantic Regional Office in Baltimore. Suburban fair housing organizations, housing information centers, and the Metropolitan Leadership Council for Open Housing took over the Chicago HOP's efforts to open white neighborhoods to Black families. Similarly, in Washington, DC, Boston, and California, projects helping individual Black families and pressuring government officials to enforce fair housing laws passed into local hands. Staff and volunteers in regional offices still responded to requests for help, however, and the CRD's national housing secretary continued to serve as a resource for other organizations and lobby for stronger federal policies. But by the late 1960s and early 1970s, the AFSC's focus had shifted from integration to improving living conditions for low-income families, as illustrated by its enthusiasm for establishing cooperatives and organizing tenants.

In rural areas, at least at first, federal programs facilitated that goal. Based on the success of the Casa de Mañana cooperative housing association working with Bard McAllister and the AFSC in California's San Joaquin Valley, the national director of the Farmer's Home Administration had recommended that FmHA agents in other states find ways to replicate that project in their areas. Soon thereafter, the New Jersey state administrator asked the AFSC for assistance launching the first self-help housing project for farmworkers on the East Coast, and the AFSC's Mid Atlantic Regional Office initiated another in Chester County in southeastern Pennsylvania. The latter introduced a new element: grants from the Office of Economic Opportunity's Migrant Section to pay for technical assistance and a construction supervisor. The Florida project initiated by the Southeast Regional Office continued this pattern, securing FmHA loans to build housing for citrus grove farmworkers using both self-help and contractors. The California *Fresno Bee* may have exaggerated when it declared that as "pioneered by the American Friends Service Committee in Goshen, self-help housing is now a War on Poverty model for the entire nation." But the AFSC programs certainly proved influential in the Office of Economic Opportunity's incorporation of self-help into rural antipoverty work in both its Community Action Program and the Migrant Section. By 1969, the Florida program was up and running, the California project had devolved to an independent organization called Self-Help Enterprises, and over fifty other self-help programs were operating in twenty-nine states and Puerto Rico, of which only a few were directly affiliated with the AFSC.[5]

However, the political winds soon turned against such grassroots work to improve the housing conditions of the poor. In January 1973, newly reelected President Nixon began efforts to shut down the antipoverty program established by the Johnson administration, targeting the Migrant Section and the Community Action Program. In addition, he imposed a moratorium on funding for low-income housing assistance that affected new construction, the rent supplement program, public housing, and college housing, severely restricting the efforts by the AFSC and other groups to produce dwellings for impoverished communities. Indeed, only FmHA section 502 loans for rural residents, the primary source of funds for farmworker self-help housing, survived the moratorium. In slipping through the cracks, rural self-help remained the only strategy that used federal funding to support low-income housing. Consequently, in some places AFSC staff helped families finish their projects with self-help when they had initially planned to use loans to pay for inexpensive commercially built homes. Switching gears and putting all their energy into self-help housing thus enabled the Florida migrant housing work, the AFSC's last housing program, to survive the Nixon cuts.[6] In 1978, the AFSC devolved the project to Florida Non-Profit Housing, a successor organization that continued self-help housing in the state and expanded it into the wider southeast region. With that, the AFSC's housing programs formally came to an end.[7]

•

When the AFSC laid down its housing work in the mid-1970s, the "freedom to live where one chooses," which Bill Moyer identified as "a basic necessity for a free, democratic community," had not been achieved. Fifty years after the passage of the Fair Housing Act, residential segregation by race continues in every major urban area, low-income families still struggle for decent and secure shelter, and housing remains at the center of inequality in American society. Community Relations Division leaders understood from the beginning of its HOPs that attaining equal opportunity in housing would prove more difficult than in employment or in schools. Their experience over the next two decades illustrated both the individual and the institutional obstacles as well as the broad social currents that made "residential segregation based on race . . . more deeply rooted and resistant to change than any other form of racial discrimination." Builders like Levitt and Klutznick would not build for or sell to African Americans. The few developers interested in open occupancy had difficulty securing land or financing. Government officials at all levels collaborated with private interests to thwart plans for integrated housing, including city councilmen and village trustees who raised the costs of sewer development in Milpitas, California, and seized land for a public park in Deerfield, Illinois; redevelopment and housing authority agents who undermined integration in public housing in Chicago or refused to build it at all in the Bay area; and FHA and VA officials who looked the other way as management brokers refused to serve Black families. Beyond specific discriminatory acts, persistent economic inequality compounded by popular and institutional racism proved to be a formidable barrier to equal access to decent housing. Finally, even when Congress and local governments adopted fair housing laws, deeply entrenched prejudices necessitated constant grassroots vigilance and pressure for enforcement.[8]

In a 1969 report to the national Community Relations Committee, Jane Reinheimer summed up the AFSC's history of two decades of work for equal housing opportunity by pointing to how the HOPs responded to these obstacles: by reassessing the "premises" of the work, abandoning "old approaches," and attempting "new methods." In short, when they found one tactic ineffective, they tried something new. When builders and government officials rebuffed the traditional Quaker approach of persuasion of those in power, the HOP directors turned their energy to helping Black families buy houses in white neighborhoods. To support such purchases and create welcoming communities, they organized fair housing councils. As they shifted gears, they learned the limitations of these approaches and gained "deepening insight into the foundations upon which" housing segregation rested. Thus, they continued to help individual home seekers, but they recognized that such efforts were too slow and too token to produce meaningful integration. Understanding that the real estate industry and its government enablers kept the gates to new housing closed to African Americans, they challenged that barrier through employing direct action and advocating for the enactment and enforcement of fair housing laws. AFSC staff also recognized that many minority families could not afford a new home in a white suburb. In response, and influenced by the national conversation about poverty, they worked to improve the housing options and conditions of low-income city residents. "This combination of trial and error, trial and gain" in search of "workable techniques" meant confronting failure realistically and finding a productive way to move on. It also suited the AFSC's goal, as a small and relatively underfunded organization, of pioneering new methods, rejecting those that failed, and developing workable models for others to follow.[9]

As much as the AFSC modeled strategies for other organizations, however, other contemporary campaigns for social change also inspired and shaped its housing activism. The history of the HOPs illustrates how social movements shared influences and adapted to changing circumstances. The AFSC's initial strategy of persuading men in industry and government to make changes had its roots in a long Quaker history of speaking truth to power, but it was also informed by an optimism it shared with other civil rights groups—short-lived, as it turned out—based on the string of victories in the Supreme Court affecting housing, transportation, political primaries, and schools. The postwar reaction against fascism had birthed a fledgling human rights movement dedicated to overcoming racial and religious bigotry. The early HOP staff members' encounters with small groups in that movement in Chicago, Philadelphia, and the Bay Area persuaded them to try fair housing council organizing. Then the mass nonviolent direct-action campaign against Jim Crow in the South inspired the AFSC to embrace the new strategies, adapt Quaker principles of peace and reconciliation to them, and employ them against housing segregation in the North. The Chicago Freedom Movement's combination of those southern tactics with Moyer's analysis of the housing problem and model for using direct action to target the real estate industry demonstrates the mutual influence between the AFSC and the Southern Christian Leadership Conference. The early housing work always had some of the hallmarks of community organizing, such as the person-to-person contacts of the Trumbull Park family visits, the nurturing of grassroots decision-making in the fair housing councils, and the devolving of programs into local hands. But the twin influences of the War on Poverty and the Black Power movement focused attention on economic inequality, forced a reconsideration of the relationship between white and Black activists, and pushed the AFSC further toward empowering marginalized people to make changes in their own communities. Finally, as the Housing Opportunities Programs wound down, the Community Relations Division affirmed its commitment to community organizing to address other priorities, including criminal justice and women's and immigrant rights. This trajectory of the HOPs and the CRD reflected the development of a distinctive strategy for change, rooted in nonviolent direct action, community organizing, and empowerment, that has influenced social justice movements since and set the future direction of AFSC programs.

In the same 1969 report, Reinheimer asked the blunt question, "In the face of obstacles seemingly beyond our powers, should we quit?" Indeed, given the intractability of residential segregation and the staff's recognition of the limitations of their strategies, what kept them going? To that question, Reinheimer offered a succinct answer: the "long history of the Society of Friends and the AFSC." Quoting the organization's cofounder Rufus Jones, she reminded her colleagues that Quakers "never lost their hold upon the central purpose of their lives—to transform this present world and these actual human fellows around them to the end that the will of God might become the will of men and that society here on Earth might take on a likeness to the Kingdom of Heaven." Besides, she added, the AFSC had never shrunk from an issue "because it seemed difficult to solve." For its founders and for the staff and volunteers who followed them, the most profound expression of faith was action. They viewed acting on the calling of one's Inner Light as a moral imperative they could not deny just because it was hard. Comparing community relations and housing work to the peace witness of the Society of Friends, Reinheimer concluded, "War is deeply intertwined in our way of life and its eradication seems often impossible. Yet to fail to speak and work against the institution of war, while helping its victims, would be a form of complicity in the institution." AFSC staff and volunteers likewise felt a responsibility to make personal witness against and to strive to overcome racial segregation and inequality.[10]

Quakers and other AFSC members not only felt called to work against social injustices, they shared a profound optimism that their actions would matter. Whether Friend or not, staff espoused basic principles:

that every human deserved dignity and equality and a chance to reach his or her potential; that reconciliation and peaceful methods could bring about fundamental change; and most important, that people had the power to make their world a better place. Faith in these principles showed up in Phil Buskirk's dogged efforts to help the Black members of the UAW secure homes in Sunnyhills. It motivated Judy Miller when she tried to bring African Americans in Trumbull Park and their South Deering neighbors together, and George Morrison when he reached out to both landlords and tenants in Roxbury. The commitment to peaceful change lay behind Bill Moyer's adaptation of nonviolent direct action to challenge the real estate system. Ultimately, Thelma Babbitt's fair housing council work and Bernard Lafayette's tenant union organizing grew from the same conviction—that people had the capacity to do good in their own communities.

All these efforts ran into obstacles and resistance, some harsher and more spiritually punishing than others. Continuing to work in those conditions, recognizing the enormity of the problems and the often only minor changes accomplished required both a "religious commitment to the worth of the individual" and a "belief in the capacities of the most underprivileged." In wrapping up the Florida migrant housing project, organizer Bill Clumpner summarized the inspiration for many AFSC activists in less spiritual terms. He recalled that the "courage of the families" who were "willing to keep going with the program," despite harassment and discrimination, because they "dream[ed] of a better house, one of their own, one that doesn't belong to 'the man,'" kept him going. Without those families, he added, he would "have called it quits months ago."[11] Such faith in the potential of people to keep going and as a result change individual lives for the better generated both perseverance and hope. That hopefulness offers the most valuable lesson those interested in social justice work can take from this history of the AFSC's housing activism: throughout the evolution of their strategies, the members' belief in nonviolence, reconciliation, and the value and potential of every person enabled them in the face of disappointment, frustration, and failure to continue to strive for the day when "people of all groups can live peaceably together."[12] That they did so reminds us that even in the face of intransigent reaction, racism, and inequality, people kept trying and made a difference, and that mattered.

Acknowledgments

I begin these acknowledgments with the person who planted the seed for this project: my husband and fellow historian, A. Glenn Crothers. One day many years ago, while he was writing an essay on Quaker antiwar activism, he said to me, "You should write a book about the American Friends Service Committee," thus setting me off on the most rewarding research and writing experience of my career. I could not have done that research without his help and encouragement, including minding the fort at home with our children, Colin and Norah, while I spent weeks at a time in Philadelphia, Chicago, and San Francisco. More important, our many, many long conversations about the AFSC and housing integration helped me through analytical and narrative problems in ways that fundamentally shaped this story. For his intellectual companionship, moral support, and faith in me, I am eternally grateful.

At two stages, this book was greatly improved by suggestions from friends, colleagues, and strangers. Kathryn Nasstrom of the University of San Francisco, who has read nearly everything I have written, often in very rough drafts, provided her usual keen editorial insights on my first attempt at putting this story together, giving me a road map for getting it in shape. More recently, Amanda Seligman and the editorial staff of the University of Chicago Press, and of course the anonymous peer reviewers, made specific, clear recommendations for revisions that pushed me to enhance the argument. Their enthusiasm for the project, an element perhaps underrated in editorial input, was greatly appreciated as well.

I also want to acknowledge the people whose work enables the research we historians do. Archivists at the Temple University Urban Archives Center, the Bancroft Library, and the University of Illinois–Chicago provided materials during my visits there and promptly and helpfully fielded email inquiries long after. The San Francisco office of the AFSC allowed me to read unprocessed housing-related materials even before they were accessioned in the organization's national archives. The History Department at the University of Louisville paid for many of the trips to those archives, and I want to express my debt to the faculty members who over the years taught the extra Distance Education courses that generated the department's travel funds: Professors Bradley Bowman, Edward McInnis, and Rebecca Devlin.

While Glenn's suggestion set me on the road to Philadelphia to dive into the AFSC archives in search of my next book project, what I encountered there kept me coming back and stirred me to finish it. On my first day, head archivist Donald Davis offered me a slice of a staff member's birthday cake. From that beginning, through all the extra scanning and mailing of documents to me, connecting me with potential interviewees, identifying hidden gems in the collection, and at the end going into the archives during a pandemic to find most of the photographs that grace these pages, he has been an invaluable resource and friend. In the collection, I found detailed, reflective, pages-long daily reports that opened a window on the past that induced both a periodic giddiness and a determination to do the story justice. I want to thank the AFSC staff people who over the years took such good notes. But in the end, I am most grateful to them for making a history that has given me hope and inspiration.

Archive Collection Abbreviations

Unless otherwise noted, all materials come from the American Friends Service Committee Archives, Philadelphia. The AFSC main collection does not include box or folder numbers. Therefore, this material is cited in the notes as author, item, date, abbreviated box name.

Unprocessed or Unboxed Materials in the AFSC Archives

AFSC NOCARO: unprocessed Northern California Regional Office files

AFSC PRO: unprocessed Pasadena Regional Office files

BIOGRAPHICAL FILES, AFSC ARCHIVES: unboxed folders of biographical material on staff members

BIOGRAPHICAL FILES [DIGITAL], AFSC ARCHIVES: digital file of biographical material on staff members

PHILADELPHIA METRO HOUSING SCANS, AFSC ARCHIVES: materials scanned and digitally housed

REFERENCE FILES INDIVIDUALS, AFSC ARCHIVES: unboxed folders of miscellaneous biographical information

STAFF/OTHER BIOGRAPHICAL INFORMATION, AFSC ARCHIVES: unboxed folder of biographical material

SUBJECT FILES: AFSC COMMUNITY RELATIONS—HOUSING, AFSC ARCHIVES: unboxed folder of miscellaneous materials related to housing

SUBJECT FILES: COMMUNITY RELATIONS, 1936–1967, AFSC ARCHIVES: unboxed folder of miscellaneous materials related to community relations

Other Archives

In notes, box and folder numbers (e.g., 88:9) or names precede abbreviation where available.

AFSC-UIC: American Friends Service Committee records, Special Collections and University Archives, University of Illinois at Chicago. Note: The Special Collections and University Archives has reorganized this collection. Box and file numbers (e.g., 50:2) used in these citations refer to the old organization.

CWSCPC-UIC: Chicago West Side Christian Parish Collection, Special Collections and University Archives, University of Illinois at Chicago

NAACP-SCRC: National Association for the Advancement of Colored People, Philadelphia Branch Records, SCRC 15, Special Collections Research Center, Temple University Libraries, Philadelphia

NCALL-BANCROFT: National Council on Agricultural Life and Labor Records, BANC MSS 67/139z, the Bancroft Library, University of California, Berkeley

NSSPC-UIC: North Shore Summer Project Collection, Special Collections and University Archives, University of Illinois at Chicago

OHC-BANCROFT: Oral History Center, the Bancroft Library, University of California, Berkeley

PFOHP: Park Forest Oral History Project, Illinois Digital Archives, https://www.parkforesthistory.org/oral-history-transcripts.html

WURSTER-BANCROFT: Catherine Bauer Wurster Papers, BANC MSS 74/163c, the Bancroft Library, University of California, Berkeley

Notes

Introduction

1. Jane Reinheimer Motz, Biographical Files, AFSC Archives; Kay Whitlock to LGBT Network, February 1, 2005, Biographical Files [digital], AFSC Archives; Jane Reinheimer to J. Theodore Peters, February 16, 1954, American Section 1954 Community Relations Housing A–Z; Jane Reinheimer to Martha B. Brown, November 27, 1953, American Section 1953 Community Relations Housing and Indians.

2. Isaac Wheeler, quoted in Jane Reinheimer Motz Biography, Biographical Files [digital], AFSC Archives; [Jane Reinheimer Motz for] CRD to BoD, June 4, 1969, AFSC Minutes 1969 Uncoded to BD Community Relations Comm, National.

3. On the origins of the AFSC, see J. William Frost, "'Our Deeds Carry Our Message': The Early History of the American Friends Service Committee," *Quaker History* 81, no.1 (Spring 1992): 1–51; Marvin R. Weisbord, *Some Form of Peace: True Stories of the American Friends Service Committee at Home and Abroad* (New York: Viking Press, 1968), 18–24; Allan W. Austin, *Quaker Brotherhood: Interracial Activism and the American Friends Service Committee, 1917–1950* (Urbana: University of Illinois Press, 2012), 9–13; Guy Aiken, "Feeding Germany: American Quakers in the Weimar Republic," *Diplomatic History* 43, no.4 (September 2019): 597–617.

4. Frost, "'Our Deeds Carry Our Message'"; AFSC, *Bulletin* no. 62, Eighth Annual Report, 1924–1925, 5–6, AFSC Archives.

5. Gerald Jonas, *On Doing Good* (New York: Charles Scribner's Sons, 1971), 15.

6. On Quaker history and principles, see A. Glenn Crothers, *Quakers Living in the Lion's Mouth: The Society of Friends in Northern Virginia, 1730–1865* (Gainesville: University Press of Florida, 2012), 19–20; Thomas Hamm, *The Quakers in America* (New York: Columbia University Press, 2003), 13–16 and chaps. 4, 5, and 6; Frost, "'Our Deeds Carry Our Message'"; Susan Sachs Goldman, *Friends in Deed: The Story of Quaker Social Reform in America* (n.p.: Highmark Press, 2012), 6–12.

7. On Quaker conflict over the AFSC, see Frost, "'Our Deeds Carry Our Message,'" 1–2; H. Larry Ingle, "'Truly Radical, Non-violent, Friendly Approaches': Challenges to the American Friends Service Committee,"

Quaker History 105, no. 1 (Spring 2016): 1–21; H. Larry Ingle, "The American Friends Service Committee, 1947–1949: The Cold War's Effect," *Peace and Change* 23, no.1 (January 1998): 27–48; and Chuck Fager, *Quaker Service at the Crossroads: American Friends, the American Friends Service Committee, and Peace and Revolution* (Falls Church, VA: Kimo Press, 1988).

8.   Kenneth T. Jackson, *Crabgrass Frontier: The Suburbanization of the United States* (New York: Oxford University Press, 1985), 232; J. Paul Mitchell, ed., *Federal Housing Policy and Programs: Past and Present* (New Brunswick, NJ: Rutgers University Center for Urban Policy Research, 1985), 5–6.

9.   Arnold R. Hirsch, *Making the Second Ghetto: Race and Housing in Chicago, 1940–60* (Chicago: University of Chicago Press, 1998), 16–22; Laura McEnaney, *Postwar: Waging Peace in Chicago* (Philadelphia: University of Pennsylvania Press, 2018), 13–53; Matthew J. Countryman, *Up South: Civil Rights and Black Power in Philadelphia* (Philadelphia: University of Pennsylvania Press, 2006), 52; James Wolfinger, *Philadelphia Divided: Race and Politics in the City of Brotherly Love* (Chapel Hill: University of North Carolina Press, 2007), 87; Stephen Thiermann to Dick Bennett, October 28, 1952, American Section 1952 Race Relations F–I; Phil Buskirk, Secretary's Report, January 12, 1953, American Section 1953 Community Relations Housing and Indians.

10.   Housing Act of 1949, https://www.loc.gov/law/help/statutes-at-large/81st-congress/session-1/c81s1ch338.pdf; Jackson, *Crabgrass Frontier*, 203–24; Mitchell, *Federal Housing Policy*, 7–11; Marc A. Weiss, "Origins of Urban Renewal," in *Federal Housing Policy and Programs: Past and Present*, ed. J. Paul Mitchell (New Brunswick, NJ: Rutgers University Center for Urban Policy Research, 1985), 254–62.

11.   Jackson, *Crabgrass Frontier*, 233; Jeannine Bell, *Hate Thy Neighbor: Move-In Violence and the Persistence of Racial Segregation in American Housing* (New York: New York University Press, 2013), 33–34.

12.   Thomas J. Sugrue, *Sweet Land of Liberty: The Forgotten Struggle for Civil Rights in the North* (New York: Random House, 2008), 201–5; Stephen Grant Meyer, *As Long as They Don't Move Next Door: Segregation and Racial Conflict in American Neighborhoods* (New York: Rowman and Littlefield, 2000), 115–32. See also Jackson, *Crabgrass Frontier*; Hirsch, *Making the Second Ghetto*; Nathan D. B. Connolly, *World Made Concrete: Real Estate and the Remaking of the Jim Crow South in South Florida* (Chicago: University of Chicago Press, 2016); David Freund, *Colored Property: State Policy and White Racial Politics in Suburban America* (Chicago: University of Chicago Press 2010); Amanda I. Seligman, *Block by Block: Neighborhoods and Public Policy on Chicago's West Side* (Chicago: University of Chicago Press, 2005); Thomas J. Sugrue, *Origins of the Urban Crisis: Race and Inequality in Postwar Detroit* (Princeton, NJ: Princeton University Press, 2005); Kevin Kruse, *White Flight: Atlanta and the Making of Modern Conservatism* (Princeton, NJ: Princeton University Press, 2007); Matthew Lassiter, *Silent Majority: Suburban Politics*

in the Sunbelt South (Princeton, NJ: Princeton University Press, 2007); Richard Rothstein, *Color of Law: The Forgotten History of How Our Government Segregated America* (New York: Liveright, 2017); Richard H. Sander, Yana A. Kucheva, and Jonathan M. Zasloff, *Moving toward Integration: The Past and Future of Fair Housing* (Cambridge, MA: Harvard University Press, 2018).

13.   Jackson, *Crabgrass Frontier*, 219–30; Hirsch, *Making the Second Ghetto*, 68–99; Bell, *Hate Thy Neighbor*, 37. On Black agency in carving out communities on the edge of the cities, see Todd M. Michney, *Surrogate Suburbs: Black Upward Mobility and Neighborhood Change in Cleveland, 1900–1980* (Chapel Hill: University of North Carolina Press, 2017).

14.   Jeffrey Gonda, *Unjust Deeds: The Restrictive Covenant Cases and the Making of the Civil Rights Movement* (Chapel Hill: University of North Carolina Press, 2015); Juliet Saltman, *Open Housing: The Dynamics of a Social Movement* (New York: Praeger, 1978); Thomas J. Sugrue, "Concord Park, Open Housing, and the Lost Promise of Civil Rights in the North," *Pennsylvania Legacies* 10, no. 2 (November 2010): 18–23; Amanda Kolson Hurley, *Radical Suburbs: Experimental Living on the Fringes of the American City* (Cleveland: Belt, 2019); Abigail Perkiss, *Making Good Neighbors: Civil Rights, Liberalism, and Integration in Postwar Philadelphia* (Ithaca, NY: Cornell University Press, 2014); Lily Geismer, *Don't Blame Us: Suburban Liberals and the Transformation of the Democratic Party* (Princeton, NJ: Princeton University Press, 2015); David J. Garrow, ed., *Chicago 1966: Open Housing Marches, Summit Negotiations, and Operation Breadbasket* (Brooklyn, NY: Carlson, 1989); James R. Ralph, *Northern Protest: Martin Luther King, Jr., Chicago, and the Civil Rights Movement* (Cambridge, MA: Harvard University Press, 1993); Patrick D. Jones, *The Selma of the North: Civil Rights Insurgency in Milwaukee* (Cambridge, MA: Harvard University Press, 2009); Luke Ritter, "The Discriminatory Priority of Integration: Open Housing Activism in St. Louis County, 1968–1977," *Journal of the Illinois State Historical Society* 106, no. 2 (Summer 2013): 224–42; Quintard Taylor, "The Civil Rights Movement in the American West: Black Protest in Seattle, 1960–1970," *Journal of Negro History* 80, no. 1 (1995): 1–15; Christopher Bonastia, *Knocking on the Door: The Federal Government's Attempt to Desegregate the Suburbs* (Princeton, NJ: Princeton University Press, 2008); Charles Lamb, *Housing Segregation in Suburban America since 1960* (New York: Cambridge University Press, 2005); Sander, Kucheva, and Zasloff, *Moving toward Integration*; W. Dennis Keating, *The Suburban Racial Dilemma: Housing and Neighborhoods* (Philadelphia: Temple University Press, 1994).

15.   Anne Braden, *The Wall Between* (Knoxville: University of Tennessee Press, 1999).

16.   Sugrue, *Sweet Land of Liberty*, 221.

17.   Susan Lynn, *Progressive Women in Conservative Times* (New Brunswick, NJ: Rutgers University Press, 1992), 163.

Chapter One

1.   J. Cassels to File, n.d. [just after October 13, 1952], 88:9, AFSC-UIC.

2.   Report to Exec Committee from CR Program for October 1, 1953–September 30, 1954, AFSC Minutes 1953 FR Quaker International.

3.   Memo from Community Relations Division Executive Committee to Board of Directors, AFSC, re: Report on AFSC Community Relations Program Evaluative Self Study, March 1965, Subject Files: Community Relations, 1936–1967, AFSC Archives.

4.   Report to Exec Committee from CR Program for October 1, 1953, to September 30, 1954, AFSC Minutes 1953 FR Quaker International.

5.   Allan W. Austin, *Quaker Brotherhood: Interracial Activism and the American Friends Service Committee, 1917–1950* (Urbana: University of Illinois Press, 2012), 19; AFSC, *Bulletin* no. 62, Eighth Annual Report, June 1, 1924–May 31, 1935, AFSC Archives; Friends and Race Relations, 1928, Florence Yarnall, Suggestions for the Work of the Interracial Committee, and An Experiment in Interracial Understanding, 1928, General Files 1928 Interracial Section to Peace Section; AFSC, *Bulletin* no. 67, Ninth Annual Report, June 1, 1925–May 31, 1926, AFSC Archives; Anna B. Griscom to Kern Bayliss, April 2, 1929, General Files 1929 Home Service to Peace Section.

6.   For the AFSC's interwar interracialism, see Austin, *Quaker Brotherhood*, 49–111; AFSC, *Bulletin* no. 78, Eleventh Annual Report, June 1, 1927, to May 31, 1928, AFSC Archives; Typed notes on AFSC Conference on Race Relations, January 8–9, 1932, General Files 1932 Interracial to Requests for Help; Summary of Minutes of the organizational meeting, March 25, 1933, General Files 1933 Interracial to Yearly Meetings; Minutes of committee to plan, March 15, 1935, General Files 1935 General.

7.   Clara I. Cox to Clarence Pickett, October 20, 1937, Esther Balderston Jones to Clarence Pickett, October 20, 1937, and similar letters, General Files 1937 Admin to Finance.

8.   L. Hollingsworth Wood to Friend, October 27, 1937, Clarence Pickett to Robert Jones, November 16, 1937, and Clarence Pickett to Friends, December 23, 1937, General Files 1937 Admin to Finance; Practical Steps in Race Relations, 1938, General Files 1938 General to Foreign Service.

9.   Minutes, September 24, 1942, AFSC Minutes 1943 Training Comm to Nominating Comm; AFSC Annual Reports 1940, 1943, AFSC Archives.

10.   Mark Wild, *Renewal: Liberal Protestants and the American City after World War II* (Chicago: University of Chicago Press, 2019), 19–26; W. Edward Orser, "Racial Attitudes in Wartime: The Protestant Church during the Second World War," *Church History* 41, no. 3 (September 1972): 337–53; Tracy E. K'Meyer, *Interracialism and Christian Community in the Postwar South: The Story of Koinonia Farm* (Charlottesville: University Press of Virginia, 1997), 16–23; Susan Lynn, *Progressive Women in Conservative Times* (New Brunswick, NJ: Rutgers University Press, 1992), 40–67.

11. Martin Zielinski, "Working for Interracial Justice: The Catholic Interracial Council of New York, 1934–1964," *U.S. Catholic Historian* 7, no. 2/3 (Spring/Summer 1988): 233–62; Clay O'Dell, "The Politics of Housing: Catholic Activism and Dissent under Archbishop Joseph McGucken of San Francisco," *American Catholic Studies* 117, no. 3 (Fall 2006): 17–31.

12. Stuart Svonkin, *Jews against Prejudice: American Jews and the Fight for Civil Liberties* (New York: Columbia University Press, 1997), especially 1–9, 41–55, and on housing 97–112.

13. AFSC Annual Reports, 1940, 1943, 1944, AFSC Archives; Report of Finding Committee, Conference on Friends and Race Relations, September 18–19, 1943, Social Industrial Section 1943 Admin to Friends Service; Homer Morris to Margaret McColloch, November 17, 1943, Proposal for Establishment of Race Relations Division, November 30, 1943, and Methods of Approach and Scope of Activities of Interracial Department of Social Industrial Section, December 15, 1943, Social Industrial Section 1943 Japanese American Relocation to Race Relations Department; Homer Morris to Margaret McCulloch, February 4, 1944, Social Industrial Section 1944 Projects to Work Camps; Race Relations Committee Minutes, February 8, 1944, AFSC Minutes 1944 General Meeting to 1945 Validating Comm.

14. G. James Fleming, History and Problems of the Race Relations Committee, 1944–1947, AFSC Minutes 1947 Peace Section to Social Industrial Section; Frank S. Loescher, "Race and Community," *Friends Intelligencer* 103, no. 34 (August 24, 1946), clipping, Report of the Race Relations Evaluation Committee, [September 1948], and C. Rufus Rorem and Frank S. Loescher, Challenge and Opportunity in Race Relations, October 17, 1951, Subject Files: Community Relations, 1936–1967, AFSC Archives.

15. During the years of the housing work, the AFSC domestic programs also included a Peace Division and a Southern Division. Although the work of these divisions at times overlapped with community relations, a full description of their structure and activities is outside the scope of this book.

16. "Deaths," *Friends Journal*, March 1992, clipping, Reference Files Individuals A–C, AFSC Archives; Minutes, January 7, 1953, AFSC Minutes 1953 Regional and National Secretaries; American Friends Service Committee Request to the Fund for the Republic for Support of its Community Relations Program, October 1952, and Staff Evaluation of Community Relations Program, February 1953, Subject Files: Community Relations, 1936–1967, AFSC Archives; Minutes, February 14, 1952, AFSC Minutes 1952 Annual Meeting to Executive Board.

17. Board of Directors Minutes, August 2, 1944, AFSC Minutes 1943 Peace Section; American Friends Service Committee, Race Relations Committee Annual Report for 1945, Subject Files: Community Relations, 1936–1967, AFSC Archives; Conference on Work of the AFSC, April 12–13, 1946, AFSC Minutes 1946 Financial Comm to Race Relations Comm; Austin, *Quaker Brotherhood*, 167–75; Stacy Kinlock Sewell, "The Best Man for the Job: Cor-

porate Responsibility and Racial Integration in the Work Place, 1945–60," *Historian* 65, no. 5 (2003): 1125–46.

18. Carleton MacDowell, quoted in Marvin R. Weisbord, *Some Form of Peace: True Stories of the American Friends Service Committee at Home and Abroad* (New York: Viking Press, 1968), 2; Clarence Pickett, *For More Than Bread: An Autobiographical Account of Twenty-Two Years' Work with the American Friends Service Committee* (Boston: Little, Brown, 1953), 44, 64; Conference concerning Fayette County Project, September 14, 1936, AFSC Minutes 1936–37. On Penn-Craft, see Alison K. Hoagland and Margaret M. Mulrooney, *Norvelt and Penn-Craft, Pennsylvania: Subsistence Homestead Communities of the 1930s* (Washington, DC: Historic American Buildings Survey, 1991).

19. Homer Morris to Cleo Blackburn, February 12, 1942, Social Industrial Section 1942 Work Camps (Little River Farm) to Year Round; Race Relations Committee Minutes, September 18, 1947, AFSC Minutes 1947 Peace Section to Social Industrial Section; The Story of Self-Help Housing: Flanner House, 1949, American Section 1949 Community Division Self-Help Counseling. For an overview of Flanner House Homes history, see Paul Mullins, "Flanner House Homes Residential Histories," *African American Suburbia*, February 26, 2016, https://africanamericansuburbia.wordpress.com/2016/02/26/flanner-house-homes-residential-histories/, and Paul Mullins, "Race and Suburban Homogeneity: The Flanner House Homes and Post Urban African America," *Archaeology and Material Culture*, May 7, 2013, https://paulmullins.wordpress.com/2013/05/07/race-and-suburban-homogeneity-the-flanner-house-homes-and-post-urban-african-america/.

20. Minutes of Friends Self-Help et al., July 7, 1949, American Section 1949 Community Division Self-Help Counseling; Friends Self-Help Housing Program in Philadelphia: A Quaker Project in Rehabilitation, 1956, in AFSC digital archives, https://www.afsc.org/sites/default/files/documents/1956%20Self%20Help%20Housing%20in%20Phila.pdf (accessed May 4, 2021); "Friends Housing Cooperative," National Register of Historic Places Registration Form, 2015, https://www.nps.gov/nr/feature/places/pdfs/15000735.pdf (accessed May 4, 2021).

21. JWW [John W. Willard], Origins of the Housing Opportunities Program in Chicago, 1945–51, [1954], 86:16, AFSC-UIC; Housing Opportunity Program, [1951], 87:20, AFSC-UIC.

22. Homer A. Jack, The Cicero Riots of 1951, American Section 1951 Community Division A–F; "Terror in Cicero," *Newsweek*, July 23, 1951, 17; "Ugly Nights in Cicero," *Time*, July 23, 1951, 10; "Cicero Nightmare," *Nation*, July 28, 1951, 64; Richard Lentz and Karla K. Gower, *The Opinions of Mankind: Racial Issues, Press, and Propaganda in the Cold War* (Columbia: University of Missouri Press, 2010), 59–63.

23. Richard Bennett to Race Relations Committee, [August 1951], Ralph Rose to File, September 13, 1951, John Willard to Dick Bennett, Au-

gust 27, 1951, and Roundtable Discussion of Contemplated Housing Program of the AFSC, October 3, 1951, American Section 1951 Community Division A–F.

24. Stephen Thiermann to Dick Bennett, October 28, 1952, American Section 1952 Race Relations F–I; Philip Buskirk, Disposition Policy for Lanham Act Housing, [May 1954], American Section 1954 Community Relations P–Z; Philip Buskirk, Summary of Statement at San Francisco Housing Conference, August 8, 1953, American Section 1953 Community Relations Housing and Indians. On Richmond's postwar housing problems, see Marilynn S. Johnson, *The Second Gold Rush: Oakland and the East Bay in World War II* (Berkeley: University of California Press, 1993), 209–33, and Shirley Ann Wilson Moore, *To Place Our Deeds: The African American Community in Richmond, California, 1910–1963* (Berkeley: University of California Press, 2000), 97–102.

25. Jovanka Beckles, "Gary Family of Richmond: Fighting for Equality and Standing for Their Rights," http://www.radiofreerichmond.com/jovanka _beckles_the_gary_family_of_richmond_fighting_for_equality_and _standing_for_their_rights_part_1 (accessed May 4, 2021); Moore, *To Place Our Deeds*, 117–18.

26. March 27, 1952, and April 17, 1952, Minutes of the Social Industrial Committee, AFSC NoCaRO; Stephen Thiermann to Dick Bennett, October 28, 1952, enclosing Prospectus concerning Demonstration Housing Opportunities, American Section 1952 Race Relations F–I; December 11, 1952, Minutes of the Social Industrial Committee, AFSC NoCaRO; Biographical Sketch: Philip Buskirk, November 1982, Staff/Other Biographical Information, AFSC Archives. On Josephine Duveneck, see Interview with Josephine Duveneck, in *Bay Area Foundation History Volume III*, by Gabrielle Morris, February 26, 1975, OHC-Bancroft.

27. Biographical Sketch: Philip Buskirk, November 1982, Staff/Other Biographical Information, AFSC Archives; Phil Buskirk, My Spiritual Journey, December 9, 1990, Reference Files Individuals A–C, AFSC Archives. A longer version of "My Spiritual Journey" can also be found in *Friends Bulletin*, May 1992, 127–29, https://westernfriend.org/friendsbulletinp608unse2/my -afsc-experience-spiritual-journey.

28. F. Kite, notes re: meeting on Morrisville, September 13, 1951, Jacques Wilmore to Ralph Rose, October 25, 1951, and Jacques Wilmore to Ralph Rose, November 8, 1951, American Section 1951 Community Division to Economic Relations.

29. Proposal to the Field Foundation: Housing Opportunities Program, March 26, 1952, American Section 1952 Race Relations F–I; James Wolfinger, *Philadelphia Divided: Race and Politics in the City of Brotherly Love* (Chapel Hill: University of North Carolina Press, 2007), 2, 20–21; Interview with Jacques Wilmore, April 3, 1968, in Rhodes College Digital Archives, https:// dlynx.rhodes.edu/jspui/handle/10267/33845; "Nigeria's First Peace Corps

Staff," https://peacecorpsworldwide.org/nigerias-first-peace-corps-staff
-part-three/ (accessed May 4, 2021).

30. Community Relations Committee Minutes, March 11, 1953, AFSC Minutes
1953 Regional and National Secretaries; AFSC Request to the Fund for the
Republic, October 1952, Subject Files: Community Relations, 1936–1967,
AFSC Archives.

31. Phil Buskirk to Dick Bennett and Jane Reinheimer, February 3, 1953, Phil
Buskirk to File, March 3, 1953, Phil Buskirk to Dick Bennett, April 9, 1953,
and Philip Buskirk to File, May 22, 1953, American Section 1953 Community
Relations Housing and Indians; April 9, 1953, and May 21, 1953, Minutes of
the Social Industrial Committee, AFSC NoCaRO.

32. Phil Buskirk to Anne Roberts, June 3, 1953, July 15, 1953, and Phil Buskirk to
File, June 5, 1953, July 2, 1953, American Section 1953 Community Relations
Housing and Indians; Housing Opportunities Program for the Month of
March [1954], American Section 1954 Community Relations Housing A–Z;
Rona Marech, "Common Ground: Affordable Living Puts Co-op Home-
owners at Richmond's Atchison Village on [sic]," *SFGate*, October 18, 2002,
http://www.sfgate.com/bayarea/article/Common-ground-Affordable-living
-puts-co-op-2783395.php.

33. J. Philip Buskirk to Catherine Bauer Wurster, March 30, 1954, in box 10,
folder AFSC Northern California Regional Office, Wurster-Bancroft; Report
of the meeting held at the Friends Meeting House, April 6, 1954, American
Section 1954 Community Relations Housing A–Z; Martin White, Report to
the Social Industrial Committee, May–June 1955, American Section 1955
Community Relations Administration Housing; Johnson, *The Second Gold
Rush*, 228–31.

34. Phil Buskirk, meeting with Dana Murdock on July 8, 1953, American Sec-
tion 1953 Community Relations Housing and Indians; Phil Buskirk, An
Informal Report on the Housing Opportunities Program of the AFSC, 1953,
Subject Files: AFSC Community Relations—Housing, AFSC Archives; Phil
Buskirk to File, RHA meeting July 2, 1953, American Section 1953 Commu-
nity Relations Housing and Indians.

35. Phil Buskirk to File, RHA meeting July 2, 1953, and Phil Buskirk, meeting
with Dana Murdock on July 8, 1953, American Section 1953 Community
Relations Housing and Indians; Phil Buskirk, An Informal Report on the
Housing Opportunities Program of the AFSC, 1953, Subject Files: AFSC
Community Relations—Housing, AFSC Archives; Martin White, Housing
Opportunities Program Report, June 1–October 1954, AFSC NoCaRO.

36. Stephen Thiermann to Dick Bennett, January 4, 1955, and Dick Bennett to
Stephen Thiermann, February 1, 1955, American Section 1955 Community
Relations Administration Housing.

37. Barbara W. Moffett, [1994], Reference Files Individuals L–Z, AFSC Archives;
Lynn, *Progressive Women*, 166–67; Susan Sachs Goldman, *Friends in Deed:
The Story of Quaker Social Reform in America* (n.p.: Highmark Press, 2012), 8;

Community Relations Roundup, February 28–March 4, 1960, AFSC Minutes 1960 Annual Meeting to Board of Directors.

38. Arnold R. Hirsch, "Massive Resistance in the Urban North: Trumbull Park, Chicago, 1953–1966," *Journal of American History* 82, no. 2 (September 1995): 522, 527–29; "A Family Moves into Trumbull Park Homes," August 1953, clipping, 50:2, AFSC-UIC.

39. Housing Committee Meeting Minutes, January 6, 1954, American Section 1954 Community Relations Housing A–Z; Joan Seever, Weekly report on Trumbull Park, August 8, 1955, 86:24, AFSC-UIC; Mary Berger to Ed Holmgren, April 20, 1956, 51:3, AFSC-UIC; Judy Miller, Report from Camp Reinberg, June 15–16, 1957, American Section 1957 Community Relations Non-project to Housing.

40. Judy Miller, Report from Camp Reinberg, June 15–16, 1957, and Judy Miller, Report from Trumbull Park, July 11, 1957, American Section 1957 Community Relations Non-project to Housing; Mary Berger to Ed Holmgren, Report of visit of March 30, 1956, to Trumbull Park Homes, 51:3, AFSC-UIC; Meeting at AFSC Office, August 1, 1957, American Section 1957 Community Relations Non-project to Housing. The AFSC reports of visits to Trumbull Park often identified female residents only by *Mrs.* and last name.

41. Mary Berger to Ed Holmgren, Report of visit of March 30, 1956, 51:3, AFSC-UIC; Mary Berger to Ed Holmgren, Report of visit of April 27, 1956, 51:3, AFSC-UIC; Judy Miller, Report from Trumbull Park, January 28, 1958, American Section 1958 Community Relations Housing to Indian Program.

42. Judy Miller, Report from Trumbull Park, July 11, 1957, and July 18, 1957, American Section 1957 Community Relations Non-project to Housing; Ed Holmgren to Rev. Martin Luther King, July 12, 1957, 50:1, AFSC-UIC; Housing Opportunities Committee Meeting, December 12, 1957, American Section 1957 Community Relations Non-project to Housing; Report from Judy Miller on visit to Trumbull Park, January 3, 1958, American Section 1958 Community Relations Housing to Indian Program. On Ed Holmgren, see biographical note in Ed Holmgren Papers, Chicago Public Library, https://www.chipublib.org/fa-edward-holmgren-papers/ (accessed May 4, 2021).

43. John Willard to Board of Directors, AFSC, March 30, 1956, American Section 1956 Community Relations Administration F–Z to Projects A–I; John Willard to Ogden Hannaford, August 27, 1956, 51:3, AFSC-UIC; Quakers Look at Trumbull Park, A Report by the Delegation, October 1956, Subject Files: AFSC Community Relations—Housing, AFSC Archives.

44. Memo to the Chicago Community Trust, October 29, 1954, 86:16, AFSC-UIC; Ed Holmgren to Barbara Moffett, January 16, 1956, 87:13, AFSC-UIC; Quakers Look at Trumbull Park: A Report by the Delegation, October 1956, Subject Files: AFSC Community Relations—Housing, AFSC Archives; John Willard to the Board of Directors, March 30, 1956, American Section 1956 Community Relations Administration F–Z to Projects A–I; Barbara Moffett to John Willard, April 11, 1956, 87:15, AFSC-UIC.

45. Housing Committee Meeting Minutes, January 6, 1954, Richard Bennett to Stephen G. Cary, July 6, 1954, John Willard to Dick Bennett, April 27, 1954, and Dick [Richard] Bennett to John Willard, August 17, 1954, American Section 1954 Community Relations Housing A–Z; Barbara Moffett to John Willard, June 26, 1957, American Section 1957 Community Relations Nonproject to Housing; Judy Miller to Barbara Moffett, August 4, 1958, and August 19, 1958, American Section 1958 Community Relations Housing to Indian Program.

46. Hirsch, "Massive Resistance," 548; Partial Summary of Remarks by Alvin E. Rose, January 17, 1959, 62:14, AFSC-UIC; Judy Miller, Report from Trumbull Park, January 28, 1958, American Section 1958 Community Relations Housing to Indian Program; Trumbull Park—a Progress Report, April 1959, American Section 1959 Community Relations Farm Labor to Housing.

47. AFSC CRO Executive Committee Minutes, September 14, 1951, and November 21, 1951, 83:28, AFSC-UIC; Hyde Park-Kenwood Community Conference, Report to the Board of Directors, January 15, 1952, American Section 1952 Race Relations F–I; J. Cassels to File, January 12–14, 1953, 86:13, AFSC-UIC; J. Cassels to File, April 29, 1953, 86:14, AFSC-UIC; Judy Miller to Ed and John W, May 9, 1957, 87:20, AFSC-UIC; Jane Weston to Suzanne Day, August 30, 1961, Community Relations 1961 Housing Program to Farm Labor Program. For a more detailed account of the Hyde Park-Kenwood Community Conference, see Muriel Beadle, *The Hyde Park-Kenwood Urban Renewal Years* (n.p.: published by the author, 1967).

48. Jane Reinheimer to File, January 9, 1953, May 26, 1953, and Jane Reinheimer to File, June 1, 1953, American Section 1953 Community Relations Housing and Indians; Jane Reinheimer to File, March 19, 1954, American Section 1954 Community Relations Housing A–Z; Jane Reinheimer to Richard Bennett, February 3, 1956, American Section 1956 Community Relations Administration F–Z to Projects A–I; Thelma Babbitt to Community Relations Program Staff, February 4, 1958, American Section 1958 Community Relations Housing to Indian Program.

49. Jane Reinheimer to File, January 14, 1954, February 3, 1954, and Minutes of the Joint Meeting of the Church Community Council and the WMAN, November 30, 1954, American Section 1954 Community Relations Housing A–Z; Minutes of Steering Committee West Mount Airy Neighbors, March 8, 1955, American Section 1955 Community Relations Administration Housing. For a detailed study of West Mount Airy Neighbors, see Abigail Perkiss, *Making Good Neighbors: Civil Rights, Liberalism, and Integration in Postwar Philadelphia* (Ithaca, NY: Cornell University Press, 2014).

50. On neighborhood stabilization, see Phyllis Palmer, *Living as Equals: How Three White Communities Struggled to Make Interracial Connections during the Civil Rights Era* (Nashville: Vanderbilt University Press, 2008). On the AFSC's decision to move away from stabilization, see Report of the Community Relations Roundup, April 7–12, 1957, Subject Files: Community

Relations, 1936–1967, AFSC Archives; Report of the Community Relations
Roundup, February 28–March 4, 1960, AFSC Minutes 1960 Annual Meeting
to Board of Directors.

51. Interview with Philip M. Klutznick by Glenda Bailey Mershon, Febru-
ary 5, 1981, PFOHP; Will Cooley, "'We Just Can't Afford to be Democratic':
Liberals, Integrationists and the Postwar Suburb of Park Forest," *Journal of
Social History* 54, no. 1 (2020): 330–57.

52. Interview with Robert Dinerstein by Glenda Bailey-Mershon, October 4,
1980, PFOHP; Traci Parker, *Department Stores and the Black Freedom
Movement: Workers, Consumers, and Civil Rights from the 1930s to the 1980s*
(Chapel Hill: University of North Carolina Press, 2019), 133; J. Cassels to
File, June 27, 1952, 88:9, AFSC-UIC; *Park Forest (IL) Reporter*, March 5, 1953,
clipping, American Section 1953 Community Relations Housing and Indians; J. Cassels to File, September 30, 1952, 88:9, AFSC-UIC.

53. J. Cassels to File, September 30, 1952, 88:9, AFSC-UIC; Dick Bennett to
Jim Cassels, November 12, 1952, 88:10, AFSC-UIC; James Cassels to Jane
Reinheimer, November 18, 1952, 88:10, AFSC-UIC; J. Cassels to File, December 22, 1952, 88:9, AFSC-UIC; Hart Perry to James Cassels, December 17,
1952, 88:10, AFSC-UIC; J. Cassels to File, October 27, 1952, 88:9, AFSC-UIC;
Phil Klutznick to Jim Cassels, February 9, 1953, 86:15, AFSC-UIC; Frank
Horne to Phil Klutznick, February 6, 1953, 86:15, AFSC-UIC; Jane Reinheimer to Dick [Bennett], February 26, 1953, and Jim Cassels to Members
of Housing Opportunities Committee, March 20, 1953, American Section
1953 Community Relations Housing and Indians; "Park Forest Human Relations Committee Dismissed," September 1953, clipping, 92:13, AFSC-UIC.

54. "William J. Levitt, 86, Pioneer of Suburbs Dies," *New York Times*, January 29,
1994; "William Levitt: The Sultan of Suburbia," *Entrepreneur*, October 10,
2008, https://www.entrepreneur.com/article/197662; Thomas J. Sugrue,
Sweet Land of Liberty: The Forgotten Struggle for Civil Rights in the North
(New York: Random House, 2008), 210–11. For more on the integration of
the Pennsylvania Levittown, see Sugrue, 211–30; James Wolfinger, "The
American Dream—for All Americans: Race, Politics, and the Campaign
to Desegregate Levittown," *Journal of Urban History* 38, no. 3 (May 2012):
430–51; David Kushner, *Levittown: Two Families, One Tycoon and the Fight for
Civil Rights in America's Legendary Suburb* (New York: Walker, 2009).

55. Jacques Wilmore to Dick Bennett, July 15, 1953, Jacques Wilmore, file
report of visit with Victor C. Adler, November 6, 1952, and Jacques Wilmore, visit with Leo Kirk, November 6, 1952, American Section 1952 Race
Relations F–I; Jane Reinheimer to File, May 5, 1953, American Section 1953
Community Relations Housing and Indians.

56. Jack Wilmore to Ralph Rose, November 7, 1951, American Section 1951
Community Division G–Z; Jacques Wilmore to Hortense Gabel, January 16,
1953, Hortense Gabel to Jacques Wilmore, January 26, 1953, and Constance
Baker Motley to Jacques Wilmore, January 21, 1953, American Section 1953

Community Relations P–Z; Jane Reinheimer to File, visit with Arthur L. Johnson, December 23, 1953, American Section 1953 Community Relations Housing and Indians.

57. Jacques Wilmore to Tom Colgan, November 2, 1951, American Section 1951 Community Division A–F; Phil Buskirk to Alphonse Miller, April 15, 1953, American Section 1953 Community Relations Housing and Indians; Housing Opportunities Program for Month of March [1954], American Section 1954 Community Relations Housing A–Z; Phil Buskirk to Dick Bennett, August 11, 1953, American Section 1953 Community Relations Housing and Indians; Social Industrial Committee meeting, September 17, 1953, AFSC Regional Office Minutes 1953; Phil Buskirk to File, November 13, 1953, American Section 1953 Community Relations Housing and Indians; Community Reaction to Jacob's Housing Project: Situation and Approach, [March 1954], and Allan C. Wood to Members of the Swarthmore Property Owners Association, American Section 1954 Community Relations Housing A–Z; Thomas E. Colgan to Lyman Riley, December 5, 1957, American Section 1957 Community Relations Projects Latin American Program to Phila; Thelma Babbitt to Community Relations Program Staff, February 4, 1958, American Section 1958 Community Relations Housing to Indian Program.

58. Thomas J. Sugrue, "Concord Park, Open Housing, and the Lost Promise of Civil Rights in the North," *Pennsylvania Legacies* 10, no. 2 (November 2010): 19–20; Florence Kite's Notes on Conversation with Frank Loescher, May 15, 1952, and Jacques Wilmore to Dick Bennett, July 14, 1952, American Section 1952 Race Relations K–P.

59. Jane Reinheimer to File, July 10, 1952, July 19, 1952, and August 29, 1952, and Jane Reinheimer to Anna McGarry, July 10, 1952, American Section 1952 Race Relations K–P; Jane Reinheimer to File, August 17 and 20, 1954, and Jane Reinheimer to Philip Buskirk, Jim Cassels, and Martin White, November 29, 1954, American Section 1954 Community Relations Housing A–Z; "Tuesday Hangout: A Tale of Two 'Cities': Concord Park, Trevose, PA," May 8, 2018, https://www.dailykos.com/stories/2018/5/8/1762591/-Tuesday -Hangout-A-Tale-of-Two-Cities-Concord-Park-Trevose-PA-5-8-18; Sugrue, "Concord Park," 21.

60. William M. Dwyer, "Experiment in Housing," *Commonweal*, n.d., clipping, 2:11, NAACP-SCRC; Eleanor Roosevelt, "My Day," July 15, 1958, https://www .gwu.edu/~erpapers/myday/displaydoc.cfm?_y=1958&_f=md004171; Sugrue, "Concord Park," 22; Eunice Grier and George Grier, *Privately Developed Interracial Housing: An Analysis of Experience, Special Report to the Commission on Race and Housing* (Berkeley: University of California Press, 1960), 197; W. Benjamin Piggot, "The Problem of the Black Middle Class: Morris Milgram's Concord Park and Residential Integration in Philadelphia's Postwar Suburbs," *Pennsylvania Magazine of History and Biography* 132, no. 2 (April 2008): 184–85.

61. Sugrue, "Concord Park," 22–23; Piggot, "The Problem," 173, 185.

62. Three Years Review: Santa Clara County Community Relations [1958], AFSC NoCaRO; Eunice Grier and George Grier, "Sunnyhills: Milpitas, California," in *Case Studies in Racially Mixed Housing* (Princeton, NJ: Princeton Conference on Equal Opportunity in Housing, 1966), 5; Typed history of Santa Clara County Community Relations Program, May 1, 1956, American Section 1956 Community Relations Projects SC to Organizations; AFSC-NCRO Executive Committee, Minutes of Meeting, February 15, 1954, AFSC NoCaRO.

63. Philip Buskirk to Norman Carpenter, March 22, 1954, American Section 1954 Community Relations Housing A–Z; Minutes of the Social Industrial Committee, November 11, 1954, AFSC NoCaRO Minutes, 1948–1959; Phil Buskirk to J. P. Traynor, October 19, 1954, American Section 1954 Community Relations Housing A–Z; Minutes, Social Industrial Committee, March 1, 1955, AFSC NoCaRO; "Work Under Way at Milpitas on Pioneer Interracial Subdivision," *Daily Palo Alto (CA) Times*, April 7, 1955, clipping, AFSC NoCaRO.

64. Phil Buskirk, Memorandum Report, December 7, 1954, and "Work Under Way at Milpitas on Pioneer Subdivision," *Daily Palo Alto (CA) Times*, April 7, 1955, clipping, AFSC NoCaRO; Minutes of Meeting, Executive Committee, April 18, 1955, AFSC Regional Office Minutes 1955.

65. Grier and Grier, "Sunnyhills," 8–14; Minutes of the Santa Clara County Community Relations Committee, April 28, 1955, "UAW Tract Sewer Fee Protested," *San Jose (CA) Mercury*, May 4, 1955, clipping, Phil Buskirk, Memorandum Report, May 9, 1955, Minutes of the Santa Clara County Community Relations Committee, June 23, 1955, Phil Buskirk, Report on Home Builders Association and the UAW, July 25, 1955, Phil Buskirk, Report on Status of UAW housing project, August 31, 1955, and Santa Clara County Community Relations Program, Report to the Social Industrial Committee, November 1955, AFSC NoCaRO.

66. Minutes of Santa Clara County Community Relations Committee, December 1, 1955, AFSC NoCaRO; Phil Buskirk, Memorandum Report, January 17, 1956, American Section 1956 Community Relations Projects SC to Organizations; Santa Clara County Community Relations Program, Report to the Social Industrial Committee, January 5, 1956, AFSC NoCaRO.

67. Grier and Grier, "Sunnyhills," 14–16; Phil Buskirk on Sunnyhills sales meeting, February 10, written February 15, 1956, AFSC NoCaRO; Minutes of the Santa Clara County Community Relations Committee, May 17, 1956, American Section 1956 Community Relations Projects SC to Organizations; Phil Buskirk, Progress report on Sunnyhills, August 16, 1956, AFSC NoCaRO; Phil Buskirk to William Oliver, November 23, 1956, American Section 1956 Community Relations Projects SC to Organizations.

68. Grier and Grier, "Sunnyhills," 17; Phil Buskirk to File, May 23, 1957, American Section 1957 Community Relations Non-project to Housing; Three Years Review: Santa Clara Community Relations, [1958], AFSC NoCaRO.

69. Phil Buskirk to File, November 13, 1957, American Section 1957 Community Relations Non- project to Housing; Three Years Review: Santa Clara County Community Relations, [1958], AFSC NoCaRO; Grier and Grier, "Sunnyhills," 19–23.

70. Grier and Grier, "Sunnyhills," 21–22; Santa Clara Community Relations Committee Activities, August 21, 1960, Community Relations 1960 Farm Labor to Housing.

71. Ed Holmgren to Barbara Moffett, September 9, 1955, 86:23, AFSC-UIC; Ed Holmgren to Barbara Moffett, January 24, 1957, Ed Holmgren to Barbara Moffett, February 1, 1957, Housing Opportunities Program Meeting Minutes, February 7, 1957, and Housing Opportunities Committee Meeting Minutes, October 24, 1957, December 12, 1957, American Section 1957 Community Relations Non-project to Housing; Ed Holmgren to those interested in the elimination of suburban housing segregation, [1958], American Section 1958 Community Relations Housing to Indian Program.

72. Chicago Regional Office, Housing Opportunities Committee Minutes, November 12, 1959, and Jane Weston to Judy Howard, November 17, 1959, American Section 1959 Community Relations Farm Labor to Housing.

73. Judy Howard to Barbara Moffett, November 23, 1959, Jane Weston to Barbara Moffett, November 24, 1959, and Jane Weston to Barbara Moffett, December 12, 1959, American Section 1959 Community Relations Farm Labor to Housing; Dr. Martin Hayes Bickham, "Decisions in Deerfield," December 23, 1959, in series 3 box 43 folder 10, AFSC-UIC (reorganized and reboxed materials).

74. Jane Weston to Barbara Moffett, December 12, 1959, American Section 1959 Community Relations Farm Labor to Housing; Dr. Martin Hayes Bickham, "Decisions in Deerfield," December 23, 1959, 3:43:10, AFSC-UIC; Jane Weston to Barbara Moffett, January 6, 1960, 86:27, AFSC-UIC; A Proposed Program in Housing Opportunities, February 1960, Community Relations 1960 Farm Labor to Housing.

75. Jane Weston to Barbara Moffett, December 12, 1959, American Section 1959 Community Relations Farm Labor to Housing; Judy Howard to Barbara Moffett, January 5, 1960, Judy Howard to Mary Berger, January 14, 1960, Judy Howard to Mary Berger, March 11, 1960, Judy Howard to Kale Williams and Jane Weston, April 29, 1960, and Jane Weston to Judy Howard, May 16, 1960, Community Relations 1960 Farm Labor to Housing; AFSC CRO HOP Minutes of Meeting, May 9, 1966, 80:37, AFSC-UIC. For a review of Milgram's career and the North Shore project, see Amanda Kolson Hurley, "'Housing Is Everybody's Problem': The Forgotten Crusade of Morris Milgram," *Places*, October 2017, https://placesjournal.org/article/housing-is-everybodys-problem/.

76. Jane Weston to File, April 23, 1964, CRD 1964 Housing Program, box 3.

77. Report of the Community Relations Roundup, April 7–12, 1957, Subject Files: Community Relations, 1936–1967, AFSC Archives; Jane Reinheimer

to J. Theodore Peters, Friends Select School, February 16, 1954, American Section 1954 Community Relations Housing A–Z.

Chapter Two

1. Thelma W. Babbitt to Community Relations Program Staff, June 2, 1958, log #8, April 4 to May 23, 1958, and July 10, 1958, log #9, May 26 to July 1, 1958, American Section 1958 Community Relations Housing to Indian Program.

2. Lester Granger, "A Hopeful Sign in Race Relations," *Survey Graphic* 33 (November 1944), 455; H. H. Giles, "Present Status and Programs of Private Intergroup Relations Agencies," *Journal of Negro Education* 20, no. 3 (Summer 1951): 408–24; Robert Burnham, "The Mayor's Friendly Relations Committee: Cultural Pluralism and the Struggle for Black Advancement," in *Race and the City: Work, Community and Protest in Cincinnati, 1820–1970*, ed. Henry Louis Taylor Jr. (Urbana: University of Illinois Press, 1993), 258–79. For more on the postwar human relations movement, see Ariana Horn, "Paved with Good Intentions: The Rise and Fall of the 'Human Relations' Movement in Milwaukee, 1934–1980" (PhD diss., University of Wisconsin, 2015), and Leah N. Gordon, *From Power to Prejudice: The Rise of Racial Individualism in Midcentury America* (Chicago: University of Chicago Press, 2015).

3. For a detailed analysis of the writing and impact of *American Dilemma*, see David W. Southern, *Gunnar Myrdal and Black-White Relations: The Use and Abuse of "An American Dilemma," 1944–1969* (Baton Rouge: Louisiana State University Press, 1987), and Walter A. Jackson, *Gunnar Myrdal and America's Conscience: Social Engineering and Racial Liberalism, 1938–1987* (Chapel Hill: University of North Carolina Press, 1990).

4. Lisa McGirr, *Suburban Warriors: The Origins of the New American Right* (Princeton, NJ: Princeton University Press, 2001); Kevin Kruse, *White Flight: Atlanta and the Making of Modern Conservatism* (Princeton, NJ: Princeton University Press, 2007); Matthew Lassiter, *Silent Majority: Suburban Politics in the Sunbelt South* (Princeton, NJ: Princeton University Press, 2007).

5. Susan Lynn, *Progressive Women in Conservative Times* (New Brunswick, NJ: Rutgers University Press, 1992); Sylvie Murray, *The Progressive Housewife: Community Activism in Suburban Queens, 1945–1965* (Philadelphia: University of Pennsylvania Press, 2003); Joanne Meyerowitz, *Not June Cleaver: Woman and Gender in Postwar America, 1945–60* (Philadelphia: Temple University Press, 1994).

6. Jane Reinheimer on meeting of NCDH in New York, December 10, 1952, American Section 1952 Race Relations F–I; Jane Reinheimer to Jacques Wilmore, January 19, 1953, American Section 1953 Community Relations P–Z; Jane Reinheimer to File, April 2, 1953, American Section 1953 Community Relations Housing and Indians; Jane Reinheimer to File, June 2, 1953, American Section 1953 Community Relations P–Z.

7. Harry Teshima, quoted in Will Cooley, "'We Just Can't Afford to be Democratic': Liberals, Integrationists and the Postwar Suburb of Park Forest," *Journal of Social History* 54, no. 1 (2020): 344; "Park Forest Human Relations Committee Dismissed," September 1953, clipping, 92:13, AFSC-UIC.

8. Ed Holmgren to Jean Berstein, June 11, 1956, 92:13, AFSC-UIC; Housing Opportunities Program Meeting Minutes, February 7, 1957, and March 7, 1957, American Section 1957 Community Relations Non-project to Housing; HOP Minutes of Meeting, June 12, 1958, 85:1, AFSC-UIC; Judy Miller to Judy Wicoff, June 13, 1958, American Section 1958 Community Relations Housing to Indian Program; Judy Miller to Barbara Moffett, January 2, 1959, Chicago Regional Office HOP Meeting Minutes, January 8, 1959, and Judy Miller to Kale Williams, July 30, 1959, American Section 1959 Community Relations Farm Labor to Housing; Interview with Robert Dinerstein, PFOHP.

9. "Integration Hassle in Pk Forest," January 14, 1960, clipping, 92:13, AFSC-UIC; Interview with Anthony Scariano by Judy Matthias, November 30, 1980, PFOHP; Interview with Bernard Cunningham by Beverly Helm, December 1980, PFOHP; Interview with Robert Dinerstein, PFOHP.

10. Interview with Robert Dinerstein, PFOHP. On white resident resistance to integration in Park Forest, see Cooley, "'We Just Can't Afford,'" 343–44.

11. "Park Forest Officials Cool to New Group," *Chicago Daily News*, January 21, 1960, clipping, 92:13, AFSC-UIC; Interview with Anthony Scariano, PFOHP; Interview with Robert Dinerstein, PFOHP; Appeal for Support of the AFSC Program in Housing Opportunities in the Chicago Metropolitan Area, February 1960, 86:28, AFSC-UIC; Cooley, "'We Just Can't Afford,'" 345–46; AFSC HOP Chicago Metropolitan Area, December 1, 1960–June 1, 1961, Community Relations 1961 Housing Program to Farm Labor Program.

12. Jane Reinheimer to File, July 7, 1953, December 20, 1953, and December 29, 1953, American Section 1953 Community Relations Housing and Indians; Jane Reinheimer to File, September 3, 1954, American Section 1954 Community Relations Housing A–Z; Jacques Wilmore to Jane Reinheimer, December 14, 1954, American Section 1954 Community Relations P–Z; Jane Reinheimer to Samuel H. Bell, June 8, 1956, American Section 1956 Community Relations Administration F–Z to Projects A–I; Jane Reinheimer to George Loveless, May 27, 1955, and Jane Reinheimer to File, August 3, 1955, American Section 1955 Community Relations Administration Housing.

13. Jane Reinheimer to File, March 17, 1953, and October 15, 1953, American Section 1953 Community Relations Housing and Indians; Jacques Wilmore to Charles Shorter, October 29, 1953, 2:11, NAACP-SCRC.

14. Jane Reinheimer to File, December 20, 1953, and December 23, 1953, American Section 1953 Community Relations Housing and Indians; Jane Reinheimer to File, May 18, 1954, American Section 1954 Community Relations Housing A–Z; Jane Reinheimer to File, June 17, 1954, and July 20, 1954, Jacques Wilmore to Jane Reinheimer, August 12, 1954, and Jacques

Wilmore to Jane Reinheimer, October 5, 1954, American Section 1954 Community Relations P–Z.

15. Thomas J. Sugrue, *Sweet Land of Liberty: The Forgotten Struggle for Civil Rights in the North* (New York: Random House, 2008), 223; Allan W. Austin, *Quaker Brotherhood: Interracial Activism and the American Friends Service Committee, 1917–1950* (Urbana: University of Illinois Press, 2012), 168.

16. Jane Reinheimer to File, October 26, 1954, American Section 1954 Community Relations Housing A–Z; Jane Reinheimer to File, September 27, 1955, American Section 1955 Community Relations Administration Housing; Jacques Wilmore to Jane Reinheimer, September 22, 1954, American Section 1954 Community Relations P–Z.

17. Jane Reinheimer to File, March 17, 1953, American Section 1953 Community Relations Housing and Indians; Rebecca Batts Butler to Jane Reinheimer, July 20, 1954, Jacques Wilmore to Jane Reinheimer, August 12, 1954, and Jane Reinheimer to File, July 27, 1954, August 21–28, 1954, and July 8 and 12, 1954, American Section 1954 Community Relations Housing A–Z; Jane Reinheimer to File, September 27, 1955, American Section 1955 Community Relations Administration Housing.

18. Barbara Moffett to Lucy Garner, Paul Blanshard, and Frank Loescher, July 25, 1957, American Section 1957 Community Relations Non-project to Housing; Thomas J. Sugrue, "Jim Crow's Last Stand: The Struggle to Integrate Levittown," in *Second Suburb: Levittown, Pennsylvania*, ed. Diane Harris (Pittsburgh: University of Pittsburgh Press, 2010), 183. For more on African American presence in the suburbs, see Andrew Wiese, *Places of Their Own: African American Suburbanization in the Twentieth Century* (Chicago: University of Chicago Press, 2005). In addition to other sources noted, the following story of the Myerses' move-in to Levittown is drawn from Sugrue, *Sweet Land of Liberty*, 224–26; James Wolfinger, *Philadelphia Divided: Race and Politics in the City of Brotherly Love* (Chapel Hill: University of North Carolina Press, 2007), 440–46; and Daisy Myers's memoir of events, *Sticks 'n Stones: The Myers Family in Levittown* (York, PA: York County Heritage Trust, 2005).

19. Myers, *Sticks 'n Stones*, 29–32; Thomas E. Colgan, "Levittown, Pennsylvania," *Friends Journal*, September 7, 1957, 585–86.

20. Myers, *Sticks 'n Stones*, 44–46.

21. Myers, 51.

22. Myers, 55.

23. Myers, 61; AFSC, "A Statement on Levittown, Pennsylvania," press release August [14] 1957, Subject Files: Community Relations, 1936–1967, AFSC Archives.

24. American Friends Service Committee Role in Levittown, October 11, 1957, Subject Files: AFSC Community Relations—Housing, AFSC Archives; Interview with Thomas Colgan by Harry Ganz, January 29, 1991, interview #302, AFSC Archives; Thomas Colgan to Emanuel Muravchaik, Septem-

ber 17, 1957, Thomas Colgan to Howard W. McKinney, September 16, 1957, Thomas E. Colgan to Pennsylvania State Department of Insurance, September 16, 1957, and Thomas E. Colgan to Joan and Ron Turner, November 7, 1957, American Section 1957 Community Relations Non-project to Housing.

25.   Thomas Colgan to Howard W. McKinney, September 16, 1957, Thomas Colgan to Thelma Babbitt, November 20, 1957, and Thomas Colgan to Barbara Moffett, October 24, 1957, American Section 1957 Community Relations Non-project to Housing; American Friends Service Committee Role in Levittown, October 1957, Subject Files: AFSC Community Relations—Housing, AFSC Archives. On the Jewish role in seeking integration of housing, see Stuart Svonkin, *Jews against Prejudice: American Jews and the Fight for Civil Liberties* (New York: Columbia University Press, 1997), 97–107.

26.   A Proposed Program in Housing Opportunities, AFSC Regional Office, February 1960, Community Relations 1960 Farm Labor to Housing; Community Relations Committee Minutes, January 21, 1961, AFSC Minutes 1961 BDG General Service to International Service.

27.   Thelma Babbitt, typesheet of responses to questions posed by Susan Lynd, n.d., Biographical Files, AFSC Archives; Richard Taylor, Staff/Other Biographical Information, AFSC Archives; Barbara Moffett to Delaware Valley Intergroup Relations Agencies, September 18, 1959, American Section 1959 Community Relations Farm Labor to Housing. On Babbitt, see also Lynn, *Progressive Women*, 72–73.

28.   Thelma Babbitt to Community Relations Program Staff, February 18, 1958, Thelma Babbitt to File, April 18, 1958, Thelma W. Babbitt to Community Relations Program Staff, June 2, 1958, and July 10, 1958, Summary of Meeting, July 2, 1958, and Minutes, Burlington County Human Relations Council Meeting, July 28, 1952, American Section 1958 Community Relations Housing to Indian Program.

29.   First Annual Report of the AFSC Metropolitan Philadelphia Housing Opportunities Program, October 1959, 70:1, AFSC-UIC; Thelma Babbitt to Community Relations Staff, July 10, 1958, log #9, May 26 to July 1, 1958, American Section 1958 Community Relations Housing to Indian Program.

30.   Thelma Babbitt to Community Relations Program Staff, June 2, 1958, log #8, April 14 to May 23, 1958, American Section 1958 Community Relations Housing to Indian Program; Thelma Babbitt, typesheet of responses to questions posed by Susan Lynd, n.d., Biographical Files, AFSC Archives.

31.   Thelma Babbitt to Community Relations Staff, July 10, 1958, log #9, May 26 to July 1, 1958, and Thelma Babbitt to Community Relations Staff, November 14, 1958, log #11, September 16 to October 25, 1958, American Section 1958 Community Relations Housing to Indian Program.

32.   Thelma Babbitt, typesheet of responses to questions posed by Susan Lynd, n.d., Biographical Files, AFSC Archives; Thelma Babbitt to Community Relations Staff, November 14, 1958, log #11, September 16 to October 25, 1958, American Section 1958 Community Relations Housing to Indian Program.

33. Thelma Babbitt to Community Relations Staff, August 19, 1958, log #10, July 1 to August 12, 1958, American Section 1958 Community Relations Housing to Indian Program; BCHRC Housing Committee Minutes, January 22, 1959, March 3, 1959, and Emerson Darnell and William H. Wells open letter, July 23, 1959, American Section 1959 Community Relations Farm Labor to Housing; Thelma Babbitt to Community Relations Program Staff, Report for May 21 to August 4, 1959, American Section 1959 Community Relations Farm Labor to Housing. On open housing pledges, see Sugrue, *Sweet Land of Liberty*, 247–48.

34. Thelma Babbitt to Community Relations Staff, July 10, 1958, log #9, May 26 to July 1, 1958, Thelma Babbitt to Community Relations Staff, August 19, 1958, log #10, July 1 to August 12, 1958, and Thelma Babbitt to William Wells, October 3, 1958, American Section 1958 Community Relations Housing to Indian Program; William Wells to Honorable David D. Furman, January 28, 1959, American Section 1959 Community Relations Farm Labor to Housing; Dick Taylor to Barbara Moffett et al., April 5, 1960, Dick Taylor to Barbara Moffett and Charlotte Meacham, January 12, 1960, BCHRC Exec Comm meeting, April 6, 1960, Dick Taylor to Charlotte Meacham, August 9, 1960, and BCHRC joint meeting of education and housing committees, October 6, 1960, Community Relations 1960 Farm Labor to Housing.

35. BCHRC joint meeting of education and housing committees, October 6, 1960, and Pam Coe to Mary Berger et al., December 7, 1960, Community Relations 1960 Farm Labor to Housing; Maurice Heckscher and Sanford Beecher to Hugh Middleton, August 10, 1961, Community Relations 1961 Housing Program to Farm Labor Program; Charlotte Meacham to Exec Comm of BCHRC, April 13, 1962, Community Relations 1962 Farm Labor Programs to Housing Programs; Charlotte Meacham to Marian Gray and Thelma Segal, February 28, 1964, CRD 1964 Housing Program.

36. First Annual Report of the American Friends Service Committee Metropolitan Philadelphia Housing Opportunities Program, October 1959, 70:1, AFSC-UIC; Summary of Meeting, Burlington, NJ, July 2, 1958, and Thelma Babbitt to Community Relations Staff, November 14, 1958, log #11, September 16 to October 25, 1958, American Section 1958 Community Relations Housing to Indian Program; Thelma Babbitt to Community Relations Staff, report for March 16 to May 14, 1959, American Section 1959 Community Relations Farm Labor to Housing; Charlotte Meacham to Community Relations Program Staff, Housing program report February 4, 1961, to February 26, 1961, and Progress report MPHOP January 1962, Community Relations 1961 Housing Program to Farm Labor Program; Dick Taylor to Barbara [April 1964], CRD 1964 Housing Program.

37. James Harvey to Merlin Myers, October 9, 1963, and Dan Safran to Merlin Myers, October 2–8, 1963, CRD 1963 Housing to MWHOP; Barbara Moffett to AFSC BoD, April 6, 1962, and enclosure, Proposal for Metro Washington HOP, April 1962, Moffett to Eunice and George Grier, July 11, 1962, and

Report from MWHOP, December 10, 1962, Community Relations 1962 Farm Labor Programs to Housing Programs; Report from Helen Baker, August 7, 1963, CRD 1963 Housing to MWHOP; Charlotte Meacham to File, April 30, 1963, and Staff Log Book, June–July 1963, CRD 1963 Housing Program. A "white noose" encircling a "Black city" was a common metaphor used by housing integration advocates. It first appeared in comments by Philadelphia mayor Richardson Dilworth in 1957. See "Mayor Says Negroes Deserve Good Homes in All Parts of the City," *Philadelphia Tribune*, February 25, 1958. On the Urban League's program, see Todd M. Michney, *Surrogate Suburbs: Black Upward Mobility and Neighborhood Change in Cleveland, 1900–1980* (Chapel Hill: University of North Carolina Press, 2017), 187–88.

38. Helen Baker to Charlotte Meacham, May 24, 1963, and Northern Virginia Fair Housing Minutes, June 2[illegible], 1963, CRD 1963 Housing to MWHOP.

39. Progress report on MWHOP, September 1964, Merlin A. Myers to Friend, July 13, 1964, and MWHP report, vol. 1, no. 2, September 1964, CRD 1964 Housing Program, box 3.

40. Progress report on MWHOP, September 1964, and Merlin A. Myers to Friend, July 13, 1964, CRD 1964 Housing Program, box 3; Progress report on MWHOP, October 1963, Subject Files: AFSC Community Relations—Housing, AFSC Archives; Draft report by Charlotte Meacham, August 6, 1963, CRD 1963 Housing Program; "Fair Housing in Virginia," *Focus*, August 7, 1965, clipping, and "The Inclusive Community," *Focus*, February 17, 1965, clipping, Subject Files: AFSC Community Relations—Housing, AFSC Archives; Advisory Committee Conference, October 17, 1964, CRD 1964 Housing Program. On Prince George's and Montgomery Counties, see Valerie C. Johnson, *Black Power in the Suburbs: The Myth or Reality of African American Suburban Political Incorporation* (Albany: State University of New York Press, 2002); David Rusk, "Suburbia: The Promised Land?," D.C. Policy Center, August 16, 2017, https://www.dcpolicycenter.org/publications/suburbia-promised-land/; Wiese, *Places of Their Own*, 244–85.

41. Charlotte Meacham, San Francisco log, July 19, 1963, CRD 1963 Housing Program; Santa Clara County Community Relations, n.d., AFSC NoCaRO.

42. An Appeal for Support of the AFSC Equal Housing Opportunities Program, January 1960, Community Relations 1960 Farm Labor to Housing; Curt Moody to Charlotte Meacham, January 23, 1962, and Fair Housing, April 1962, Community Relations 1962 Farm Labor Programs to Housing Programs.

43. J. Cassels to File, April 2, 1953, 86:13, AFSC-UIC; J. Cassels to File, n.d., re: Homer J. Lewis of the North Shore Citizens Committee, 86:14, AFSC-UIC; Ed Holmgren to File, September 1, 1955, 86:23, AFSC-UIC; Housing Opportunities Committee Meeting Minutes, May 2, 1957, American Section 1957 Community Relations Non-project to Housing; CRO Housing Opportunities Committee Minutes, March 19, 1959, American Section 1959 Commu-

nity Relations Farm Labor to Housing; AFSC HOP, Freedom of Residence in Deerfield, November 1960, 86:27, AFSC-UIC; Jane Weston to Catherine Naysmith, January 4, 1961, 86:29, AFSC-UIC; Maxwell Hahn to Hugh Middleton, April 22, 1960, 86:28, AFSC-UIC.

44. On Eichholz meetings, see for example HOP Minutes of Meeting, May 11, 1961, Community Relations 1961 Housing Program to Farm Labor Program; Al Eichholz to Kale Williams and Jane Weston, May 10, 1961, Al Eichholz to HOP Committee, May 10, 1961, June 27, 1961, August 4, 1961, and November 8, 1961, 86:31, AFSC-UIC.

45. Al Eichholz to Kale Williams and Jane Weston, June 9, 1961, 86:31, AFSC-UIC; Al Eichholz to Kale Williams and Jane Weston, March 22, 1962, Community Relations 1962 Farm Labor Programs to Housing Programs; Al Eichholz to Kale Williams and Jane Weston, June 12, 1962, Al Eichholz to Kale Williams and Jane Weston, January 29, 1962, and Al Eichholz to Kale Williams and Jane Weston, February 12, 1962, 87:4, AFSC-UIC; AFSC HOP Chicago Metro Area, December 1, 1962, to June 1, 1963, CRD 1963 Housing Program.

46. Jane Weston to Al Eichholz, November 29, 1962, 87:4, AFSC-UIC; Housing Opportunities Program, September 1962, 87:2, AFSC-UIC; AFSC CRO HOP Minutes of Meeting, January 10, 1963, 80:37, AFSC-UIC.

47. Form letter from HOME Inc. to Friend, November 10, 1959, Minutes of Board Meeting, October 1, 1959, and Questions and Answers about Home Opportunities Made Equal, Inc., December 21, 1959, 42:11, AFSC-UIC; Jane Weston to Barbara Moffett and Charlotte Meacham, August 30, 1961, and Pam Coe to Mary Berger et al., August 30, 1961, Community Relations 1961 Housing Program to Farm Labor Program; Housing Opportunities Program, September 1962, 87:2, AFSC-UIC; Jane Weston to Charlotte Meacham, February 20 1964, CRD 1964 Housing Program, box 3; Santa Clara County Community Relations, n.d., AFSC NoCaRO.

48. Dick Taylor, NAIRO Interne day to day, May 19–28, 1958, American Section 1958 Community Relations Housing to Indian Program; Thelma W. Babbitt, Report of Events surrounding the Move of the Second Negro Family to Levittown, Pennsylvania, August 6, 1958, Subject Files: AFSC Community Relations—Housing, AFSC Archives.

49. AFSC staff logs and reports often left out the name of the Black pioneer families to protect their privacy.

50. HOP Minutes of Meeting, February 9, 1961, Jane Weston to Barbara Moffett and Charlotte Meacham, August 30, 1961, and Pam Coe to Housing Staff, May 3, 1961, Community Relations 1961 Housing Program to Farm Labor Program; Jane Weston to HOP Staff, March 4, 1963, CRD 1963 Housing Program.

51. Charlotte Meacham and Margaret Fisher, *Fair Housing Handbook* (Philadelphia: American Friends Service Committee; New York: National Committee against Discrimination in Housing, 1965), AFSC Archives.

52. Paul B. Sheatsley, "White Attitudes toward the Negro," *Daedalus* 95, no.1 (1966): 217–8; Sugrue, *Sweet Land of Liberty*, 247–48; Eunice Grier and George Grier, *In Search of Housing: A Study of Experiences of Negro Professional and Technical Personnel in New York State* (New York: New York State Commission for Human Rights, 1965), 38–39; Andrew Kohut, "50 Years Ago: Mixed Views about Civil Rights but Support for Selma Demonstrators," *Factank: News in the Numbers*, March 5, 2015, https://www.pewresearch .org/fact-tank/2015/03/05/50-years-ago-mixed-views-about-civil-rights-but -support-for-selma-demonstrators/.

53. C. H. Yarrow, Annual Report to Shareholders and Friends, May 7, 1968, [misfiled in] American Section 1959 Community Relations Farm Labor to Housing; Housing Opportunities Program: A Report to AFSC Chicago Office Executive Committee on January 19, 1966, CRD 1966 Housing Program ROs Chicago to Seattle; Present Status Northwest Suburban Area Housing Opportunities, April 12, 1962, 87:4, AFSC-UIC.

54. Interview with Keith Harvey by Tracy E. K'Meyer, June 5, 2015, AFSC Archives; Jane C. Reinheimer to File, March 17, 1953, American Section 1953 Community Relations Housing and Indians; Grier and Grier, *In Search of Housing*, 17–18.

55. Jane Reinheimer to Lorraine Cleveland, July 14, 1954, American Section 1954 Community Relations P–Z; Jane Reinheimer to File, April 11, 1955, American Section 1955 Community Relations Administration Housing; Tom Colgan to Barbara Moffett, November 8, 1957, American Section 1957 Community Relations Non-project to Housing.

56. Thelma Babbitt to Community Relations Program Staff, April 18, 1958, log #7, March 3 to April 11, 1958, American Section 1958 Community Relations Housing to Indian Program; Thelma Babbitt to File, April 16, 1958, 70:1, AFSC-UIC.

57. Tom Colgan to Florence Kite, November 8, 1957, American Section 1957 Community Relations Non-project to Housing; Judy Wicoff to Phil Buskirk, January 10, 1958, and Leonard Menard to Robert Bullock, June 18, 1958, American Section 1958 Community Relations Farm Labor to High School Program; HOP Subcommittee Minutes, March 4, 1958, AFSC Minutes 1958 AEA Ed Advisory Comm to FIS International Student House Comm; Thelma Babbitt to Community Relations Program Staff, March 3, 1958, log #6, February 17 to March 3, 1958, American Section 1958 Community Relations Housing to Indian Program; Tom Colgan to Barbara Moffett, November 8, 1957, American Section 1957 Community Relations Non-project to Housing.

58. Pam Coe to Mary Berger et al., December 7, 1960, BCHRC Exec Committee, February 17, 1960, and BCHRC subcommittee on workshops, November 3, 1960, Community Relations 1960 Farm Labor to Housing; Arthur L. Smith to resource people, January 20, 1961, Press Release, April 15, 1961, and

BCHRC Executive Committee Minutes, April 27, 1961, Community Relations 1961 Housing Program to Farm Labor Program.

59. Progress report of the AFSC Metropolitan Housing Opportunities Program to the Dolfinger-McMahon Foundation, January 1961, and Charlotte Meacham to Community Relations Program Staff, November 3, 1960, to February 5, 1961, Community Relations 1961 Housing Program to Farm Labor Program.

60. HOP Minutes, February 9, 1961, Jane Weston to Pam Coe, June 23, 1961, and Judy Howard to Jane Weston, October 10, 1961, Community Relations 1961 Housing Program to Farm Labor Program.

61. Will Cooley, "Moving on Out: Black Pioneering in Chicago, 1915–1950," *Journal of Urban History* 36, no. 4 (2010): 485–506.

62. Helen Baker Report, July 17–18, 1962, Community Relations 1962 Farm Labor Programs to Housing Programs.

63. Jane Weston to Barbara Moffett, May 31, 1962, 87:5, AFSC-UIC; Jane Weston to Kale Williams, February 26, 1962, Community Relations 1962 Farm Labor Programs to Housing Programs; Mary Lou Finley, Bernard Lafayette Jr., James R. Ralph, and Pam Smith, eds., *The Chicago Freedom Movement: Martin Luther King and Civil Rights Activism in the North*, with a foreword by Clayborne Carson (Lexington: University Press of Kentucky, 2016), 158; Mark Engler and Paul Engler, "Surviving the Ups and Downs of Social Movements," *Waging Nonviolence: People Powered News and Analysis*, September 2, 2014, https://wagingnonviolence.org/2014/09/surviving-ups-downs-social-movements/; Barbara Moffett to Jane Weston and Kale Williams, May 25, 1962, 87:5, AFSC-UIC; Housing Opportunities Program Report, September 1962, 87:2, AFSC-UIC.

64. Report by Bill Moyer, September 26–October 5, 1962, and October 8–15, 1962, Community Relations 1962 Farm Labor Programs to Housing Programs; AFSC HOP Chicago Metropolitan Area, June 1–December 1, 1962, General Administration 1962 Regional Offices to Information Services; AFSC CRO HOP Minutes, March 14, 1963, 80:37, AFSC-UIC; Report by Bill Moyer, April 1–8, 1963, CRD 1963 Housing Program.

65. AFSC HOP Chicago Metropolitan Area, December 1, 1962, to June 1, 1963, and Draft Report by Charlotte Meacham, August 6, 1963, CRD 1963 Housing Program; Proposal to the Field Foundation from the AFSC CRO Housing and Urban Affairs Program, April 1964, 88:12, AFSC-UIC.

66. Sherry Wilson Brown, "Bert Ransom Creates a Chorus of Hope," *Alexandria (VA) Gazette Packet*, January 22, 2009, http://www.tisaraphoto.com/legends/Ransom.htm; Elbert Ransom, September 8–20, 1964, and December 7–11, 1964, CRD 1964 Housing Program, box 3; Report by Elbert Ransom, September 21–26, 1964, 88:11, AFSC-UIC; Bert Ransom to HOP Committee, October 1965, 81:16, AFSC-UIC; ERMF-NAIRO Internship Program, Supervisor's Third Quarter Report, May 25, 1965, 86:3, AFSC-UIC;

Report to the Field Foundation on Chicago Metropolitan Area Housing Opportunities Program, October 1, 1964, to September 20, 1965, CRD 1965 Housing Program to Rights of Conscience Program.

67. Elbert Ransom, September 28 to October 3, 1964, Bert Ransom, October 12 to November 6, 1964, and First Chicago Area Housing Opportunities Conference background and evaluation, n.d., CRD 1964 Housing Program, box 3; Report by Bert Ransom, December 14 to February 19, 1965, AFSC CRO HOP, 86:3, AFSC-UIC; Bert Ransom to HOP Committee, October 1965, 81:16, AFSC-UIC.

68. Donald Moffitt, "Fair-Housing Flop?," *Wall Street Journal*, February 2, 1965; Report by Bert Ransom, October 12 to November 6 and November 30 to December 4, 1964, CRD 1964 Housing Program, box 3; Grier and Grier, *In Search of Housing*, 8, 27–33.

69. Dick Taylor to Barbara [Moffett], [April 1964], CRD 1964 Housing Program.

70. Barbara Krasner, False Assumptions about the Fair Housing Movement, Metropolitan Philadelphia, February 1966, CRD 1966 Housing Program Metro Philly to Metro Washington; Isabel Gehr, Final Report, June 23, 1966, CRD 1966 Housing Program ROs Chicago to Seattle.

71. Sugrue, *Sweet Land of Liberty*, 247–48; Grier and Grier, *In Search of Housing*, 17; George B. Nesbitt and Elfriede Hoeber, "The Fair Housing Committee: Its Need for a New Perspective," *Land Economics* 41, no. 2 (May 1965): 97–110.

72. Minutes of HOP subcommittee on future of program, January 6, 1966, 80:8, AFSC-UIC.

Chapter Three

1. North Shore Summer Project Statement of Purpose, [Spring 1965], CRD 1965 Housing Program to Rights of Conscience Program.

2. Gerda Lerner, *Nonviolent Resistance: The History of an Idea*, Harvey Wish Memorial Lecture Series (Cleveland: Department of History, Case Western University, 1983), 13; Anthony C. Siracusa, "From Pacifism to Resistance: The Evolution of Nonviolence in Wartime America," *Journal of Civil and Human Rights* 3, no. 1 (Spring/Summer 2017): 62; Joseph Kip Kosek, "Richard Gregg, Mohandas Gandhi, and the Strategy of Nonviolence," *Journal of American History* 91, no. 4 (March 2005): 1338–39; Richard B. Gregg, *The Power of Nonviolence* (Philadelphia: Lippincott, 1934); Minutes of the Committee to Plan for the Institute of Race Relations, March 15, 1935, and Institute of Race Relations, program, July 1–29, 1935, General Files 1935 General; Minutes of the Social Industrial Section, November 7, 1935, AFSC Minutes 1933–35.

3. Kosek, "Richard Gregg," 1341; Siracusa, "From Pacifism to Resistance," 63–66; Irva Jane Sampson to Ed Miller, July 27, 1942, Irva Jane Sampson to Ed Miller, August 10, 1942, and William H. Kuenning, August 20, 1942, Social

Industrial Section 1942 Work Camps to Indianapolis, Ind. On the founding and early activities of CORE, see August Meier and Elliott Rudwick, *CORE: A Study in the Civil Rights Movement, 1942–1968* (New York: Oxford University Press, 1973), 4–39.

4. Kosek, "Richard Gregg," 1343–45; Clarence Pickett, "Three Quakers in Montgomery," *Friends Journal*, May 5, 1956, 280–81; Community Relations Committee Minutes, March 7, 1956, AFSC Minutes 1956 Annual Meeting to BB Bequest Comm; Report of the Community Relations Roundup, April 7–12, 1957, and Introductory Remarks by Community Relations Division Executive Committee Chairman, Richard K. Bennett, December 5, 1962, Subject Files: Community Relations, 1936–1967, AFSC Archives. On James Lawson's experience in India and reaction to Montgomery, see David Halberstam, *The Children* (New York: Random House, 1998), 11–50.

5. Report of the Community Relations Roundup, April 7–12, 1957, Subject Files: Community Relations, 1936–1967, AFSC Archives; Judy Miller, untitled essay, May 19, 1958, 97:12, AFSC-UIC.

6. Representative Council Minutes, February 22–27, 1959, circulated in Barbara Moffett to Board of Directors, April 1, 1959, 92:12, AFSC-UIC.

7. "Minutes from Last Session," [n.d. but filed with 1959 Spring Roundup materials], 97:12, AFSC-UIC; AFSC Sub Committee on Southern Programs Minutes, April 19, 1960, AFSC Minutes 1960 Annual Meeting to Board of Directors; Judy Howard to Community Relations Staff et al., re: Roundup November 12–16, 1961, AFSC Minutes 1962 Program Priorities Comm to Social and Technical Assistance Comm; American Friends Service Committee, press release March 31, 1960, Subject Files: Community Relations, 1936–1967, AFSC Archives; Community Relations Division Exec Comm Minutes, March 21, 1967, AFSC Minutes 1967 BD General Service Comm to Peace Education Div; The Theory and Practice of Civil Disobedience, October 21, 1968, AFSC Minutes 1968 Community Relations Exec Comm to International Conferences. On Jean Fairfax, see Susan Lynn, *Progressive Women in Conservative Times* (New Brunswick, NJ: Rutgers University Press, 1992), 76–77, 109–10.

8. Kosek, "Richard Gregg," 1345; Halberstam, *The Children*, 50; Siracusa, "From Pacifism to Resistance," 57–59.

9. Housing Opportunities Program, April 1957, 87:20, AFSC-UIC; Meeting at YMCA, August 2, 1957, Committee on Non-violence meeting at YMCA, September 13, 1957, and Housing Opportunities Committee meeting December 12, 1957, American Section 1957 Community Relations Non-project to Housing; An Institute on Non-violence and Integration, December 7, 1957, 87:21, AFSC-UIC.

10. Lawrence S. Aspey, The Emphasis and Balance of an AFSC Program on Non-violence, September 16, 1961, and Stewart Meacham to Peace Education Secretaries, November 5, 1962, PED 1962 Friends Peace Service to Program on Nonviolence; AFSC NERO, Nonviolence in Theory and Practice,

October 1962, 4:19, AFSC-UIC; AFSC NCRO Executive Committee Minutes, June 15, 1964, AFSC Regional Office Minutes 1964 Pasadena to Seattle.

11. For example, the Metropolitan Philadelphia HOP staff organized demonstrations in 1965 in the suburbs west of the city, and the Metropolitan Washington HOP staff participated in sit-ins in 1967 calling for Defense Secretary Robert McNamara to order the desegregation of off-base military housing.

12. James R. Ralph, *Northern Protest: Martin Luther King, Jr., Chicago, and the Civil Rights Movement* (Cambridge, MA: Harvard University Press, 1993), 82, 102; Report by Bill Moyer, March 18–23, 1963, June 17–24, 1963, June 25–July 2, 1963, CRD 1963 Housing Program; AFSC to Key Leaders Concerned with Non-violent Direct Action for Civil Rights, June 28, 1963, 87:7, AFSC-UIC; Leadership Consultation on Need for Training in Non-violent Direct Action, July 14, 1963, 4:19, AFSC-UIC; Jane Weston to HOP Committee, August 1, 1963, CRD 1963 Housing Program.

13. Kale Williams to Executive Committee, August 9, 1963, 78:6, AFSC-UIC. Bill Moyer Logs from July to October 1963, CRD 1963 Housing Program; AFSC CRO HOP Minutes, December 12, 1963, 80:37, AFSC-UIC; Carl Zietlow to Glenn Smiley, March 11, 1964, 78:4, AFSC-UIC; Jim Bristol to Carl Zietlow, March 16, 1964, 4:19, AFSC-UIC; Weekend Workshops in Nonviolence, 105:8, AFSC-UIC; Jane Weston to Charlotte Meacham, April 24, 1964, CRD 1964 Housing Program, box 3; Barbara Moffett to National Community Relations Committee, September 1976, Reference Files Individuals, AFSC Archives.

14. AFSC CRO HOP Minutes, December 12, 1963, 80:37, AFSC-UIC; Minutes, February 25, 1964, AFSC Minutes 1964 Representative Council to CRI National Indian Program; Kale Williams to Executive Committee of the AFSC Chicago Reginal Office, March 20, 1964, CRD 1964 Housing Program, box 3. Graydon Megan, "Kale Williams, Fair Housing Leader in Chicago, Dies at 90," *Chicago Tribune*, January 20, 2016, https://www.chicagotribune.com/news/obituaries/ct-kale-williams-obituary-20160120-story.html.

15. Bernard Lafayette Jr. and Kathryn Lee Johnson, *In Peace and Freedom: My Journey in Selma* (Lexington: University Press of Kentucky, 2013), xi–xiii; Mary Lou Finley, Bernard Lafayette Jr., James R. Ralph, and Pam Smith, eds., *The Chicago Freedom Movement: Martin Luther King and Civil Rights Activism in the North*, with a foreword by Clayborne Carson (Lexington: University Press of Kentucky, 2016), 389–90; Interview with Bernard Lafayette by Tracy E. K'Meyer, October 12, 2014, AFSC Archives.

16. Allan W. Austin, *Quaker Brotherhood: Interracial Activism and the American Friends Service Committee, 1917–1950* (Urbana: University of Illinois Press, 2012), 9; H. Larry Ingle, "The American Friends Service Committee, 1947–1949: The Cold War's Effect," *Peace and Change* 23, no.1 (January 1998): 29.

17. "African American Folklorist: Gerald L. Davis," Notable Folklorists of

Color, https://notablefolkloristsofcolor.org/portfolio/gerald-l-davis/ (accessed May 6, 2021).

18. Judy Howard to Community Relations Staff, Committee, and Roundup Participants, November 12–16, 1961, AFSC Minutes 1962 Program Priorities Comm to Social and Technical Assistance Comm. On the tensions in the AFSC over non-Quaker staff, see H. Larry Ingle, "'Truly Radical, Non-violent, Friendly Approaches': Challenges to the American Friends Service Committee," *Quaker History* 105, no. 1 (Spring 2016): 3–4; J. William Frost, "'Our Deeds Carry Our Message': The Early History of the American Friends Service Committee," *Quaker History* 81, no.1 (Spring 1992): 1; Gregory A. Barnes, *A Centennial History of the American Friends Service Committee* (Philadelphia: Friends Press, 2016), 270, 282–83.

19. Review of Intensive Program to Strengthen Nonviolence in the Civil Rights Struggle, June 1–September 30, 1964, and Minutes, October 27, 1964, AFSC Minutes 1964 Representative Council to CRI National Indian Program; Finley et al., *The Chicago Freedom Movement*, 294; Interview with Bernard Lafayette, AFSC Archives.

20. Meier and Rudwick, *CORE*, 6, 28; Alderman Leon M. Despres, Why the Sit-Ins in Our Community, January 30, 1962, 104:12, AFSC-UIC; Report by Bill Moyer, March 18–23, 1963, April 8–12, 1963, and June 25–July 2, 1963, CRD 1963 Housing Program; Santa Clara County Community Relations Committee, March 21, 1962, AFSC Regional Office Minutes 1962 Portland to Seattle; Dan Safran to Merlin Myers, program activities, August 12–16, 1963, CRD 1963 Housing to MWHOP; Staff logbook, June and July 1963, CRD 1963 Housing Program; Kale Williams to Clerks and Pastors of Friends Meetings, August 9, 1963, 87:6, AFSC-UIC.

21. AFSC CRO HOP Minutes of Meeting, May 14, 1964, 81:11, AFSC-UIC.

22. AFSC HOP Chicago metropolitan area, June 1, 1963, to June 30, 1964, Bill Moyer to Charlotte Meacham, August 3, 1964, and AFSC CRO HOP Minutes of Meeting, August 13, 1964, CRD 1964 Housing Program, box 3.

23. For Discussion by HOP Committee: North Shore Summer Project, February 11, 1965, 86:4, AFSC-UIC; HOP Chicago to Kale Williams, March 10, 1965, with enclosure Prospectus of the North Shore Summer Project, CRD 1965 Housing Program to Rights of Conscience Program.

24. Report by Bill Moyer, January 28 to February 3, 1963, CRD 1963 Housing Program; HOP Chicago to Kale Williams, March 10, 1965, with enclosure, Prospectus of the North Shore Summer Project, and Carol Kleinman, "Mission in Suburbia," *Renewal*, April 1965, clipping, CRD 1965 Housing Program to Rights of Conscience Program.

25. Carol Kleinman, "Mission in Suburbia," *Renewal*, April 1965, clipping, and North Shore Summer Project Statement of Purpose, CRD 1965 Housing Program to Rights of Conscience Program.

26. AFSC CRO HOP Minutes of Meeting, May 13, 1965, and June 10, 1965, 81:16, AFSC-UIC; Bill Moyer, North Shore home seekers handout, April 22, 1965,

CRD 1965 Housing Program to Rights of Conscience Program; Jack Mabley, "Can Love Win over Fear on North Shore?," *Chicago's American*, May 14, 1965, clipping, 1:1, NSSPC-UIC; "Over Rollo's Desk," *Skokie [IL] News*, May 6, 1965, clipping, CRD 1965 Housing Program to Rights of Conscience Program.

27. North Shore Summer Project newsletter, June 25, July 14, and July 23, 1965, CRD 1965 Housing Program to Rights of Conscience Program; Sally Olds, news release for the North Shore Summer Project, July 17, 1965, 1:2, NSSPC-UIC; Jerome Watson, "Plan 'Escalation' in Drive on N. Shore," *Chicago Sun-Times*, August 2, 1965, clipping, 86:4, AFSC-UIC; Thomas Fitzpatrick, "Winnetka Crowd Hears King," *Chicago Tribune*, July 26, 1965, clipping, 1:1, NSSPC-UIC; Charlotte Meacham to File, August 3, 1965, CRD 1965 Housing Program, box 1; North Shore Summer Project Summary Report, August 29, 1965, CRD 1965 Housing Program to Rights of Conscience Program.

28. Emory Davis to Lewis Pfaff, June 29, 1965, 86:4, AFSC-UIC; North Shore Summer Project newsletter, July 14, 1965, CRD 1965 Housing Program to Rights of Conscience Program; North Shore Summer Project newsletter, July 23, 1965, 1:3, NSSPC-UIC; Jerome Watson, "Plan 'Escalation' in Drive on N. Shore," *Chicago Sun-Times*, August 2, 1965, clipping, 86:4, AFSC-UIC; Charlotte Meacham to File, August 3, 1965, CRD 1965 Housing Program, box 1.

29. Sally Olds, news release for North Shore Summer Project, July 17, 1965, 1:2, NSSPC-UIC; North Shore Summer Project newsletter, July 23, 1965, 1:3, NSSPC-UIC; North Shore Summer Project: A Public Witness, 1:12, NSSPC-UIC; Sally Olds, news release for North Shore Summer Project, August 24, 1965, 1:2, NSSPC-UIC; Jerome Watson, "Plan 'Escalation' in Drive on N. Shore," *Chicago Sun-Times*, August 2, 1965, clipping, 86:4, AFSC-UIC.

30. Joan Wilson, "Veterans' Housing," North Shore Summer Project newsletter, September 14, 1965, 1:3, NSSPC-UIC; Activities of HOP/Chicago's new assistant director, or footsteps of neophyte Jerry Davis, September 20–October 3, 1965, Jerry Davis, log, October 4–17, 1965, and Susannah Gross, Report, October 11–28, 1965, CRD 1965 Housing Program to Rights of Conscience Program.

31. AFSC CRO HOP Minutes of Meeting, October 14, 1965, 81:26, AFSC-UIC; "Why a NON-VIOLENT Movement," n.d. [1966], 1:5, CWSCPC-UIC; Finley et al., *The Chicago Freedom Movement*, 124–25.

32. Activities of HOP/Chicago's new assistant director, or footsteps of neophyte Jerry Davis, September 20–October 3, 1965, CRD 1965 Housing Program to Rights of Conscience Program; AFSC CRO HOP Minutes of Meeting, October 14, 1965, 81:16, AFSC-UIC.

33. [Bill Moyer], Housing Opportunities Program: A Report to AFSC Chicago Office Exec Committee, January 19, 1966, CRD 1966 Housing Program ROs Chicago to Seattle; AFSC CRO HOP Minutes of Meeting, February 17, 1966, 80:8, AFSC-UIC.

34. AFSC CRO HOP Minutes of Meeting, April 14, 1966, and June 9, 1966, 80:8, AFSC-UIC.

35. AFSC CRO HOP Minutes of Meeting, February 17, 1966, March 10, 1966, May 12, 1966, and June 9, 1966, 80:8, AFSC-UIC; Carl P. Zietlow to Friend, June 30, 1966, 1:8, NSSPC-UIC. On Oak Park, see Carole Goodwin, *The Oak Park Strategy: Community Control of Racial Change* (Chicago: University of Chicago Press, 1979).

36. "Why a NON-VIOLENT Movement," n.d. [1966], 1:5, CWSCPC-UIC; Bill Moyer, An Analysis of the System of Housing Negroes in Chicago, February 18, 1966, CRD 1966 Housing Program ROs Chicago to Seattle; AFSC CRO HOP Minutes of Meeting, March 10, 1966, 80:8, AFSC-UIC; HOP Chicago to Kale Williams, March 10, 1965, with enclosure Prospectus of the North Shore Summer Project, CRD 1965 Housing Program to Rights of Conscience Program; Finley et al., *The Chicago Freedom Movement*, 44–45; AFSC CRO HOP Minutes of Meeting, June 9, 1966, 80:8, AFSC-UIC; Carl P. Zietlow to Friend, June 30, 1966, 1: 8, NSSPC-UIC. In his study of the Chicago open housing movement, James R. Ralph likewise credits Moyer with persuading Bevel and SCLC to use direct action against the real estate industry as a strategy for ending the slums. See Ralph, *Northern Protest*, 99–101.

37. Carl Zietlow to Friend, June 30, 1966, 1:8, NSSPC-UIC; Urban Affairs Weekly Report, July 10, 1966, and Notes on Barbara Moffett's Conversation with Kale Williams, July 13, 1966, CRD 1966 Housing Program ROs Chicago to Seattle; Ralph, *Northern Protest*, 105–7.

38. Mary Lou Finley, "The Open Housing Marches: Chicago, Summer '66," in *Chicago 1966: Open Housing Marches, Summit Negotiations, and Operation Breadbasket*, ed. David J. Garrow (Brooklyn, NY: Carlson, 1989), 4–7, 10, 16–17, 42. On the Chicago movement, see Ralph, *Northern Protest*, and Garrow, *Chicago 1966*. The following account focuses on the involvement of AFSC representatives in the direct-action campaign of the summer of 1966.

39. Urban Affairs Weekly Report, July 17, 1966, CRD 1966 Housing Program ROs Chicago to Seattle; Ralph, *Northern Protest*, 109–13; Amanda I. Seligman, "'But Burn—No': The Rest of the Crowd in Three Civil Disorders in 1960s Chicago," *Journal of Urban History* 37, no. 2 (2011): 230–55.

40. Urban Affairs Weekly Report, July 17 and 24, 1966, CRD 1966 Housing Program ROs Chicago to Seattle; Ralph, *Northern Protest*, 114; Finley, "The Open Housing Marches," 21.

41. Urban Affairs Weekly Report, July 24 and 31, 1966, CRD 1966 Housing Program ROs Chicago to Seattle.

42. Ralph, *Northern Protest*, 114–16; Urban Affairs Weekly Report, July 24 and 31, 1966, CRD 1966 Housing Program ROs Chicago to Seattle.

43. Ralph, *Northern Protest*, 119–20; Urban Affairs Weekly Report, July 31, 1966, CRD 1966 Housing Program ROs Chicago to Seattle.

44. Ralph, *Northern Protest*, 120–23; Urban Affairs Weekly Report, July 31, 1966,

and Notes on talk with Kale Williams, August 1, 1966, CRD 1966 Housing Program ROs Chicago to Seattle.

45. James A. Colaiaco, "Martin Luther King, Jr. and the Paradox of Nonviolent Direct Action," *Phylon* 47, no. 1 (1986): 16–28; Maria Pappalardo, Chicago Report, November 22, 1966, CRD 1966 Housing Program ROs Chicago to Seattle; Ralph, *Northern Protest*, 133–34; Finley, "The Open Housing Marches," 10–12, 27–28.

46. Maria Pappalardo to Barbara Moffett et al., July 29, 1966, Maria Pappalardo to File, Chicago Logs, August 12, 1966, Maria Pappalardo to File, August 19, 1966, and AFSC Chicago Regional Office: Appeal for Support of Urban Community Relations Work, September 1966, CRD 1966 Housing Program ROs Chicago to Seattle.

47. Maria Pappalardo to Barbara Moffett et al., July 29, 1966, and Report signed "Maria," Saturday, August 13, 1966, CRD 1966: Housing Program ROs Chicago to Seattle; HOP Minutes, February 9, 1967, AFSC Regional Office Minutes 1967 Cambridge to Pasadena.

48. Ralph, *Northern Protest*, 136–37; Maria Pappalardo to Barbara Moffett et al., July 29, 1966, Maria Pappalardo to File, August 19, 1966, [Maria Pappalardo], August 19, 1966, Maria Pappalardo to Log, August 24, 1966, and AFSC HOP Chicago Metropolitan Area Report, October 1965–66, CRD 1966 Housing Program ROs Chicago to Seattle; Marlene Thompson to AFSC, July–August 1966, 86:6, AFSC-UIC.

49. Urban Affairs Weekly Report, August 7, 1966, CRD 1966 Housing Program ROs Chicago to Seattle; Ralph, *Northern Protest*, 122–23. Note that the Urban Affairs report was unsigned, but these reports were Lafayette's responsibility and he typically wrote them.

50. Maria Pappalardo, [Report], August 13, 1966, Urban Affairs Weekly Report, August 14, 1966, and Maria Pappalardo, [Report], August 14, 1966, CRD 1966 Housing Program ROs Chicago to Seattle.

51. Maria Pappalardo to File, Friday, August 12, 1966, CRD 1966 Housing Program ROs Chicago to Seattle; Ralph, *Northern Protest*, 142–50.

52. Ralph, *Northern Protest*, 153–58; To Achieve Justice and Make Chicago an Open City, August 17, 1966, CRD 1966 Housing Program ROs Chicago to Seattle.

53. Maria Pappalardo, [Report], August 18, 1966, August 19, 1966, and August 20, 1966, Urban Affairs Weekly Report, August 21, 1966, and Maria Pappalardo to File, August 22, 1966, CRD 1966 Housing Program ROs Chicago to Seattle.

54. Maria Pappalardo, [Report], August 18, 1966, August 22, 1966, and August 23, 1966, and Report of the Subcommittee to the Conference on Fair Housing convened by the Chicago Conference on Religion and Race, August 26, 1966, CRD 1966 Housing Program ROs Chicago to Seattle.

55. Report of the Subcommittee to the Conference on Fair Housing Convened by the Chicago Conference on Religion and Race, August 26, 1966, CRD 1966 Housing Program ROs Chicago to Seattle.

56. John McKnight, "The Summit Negotiations," in *Chicago 1966: Open Housing Marches, Summit Negotiations, and Operation Breadbasket*, ed. David J. Garrow (Brooklyn, NY: Carlson, 1989), 138, 141–45; Ralph, *Northern Protest*, 168–71.

57. Maria Pappalardo to File, September 2, 1966, CRD 1966 Housing Program ROs Chicago to Seattle; AFSC CRO HOP Minutes, August [?], 1966, 80:8, AFSC-UIC.

58. Maria Pappalardo to File, September 2, 1966, A Proposal for Participation in Project Open Housing for the Chicago Commission on Human Relations, September 12, 1966, Urban Affairs Weekly Report, September 18 and 25, 1966 [combined report], and Appeal for Support of Urban Community Relations Work, September 1966, CRD 1966 Housing Program ROs Chicago to Seattle; AFSC CRO HOP Minutes, August [?], 1966, 80:8, AFSC-UIC; Chicago Regional Office: Program Affecting Housing in the Chicago Metropolitan Area, October 12, 1966, 86:6, AFSC-UIC.

Chapter Four

1. *Quaker Faith and Action*, 5th ed., http://qfp.quaker.org.uk/passage/23-02/ (accessed May 6, 2021).

2. Thomas Hamm, *The Quakers in America* (New York: Columbia University Press, 2003), 29–31, 157–60; E. Raymond Wilson, *Uphill for Peace: Quaker Impact on Congress* (Richmond, IN: Friends United Press, 1975), 3; Stephen Cary et al., *Speak Truth to Power: A Quaker Search for an Alternative to Violence* (Philadelphia: American Friends Service Committee, 1955), http://www.quaker.org/sttp.html (accessed, May 6, 2021). For more on the history of the phrase "speak truth to power," see Guy Aiken, "When Not to Speak Truth to Power: Thoughts on the Historiography of the Social Gospel," http://usreligion.blogspot.com/2017/08/when-not-to-speak-truth-to-power.html (accessed May 6, 2021).

3. Marvin R. Weisbord, *Some Form of Peace: True Stories of the American Friends Service Committee at Home and Abroad* (New York: Viking Press, 1968), xvii–xviii, 4–5; AFSC, *Bulletin* no. 92, Fifteenth Annual Report, June 1, 1931–December 1, 1932, AFSC Archives.

4. John Willard to Dick Bennett, August 27, 1951, American Section 1951 Community Division A–F; J. Cassels to File, December 22, 1952, 88:9, AFSC-UIC; Phil Buskirk to Richard Bennett, January 20, 1955, in box 10, folder AFSC Northern California Regional Office, Wurster-Bancroft; HOP Minutes of Meeting, May 11, 1961, and Report of the Community Relations Roundup, April 7–12, 1957, Subject Files: Community Relations, 1936–1967, AFSC Archives; Summary of Meeting, July 2, 1958, American Section 1958 Community Relations Housing to Indian Program.

5. For a history of the Friends Committee on National Legislations, see Wilson, *Uphill for Peace*.

6. Ruth Morton to Dick Bennett et al., February 21, 1952, and Ruth Morton to Dick Bennett et al., March 26, 1952, American Section 1952 Race Relations F–I; Richard Bennett to the President, January 20, 1954, and Jane Reinheimer to William Stansbury, March 24, 1954, American Section 1954 Community Relations Housing A–Z.

7. Henry Patterson to Maxwell M. Rabb, April 9, 1954, American Section 1954 Community Relations, P–Z; Robert Fredrick Burk, *The Eisenhower Administration and Black Civil Rights* (Knoxville: University of Tennessee Press, 1984), 70; Jane Reinheimer to Dick Bennett, April 29, 1954, and Dick Bennett to Jane Reinheimer, May 13, 1954, American Section 1954 Community Relations P–Z.

8. Jane Reinheimer to File, May 26, 1954, Jane Reinheimer to Dick Bennett, May 25, 1954, Jim Cassels to Jane Reinheimer, June 10, 1954, and Dick Bennett to Maxwell Rabb, July 1, 1954, American Section 1954 Community Relations P–Z.

9. Jane Reinheimer to Dick Bennett, July 14, 1954, and Richard K. Bennett to Henry Patterson, September 16, 1954, American Section 1954 Community Relations P–Z.

10. Burk, *The Eisenhower Administration*, 16. On the Eisenhower administration's approach to housing, see Burk, 109–27; Arnold R. Hirsch, "'Containment' on the Homefront: Race and Federal Policy from the New Deal to the Cold War," *Journal of Urban History* 26, no. 2 (January 2000): 158–89; Charles Lamb and Adam W. Nye, "Do Presidents Control Bureaucracy?: The Federal Housing Administration during the Truman-Eisenhower Era," *Political Science Quarterly* 127, no. 3 (2012): 445–64.

11. Barbara Moffett to Clarence Pickett, April 25, 1955, Subject Folder: AFSC Community Relations—Housing, AFSC Archives; Phil Buskirk to Richard Bennett, June 4, 1954, American Section 1954 Community Relations P–Z.

12. Rough notes on meeting re: Morrisville, September 13, 1951, by F. Kite [Florence], and Jack Wilmore to Ralph Rose, December 11, 1951, American Section 1951 Community Division to Economic Relations; Jacques Wilmore to Dick Bennett, June 3, 1952, Jacques Wilmore to Dick Bennett, July 15, 1952, Jacques Wilmore, file report of visit with Victor C. Adler, regional director of Housing and Home Financing Agency for Philadelphia, November 6, 1952, and Jacques Wilmore, file report of visit with Leo Kirk in the FHA regional office, November 6, 1952, American Section 1952 Race Relations F–I.

13. J. Philip Buskirk to Albert M. Cole, May 24, 1954, and Disposition Policy for Lanham Act Housing, in box 10, folder AFSC Northern California Regional Office, Wurster-Bancroft; Phil Buskirk to Richard Bennett, June 4, 1954, American Section 1954 Community Relations P–Z.

14. Ed Holmgren to File, August 2, 1955, American Section 1955 Community Relations Administration Housing; Recommendations of the AFSC to Mayor Richard J. Daley, March 12, 1956, 1:3, AFSC-UIC; Housing Opportunities Program meeting, March 15, 1956, American Section 1956 Community

Relations Administration F–Z to Projects A–I; Lucy P. Carner et al., [report on mission to Trumbull Park], October 1956, Subject Folder: AFSC Community Relations—Housing, AFSC Archives.

15. Trumbull Park—a Progress Report, April 1959, and Kale Williams to File, February 3, 1959, American Section 1959 Community Relations Farm Labor to Housing. On the political impact of white resistance on the Chicago Housing Authority, see Arnold R. Hirsch, "Massive Resistance in the Urban North: Trumbull Park, Chicago, 1953–1966," *Journal of American History* 82, no. 2 (September 1995): 522–55.

16. Thelma W. Babbitt, Testimony Prepared for Governor's Citizens Committee on Discrimination in Housing, December 2, 1958, American Section 1958 Community Relations Housing to Indian Program; Charlotte C. Meacham, Testimony Prepared for a Public Hearing on Fair Housing before the Committee on Revision and Amendment of Laws, State of New Jersey, April 10, 1961, Subject Folder: AFSC Community Relations— Housing, AFSC Archives; Jane Weston, Statement Prepared for a Public Hearing on HB 755, May 8, 1963, 87:9, AFSC-UIC.

17. Charlotte C. Meacham, Testimony Prepared for a Public Hearing on Fair Housing before the Committee on Revision and Amendment of Laws, State of New Jersey, April 10, 1961, Subject Folder: AFSC Community Relations—Housing, AFSC Archives; Jane B. Weston, Statement Prepared for a Public Hearing Held by the Committee on Judiciary of the City Council of Chicago, Illinois, July 19, 1963, 87:9, AFSC-UIC.

18. Ed Holmgren to John Willard, March 25, 1958, 87:25, AFSC-UIC; Jane Weston to Pam Coe, March 24, 1961, Jane Weston to Pam Coe, May 3, 1961, and Jane Weston to Pam Coe, June 23, 1961, Community Relations 1961 Housing Program to Farm Labor Program.

19. Judy Howard to Community Relations Division Executive Committee, April 19, 1962, AFSC Minutes 1962 Program Priorities Comm to Social and Technical Assistance Comm; Housing Opportunities Program, September 1962, 87:2, AFSC-UIC.

20. I have found only one reference to passage of the Chicago ordinance in either the AFSC Archives in Philadelphia or the Chicago Regional Office files at the University of Illinois–Chicago. On the Chicago Fair Housing Ordinance, see "September 11, 1963—Open Housing Ordinance Passes in City Council," *Connecting the Windy City*, September 11, 2017, http://www .connectingthewindycity.com/2017/09/september-11-1963-open-housing .html; James R. Ralph, *Northern Protest: Martin Luther King, Jr., Chicago, and the Civil Rights Movement* (Cambridge, MA: Harvard University Press, 1993), 82, 102, 115, 209; AFSC HOP Chicago Metro Area, June 1, 1963, to June 30, 1964, CRD 1964 Housing Program, box 3.

21. AFSC CRO HOP Minutes of Meeting, August 13, 1964, Jane Weston to Bill Berry et al., August 27, 1964, and Jane Weston to Charlotte Meacham, October 14, 1964, CRD 1964 Housing Program, box 3.

22. Clay O'Dell, "The Politics of Housing: Catholic Activism and Dissent under Archbishop Joseph McGucken of San Francisco," *American Catholic Studies* 117, no. 3 (Fall 2006): 21; Santa Clara County Community Relations, December 1960 to January 1961 Report, Community Relations 1961 Housing Program to Farm Labor Program; Santa Clara County Community Relations, December 1961 to January 1962 Report, Minutes of the Santa Clara County Community Relations Committee Meeting, March 21, 1962, Santa Clara County Community Relations Report, February–March 1962, Minutes of the Santa Clara Community Relations Committee Meeting, May 16, 1962, Santa Clara Community Relations Report, July-August-September 1962, and Santa Clara County Community Relations Committee Meeting, February 20, 1963, AFSC NoCaRO; Stephen Thiermann to Barbara Moffett, April 16, 1963, CRD 1963 Housing Program; Community Relations Committee Minutes, June 11, 1963, AFSC Regional Office Minutes 1963 Houston to Seattle. On the Berkeley fair housing fight, see David B. Oppenheimer, "California's Anti-Discrimination Legislation, Proposition 14, and the Constitutional Protection of Minority Rights: The Fiftieth Anniversary of the California Fair Employment and Housing Act," *Golden Gate University Law Review* 40, no. 2 (January 2010): 117–27; W. J. Rorabaugh, *Berkeley at War: The 1960s* (New York: Oxford University Press, 1989), 56–58.

23. For a review of California's open housing legislation in this period and the launching of the Proposition 14 campaign, see Oppenheimer, "California's Anti-Discrimination Legislation," and Raymond E. Wolfinger and Fred I. Greenstein, "Repeal of Fair Housing in California: An Analysis of Referendum Voting," *American Political Science Review* 62, no. 3 (August 1968): 753–69.

24. *Fair Housing*, newsletter of the AFSC Southern California Regional Office, May 1964, AFSC PRO; Charlotte Meacham to Barbara Moffett et al., March 3, 1964, and [?] to Colin W. Bell, March 20, 1964, CRD 1964 Housing Program, box 3.

25. Community Relations Committee Minutes, December 10, 1963, AFSC Regional Office Minutes 1963 Houston to Seattle; AFSC NCRO Exec Comm Minutes, March 16, 1964, April 20, 1964, and May 18, 1964, AFSC Regional Office Minutes 1964 Pasadena to Seattle; *Fair Housing*, newsletter of the AFSC Southern California Regional Office, Summer 1964, AFSC PRO.

26. AFSC NCRO Executive Committee Minutes, April 20, 1964, AFSC Regional Office Minutes 1964 Pasadena to Seattle; *Fair Housing*, newsletter of the AFSC Southern California Regional Office, February 1964, March 15, 1964, and Summer 1964, and Lou Ruby to Bob Mang, March 16, 1964, AFSC PRO; AFSC NCRO Executive Committee Minutes, May 18, 1964, AFSC Regional Office Minutes 1964 Pasadena to Seattle.

27. Exec Comm Minutes, November 16, 1964, AFSC Regional Office Minutes 1964 Pasadena to Seattle; Isabel Gehr to Charlotte Meacham, December 19, 1964, CRD 1964 Housing Program, box 3; Temporary steering committee

for the Bay Area Fair Housing Council to Bay Area fair housing groups, July 25, 1966, CRD 1966 Housing Program ROs Chicago to Seattle; Charlotte Meacham, visit to Pasadena, June 1965, CRD 1965 Housing Program, box 1; Isabel Gehr, final report, June 23, 1966, CRD 1966 Housing Program ROs Chicago to Seattle.

28. For a history of the development of an affirmative action approach to racial equality, see Paul D. Moreno, *From Direct Action to Affirmative Action: Fair Employment Law and Policy in America, 1933–1972* (Baton Rouge: Louisiana State University Press, 1997).

29. AFSC HOP Chicago Metro Area, December 1, 1962, to June 1, 1963, CRD 1963 Housing Program; Kale Williams to Housing Program Files, October 30, 1964, CRD 1964 Housing Program, box 3.

30. AFSC CRO HOP Minutes of Meeting, August 11, 1966, 80:8, AFSC-UIC; Robert Howard, "Governor Kerner Issues Fair Practices Code," *Chicago Tribune*, July 11, 1963, https://www.newspapers.com/clip/22228061/fair-practices -code/; "Alton NAACP Leader Lauds Law," *Alton (IL) Evening Telegraph*, July 14, 1966, https://www.newspapers.com/newspage/14827340/; Maria Pappalardo to Barbara Moffett, Charlotte Meacham, et al., July 29, 1966, CRD 1966 Housing Program ROs Chicago to Seattle.

31. Bert Ransom to Charlotte Meacham, May 26, 1966, CRD 1966 Housing Program ROs Chicago to Seattle; AFSC CRO HOP Minutes of Meeting, June 9, 1966, 80:8, AFSC-UIC; Maria Pappalardo to File, Chicago Logs, Friday, August 12, 1966, CRD 1966 Housing Program ROs Chicago to Seattle.

32. Maria Pappalardo to File, September 2, [1966], CRD 1966 Housing Program ROs Chicago to Seattle; AFSC CRO HOP Minutes of Meeting, August 8, 1966, 80:8, AFSC-UIC; Chicago Regional Office: Program Affecting Housing in the Chicago Metropolitan Area, October 12, 1966, 86:6, AFSC-UIC; AFSC CRO HOP Minutes of Meeting, October 13, 1966, 80:8, AFSC-UIC; William H. Moyer to CCCO Delegates Retreat, October 23, 1966, and AFSC HOP Chicago Metropolitan Area, October 1965–66, CRD 1966 Housing Program ROs Chicago to Seattle.

33. William H. Moyer to CCCO Delegates Retreat, October 23, 1966, and AFSC HOP Chicago Metropolitan Area, October 1965–66, CRD 1966 Housing Programs ROs Chicago to Seattle; Jerry Lipson, "2 Say City Broke Pact on Housing," *Chicago Daily News*, March 15, 1967, clipping, CRD 1967 Housing and Urban Affairs Metro Phila Reports to Regional Office.

34. Metropolitan Program Committee Minutes, June 10, 1968, AFSC Regional Office Minutes 1968 Baltimore to Chicago; Jim Reedy to Kale Williams, July 31, 1968, CRD 1968 Housing and Urban Affairs Regional Offices to Rights of Conscience; "Ransom, Jr., Elbert 'Bert,'" Living Legends of Alexandria, https://alexandrialegends.org/elbert-ransom-jr/ (accessed May 19, 2021); Wikipedia, s.v. "William Moyer," https://en.wikipedia.org/ wiki/William_Moyer, last modified November 25, 2020; Bill Moyer, "History Is a Weapon," Spring 1987; revised version of article originally published

in *Dandelion* (Fall 1986), http://www.historyisaweapon.com/defcon1/ moyermap.html; William H. Moyer, JoAnn McAllister, Mary Lou Finley, and Steven Soit, *Doing Democracy: The MAP Model for Organizing Social Movements* (Gabriola Island, BC: New Society Publishers, 2001); Open Communities Committee meeting, January 6, 1969, AFSC Regional Office Minutes 1969 Baltimore to Pasadena; James Reedy, Open Housing Compliance Testing Program, February 1969, CRD 1969 Housing and Urban Affairs Regional Offices.

35. Text of the Summit Agreement—Agreement of the Subcommittee to the Conference on Fair Housing Convened by the Chicago Conference on Religion and Race—is online at http://cfm40.middlebury.edu/node/ 48 (accessed May 10, 2021). Kale Williams to Exec Comm of the Chicago Regional Office, January 13, 1967, AFSC Regional Office Minutes 1967 Cambridge to Pasadena; John A. McDermott, "Kale Williams' Legacy to Chicago," *Chicago Tribune*, November 15, 1992, https://www.chicagotribune .com/news/ct-xpm-1992-11-15-9204130456-story.html; Brian White, "The Leadership Council for Metropolitan Open Communities: Chicago and Fair Housing," in *The Chicago Freedom Movement: Martin Luther King and Civil Rights Activism in the North*, ed. Mary Lou Finley, Bernard Lafayette Jr., James R. Ralph, and Pam Smith, with a foreword by Clayborne Carson (Lexington: University Press of Kentucky, 2016), 131–53; Andrea M. K. Gill, "Moving to Integration?: The Origins of Chicago's *Gautreaux* Program and the Limits of Voucher-Based Housing Mobility," *Journal of Urban History* 38, no. 4 (2012): 662–86.

36. Barbara Moffett to Dick Bennett, February 10, 1965, CRD 1965 Housing Program, box 1; Charlotte Meacham to Harold Fleming, November 24, 1964, and Charlotte Meacham to Commissioner Philip Brownstein, June 24, 1964, CRD 1964 Housing Program; Charlotte Meacham, Housing and Related Programs, Community Relations Division, AFSC, September 1965, CRD 1965 Housing Program, box 1.

37. Charlotte Meacham to National Housing Program Committee, November 6, 1964, CRD 1964 Housing Program; FHA private agency pilot project to increase . . . , January 28, 1965, and Barbara Moffett to Dick Bennett, February 10, 1965, CRD 1965 Housing Program, box 1.

38. Charlotte Meacham to File, January 17, 1966, and Charlotte Meacham to File re: visit with Philip Brownstein, January 17, 1966, CRD 1966 Housing Program to Metro Philadelphia; Minutes, February 10, 1966, AFSC Minutes 1966 Board of Directors to CRS.

39. Interview with Barbara Krasner by Tracy E. K'Meyer, July 17, 2014, AFSC Archives; Julia Robinson, week of December 6, 1965, and Barbara Krasner, Log for December 13, 1965, CRD 1965 Housing Program, box 1; Minutes, February 10, 1966, AFSC Minutes 1966 Board of Directors to CRS; Nathan Greene to MPHP Research Advisory Committee re: meeting March 24, 1966, Minutes of MPHP Research Advisory Committee, March 24, 1966, and

Minutes of MPHP Advisory Committee, April 29, 1966, CRD 1966 Housing Program to Metro Philadelphia.

40. Julia Robinson, Staff Meeting, January 10, 1966, Staff Meeting for March 28, and Nathan Greene to MPHP Field Staff, May 3, 1966, CRD 1966 Housing Program to Metro Philadelphia.

41. Interview with Barbara Krasner, AFSC Archives; Julia Robinson, Log, May 23, 1966, and Barbara Krasner, Log, May 24, 1966, CRD 1966 Housing Program Metro Philly to Metro Washington; Minutes June 15, 1966, AFSC Minutes 1966 Board of Directors to CRS; AFSC to Thomas Gallagher and Michael Albert, July 6, 1966, CRD 1966 Housing Program to Metro Philadelphia; American Friends Service Committee, *A Report to the President: AFSC Experience and Recommendations re: Executive Order 11063 on Equal Opportunity in Housing* (Philadelphia: American Friends Service Committee, 1967), xxx.

42. AFSC, *Report to the President*, xxxi; AFSC to Thomas Gallagher and Michael Albert, July 6, 1966, CRD 1966 Housing Program to Metro Philadelphia.

43. Minutes, June 15, 1966, AFSC Minutes 1966 Board of Directors to CRS; Charlotte Meacham to Thomas Gallagher, July 6, 1966, and AFSC to Thomas Gallagher and Michael Albert, July 6, 1966, CRD 1966 Housing Program to Metro Philadelphia.

44. Charlotte Meacham to Thomas Gallagher, July 6, 1966, and AFSC to Thomas Gallagher and Michael Albert, July 6, 1966, CRD 1966 Housing Program to Metro Philadelphia.

45. Nathan Greene, Log, July 19, 1966, and August 8, 1966, and Nate Green to MPHP, August 17, 1966, CRD 1966 Housing Program to Metro Philadelphia.

46. Staff meeting, July 11, 1966, John Silard to Arthur Levin, Potomac Institute, July 13, 1966, Arthur J. Levin to Charlotte Meacham, July 15, 1966, Nathan Greene to Philip N. Brownstein, September 3, 1966, Nathan Greene, Log, July 19, 1966, and Nate Green to Metro Philadelphia Housing Program, August 17, 1966, CRD 1966 Housing Program to Metro Philadelphia.

47. Thomas J. Gallagher to FHA sales brokers, August 18, 1966, Nathan Greene to Philip N. Brownstein, September 3, 1966, Nathan Greene to Philip N. Brownstein, December 14, 1966, and Nathan Greene to MPHP Advisory Committee, additions to July 6 memo, CRD 1966 Housing Program to Metro Philadelphia; James Harvey to B. T. McGraw, February 20, 1967, and Nathan Greene, Log, February 20, 1967, CRD 1967 Education Program to Housing and Urban Affairs Correspondence.

48. Nathan Greene to MPHP Advisory Committee, December 1966, CRD 1966 Housing Program to Metro Philadelphia; AFSC, *Report to the President*; Proposal for Additional Follow Up on the AFSC Report to the President, February 13, 1968, CRD 1968 Education Program to Housing and Urban Affairs.

49. James H. Harvey to AFSC Regions, Housing and Urban Affairs Programs, and Metro Fair Housing Programs, August 31, 1967, and Congressional

Conference Report on Equal Opportunity in Housing, September 13, 1967, CRD 1967 Housing and Urban Affairs Metro Phila Reports to Regional Office; Proposal for Additional Follow Up on the AFSC Report to the President, February 13, 1968, CRD 1968 Education Program to Housing and Urban Affairs.

50. Proposal for Additional Follow Up on the AFSC Report to the President, February 13, 1968, CRD 1968 Education Program to Housing and Urban Affairs.

51. Evaluative Report, MWHP, March 1967, CRD 1967 Housing and Urban Affairs Metro Phila Reports to Regional Office; Isabel Gehr, Final Report, June 23, 1966, and Isabel Gehr, AFSC Pacific Southwest Region Fair Housing Program, January 26, 1966, CRD 1966 Housing Program ROs Chicago to Seattle; Housing/Employment Program, second draft, February 1967, CRD 1967 Housing and Urban Affairs Regional Office High Point/Atlanta to Seattle.

Chapter Five

1. Barbara Moffett to Jane Weston, February 7, 1969, and Barbara Moffett to Regional Office Secretaries, February 20, 1969, CRD 1969 Housing and Urban Affairs.

2. Report to Exec Committee from CR program, September 30, 1954, AFSC Minutes 1953 FR Quaker International; Report of the Community Relations Roundup, April 7–12, 1957, and Community Relations Division Review for Board of Directors, December 1962, Subject Files: Community Relations, 1936–1967, AFSC Archives.

3. Barbara Moffett to Regional Office Exec Secretaries and Community Relations Staff, March 20, 1963, and Minutes of the Joint Meeting of Community Relations Committees, October 4, 1963, AFSC Minutes 1963 BDP Program Priorities Comm; Memo from the Community Relations Division Executive Committee to Board of Directors, AFSC, March 1965, Subject Files: Community Relations, 1936–1967, AFSC Archives.

4. Nancy L. Roberts, *Dorothy Day and the Catholic Worker* (Albany: State University of New York Press, 1984); Mark Wild, *Renewal: Liberal Protestants and the American City after World War II* (Chicago: University of Chicago Press, 2019); Ernesto Galarza, *Farm Workers and Agribusiness in California, 1947–1960* (Notre Dame, IN: University of Notre Dame Press, 1977), 205.

5. Maurice Isserman, *The Other American: The Life of Michael Harrington* (New York: Public Affairs, 2000), 176–78.

6. Isserman, 178–79, 181–82, 208–9.

7. On the origins of the War on Poverty and the Community Action Program, see Annelise Orleck and Lisa Gayle Hazirjian, *The War on Poverty: A New Grassroots History* (Athens: University of Georgia Press, 2011), 5–6, 9–18; Anne Bradstreet Wallace Effland, "The Emergence of Federal Assistance

Programs for Migrant and Seasonal Farm Workers in Post–World War II America" (PhD diss., Iowa State University), 1991, 126–30; Carlton Basmajian and Jan Rongerude, "Hiding in the Shadows of Wagner-Steagall," *Journal of the American Planning Association* 78, no. 4 (2012): 411; David Tostensson, "Beyond the City: Lyndon Johnson's War on Poverty in Rural America," *Journal of Policy History* 25, no. 4 (2013): 587–613; Office of Economic Opportunity, "The Migrant and the Economic Opportunity Act: An Explanation of the Assistance Available under the Economic Opportunity Act to Assist the Migrant and Seasonal Agricultural Worker and His Family," February 1965, http://digitalassets.lib.berkeley.edu/irle/ucb/text/lb001024.pdf (accessed May 10, 2021).

8.   Bob Moses and Charles E. Cobb Jr., *Radical Equations: Civil Rights from Mississippi to the Algebra Project* (Boston: Beacon Press, 2001), 112; On Saul Alinsky, see Saul David Alinsky, *Rules for Radicals: A Practical Primer for Realistic Radicals* (New York: Vintage Books, 1989), and P. David Fink, *The Radical Vision of Saul Alinsky* (New York: Paulist Press, 1984). On Myles Horton, see Frank Adams and Myles Horton, *Unearthing Seeds of Fire: The Idea of Highlander* (Winston-Salem, NC: J. F. Blair, 1975).

9.   Memo from Community Relations Division Executive Committee to Board of Directors, March 1965, and Helen E. Baker, AFSC Testimony Prepared for Special Sub-Committee, Committee on Education and Labor, House of Representatives, regarding the Economic Opportunity Act of 1964, April 20, 1964, Subject Files: Community Relations, 1936–1967, AFSC Archives.

10.   Interview with Josephine Duveneck, OHC-Bancroft; Stephen H. Thiermann, *Welcome to the World: Discoveries with the American Friends Service Committee on the Frontiers of Social Change* (San Francisco: American Friends Service Committee, 1968), 32–36; Eleanor Eaton, Community Relations Division Review for Board of Directors, December 1962, Community Relations 1962 Farm Labor Programs to Housing Programs.

11.   Bard McAllister to Catherine Bauer, July 2, 1956, in box 10, folder AFSC Northern California Regional Office, Wurster-Bancroft.

12.   For a fuller story of the California self-help housing project, see *The Beginning of Self-Help Housing in the San Joaquin Valley: The Story of Self-Help Enterprises, 1965–1970*, AFSC Archives. For an introduction to self-help housing during this period, see Nancy H. Kwak, *A World of Homeowners: American Power and the Politics of Housing Aid* (Chicago: University of Chicago Press, 2015), 195–201.

13.   Program Priority Review attached to PPC Proposal for Boston "Inner Ring" Project: Expansion of Non-discriminatory Housing for Low-Income Negroes, [January 1963], Subject Files: AFSC Community Relations—Housing, AFSC Archives; John A. Sullivan to Barbara Moffett, November 9, 1962, Community Relations 1962 Farm Labor Programs to Housing Programs.

14.   Minutes of Community Relations Division Exec Comm, June 26, 1962, Community Relations 1962 Farm Labor Programs to Housing Programs;

PPC Proposal for Boston "Inner Ring" Project, [January 1963], Subject Files: AFSC Community Relations—Housing, AFSC Archives.

15. PPC Proposal for Boston "Inner Ring" Project, [January 1963], Subject Files: AFSC Community Relations—Housing, AFSC Archives; Boston Exploration, [Spring 1963], and Metropolitan Boston Low-Income Housing Proposal, September 30, 1963, CRD 1963 Housing Program.

16. Summary Community Relations Committee Thinking on the Grier Report and Draft Proposal for Implementation of the Report, October 1, 1963, and George Grier to Charlotte Meacham, July 17, 1963, CRD 1963 Housing Program; John A. Sullivan to Nancy St. John and the Proposal Implementation Committee, October 4 and 5, 1964, and Statement of Aims and Goals for the Community Relations Program in the Greater Boston Area, October 9, 1964, CRD 1964 Housing Program, box 3.

17. Report on Site Selection Process, and First Progress Report of the Metropolitan Boston Housing Program Staff, October 2, 1964, CRD 1964 Housing Program, box 3.

18. John A. Sullivan, Second Progress Report, May 28, 1965, CRD 1965 Housing Program, box 2; Duncan Howlett, *No Greater Love: The James Reeb Story* (New York: Harper and Row, 1966), 190–92.

19. Dan Richardson, Speech on Boston Common, March 14, 1965, CRD 1965 Housing Program, box 2.

20. Bob Gustafson to Barbara Moffett, January 28, 1966, Charlotte Meacham to Boston Housing Staff, May 25, 1966, and Call for Action: A Description of the Call for Action Program, AFSC, July 11, 1966, CRD 1966 Housing Program Metro Washington to ROs Cambridge; "RAP to Expand Call for Action," CRD Program News Memo, issue 23, January 1969, CRD 1969 Housing and Urban Affairs to Reference.

21. Thelma Babbitt, Greater Boston Low-Income Housing Program Progress Report, February 1967, CRD 1967 Housing and Urban Affairs Metro Phila Reports to Regional Office.

22. Community Relations Committee Meeting Minutes, January 11, 1966, and January 21, 1966, AFSC Regional Office Minutes 1966 Cambridge to High Point; Charlotte Meacham to File, April 14–15, 1966, CRD 1966 Housing Program to Metro Philadelphia; Charlotte Meacham to Boston housing staff, May 25, 1966, CRD 1966 Housing Program Metro Washington to ROs Cambridge; Thelma Babbitt, Greater Boston Low-Income Housing Program Progress Report, February 1967, CRD 1967 Housing and Urban Affairs Metro Phila Reports to Regional Office.

23. Michael F. Bennett, "Does State Sanitary Code Cover Public Housing," *Sunday Herald* (Boston), February 5, 1967, clipping, and Janet Riddell, "Can City Be a Slumlord?," *Morning Globe* (Boston), February 4, 1967, clipping, CRD 1967 Housing and Urban Affairs Metro Phila Reports to Regional Office; Executive Committee Minutes, February 17, 1967, AFSC Regional Office Minutes 1967 Cambridge to Pasadena; Bob Gustafson, Log, Febru-

ary 17, 1967, CRD 1967 Housing and Urban Affairs Metro Phila Reports to Regional Office.

24. Charlotte Meacham to File, April 14–15, 1966, CRD 1966 Housing Program to Metro Philadelphia; Bob Gustafson, Log, November 28, 1966, CRD 1966 Housing Program Metro Washington to ROs Cambridge; AFSC Housing Program newsletter, February 1967, CRD 1967 Housing and Urban Affairs Metro Phila Reports to Regional Office.

25. George Morrison, Statement on the Owners' Group, July 18, 1967, AFSC New England Regional Office, 1967–1971; Community Relations Committee, November 16, 1966, AFSC Regional Office Minutes 1966 Cambridge to High Point; George Morrison, response to Joseph Kahan's article, January 1967, CRD 1967 Housing and Urban Affairs Metro Phila Reports to Regional Office.

26. Urban Affairs Program, March 20, 1964, 88:14, AFSC-UIC; Proposal to the Field Foundation from the AFSC CRO Housing and Urban Affairs Program, April 1964, 88:12, AFSC-UIC.

27. "East Garfield Park," *Encyclopedia of Chicago*, http://www.encyclopedia .chicagohistory.org/pages/404.html (accessed May 10, 2021); AFSC Chicago Regional Office Appeal to the Field Foundation, Feb 1966, CRD 1966 Housing Program ROs Chicago to Seattle; Judy Miller to Ed and John W., May 9, 1957, 87:20, AFSC-UIC; "Why a NON-VIOLENT Movement," n.d. [1966], 1:5, CWSCPC-UIC; Herman Jenkins, "Tenant Unions during the Chicago Freedom Movement," in *The Chicago Freedom Movement: Martin Luther King and Civil Rights Activism in the North*, ed. Mary Lou Finley, Bernard Lafayette Jr., James R. Ralph, and Pam Smith, with a foreword by Clayborne Carson (Lexington: University Press of Kentucky, 2016), 185.

28. Minutes of Program Committee Meeting, CRO Urban Affairs Program, January 10, 1966, 80:5, AFSC-UIC; Report to Executive Committee, January 19, 1966, from the Urban Affairs Committee, 86:8, AFSC-UIC.

29. Bernard Lafayette, Urban Affairs Program of the AFSC CRO, June 1964, CRD 1964 Housing Program, box 3.

30. Bernard Lafayette, Urban Affairs Program of the AFSC CRO, June 1964, CRD 1964 Housing Program, box 3; Summer Project Proposal: Urban Affairs and Community Organizational Project, Chicago, Illinois, [Winter 1965], and Urban Affairs Project, Chicago, Illinois, [Summer 1965], 105:10, AFSC-UIC.

31. Newsletter #1, US Projects Program, AFSC July 14, 1965, 105:9, AFSC UIC; Will Hartzler to Carl Zietlow, Marcy 18, 1965, 105:10, AFSC-UIC; Charlotte Meacham to File, August 4, 1965, CRD 1965 Housing Program, box 1. On block clubs, see Amanda I. Seligman, *Chicago's Block Clubs: How Neighbors Shape the City* (Chicago: University of Chicago Press, 2016).

32. Bernard Lafayette, Monthly Report for August 1965, CRD 1965 Housing Program to Rights of Conscience Program; Minutes of Program Committee Meeting, CRO Urban Affairs Program, January 10, 1966, 80:5, AFSC-UIC;

Projected Plans for an Intensive Lead Poisoning Campaign in East Garfield Park, February 14, 1966, 86:7, AFSC-UIC; AFSC Chicago Regional Office Urban Affairs Program, March 14, 1966, CRD 1966 Housing Program ROs Chicago to Seattle; Interview with Bernard Lafayette, AFSC Archives.

33. Housing Resolutions, East Garfield Park People's Conference, February 5, 1966, 86:7, AFSC-UIC.

34. Joel Schwartz, "The New York City Rent Strikes of 1963–64," *Social Service Review* 57, no. 4 (December 1983): 545–64. For a broader history of tenant council organizing, see Roberta Gold, *When Tenants Claimed the City: The Struggle for Citizenship in New York Housing* (Urbana: University of Illinois Press, 2014). In Lafayette's description of the founding of the tenant organizing effort, he does not acknowledge any influence of this history. See Interview with Bernard Lafayette, AFSC Archives.

35. Kale Williams to Barbara Moffett, December 9, 1966, CRD 1966 Housing Program ROs Chicago to Seattle.

36. Kale Williams to Barbara Moffett, December 9, 1966, CRD 1966 Housing Program ROs Chicago to Seattle; Minutes of UAP Committee Meeting, April 18, 1966, 80:5, AFSC-UIC; Urban Affairs Program Report for Week Ending June 12, 1966, and June 19, 1966, and Join the Union to End Slums [flyer], CRD 1966 Housing Program ROs Chicago to Seattle; Jenkins, "Tenant Unions during the Chicago Freedom Movement," 189; Interview with Bernard Lafayette, AFSC Archives; UAP Report, July 19, 1966, 86:10, AFSC-UIC.

37. Minutes of UAP Committee Meeting, April 18, 1966, and June 13, 1966, 80:5, AFSC-UIC; EGP Union to End Slums Newsletter, September 10, 1966, CRD 1966 Housing Program ROs Chicago to Seattle.

38. Urban Affairs Weekly Report, December 9, June 19, June 26, July 3, and July 10, 1966, CRD 1966 Housing Program ROs Chicago to Seattle; James R. Ralph, *Northern Protest: Martin Luther King, Jr., Chicago, and the Civil Rights Movement* (Cambridge, MA: Harvard University Press, 1993), 63.

39. Sally Olds, "Tenant Unions Seek to Put an End to Slums," *Christian Century*, December 6, 1967, clipping, CRD 1967 Housing and Urban Affairs Metro Phila Reports to Regional Office; typed sheet starting "On July 12, 1966, the East Garfield Park Union to End Slums. . . . ," and Urban Affairs Weekly Report, July 17 and October 16, 1966, CRD 1966 Housing Program ROs Chicago to Seattle; Ralph, *Northern Protest*, 262n63.

40. Urban Affairs Weekly Report, July 21 and August 7, 1966, CRD 1966 Housing Program ROs Chicago to Seattle.

41. Jenkins, "Tenant Unions during the Chicago Freedom Movement," 183; Sally Olds, "Tenant Unions Seek to Put an End to Slums," *Christian Century*, December 6, 1967, clipping, CRD 1967 Housing and Urban Affairs Metro Phila Reports to Regional Office.

42. Peter H. Prugh, "Chicago Tenant Unions Grow: Force Landlords to Improve Apartments," *Wall Street Journal*, November 16, 1966, clipping,

and Urban Affairs Weekly Report, September 4, 1966, CRD 1966 Housing Program ROs Chicago to Seattle.

43. Urban Affairs Weekly Report, August 21, September 18, September 25, October 2, October 16, October 23, October 30, November 6, November 13, and November 20, 1966, CRD 1966 Housing Program ROs Chicago to Seattle; Urban Affairs Weekly Report, October 9, 1966, 86:10, AFSC-UIC; Jenkins, "Tenant Unions during the Chicago Freedom Movement," 191.

44. Urban Affairs Weekly Report, August 14 and 21, September 18 and 25, October 2, and December 11, 1966, CRD 1966 Housing Program ROs Chicago to Seattle; Urban Affairs Weekly Report, October 9, 1966, 86:10, AFSC-UIC; Urban Affairs Weekly Report, April 23, 1967, CRD 1967 Housing and Urban Affairs Metro Phila Reports to Regional Office.

45. Urban Affairs Weekly Report, August 21, October 16, October 30, and November 13, 1966, CRD 1966 Housing Program ROs Chicago to Seattle; Urban Affairs Weekly Report, October 9 and 23, 1966, 86:10, AFSC-UIC.

46. Urban Affairs Weekly Report, February 5, February 19, March 10, March 12, April 9, April 23, April 30, May 21, and May 28, 1967, CRD 1967 Housing and Urban Affairs Metro Phila Reports to Regional Office.

47. Jane Weston to File, February 24, 1964, CRD 1964 Housing Program, box 3; Ad Hoc Urban Affairs Committee Meeting, August 4, 1965, CRD 1965 Housing Program to Rights of Conscience Program; "Material for Discussion of Low Income Housing," November 15, 1965, 86:5, AFSC-UIC; Minutes of Program Committee Meeting, CRO UAP, January 10, 1966, AFSC-UIC.

48. Memo: Re Urban Affairs Committee Meeting, August 4, 1965, 81:25, AFSC-UIC; Jane Weston to Participants in Staff Committee Seminar on Program Planning, November 26, 1965, 81:17, AFSC-UIC.

49. Charlotte Meacham to File, October 13, 1965, and Jane Weston to Kale Williams, October 18, 1965, CRD 1965 Housing Program to Rights of Conscience Program; Minutes of Program Committee Meeting, February 14, 1966, 80:5, AFSC-UIC.

50. Urban Affairs Weekly Report, December 11, 1966, CRD 1966 Housing Program ROs Chicago to Seattle.

51. Kale Williams to Barbara Moffett, May 1, 1967, Urban Affairs Weekly Report, June 11, 1967, and An Appeal for Support of the Housing and Urban Affairs Program, September 1967, CRD 1967 Housing and Urban Affairs Metro Phila Reports to Regional Office. On the Community Renewal Foundation, see Wild, *Renewal*, 133–34.

52. Urban Affairs Weekly Report, August 14 and September 18 and 25, 1966, CRD 1966 Housing Program ROs Chicago to Seattle; Urban Affairs Weekly Report, October 9, 1966, 86:10, AFSC-UIC; Lafayette to CCCO delegates, October 23, 1966, CRD 1966 Housing Program ROs Chicago to Seattle; Urban Affairs Weekly Report, April 23, 1967, CRD 1967 Housing and Urban Affairs Metro Phila Reports to Regional Office; Exec Comm Minutes, August 16, 1967, AFSC Regional Office Minutes 1967 Cambridge to Pasadena.

53. For an overview of the long Black Power movement, see Rhonda K. Williams, *Concrete Demands: The Search for Black Power in the 20ᵗʰ Century* (New York: Routledge, 2015). For an introduction to the field of Black Power studies, see Peniel E. Joseph, "Black Liberation without Apology: Reconceptualizing the Black Power Movement," *Black Scholar* 31, no. 3/4 (Fall/Winter 2001): 2–20.

54. Minutes, September 16, 1966, AFSC Regional Office Minutes 1966 Cambridge to High Point; Report by the Continuation Committee on Racial Crisis, January 6, 1967, AFSC New England Regional Office, 1967–1971.

55. Peace Education Committee Minutes, March 11, 1967, AFSC Regional Office Minutes 1967 Cambridge to Pasadena; Report of Special Meeting on Avon Institute, August 10, 1967, AFSC New England Regional Office, 1967–1971.

56. Report of Special Meeting on Avon Institute, August 10, 1967, and A Quaker Approach to the Urban Crisis—Action Needed Now, notes of Patricia Petremont, July 29–August 5, 1967, AFSC New England Regional Office, 1967–1971; Bob Gustafson to Bob Lyon, August 8, 1967, CRD 1967 Housing and Urban Affairs Metro Phila Reports to Regional Office.

57. A Quaker Approach to the Urban Crisis—Action Needed Now, notes of Patricia Petremont, July 29–August 5, 1967, and Report of Special Meeting on Avon Institute, August 10, 1967, AFSC New England Regional Office, 1967–1971; Bob Gustafson to Bob Lyon, August 8, 1967, CRD 1967 Housing and Urban Affairs Metro Phila Reports to Regional Office.

58. Barbara Moffett to Community Relations Division Exec Comm, September 18, 1967, and Barbara Moffett to Ken Kirkpatrick, September 21, 1967, CRD 1967 Administration; "Barbara W. Moffett," and Linda Wright Moore, "Justice Lost a Tireless Worker with Barbara Moffett's Death," *Philadelphia Daily News*, October 13, 1994, clipping, Reference Files Individuals, AFSC Archives; Community Relations Division Exec Comm Minutes, September 26, 1967, AFSC Minutes 1967 BD General Service Comm to Peace Education Div.

59. Percy Baker to Barbara Moffett, September 10, 1967, CRD 1967 Administration; Ruth Smith to Regional Exec Secretaries, October 9, 1967, Report of Special Meeting, September 11, 1967, and Community Relations Division Exec Comm Minutes, September 26, 1967, AFSC Minutes 1967 BD General Service Comm to Peace Education Div.

60. Report by the Continuation Committee on the Racial Crisis, January 6, 1967, AFSC New England Regional Office, 1967–1971; Report of Special Meeting, September 11, 1967, and CRD Exec Comm to NERO, October 3, 1967, AFSC Minutes 1967 BD General Service Comm to Peace Education Div; Percy Baker to Barbara Moffett, September 10, 1967, CRD 1967 Administration.

61. Report of Special Meeting, September 11, 1967, and Community Relations Division Exec Comm Minutes, September 26, 1967, AFSC Minutes 1967 BD General Service Comm to Peace Education Div; To the Avon Institute Par-

ticipants and the American Friends Service Committee, to be responded to by Friday evening August 2, 1968, AFSC New England Regional Office, 1967–1971; Percy Baker to Barbara Moffett, September 10, 1967, CRD 1967 Administration; A Statement by Representatives of the American Friends Service Committee to the Avon Institute, August 2, 1968, AFSC New England Regional Office, 1967–1971.

62. Barbara Moffett to Percy Baker, George Grier, and Perry Ottenberg, September 29, 1967, CRD 1967 Administration; An Appeal for Support of the Housing and Urban Affairs Program, September 1967, CRD 1967 Housing and Urban Affairs Metro Phila Reports to Regional Office; Ruth Smith to Regional Executive Secretaries, October 9, 1967, AFSC Minutes 1967 BD General Service Comm to Peace Education Div.

63. Report of the Special Meeting, September 11, 1967, AFSC Minutes 1967 BD General Service Comm to Peace Education Div; Barbara Moffett to Percy Baker, George Grier, and Perry Ottenberg, September 29, 1967, CRD 1967 Administration; Barbara Moffett to Regional Office Executive Secretaries and Community Relations Staff, April 23, 1968, AFSC Minutes 1968 Community Relations Exec Comm to International Conferences.

64. Community Relations Committee Minutes, September 20, 1967, and Exec Comm Minutes, October 20, 1967, AFSC Regional Office Minutes 1967 Cambridge to Pasadena; Barbara Moffett and James Harvey to Bob Lyon, October 31, 1967, and Report to the Exec Comm by the Exec Comm Sub Comm and the Roxbury Community Committee, December 6, 1967, CRD 1967 Housing and Urban Affairs Metro Phila Reports to Regional Office.

65. "Statement of Purpose," NERO/AFSC March 8, 1968, and Robert Lyon to Barbara Moffett, May 15, 1968, CRD 1968 Housing and Urban Affairs Regional Offices to Rights of Conscience.

66. Friends and the Roxbury Action Program, June 9, 1970, CRD 1970 Housing and Urban Affairs Comms and Orgs to Regional Offices; On the Roxbury Action Program, see Stewart E. Perry, *Building a Model Black Community: The Roxbury Action Program* (Cambridge, MA: Center for Community Economic Development, 1978).

67. Jim Harvey to Bob Lyon, August 5, 1968, Robert Lyon to all staff, November 6, 1968, and Deck Mclean, "New Head Tenant Aid Plan," *Boston Globe*, December 8, 1968, clipping, CRD 1968 Housing and Urban Affairs Regional Offices to Rights of Conscience; AFSC Board of Directors Minutes, September 19–20, 1969, and Bronson P. Clark to George Morrison, October 24, 1969, CRD 1969 Housing and Urban Affairs Regional Offices; Friends and the Roxbury Action Program, June 9, 1970, and Barbara Moffett to Bob Lyon, June 17, 1970, CRD 1970 Housing and Urban Affairs Comms and Orgs to Regional Offices.

68. Urban Affairs Weekly Report, July 10, 1966, CRD 1966 Housing Program ROs Chicago to Seattle; An Appeal for Support of the Housing and Urban

Affairs Program, September 1967, CRD 1967 Housing and Urban Affairs
Metro Phila Reports to Regional Office; Metropolitan Program Commit-
tee Minutes, April 8, 1968, AFSC Regional Office Minutes 1968 Baltimore
to Chicago; Barbara Moffett to Regional Office Executive Secretaries and
Community Relations Staff, April 23, 1968, AFSC Minutes 1968 Community
Relations Exec Comm to International Conferences.

69. Urban Affairs Weekly Report, August 14, 1966, September 18 and 25, 1966,
CRD 1966 Housing Program ROs Chicago to Seattle; AFSC-CRO, On the
West Side, December 1968, CRD 1968 Housing and Urban Affairs Regional
Offices to Rights of Conscience; R. Ogden Hannaford to John Musser,
August 29, 1969, enclosure Report and Proposal to the General Service
Foundation, August 1969, CRD 1969 Housing and Urban Affairs Regional
Offices.

70. "Garfield Pk 'Tent-In' Staged to Protest W. Side Housing," October 5, 1968,
clipping, Marge Bacon to Barbara Moffett and James Harvey, October 7,
1968, Chicago Tenant Union's Demands, October 23, 1968, "Protest Condemnation of Garfield Pk Homes," *Chicago Sun-Times*, October 24, 1968,
clipping, and AFSC-CRO, On the West Side, December 1968, CRD 1968
Housing and Urban Affairs Regional Offices to Rights of Conscience.

71. Chicago Tenant Union Funding Proposal, January 1969, AFSC Chicago
Regional Office 1969 Administration to Metro; Jenkins, "Tenant Unions
during the Chicago Freedom Movement," 192–93. On the Bedford Stuyvesant project, see Brian Purcell, "'What We Need Is Brick and Mortar': Race,
Gender and Early Leadership of the Bedford Stuyvesant Restoration Corporation," in *The Business of Black Power: Community Development, Capitalism, and Corporate Responsibility in Postwar America*, ed. Laura Warren Hill
and Julia Rabig (Rochester, NY: University of Rochester Press, 2012), 217–44.

72. Urban Affairs Weekly Report, August 14, 1966, CRD 1966 Housing Program
ROs Chicago to Seattle; Anthony R. Henry and Frank Boykin, April 22,
1969, CRD 1969 Housing and Urban Affairs; Exec Comm Minutes, July 30,
1069, December 17, 1969, and attachment Progress Report on Recent
Important Developments of Chicago Tenant Union Activities, January
1970, AFSC Regional Office Minutes 1969 Baltimore to Pasadena; R. Ogden
Hannaford to John Musser, August 29, 1969, enclosure Report and Proposal
to General Service Foundation, CRD 1969 Housing and Urban Affairs
Regional Offices; Urban Programs Proposal to the Wieboldt Foundation, August 1970, and Kale Williams to Ernest C. Stevens, September 30,
1970, CRD 1970 Housing and Urban Affairs Comms and Orgs to Regional
Offices.

73. Kale Williams to John Musser, November 4, 1970, CRD 1970 Housing and
Urban Affairs Comms and Orgs to Regional Offices.

74. Jane Weston to Metropolitan Program Committee, January 30, 1969, AFSC
Regional Office Minutes 1969 Baltimore to Pasadena; Barbara Moffett to
Jane Weston, February 7, 1969, Barbara Moffett to Regional Office Exec Sec-

retaries, February 20, 1969, AFSC and the National Tenants Organization—
Draft, November 1969, Barbara Moffett to Tony Henry, November 5, 1969,
and William Steif, "The Squat-In: Revolution in Low-Cost Housing,"
Columbus (Ohio) Citizen Journal, November 29, 1969, clipping, CRD 1969
Housing and Urban Affairs.

75. Proposal for VISTA Training by NTO, April 1969, Anthony R. Henry and
Frank Boykin, Activity Report, April 22, 1969, and Ed Darden, Proposal
for a National Seminar on Housing Problems and Tenant Organization,
May 27, 1969, CRD 1969 Housing and Urban Affairs; Brief Description of
NTO, January 1971, Earle Edwards to Edmund A. Rosenthal, February 17,
1971, Thelma Segal to File, March 22, 1971, "Score One for the Tenants:
They Win a Standard Lease for Public Housing," *House and Home Magazine*, April 1971, clipping, and "Model Lease for Public Housing Runs into
Trouble," *Economic Opportunity Report*, August 23, 1971, clipping, CRD 1971
Education Program to Housing and Urban Affairs.

76. Robert Gustafson to Barbara Moffett, January 28, 1966, CRD 1966 Housing Program Metro Washington to ROs Cambridge; Bernard Lafayette to
CCCO Delegates, October 23, 1966, CRD 1966 Housing Program ROs Chicago to Seattle.

Conclusion

1. A Construction and Advocacy Program to Increase the Housing Available
to Rural Poor People in Florida, Draft-Discussion Paper, September 3, 1974,
CRD 1974 Economic and Rural Affairs.

2. *Report of the National Advisory Commission on Civil Disorders* (Washington,
DC: US Government Printing Office, 1968).

3. Gregory A. Barnes, *A Centennial History of the American Friends Service
Committee* (Philadelphia: Friends Press, 2016), 250, 271–72, 185–86; Interview with Tony Henry by "interviewer," n.d., AFSC Archives.

4. Minutes, CRD Exec Comm, October 23, 1970, FSC Minutes 1970 BDB
Bequest Comm to YAD; CRD Committee Minutes, March 19, 1971, and
Barbara Moffett to National Community Relations Committee, March 12,
1971, enclosing Search for Justice proposal, AFSC Minutes 1971 Board Exec
Comm to Peace Education; Barnes, *A Centennial History*, 254, 257, 275–79,
284–85, 305; Cushing Dolbeare to National Community Relations Committee, September 26, 1973, AFSC Minutes 1973 BDE Exec Comm to Third
World Peace Ed.

5. Community Relations Program in Southern New Jersey, September 15,
1964, CRD 1964 Farm Labor and Rural Affairs; Eleanor Eaton to Barbara
Moffett, October 31, 1963, CRD 1963 American Indians to Farm Labor; Minutes, Community Relations Executive Committee, December 3, 1963, AFSC
Minutes 1963 BDP Program Priorities Comm; "Interest in 'Self-Help' Housing Grows, but 20 Families Needed," *Kennett News and Advertiser* (Kennett

Square, PA), June 8, 1965, clipping, CRD 1965 Farm Labor and Rural Affairs; Eleanor Eaton to Elizabeth Herring, January 22, 1963, 3:18, NCALL-Bancroft; Eleanor Eaton to Barbara Moffett, October 31, 1963, CRD 1963 American Indians to Farm Labor; Ron Taylor, "Slum Today; Own Housing Tomorrow," *Fresno (CA) Bee*, March 27, 1966, clipping, CRD 1968 Economic Security and Rural Affairs Comms and Orgs to Projects; Richard J. Margolis, *Something to Build On: The Future of Self-Help Housing in the Struggle against Poverty* (Washington, DC: International Self-Help Housing Associates and the American Friends Service Committee, 1967), 23 and appendix; *OEO Programs for Migrants and Seasonal Farm Workers*, United States Department of Health, Education and Welfare, 1969, http://files.eric.ed.gov/fulltext/ED028877.pdf.

6. Chris Bonastia, "Hedging His Bets: Why Nixon Killed HUD's Desegregation Efforts," *Social Science History* 28, no. 1 (Spring 2004): 36–38; Jim Upchurch to Wil Hartzler, February 22, 1973, CRD 1973 Economic and Rural Affairs.

7. "Who We Are," Florida Non-Profit Housing, https://www.fnph.org/copy -of-who-we-are, (accessed May 11, 2021); Bob Marshall, "Looking Back: The Beginnings and Evolution of USDA's Self-Help Housing Movement," Housing Assistance Council, http://www.ruralhome.org/sct-information/ rural-voices/rv-digital/161-rvsu-2015/1191-looking-back-the-beginnings-and -evolution-of-usdas-self-help-housing-movement (accessed May 11, 2021).

8. Bill Moyer, Open Communities: A Prospectus for a Project to Achieve Open Occupancy through the Chicago Area, March 1966, CRD 1966 Program ROs Chicago to Seattle; Final Priority Proposals to Board Program Priorities Committee, [January 21, 1961], AFSC Minutes 1961 BDG General Service to International Service.

9. [Jane Reinheimer Motz] to BoD, June 4, 1969, AFSC Minutes 1969 Uncoded to BD Community Relations Committee, National.

10. [Jane Reinheimer Motz] to BoD, June 4, 1969, AFSC Minutes 1969 Uncoded to BD Community Relations Committee, National.

11. Stephen Thiermann to Dick Bennett, January 4, 1955, American Section 1955 Community Relations Administration Housing; Judy Howard to Community Relations Staff et al., CA Roundup, November 12–16, 1961, AFSC Minutes 1962 Program Priorities Comm to Social and Technical Assistance Comm; Bill Clumpner to AFSC and RHA, August 23, 1973, CRD 1973 Economic and Rural Affairs.

12. Memo to Race Street Yearly Meeting, June 5, 1953, American Section 1953 Community Relations Housing and Indians.

Index